THE LEGAL WORD BOOK

SECOND EDITION

Compiled by
Frank S. Gordon,
Thomas M. S. Hemnes, and
Charles E. Weinstein

 Houghton Mifflin · Boston

Thomas M. S. Hemnes and Charles E. Weinstein are affiliated with Foley, Hoag & Eliot, Boston, Massachusetts.

All correspondence and inquiries should be directed to
Reference Division, Houghton Mifflin Company
One Beacon Street, Boston MA 02108

Library of Congress Cataloging in Publication Data

Hemnes, Thomas M. S., 1948–
  The legal word book.

  Rev. ed. of: The legal word book/compiled by
Frank S. Gordon and Thomas M. S. Hemnes. c1978.
  1. Law—United States—Terms and phrases.
I. Weinstein, Charles E.   II. Gordon, Frank S.,
1952–   .   III. Gordon, Frank S., 1952–
Legal word book.   IV. Title.
KF156.H44   1982   340′.14   82-18709
ISBN 0-395-32942-6

CONTENTS

HOW TO USE THIS BOOK

The Legal Word Book, Second Edition has been prepared in order to fill the long-standing need for an adequate, convenient speller of terms used in the legal profession and for a quick-reference guide to the preparation of legal forms, documents, and citations.

Twenty-five thousand terms are listed in alphabetical order and in the clearest and most useful possible way. Many of the entries included are in common usage, but each has a specific legal meaning or use. Information is provided on how to spell the words, how to divide them into syllables, and which syllables are stressed when the words are pronounced.

The Legal Word Book, Second Edition contains a comprehensive list of abbreviations that includes those for court reports and law journals. Directories — with addresses — are provided for the federal court system, for federal agencies, for embassies and consulates of the United States, and for the counties and county seats of the states of the United States. Also entered are section on forms of acknowledgment and address; proofreaders' marks; Roman numerals; a perpetual calendar; postal abbreviations; and telephone area codes for many cities in the United States and other countries.

ORDER OF ENTRIES

The list of entries is given in strict alphabetical order for quick and easy access.

Each entry appears in the form in which it is most commonly used, for example, the plural of a noun (*reprisals; consular courts*), the present participle of a verb (*charging lien*), and so on; some words are entered in both the singular and the plural (*damage; damages*).

Series of multiword phrases sharing a common element — be it first, middle, or last — are listed under the key word in the following style:

> bill
> — for a new tri′al
> — in na′ture of a — of re·view′
> sup′ple·men′tal —

> ab i·ni′ti·o′
> — mun′di′

In such a series the dash functions as a sort of ditto mark and indicates that the key word or phrase (in the cases above, the word *bill* and the phrase *ab initio*) is repeated in each subsequent phrase in place of the dash: *bill for a new trial, bill in nature of a bill of review*, and *supplemental bill; ab initio mundi*.

In some phrases the same key word functions in more than one part of speech. In such cases the key word of the main entry is followed by a part-of-speech label (*n.*, noun; *v.*, verb; *adv.*, adverb; and *adj.*, adjective), and each phrase is entered under the part of speech to which it belongs:

> hon′or *v.*
> hon′or *n.*
> — courts
> of′fice of —

Sometimes the key word has both a capitalized form and a lower-case form. Phrases are entered under the appropriate main-entry form:

> court
> civ′il —
> crim′i·nal —
> — of ap·peals′

> Court
> — of Ad′mi·ral·ty
> Su·preme′ Ju·di′cial —
> Su·preme′ — of Er′rors

These would be written *civil court, criminal court, court of appeals; Court of Admiralty, Supreme Judicial Court*, and *Supreme Court of Errors*.

DIVISION OF WORDS

The Legal Word Book, Second Edition shows how words may correctly be divided into syllables. With the exception of law French and a few foreign words not yet assimilated into the language, all words have been analyzed and divided according to the same criteria applied in *The American Heritage Dictionary, Second College Edition*, a recognized authority on words, and in *The Word Book* (Houghton Mifflin Company, 1976), a speller presenting a list of the most commonly used words in the English language and a useful adjunct to *The Legal Word Book, Second Edition*. Law Latin terms have been included in this system of division because they are part of the legal lexicon of native speakers of English and are pronounced accordingly.

Divisions are shown by means of a centered dot, an accent mark, or a hyphen:

pac'tum   blue'-sky' law   cur'so·ry ex·am'i·na'tion

STRESS

Two different stress marks are used; the first, a boldface stress, indicates the syllable that has the primary stress in the word:

as'signs   hin'der and de·lay'

The second mark, a lighter stress, indicates syllables that are pronounced with less stress than those marked with a primary stress but with a stronger stress than unmarked syllables:

de·fam'a·cast'   co·ju'di·ces'   heir'ship'

At times stress shifts when a word is used as a different part of speech:

pur'port' n.   rec'ord n.
pur·port' v.   re·cord' v.

Forms given are identified by the applicable part-of-speech label in italics.

VARIANTS

Variant, or alternate, spellings of a word are given after the preferred spelling form and appear as follows:

as·size' or as·sise'   en·dorse' or in·dorse'

A

ab·ac'tion
ab'ac'tor
a·ban'don
a·ban'don·ee'
a·ban'don·ment
ab an'te
ab an·ti'quo'
a·bat'a·ble nui'sance
a·bate'
a·bate'ment
a·ba'tor
ab'bey
ab'bot
ab·bre'vi·ate'
ab·bre'vi·a'tions
ab·bre'vi·a'tors
ab·broch'ment or ab·
 broch'ment
ab'di·cate'
ab'di·ca'tion
ab'di·to'ri·um
ab·duc'tion
a·bear'ance
ab'er·ra'tion
ab'er·ra'tion·al
a·bet'
a·bet'tor
ab ex'tra
a·bey'ance
a·bide'
a·bil'i·ty
ab i·ni'ti·o'
 — mun'di'
ab in'tra
a·bish'er·ing or a·bish'-
 ers·ing
ab·ju'di·ca'ti·o'
ab'ju·ra'tion
ab·jure'
a'ble-bod'ied
 — sea'man
a'ble sea'man
ab'le·gate'
ab'ne·gate'
ab'ne·ga'tion
a·bode'
a·bol'ish
ab'o·li'tion

ab'o·li'tion·ist
à bon droit
ab'o·rig'i·nal
 — ti'tle
a·bor'ti·fa'cient
a·bor'tion
a·bor'tion·ist
a·bor'tive
a·bor'tus
a·bout'
a·bove'
a·bridge'
a·bridg'ment
a·broach'ment
a·broad'
ab'ro·gate'
ab'ro·ga'tion
ab'ro·ga'tor
ab·scond'
ab'sence
ab'sent
ab'sen·tee'
 — land'lord'
 — vot'ing
ab'sen·tee'ism
ab'so·lute'
 — deed
 — li'a·bil'i·ty
ab'so·lute'ly
ab'so·lu'tion
ab'so·lut'ism
ab·solve'
ab·sorb'
ab·sorp'tion
abs'que
 — hoc
ab·sten'tion
ab'sti·nence
ab'stract' n.
 — of ti'tle
ab·stract' adj.
 — ques'tion
ab·stract' v.
ab·strac'tion
ab·strac'tor
ab·surd'i·ty
a·buse' v.
a·buse' n.
 — of proc'ess'
a·bu'sive
a·but'

a·but'ments
a·but'tals
a·but'ter
ac'a·deme'
ac'a·dem'ic
a·cad'e·my
ac·cede'
ac·cel'er·at'ed
 — de·pre'ci·a'tion
ac·cel'er·a'tion
 — clause
ac·cept'
ac·cep'tance
ac·cep'tor
ac·cess'
ac·ces'si·bil'i·ty
ac·ces'si·ble
ac·ces'sion
ac·ces'so·ry
ac'ci·dent
ac'ci·den'tal
ac·com'mo·date'
ac·com'mo·da'tion
 — en·dors'er
 — mak'er
 — note
 — par'ty
ac·com'pa·ny
ac·com'plice
ac·cord' v.
ac·cord' n.
 — and sat'is·fac'tion
ac·cor'dance
ac·cor'dant
ac·couche·ment'
ac·count'
 — book
 — pay'a·ble
 — re·ceiv'a·ble
 — stat'ed
ac·count'a·ble
ac·count'ant
ac·count'ing
ac·counts'
 — pay'a·ble
 — re·ceiv'a·ble
ac·cred'it
ac·cred'i·ta'tion
ac·cre'tion
ac·cru'al
 — ba'sis

ac·crue'
ac·cru'ing
ac·cu'mu·late'
ac·cu'mu·la'tions
ac·cu'mu·la'tive
ac·cus'al
ac'cu·sa'tion
ac·cu'sa·to'ry part
ac·cuse'
ac·cused'
ac·cus'er
ac·cus'tomed
ac'id test
ac·knowl'edge
ac·knowl'edg·ment
a coe'lo us'que ad
  cen'trum
ac'o·lyte'
a con·trar'i·o'
ac·quain'tance
ac·quaint'ed
ac·quest'
ac'qui·esce'
ac'qui·es'cence
  — in pais
  — of God
ac·quire'
ac'qui·si'tion
ac·quit'
ac·quit'tal
ac·quit'tance
ac·quit'ted
a'cre
a'cre·age
a·cross'
act
  — in pais
act'ing
ac'tion
  — for mon'ey had and
    re·ceived'
  — in per·so'nam
  — in rem
  — qua'si' in rem
  — to qui'et ti'tle
ac'tion·a·ble
ac'tive
ac·tiv'i·ty
ac'tor
ac'tu·al
ac'tu·al'i·ty

ac'tu·al·i·za'tion
ac'tu·al·ize'
ac'tu·ar'i·al
ac'tu·ar'i·al·ly
ac'tu·ar'y
ac'tu·ate'
ac'tum
ac'tus
ad'ap·ta'tion
a·dapt'ed
ad cul'pam
ad cu'ri·am
add
ad dam'num
ad·den'da
ad·den'dum
ad·dict' v.
ad'dict n.
ad·dict'ed
ad·dic'tion
ad di'em
ad·di'tion
ad·di'tion·al
  — in·sured'
ad·di'tur
ad'dled
ad·dress'
ad'dress·ee'
ad·duce'
a·deem'
a·demp'tion
a·dept'
ad'e·quate
ad·her'ence
ad·her'ing
ad·he'sion
  — con'tract'
ad hoc
ad hom'i·nem
ad in'fi·ni'tum
ad'i·po·cere'
ad'i·ra'tus
ad'it
ad'i·tus
ad·ja'cent
ad'jec·tive law
ad·join'ing
ad·journ'
ad·journ'ment
ad·judge'
ad·ju'di·cate'

ad·ju'di·ca'tion
ad·ju'di·ca·to'ry
ad'junct'
ad·ju·ra'tion
ad·jure'
ad·just'
ad·just'er
ad·just'ment
ad'ju·tant gen'er·al
ad·le'gi·a're'
ad li'tem
ad·meas'ure·ment
ad·min'is·ter
ad·min'is·tra'tion
ad·min'is·tra'tive
ad·min'is·tra'tor
  — de bo'nis non
ad·min'is·tra'trix
ad'mi·ral
ad'mi·ral·ty
ad·mis'si·bil'i·ty
ad·mis'si·ble
ad·mis'sion
ad·mis'sions
ad·mit'
ad·mit'tance
ad·mit'ted
ad·mix'ture
ad·mon'ish
ad'mo·ni'tion
ad·mon'i·to'ry
ad nau'se·am
a·do'be
ad'o·les'cence
a·dopt'
a·dop'tion
ad pro'se·quen'dum
ad quem
ad rec'tum
ad re'spon·den'dum
a·drift'
a·dult'
a·dul'ter·a'tion
a·dul'ter·er
a·dul'ter·ess
a·dul'ter·ous
a·dul'ter·y
ad va·len'ti·am
ad va·lo'rem
ad·vance'
ad·vance'ment

ad·vanc'es
ad·van'tage
ad·ven·ti'tious
ad·ven'ture
ad·ven'tur·er
ad'ver·sar'y
— pro·ceed'ing
ad·verse'
— in'ter·est
— par'ty
— pos·ses'sion
ad'ver·tise'
ad'ver·tise'ment
ad·vice'
ad·vise'
ad·vised'
ad·vis'ed·ly
ad·vise'ment
ad·vi'so·ry
— o·pin'ion
ad'vo·ca·cy
ad'vo·cate' v.
ad'vo·cate n.
aer'o·drome'
aer'o·naut'
aer'o·stat'ics
aes·thet'ic or es·thet'ic
af·fair'
af·fairs'
af·fect'
af·fec'tion
af·fec'tus
af·feer'
af·fi'ance
af·fi'ant
af'fi·da're'
af'fi·da'vit
— of serv'ice
af·fil'i·ate'
af·fil'i·a'tion
af·fin'i·ty
af·firm'
af·fir'mance
af·fir'mant
af'fir·ma'tion
— of fact
af·fir'ma·tive
— ac'tion
— de·fense'
— proof
— re·lief'

af·fix'
af'fix·a'tion
af·fix'ing
af·flic'tion
af·fray'
af·freight'ment
af·front'
a·fore'men'tioned
a·fore'said'
a·fore'thought'
a for'ti·o'ri'
af'ter
— sight
af'ter-ac·quired'
— ti'tle
af'ter-born child
af'ter-dis·cov'ered
— ev'i·dence
af'ter·math'
af'ter·noon'
af'ter·thought'
af'ter·ward or af'ter·
wards
a·gainst'
a·gal'ma
age
a'gen·cy
— cou'pled with in'ter·
est
a·gen'da
a'gent
a'ger
ag'gra·vat'ed as·sault'
ag'gra·vat'ing
ag'gra·va'tion
ag'gre·gate'
ag'gre·gates'
ag'gre·ga'tion
ag·gres'sion
ag·gres'sive·ly
ag·gres'sor
ag·grieved'
— par'ty
ag'i·o'
ag'o'tage
a·gist'
a·gist'er
a·gist'ers
a·gist'ment
a·gis'tor
ag'i·ta'tor

ag·no'men
ag·nom'i·na'tion
ag'o·ny
a·graph'i·a
a·grar'i·an
— laws
a·grar'i·um
a·gree'
a·greed'
— case
— or·der
— state'ment of facts
a·gree'ment
— not to be per·formed'
with·in' a year
a·gre·er'
ag'ri·cul'tur·al
— lien
ag'ri·cul'ture
aid n.
— and com'fort
aid v.
— and a·bet'
— and as·sist'
aid'er
— and a·bet'tor
aids
ail'ment
air
— cours'es
air'-con·di'tion
air'craft'
air'plane'
air'port'
air'ship'
air'way'
a·journ'ment or a·
journe'ment
a·kin'
al'co·hol'ic bev'er·age
al'co·hol'ism
al'der·man
a'le·a·to'ry con'tract'
a'li·a
a'li·a·men'ta
a'li·as
— dic'tus
— ex'e·cu'tion
— sub·poe'na
— sum'mons
— tax war'ant

— writ
— writ of ex'e·cu'tion
al'i·bi'
a'li·en
— a·mi' or a·my'
— and se·di'tion laws
— friend
al'ien·a·ble
al'ien·age
al'ien·ate'
al'ien·a'tion
— of af·fec'tions
al'ien·ee'
al'ien·ism
al'ien·ist
al'ien·or'
a·lign'ment
a·like'
al'i·men·ta
al'i·mo'ny
al'i·quot'
al'i·ter
a'li·un'de'
ev'i·dence —
— rule
a·live
all
— and sin'gu·lar
— faults
— fours
All-A·mer'i·can
al'le·ga'tion
— of fact
al·lege'
al·leged'
al·leg'ed·ly
al·le'giance
al'le·gi·a're'
al'ler·gy
al'ley
al·li'ance
al·li'sion
al'lo·ca·ble
al'lo·cate'
al'lo·ca'tion
al'lo·ca'tur'
al'lo·cu'tion
al'lo·di·al
al'lo·graph'
al·longe'
al'lo·path'ic prac'tice

al·lot'
al·lot'ment
al·lot'tee'
al·low'
al·low'a·ble
al·low'ance
— pen·den'te' li'te'
al'loy'
al·lude'
al·lu'sion
al·lu'sive
al·lu'vi·al
al·lu'vi·o' ma'ris
al·lu'vi·on
al'ly
al'ma·nac'
al'ma·ri·a
alms
alms'house'
a·lone'
a·long'
al'so
al'ter
al'ter·a'tion
al'ter·ca'tion
al'ter e'go
al'ter·nat
al'ter·nate' v.
al'ter·nate n.
al·ter·na·tive
— plead'ing
— re·lief'
— re·main'ders
a·lum'na
a·lum'nae'
a·lum'ni'
a·lum'nus
a·mal'ga·ma'tion
a·man'u·en'sis
am·bas'sa·dor
am·bas'sa·do'ri·al
am'bi·dex'ter
am'bi·dex'trous
am'bi·gu'i·ty
— up·on' the fac'tum
am·big'u·ous
am'bit
am·blot'ic
am'bu·lance
— chas'er
— chas'ing

am'bu·la·to'ry
am'bush'
a·me'lio·rat'ing waste
a·me'lio·ra'tions
a·me'na·ble
a·mend'
a·mend'ment
a·mends'
a·men'i·ty
a men'sa et tho'ro'
a·merce'
a·merce'ment
A·mer'i·can
A·mer'i·can Bar As·so'-
  ci·a'tion
a·mi' or a·my'
am'i·ca·ble
am'i·ca·bly
a·mi'cus cu'ri·ae'
am·ne'si·a
am'nes·ty
a·mong'
am'or·tiz'a·ble
am'or·ti·za'tion
am'or·tize'
a·mo'tion
a·mount'
— in con'tro·ver·sy
— in dis·pute'
am·phet'a·mine'
am'pli·fi·ca'tion
am'pli·fy'
am'pu·tate'
am'pu·ta'tion
a·muse'ment
an'a·graph'
a·nal'o·gous
an'a·logue'
a·nal'o·gy
a·nal'y·ses'
a·nal'y·sis
an'a·lyt'ic
an'a·lyt'i·cal
an'a·lyze'
an·aph'ro·dis'i·a
an·aph'ro·dis'i·ac'
an'ar·chist
an'ar·chy
a·nath'e·ma
a·nath'e·ma·tize'
an'ces'tor

an·ces'tral
an'chor
an'chor·age
an'cient
— deed
— doc'u·ments
— lights
— wa'ter·course'
— writ·ings
an'cients
an'cil·lar'y
— ad·min'is·tra'tion
— at·tach'ment
— ju'ris·dic'tion
— pro·ceed'ing
— re·ceiv'er
an'es·the'si·a or an'aes·the'si·a
an'es·the'si·ol'o·gist or an'aes·the'si·ol'o·gist
an'es·thet'ic or an'aes·thet'ic
an'eu·rysm or an'eu·rism
a·new'
an'ga·ry
right of —
an'ger
an·gi'na pec'to·ris
an'gling
an'guish
an'i·mal
an'i·mos'i·ty
an'i·mus
— do·nan'di'
— fu·ran'di'
— tes·tan'di'
an'nals
an'nex
an'nex·a'tion
an'ni·ver'sa·ry
an'no' Dom'i·ni'
an'no·tat'ed
— stat'utes
an'no·ta'tion
an·nounced'
an·nounce'ment
an·nounc'er
an·noy'ance
an'nu·al
— as·say'
— de·pre'ci·a'tion

an'nu·al·ly
an·nu'i·tant
an·nu'i·ties
an·nu'i·ty
an·nul'
an·nul'ment
a·nom'a·lous
a·nom'a·ly
an·o·nym'i·ty
a·non'y·mous
an'swer
an'swer·a·ble
an'te
an'te·ce'dent
an'te·date'
an·ten'na
an·ten'nae'
an'te·nup'tial
— con'tract'
— set'tle·ments
an'thra·co'sis
an'thro·pom'e·try
an'ti·bi·ot'ic
an·tic'i·pa'tion
an·tic'i·pa·to'ry
— breach of con'tract'
— re·pu'di·a'tion
an'ti·dote'
an·tig'ra·phy
an·tin'o·my
an'ti·sep'tic
an'ti·so'cial
an'ti·trust' acts
a pais
a·part'ment
a'pex'
a·pha'si·a
a·pho'ni·a
ap'o·ge'an tides
ap'o·lo'gi·a
a·pol'o·gize'
a·pol'o·gy
ap'o·plex'y
a·pos'ta·sy
a pos·te'ri·o'ri
a·pos'tles
a·poth'e·car'y
ap·pa·ra'tus
ap·par'el
ap·par'ent
— a'gen·cy

— au·thor'i·ty
— dan'ger
ap·peal'
— bond
— in for'ma pau'per·is
ap·pealed'
ap·pear'
— of rec'ord
ap·pear'ance
ap·pel'lant
ap·pel'late
— court
— ju'ris·dic'tion
ap'pel·lee'
ap·pend'
ap·pend'age
ap·pen'dant
ap·pen'di·ces'
ap·pen'dix
ap'per·tain'
ap'per·tain'ing
ap·pli'ance
ap·pli·ca·ble
ap·pli·cant
ap·pli·ca'tion
ap·ply'
ap·point'
ap·point'ee'
ap·point'ive
ap·point'ment
ap·poin'tor
ap·por'tion
ap·por'tion·ment
ap·prais'al
ap·praise'
ap·praise'ment
ap·prais'er
ap·pre'cia·ble
ap·pre'ci·ate'
ap·pre'ci·a'tion in val'ue
ap'pre·hend'
ap'pre·hen'sion
ap·pren'tice
ap·pren'tice·ship'
ap·prise'
ap·proach'
right of —
ap·proach'es
ap·pro'pri·ate *adj.*
ap·pro'pri·ate' *v.*

ap·pro′pri·a′tion
  — bill
ap·pro′pri·a′tor
ap·prov′al
ap·prove′
ap·prove′ment
ap·prov′er
ap·prox′i·mate
ap·prox′i·ma′tion
ap·pur′te·nance
ap·pur′te·nant
a·prax′i·a
à pren′dre
a pri·o′ri
ap′ro·pos′
apt
a·quat′ic
a quo
ar′a·ble land
ar′bi·ter
ar′bi·tra·ble
ar′bi·trage′
ar′bi·tra·geur′
ar·bit′ra·ment
ar′bi·trar′i·ly
ar′bi·trar′i·ness
ar′bi·trar′y
ar′bi·trate′
ar′bi·tra′tion
  — clause
ar′bi·tra′tor
ar′bor
arch·bish′op
arch·dea′con
ar′che·type′
ar′chi·tect′
ar·chi′val
ar′chives′
ar′chi·vist
ar′e·a
ar′e·a·way′
à ren′dre
Ar′e·op′a·gus
a·rere′
ar′gu·en′do′
ar′gu·ment
ar′gu·men′ta·tive
a·rise′
ar′is·toc′ra·cy
armed
ar′mi·stice

arm of the sea
ar′mor·y
arms
arm′s′-length′ trans·
  ac′tion
ar′my
a·round′
ar·raign′
ar·raign′ment
ar·range′ment
ar·ray′
ar·rear′ag·es
ar·rears′
ar·rest′
  — of judg′ment
ar·ri′val
ar·rive′
ar′ro·gate′
ar′ro·ga′tion
ar′se·nals
ar′son
art
  pri′or —
  words of —
ar·te′ri·o·scle·ro′sis
ar·te′sian well
ar′ti·cle
ar′ti·cled clerk
ar′ti·cles
  — of a·gree′ment
  — of as·so′ci·a′tion
  — of faith
  — of im·peach′ment
  — of in·cor′po·ra′tion
  — of part′ner·ship′
ar·tic′u·late′ v.
ar·tic′u·late adj.
ar·tic′u·la′tion
ar′ti·fice
ar·tif′i·cer
ar′ti·fi′cial
  — in·sem′i·na′tion
  — pre·sump′tions
ar′ti·fi′cial·ly
ar′ti·san
as a·gainst′
as be·tween′
as·cend′
as·cen′dan·cy or as·cen′-
  den·cy
as·cen′dants

as·cent′
as′cer·tain′
as′cer·tain′a·ble
as·crib′a·ble
as·cribe′
as is
ask
as′pect′
as per
as·per′sions
as′phalt′
as·phyx′i·a
as·phyx′i·a′tion
as′pi·rin
as′por·ta′tion
as·sail′
as·sail′a·ble
as·sail′ant
as·sas′sin
as·sas′si·na′tion
as·sault′
  — and bat′ter·y
  — with in·tent′ to com·
    mit′ man′slaugh′ter
  — with intent to commit
    mur′der
  — with intent to commit
    rape
  — with intent to commit
    rob′ber·y
as·say′
  — of′fice
as·say′er
as·sem′blage
as·sem′ble
as·sem′bly
  un·law′ful —
as·sem′bly·man
as·sent′
as·sert′
as·ser′tion
as·ser′tive·ness
as·sess′
as·sess′a·ble
  — stock
as·sessed′
  — val′u·a′tion
as·sess′ment
  — dis′trict
  — la′bor
  — list

— pe′ri·od
— roll
as·ses′sor
as′sets′
as′sev·er·a′tion
as·sign′
as·sign′a·bil′i·ty
as·sign′a·ble
as·sign·ee′
— for the ben′e·fit of
  cred′i·tors
as·sign′ment
as·sign′or′
as·signs′
as·sist′
as·sis′tance
— of coun′sel
as·sis′tant
as·size′ *or* as·sise′
as·siz′es *or* as·sis′es
as·so′ci·ate′
as·so′ci·a′tion
as such
as·sume′
as·sump′sit
— for mon′ey had and
  re·ceived′
— on quan′tum me·ru′it
as·sump′tion
— of in·debt′ed·ness
— of risk
as·sur′ance
as·sure′
as·sured′
as·tip′u·la′tion
a·sy′lum
at arm′s length
at bar
a te′ner·is an′nis
a terme
a′the·ism
a′the·ist
a′the·is′tic
at large
at law
at′om·ize′
a·tro′cious as·sault′
  and bat′ter·y
a·troc′i·ty
at′ro·pine′
at·tach′

at·tach′a·ble
at·ta·ché′
at·tached′
at·tach′ing cred′i·tor
at·tach′ment
— ex′e·cu′tion
writ of —
at·tain′
at·tain′der
at·tempt′
at·ten′dant *n.*
at·ten′dant *adj.*
— terms
at·ten′tion
at·test′
at′tes·ta′tion
— clause
— of will
at·test′ed cop′y
at·test′ing wit′ness
at·tes′tor
at·torn′
at′tor·na′re′
at·tor′ney
— at law
— gen′er·al
— in fact
let′ter of —
— of rec′ord
pow′er of —
at·tor′ney·ship′
at·tor′ney′s lien
at·trac′tive nui′sance
  doc′trine
at·trib′ut·a·ble
at′trib·ute′ *n.*
at·trib′ute *v.*
at′tri·bu′tion
a·typ′i·cal
au be·soin′
au con·traire′
auc′tion
auc′tion·eer′
au′di·ence
au′dit
au′di·ta quer′e·la
au′di·tor
aug′men·ta′tion
aunt
au·then′tic
au·then′ti·ca′tion

au′then·tic′i·ty
au′thor
au·thor′i·ties
au·thor′i·ty
ap·par′ent —
ex·press′ —
gen′er·al —
im·plied′ —
au′thor·i·za′tion
au′thor·ize′
au′to-op′tic ev′i·dence
au·toc′ra·cy
au′to·crat′ic
au′to·graph′
au′to·graph′ic
au′to·mat′ic
au·tom′a·tism
au·tom′a·ton
au′to·mo·bile′
au′to·mo′tive
au·ton′o·mous
au·ton′o·my
au′top′sy
au·top′tic prof′er·ence
au′tre
— droit
— vie
aux·il′ia·ry
a·vail′a·ble
a·vails′
av′e·nue′
a·ver′
av′er·age
a·ver′ment
a·verse′
a·ver′sion
a′vi·a′tion
a vin′cu·lo mat′ri·mo′-
  ni·i′
a·vo·cat′
av′o·ca′tion
a·void′
a·void′a·ble con·se·
  quenc·es
a·void′ance
av′oir·du·pois′
a·vouch′
a·vouch′er
a·vow′
a·vow′al
a·vow′ed·ly

a·vow'ry
a·vul'sion
a·wait'
a·ward'
ax'i·om
ax'i·o·mat'ic

B

bach'e·lor
back'dat'ing
back'ing
back'log'
back'-pay' a·wards'
back'-seat' driv'er
back tax'es
back'-to-work' a·gree'-
  ment
back'ward·a'tion or
  back'a·da'tion
back'ward
  for'ward and — at sea
back'wards
back'wa'ter
bad
  — debt
  — faith
  — mo'tive
  — ti'tle
badge
  — of fraud
bag
bag'gage
  — car
bail v.
bail n.
  — bond
bail'a·ble
  — ac'tion
  — of·fense'
  — proc'ess'
bail·ee'
bail'iff
bail'i·wick'
bail'ment
  ac'tu·al —
  con·struc'tive —
  — for hire
  — for mu'tu·al ben'e·fit

gra·tu'i·tous —
in·vol'un·tar'y —
  — lease
bail'or
bail'out'
bait
  — and switch
bak'er
bak'er·y
bal'ance
  net —
  — of con·ven'ience
  — of pow'er
  — sheet
bal'anc·ing
  — of in'ter·ests
  — test
  — the eq'ui·ties
bal'co·nies
bale
bal'last
bal'la·stage'
bal·lis'tics
bal·loon'
  — mort'gage
bal'lot
  — box
  Mas'sa·chu'setts —
ban
ba·nal'
ba·nal'i·ty
banc
ban'dit
bane
ban'ish·ment
ban'is·ter and rail'ing
bank
  — ac·count'
  — check
  cor're·spon'dent —
  de·pos'i·to·ry —
  — draft
  joint'-stock' —
  — note
  sav'ings —
bank'a·ble pa'per
bank'book'
bank'er
bank'er's
  — ac·cep'tance
  — lien

  — note
bank'ing
  — hours
bank'rupt'
  — law
bank'rupt'cy
  ad·ju'di·ca'tion of —
  — dis'charge'
  — pro·ceed'ings
  trus·tee' in —
  vol'un·tar'y —
ban'ner
banns of mat'ri·mo'ny
bar
  — as·so'ci·a'tion
bar'ba·rous
bar'ber
bar·bi'tu·rate
bare
  — li'cen·see'
  — pat'ent li'cense
  — trus·tee'
bar'gain
  — and sale
  plea —
bar'gain·ee'
bar'gain·or'
bark
barn
Barn'ard's Inn
bar'on
bar'on·et
bar'o·ny
bar'ra·tor or bar're·tor
bar'ra·trous
bar'ra·try or bar're·try
barred
bar'rel
bar'ren mon'ey
bar'ren·ness
bar'ri·cade'
bar'ri·er
bar'ris·ter
bar'ter
bas'al frac'ture
base
  — line
based
  — up·on'
base'ball'
base'ment

ba'ses' n.
bas'es v. & n.
ba·sil'i·ca
ba'sin
ba'sis
  ad·just'ed —
  stepped'-up' —
  sub'sti·tute' —
bas'tard
bas'tard·ize'
bas'tard·y
  — proc'ess'
Bas·tille'
bat'tel
bat'tered
  — child
  — wife
bat'ter·y
bat'tle of the forms
baux'ite'
bawd
bawd'y·house'
bay
  — win'dow
bay'gall'
bay'ou
beach
bea'con
bea'con·age
bea'dle
bear v.
  — arms
  — in'ter·est
bear'er
  — bond
  — in'stru·ment
  — pa'per
bear'ers
bear'ing date
bear mar'ket
beast
beat
be·come'
bed
bed'ding
bede'house'
be'del
bed'lam
beef
beer
be·get'

beg'gar
be·gin'
be·got'ten
be·gun'
be·half'
be·hav'ior
be·hoof'
be·hooves'
be·lief'
bel·lig'er·en·cy
bel·lig'er·ents
bel'lum
be·long'
be·long'ings
be·low'
bench
  — mark
  — tri'al
  — war'rant
ben'e·fac'tor
ben'e·fac'tress
ben'e·fice
ben'e·fi'cial
  — as·so'ci·a'tion
  — en·joy'ment
  — es·tate'
  — in'ter·est
  — own'er
  — pow'er
  — use
ben'e·fi'ci·ar·y
  change of —
  — heir
ben'e·fit
  — of bar'gain rule
  — of cler'gy
  — of coun'sel
  — of dis·cus'sion
be·nev'o·lence
be·nev'o·lent
  — as·so'ci·a'tions
  — cor'po·ra'tion
  — so·ci'e·ty
be·queath'
be·quest'
  con·di'tion·al —
  spe·cif'ic —
berm bank
Bern'stein' test
ber'ton
be·seech'

be·soin'
be·sot'
bes'se·mer·iz'ing
best
  — ev'i·dence
bes'ti·al'i·ty
be·stow'
bet
be·tray'al
be·troth'al
be·trothed'
be·troth'ment
bet'ter·ment
  — acts
bev'er·age
be·yond' a rea'son·a·
  ble doubt
bi·an'nu·al
bi'as
Bi'ble
bi·cam'er·al sys'tem
bid
  — in
  — off
  up·set' —
bid'der
bid'dings
  — com·pet'i·tive
biel'brief'
bi·en'ni·al·ly
biens
big'a·mist
big'a·my
big'ot
bi·lan'
bi·lat'er·al con'tract'
bil'boes
bilged
bill
  ap·pro'pri·a'tions —
  cross —
  — for a new tri'al
  — for fore·clo'sure
  — for fraud
  — in aid of ex'e·cu'tion
  — in na'ture of a — of
    re·view'
  — in nature of a — of
    re·viv'or
  — in nature of a sup'ple·
    men'tal —

— in nature of in'ter·
plead'er
— o·blig'a·to'ry
— of ad·ven'ture
— of at·tain'der
— of con·form'i·ty
— of costs
— of cred'it
— of debt
— of dis·cov'er·y
— of en'try
— of ex·cep'tions
— of ex·change'
— of gross ad·ven'ture
— of health
— of in·dict'ment
— of in'for·ma'tion
— of in'ter·plead'er
— of lad'ing
— of pains and pen'al·
ties
— of par·tic'u·lars
— of peace
— of re·view'
— of re·viv'or
— of revivor and sup'-
ple·ment
— of rights
— of sale
— of sight
— pay'a·ble
— pe'nal
pri·vate —
— qui'a tim'et
— re·ceiv'a·ble
— sin'gle
sup'ple·men'tal —
— to car'ry a de·cree'
in'to ex'e·cu'tion
— to per·pet'u·ate' test'-
ti·mo'ny
— to qui'et pos·ses'sion
and ti'tle
— to sus·pend' a de·cree'
— to take tes'ti·mo'ny
de be·ne' es'se'
bill'board'
billed
bil'let
bil'liard ta'bles
bill'ings

bil'ly
bi·me·tal'lic
bi·met'al·lism
bind
— out
bind'er
bind'ing
— a·gree'ment
— in·struc'tion
— o'ver
bi'op'sy
bi·par'tite'
birth
— cer·tif'i·cate
— con·trol'
bis
bish'op
bish'op·ric
bi·tu'men
bi·tu'mi·nous coal
black a'cre and white
a'cre
black'jack'
black'-let'ter law
black'list'
black'mail'
Black Ma·ri'a
black'smith' shop
blanc seign
blank
— ac·cep'tance
— check
— en·dorse'ment
blan'ket
— bond
— in·sur'ance
— mort'gage
— pol'i·cy
blanks
blas'phe·my
blast'ing
bleach'ers
blees
blend'ed price
ble'ta
blind
— car
— cor'ner
— nail'ing
— wag'on
blind'craft'

block
— book sys'tem
— of sur'veys'
— to — rule
block·ade'
block'age
— rule
block'-book'ing
block'head'
blood
— group'ing test
blood'hounds'
bludg'eon
blue
— laws
— notes
— rib'bon
blue'-chip' in·vest'ment
blue'-sky' law
bluff
blum'ba
blun'der
blun'der·buss'
board
— meas'ure
— of al'der·men
— of ap·peals'
— of bar o'ver·se'ers
— of di·rec'tors
— of ed'u·ca'tion
— of ex·am'in·ers
— of health
— of med'i·cal ex·am'in·
ers
— of re'gents
— of reg'is·tra'tion
— of re·view'
— of trade
board'er
board'ing house
boat
boat'a·ble
boat'ing
boat'swain
bob'bies
bob'tail' driv'er
bob'tailed ca·boose'
bob'tails'
bod'i·ly
bod'y
— cor'po·rate

— ex'e·cu'tion
— heirs
— of a coun'ty
— of an in'stru·ment
— of laws
— of the of·fense'
— pol'i·tic
bo'gus
boil'ar·y
boil'er
boi'ler·plate'
boil'er-room' trans·ac'-
  tion
bolt
bolt'ing
bo'na' *pl.n.*
bo'na *adj.*
  — fide
  — fide pur'chas·er
  — fides
bo·nan'za
bond
  — and mort'gage
  an·nu'i·ty —
  ap·peal' —
  ar'bi·trage'
  —at·tach'ment —
  claim —
  con·vert'i·ble —
  cor'po·rate —
  — cred'i·tor
  de·ben'ture —
  — for deed
  forth·com'ing—
  — for ti'tle
  gen'er·al mort'gage —
  in'come' —
  in·dem'ni·ty —
  in·dus'tri·al de·vel'op·
    ment —
  — is'sue
  li'a·bil'i·ty —
  Lloyd's —
  mu·nic'i·pal —
  — of in·debt'ed·ness
  per·form'ance —
  — pre'mi·um
  re'de·liv'er·y —
  sim'ple —
  sin'gle —
  straw —

treas'ur·y —
U.S. Sav'ings —
  — with sure'ty
bond'age
bond'ed
  — in·debt'ed·ness
  — ware'house'
bonds'man
bon'i·fi·ca'tion
bo'nus
  — stock
bon'y
boo'by trap
boo'dle
boo'dling
book
  — ac·count'
  — debt
  — of o·rig'i·nal en'tries
  — val'ue
booked
book'ing con'tract'
book'keep'ing
book'mak'er
book'mak'ing
books
  — and pa'pers
  — of ac·count'
boom
boom'age
boot
boot'ing-corn' *or* bot'-
  ing-corn'
boot'leg'ger
boot'leg'ging
boot'strap'
boo'ty
booze
bor'der
  — search
  — war'rant
born
  — a·live'
  — out of wed'lock'
bor'ough
bor·ras'ca
bor'row
bor'row·er
bor'row·ings
Bos·ton in'ter·est
both

bot'tle
bot'tom land
bot'tom·ry
bot'u·lism
bou'doir'
bought
  — and sold notes
boul'e·vard'
boul'e·vare'ism
bounc'er
bound
bound'a·ry
bound'ers
bounds
boun'ty
bour·geois'
bourse
bo'vine
boy'cott'
  sec'ond·ar'y —
Boyd rule
brain death
brain'wash'
brake
branch
  — bank
  — of the sea
  — pi'lot
brand
Bran'deis brief
brand'ing
bran'dish
bra·va'do
bra·vu'ra
brawl
breach
  — of close
  — of con'tract'
  — of cov'e·nant
  — of du'ty
  — of prom'ise
  — of the peace
  — of trust
  — of war'ran·ty
break
  — and take
break'age
break'ing
  — and en'ter·ing
  — bail
  — bulk

— jail
breath
breath'a•lyz'er test
breath'ing
breed
breth'ren
breve
bre•vet'
bre'vi•a
bre'vi•ate n.
bre'vi•ate' v.
brew'er
bribe
brib'er•y
  com•mer'cial —
Bride'well
bridge
  — mas'ters
brief
  — of ti'tle
brief'ly
brig'and
brig'and•age
brine
bring
  — a•bout'
  — suit
bring'ing er'ror
broad in•ter'pre•ta'tion
broad'side' ob•jec'tion
bro•cage'
bro'ken
  — lot
bro'ker
bro'ker•age
  — con'tract'
  — list'ing
bro'ker-deal'er
broth'el
broth'er
broth'er-in-law'
broth'er-sis'ter cor'po•
  ra'tion
brought
  — to tri'al
bru'tum ful'men
bub'ble
buck'et•ing
budg'et
budg'et•ar'y
buff'er

— zone
buf•fet'
bug'ger•y
build
build'er
build'ing
  — and loan as•so'ci•
    a'tion
  — code
  — lien
  — loan agree'ment
  — per'mit
  — site
bulk
  — sales acts
  — trans'fers
bull
  — mar'ket
bul'le•tin
bul'lion
  — fund
bull'pen'
bum•bail'iff
bump'ing
bun'co' game
bun'dle
buoy
bur'den
  — of go'ing for'ward
  — of per•sua'sion
  — of pro•duc'ing ev'i•
    dence
  — of proof
bu'reau
bu•reauc'ra•cy
Bur'ford ab•sten'tion
burg or burgh
bur'gage
  — hold'ing
  — ten'ure
bur'gess
bur'glar
bur•glar'i•ous•ly
bur'glar•y
  — in the first de•gree'
bur'go•mas'ter
bur'i•al
burk'ing
burk'ism
bur'law courts
bur•lesque'

burn
bur•ro'chi•um
bur'sa
bur'sar
bur•sar'i•a
bur'y•ing ground
bush'el
busi'ness
  — a'gent
  — bad debts
  — cor'po•ra'tion
  — en'ter•prise'
  — en'try rule
  — hours
  — in'vi•tee'
  — judg'ment rule
  — loss'es
  — name
  or'di•nar'y course of —
  — rec'ords ex•cep'tion
  — trust
butch'er
but'-for' test
butt
but'tals
butte
butt'ed
  — and bound'ed
butts
  — and bounds
buy
  — and sell a•gree'ment
  — in
  — long
  — on mar'gin
buy'er
  — in the or'di•nar'y
    course of busi'ness
buy'ing
  — long
  — ti'tles
by'-bid'der
by'-bid'ding
by law
by'law' men
by'laws'
by op'er•a'tion of law
by'-pass'ing
by rea'son of
by'stand'er
by vir'tue of

C

ca·bal'
cab'al·lar'i·a
ca·ban'a
cab'a·ret'
cab'i·net
  — coun'cil
ca'ble
  — trans'fer
cab'o·tage'
cache
ca·dav'er
ca·dav'er·ous
ca·de·re'
ca'det
ca'dit
ca·du'ca
ca·du'ca'ry
Cae·sar'e·an *or* cae·sar'-
  e·an
cae'ter·or'um
cae'ter·us
ca·fé'
caf'e·te'ri·a plan
cag'ey *or* cag'y
ca·hoots'
ca·jole'
cal'a·boose'
ca·lam'i·ty
cal'cu·late'
cal'cu·lat'ed
cal'en·dar
call
  — loan
  — op'tion
call'a·ble
  — bonds
call'ers
call'ing
  — an e·lec'tion
  — the dock'et
  —the ju'ry
  — to tes'ti·fy'
  — to the bar
ca·lum'ni·a
ca·lum'ni·a'tor
cal'um·ny
cam'er·a
  in —

cam'er·a·lis'tics
cam'ou·flage'
camp
cam·paign'
cam'pa·nar'i·um
cam'pa·ni'le'
camp'ers
ca·nal'
can'cel
can'cel·la'tion
  — clause
can'celled
  — check
can'di·date'
can'na·bis
can'on
  — law
ca·non'i·cal
  — dis'a·bil'i·ty
can'on·ist
can'ons
  — of con·struc'tion
  — of eth'ics
can'tel *or* can'tle
can'tred
can'vass
can'vass·er
ca'pa·ble
ca·pac'i·ty
ca'pax'
  — do'li'
  — ne·go'ti·i'
cape
ca'pi·as
  — ad au'di·en'dum ju·
    dic'i·um
  — ad com'pu·tan'dum
  — ad pro'se·quen'dum
  — ad re'spon·den'dum
  — ad sat'is·fac'i·en'dum
  — ex'ten·di' fa'ci·as
  — in with'er·nam'
  — pro fi'ne'
  — ul'la·ga'tum
cap'i·a·tur' pro fi'ne'
cap'i·ta
 per —
cap'i·tal *n.*
 paid'-in' —
 stat'ed —
cap'i·tal *adj.*

  — ac·count'
  — as'sets'
  — case *or* crime
  — con'tri·bu'tion
  — ex·pen'di·ture
  — gains
  — im·pair'ment
  — in·crease'
  — in·vest'ment
  — mar'ket
  — out'lay'
  — pun'ish·ment
  — re·cov'er·y
  — re·turn'
  — stock
  — stock tax
  — struc'ture
  — sur'plus
  — trans·ac'tion
cap'i·tal·ist
cap'i·tal·i·za'tion
 meth'od
cap'i·tal·ize'
cap'i·ta'tim
cap'i·ta'tion tax
cap'i·tol
ca·pit'u·la
ca·pit'u·la'tion
cap'tain
cap'tain·cy
cap·ta'tion
cap'ta·tor
cap'tion
cap'tives
cap'tor
cap'ture
cap'ut
car'at
car·ca'num
car'cass
car·ca'tus
car'cel·age
car'cer
car·cin'o·gen
car·ci·no·gen'ic
card'hold'er
car'di·nal
car'di·ol'o·gy
car'di·o·vas'cu·lar
care
 or'di·nar'y —

rea'son·a·ble —
care'less
care'less·ly
car'go
Car'lisle ta'bles
car'load'
Car'mack Act
car'nal
— a·buse'
— knowl'edge
car'nal·i·ter
car'nal'i·ty
car'nal·ly knew
car'riage
Car'riage of Goods by
    Sea Act
car'ri·er
car'ri·er's lien
car'ry
— a mem'ber
— an e·lec'tion
— back
— costs
— on trade or busi'ness
car'ry·ing
— a·way'
— charge
cart
— bote
car'ta
carte blanche
car·tel'
car'tu·lar'y
car'u·cate
case
— in chief
— law
— sys'tem
case'ment
cas'es
— and con'tro·ver'sies
case'work'er
cas for·tu'it
cash
— ac·count'
— book
— con'tract'
— dis'count'
— mar'ket val'ue
— note
— price

— sale
— sur·ren'der val'ue
— val'ue
— value op'tion
cash·ier'
cash·iered'
cash·ier's' check
cas'ing-head' gas
cas'ket
cas·sa're'
cast
— a·way'
cast'a·way'
cas'ti·ga·to'ry
cast'ing vote
cas'u·al
— em·ploy'ment
— pau'per
— poor
cas'u·al·ty
— in·sur'ance
— loss
ca'su·is'tic or ca'su·is'ti·
    cal
ca'su·ist'ry
ca'sus
— bel'li'
— foe'de·ris
— for·tu'i·tus
— ma'jor
— o·mis'sus
cat'al·la
cat'als
ca·tas'tro·phe
catch'ings
catch'land'
catch'poll'
cat'e·gor'i·cal
cat'e·gor'i·cal·ly
ca·the'dral
cat'tle
— gate
— pass
— range
— rus'tling
cat'tle·guard
Cau·ca'sian
cau'cus
cau'sa
— list
— mor'tis

— pat'et
— prox'i·ma
— re·mo'ta
— si'ne' qua non
— tur'pis
caus'al
cau·sal'i·ty
cau·sa'tion
cau·sa·tor
cause v.
— suit to be brought
cause n.
— books
— in fact
— list
— of ac'tion
— of in'ju·ry
causes cé·lèbres'
cause'way'
cau'tion
cau'tion·ar'y
—in·struc'tion
— judg'ment
cau'tious
ca've·at'
— ac'tor
— emp'tor'
— to will
— ven'di·tor'
— vi'a·tor'
ca've·a'tor
ca·ve're'
cease
— and de·sist' or'der
cede
cel·a'tion
cel'e·bra'tion of mar'-
    riage
cel'i·ba·cy
cel'i·bate
cem'e·ter'y
ce'ne·gild'
cen·si'taire'
cen'sive
cen'sor
cen'sor·ship'
cen'sur·a·ble
cen'sure
cen'sus
— bu'reau
— re'ga'lis

cent
cen'tal
cen'te·na
cen'ter
cen·time'
cen'tral·i·za'tion
Cen'tral In·tel'li·gence
 A'gen·cy
cen'tu·ry
ceorl
ce'pi
ce'pit
— et ab·dux'it
— et as'por·ta'vit
— in a'li·o' lo'co'
ce'ra or ce're
— im·pres'sa
cer'e·bel'lum
cer'e·bral
cer'e·brum
cer'tain
 sum —
cer'tain·ty
cer'ti·fi'a·ble
cer'ti·fi'a·bly
cer·tif'i·cate
— of de·pos'it
— of in·cor'po·ra'tion
— of need
— of oc'cu·pan·cy
— of pub'lic con·ven'-
  ience and ne·ces'si·ty
— of reg'is·try
— of stock
— of title
cer'ti·fi·ca'tion
— mark
— of ques'tions of law
cer'ti·fied'
— car'ri·ers
— check
— cop'y
— mail
— pub'lic ac·count'ant
— ques'tion
cer'ti·fy'
cer'ti·o·ra'ri
ces·sa're'
ces'sion
— of goods
cess'ment

ces'sor
ces·tui'
— que trust
— que use
— que vie
ces·tuy'
chace
chace'a·ble
chac'er
chain
— of cus'to·dy
— of pos·ses'sion
— of ti'tle
chair'man
chal'dron or chal'dern or
 chal'der
chal'lenge v.
chal'lenge n.
— for cause
gen'er·al —
per·emp'to·ry —
prin'ci·pal —
— prop'ter af·fec'tum
— propter de·fec'tum
— propter de·lic'tum
— propter ho·no'ris re·
  spec'tum
— to the ar'ray
— to the fa'vor
— to the pan'el
— to the poll
cham'ber
— of com'merce
star —
— sur'veys'
cham'ber·lain
cham'bers
in —
cham'fer
cha·motte'
cham'per·tor
cham'per·tous
cham'per·ty
cham'pi·on
chance
chance'-med'ley
chan'cel·lor
chan'cel·lor·ship'
chan'cer
chan'cer·y
change

— of ben'e·fi'ci·ar'y
— of dom'i·cile'
— of ven'ue
chan'nel
chap'el
chap'er·on'
chap'lain
chap'lain·cy
chap'lain·ship'
chap'ter
char'ac·ter
— ev'i·dence
charge v.
charge n.
— and dis'charge'
gen'er·al —
— sheet
spe'cial —
charge'a·ble
charge ac·count'
re·volv'ing —
char·gé' d'af·faires'
charge'-off'
charg'es
charg'ing lien
char'i·ta·ble
— be·quest'
— con'tri·bu'tion
— cor'po·ra'tion
— de·duc'tion
— foun·da'tion
— im·mu'ni·ty
— in'sti·tu'tion
— or'gan·i·za'tion
— re·main'der
— trust
char'i·ty
char'la·tan
char'la·tan·ism
chart
char'ta
char'ter v.
char'ter n.
— boat
— par'ty
char'ter·er
char'ter·house'
chase
chas'sis
chaste
— char'ac·ter

chas'ti·ty
chat'tel
  — mort'gage
  — pa'per
chat'tels
 real —
chaud'-med'ley
chauf'feur
cheat
cheat'ers
check v.
check n.
 blank —
 cash·ier's' —
 trav'el·er's —
check'book'
check'-off sys'tem
check'-roll'
checks and bal'anc·es
cheque
Cher'o·kee' Na'tion
che'vage
Chi·ca'go Board of
  Trade
chi·cane'
Chick'a·saw' Na'tion
chief
 dec'la·ra'tion in—
 ex·am'i·na'tion in —
 — judge
 — jus'tice
 — mag'is·trate'
  ten'ant in—
child
 — a·buse'
 — la'bor laws
 post'hu·mous—
 qua'si' post'hu·mous —
 — sup·port'
chil'dren
child's part
chill'ing
 — a sale
 — ef·fect'
chi·rop'o·dist
chi·rop'o·dy
chi'ro·prac'tic
chi'ro·prac'tor
chi·rur'geon
chiv'al·rous
chiv'al·ry

choate lien
choice of law
chops
chose
 — in ac'tion
 — in pos·ses'sion
cho'sen free'hold'ers
Chris'tian
 — name
Chris'ti·an'i·ty
chron'ic
 — al'co·hol'ism
chro·nol'o·gy
chron'o·log'i·cal
church
 — prop'er·ty
 — war'dens
churl
cic'a·trix'
ci'der
ci'pher
cir'ca
cir'cuit
 — courts
 — courts of ap·peals'
 — judge
 — jus'tice
cir·cu'i·tous
cir·cu'i·ty of ac'tion
cir'cu·lar
 — let'ter of cred'it
 — notes
cir'cu·la'ted
cir'cu·la'tion
cir·cum'fer·ence
cir·cum'fer·en'tial
cir'cum·lo·cu'tion
cir'cum·loc'u·to'ry
cir'cum·scribe'
cir'cum·spect'
cir'cum·stanc'es
cir'cum·stan'tial ev'i·
  dence
cir'cum·ven'tion
cir'cus
cis'ta
ci·ta'tion
 — of au·thor'i·ties
ci·ta'tors
cite
cit'i·zen

cit'i·zen's ar·rest'
cit'i·zen·ship'
cit'y
 — coun'cil
 — e·lec'tion
civ'ic
 — en'ter·prise'
civ'il
 — ac'tion
 — com·mit'ment
 — con·spir'a·cy
 — con·tempt'
 — dam'age acts
 — dis'o·be'di·ence
 — en·force'ment pro·
  ceed'ing
 — in'for·ma'tion
 — in'quest'
 — li'a·bil'i·ty
 — lib'er·ties
 — nui'sance
 — ob'li·ga'tion
 — of'fice
 — of'fi·cer
 — pro·ce'dure
 — rights
 — serv'ice
 — side
 — town'ship'
ci·vil'ian
ci'vi·lis
ci·vil'i·ter
 — mor'tu·us
civ'i·li·za'tion
Civ'il Law
claim v.
claim n.
 — ac·crued'
 — and de'liv'er·y
 — bond
 — in eq'ui·ty
 — of own'er·ship', right,
  and ti'tle
 — prop'er·ty bond
claim'ant
claims
 — ad·just'er
clam'or
clan·des'tine
class
 — ac'tion

— gift
— leg'is·la'tion
— rep're·sen·ta'tion
clas'si·fi·ca'tion
— of risks
clas'si·fied'
clas'si·fy'
clause
clau'sum
—fre'git
Clay'ton Act
clean
—bill of lad'ing
— hands
clean'-air' acts
clear
— and con·vinc'ing
   proof
— and pres'ent dan'ger
— an·nu'i·ty
— chance
— days
— ev'i·dence
— mar'ket val'ue
— proof
— ti'tle
— val'ue
clear'ance
clear'ing
— ti'tle
clear'ing-house'
clear'ings
clear'ly
— er·ro'ne·ous
cler'gy
cler'gy·man
cler'i·cal
— er'ror
— mis·pri'sion
cler'i·cus
— mer·ca'ti'
— pa·ro'chi·a'lis
clerk
— of ar·raigns'
— of as·size'
— of court
— of en·roll'ments
— of in·dict'ments
— of rec'ords and writs
— of seats

— of the crown in
   chan'cer·y
— of the House of
   Com'mons
— of the mar'ket
— of the par'lia·ments
— of the peace
— of the pet'ty bag
— of the priv'y seal
— of the sig'net
— of the ta'ble
clerk'ship'
cli'ent
cli'en·te'la
cli'en·tele'
Clif'ford's Inn
Clif'ford Trust
clin'i·cal
clipped sov'er·eign·ty
clo'ere
close v.
close n.
close adj.
— cor'po·ra'tion
— jail ex'e·cu'tion
closed
— shop
— shop con'tract'
— trans·ac'tion
closed'-end' mort'gage
close-hauled
clos'ing
— ar'gu·ment
— costs
— state'ment
clo'ture
cloud on ti'tle
clough
club
— law
clue
clus'ter zon'ing
clutch
clyp'e·us or clip'e·us
coach
co'ad·ju'tor
co'ad·min'is·tra'tor
co'ad·ven'tur·er
co'a·li'tion
co'as·sign·ee'
coast v.

coast n.
— guard
— wa'ters
coast'er
coast'ing
— trade
coast'wise'
cock'bill'
cock'et
cock'pit'
co'con·spir'a·tor
code
— ci·vil'
— d'in·struc·tion' cri·mi·
   nelle'
— noir
— pé·nal'
Code
— Na·po·lé·on'
— of Fed'e·ral Reg'u·la'·
   tions
— of Jus·tin'i·an
— of Mil'i·tar'y Jus'tice
— of Pro·fes'sion·al Re·
   spon'si·bil'i·ty
co'de·fen'dant
co'dex
— Gre·go'ri·a'nus
— Her·mog'e·ni·a'nus
— Ju'ris Ca·non'i·ci'
— Jus·tin'i·a'ne·us
— Re·pet'i·tae' Prae·lec'·
   ti·o'nis
— The·o·do'si·a'nus
— Vet'us
cod'i·cil
cod'i·fi·ca'tion
co·emp'tion
co·e'qual
co·erce'
co·er'cion
co·ex·ec'u·tor
cof'er·er of the queen's
   house'hold'
cog'nates'
cog·ni'ti·o'
cog·ni'ti·o·nes'
cog·ni'ti·o'ni·us mit·
   ten'dis
cog'ni·tive
cog'ni·za·ble

cog'ni·zance
cog·ni·zee'
cog'ni·zor
cog·no'men
cog·no'vit
— ac'ti·o'nem
— note
co·hab'it
co·hab'i·tant
co·hab'i·ta'tion
Co'han Rule
co·heir'
co·heir'ess
coif
coin
coin'age
co'in·sur'ance
co'i·tus
co·ju'di·ces'
Coke's in'sti·tutes'
cold blood
co'li·ber'tus
col·lab'o·ra'tion
col·laps'i·ble cor'po·ra'-
   tion
col·late'
col·lat'er·al
— at·tack'
— con'tract'
— es·top'pel
— facts
— fraud
— im·peach'ment
— in·her'i·tance tax
— is'sues
— kins'men
— line
— loan
— mort'gage
— prom'ise
— se·cu'ri·ty
— source rule
— un'der·tak'ing
col·la'ti·o'
— bo·no'rum
— sig·no'rum
col·la'tion
col·la'ti·o·ne' he·rem'i·
   ta'gi·i'
col·lect'
— on de·liv'er·y

col·lect'i·ble
col·lec'tive
— bar'gain·ing
— bargaining a·gree'-
   ment
— bargaining u'nit
— la'bor a·gree'ment
— mark
col·lec'tor
col·leg'a·tar'y
col'lege
col·le'gi·a
col·le'gi·al
col·lide'
col'lier·y
col·li'sion
col'lo·cate'
col'lo·ca'tion
col·lo'qui·um
col·lu'sion
col·lu'sive
— ac'tion
— join'der
colne
col'o·ny
col'or
— of au·thor'i·ty
— of law
— of of'fice
— of ti'tle
un'der — of state law
col'or·a·ble
— claim
— im'i·ta'tion
col'ored
col'pic·es
colt
com'bar·o'nes'
com'bat
com·bi·na'tion
— in re·straint' of trade
— pat'ent
com·bus'ti·o'
co'mes'
comes and de·fends'
com'fort
com'i·ta'tus
com'i·tes'
co'mi·tis'sa
co'mi·ti'va
com'i·ty

com'ma
com·mand'
com·mand'er in chief
com·mand'er·y
com·mand'ment
com·mence'
com·mence'ment
— of ac'tion
— of a dec'la·ra'tion
com'men·da'tion
com·men'da·to'ry
com'ment'
— up·on' the ev'i·dence
com'merce
— a·mong' the states
— clause
do·mes'tic —
for'eign —
in'ter·na'tion·al —
in'ter·state' —
in'tra·state' —
— with for'eign na'tions
— with In'di·an tribes
Com'merce De·part'-
   ment
com·mer'ci·a bel'li'
com·mer'cial
— a'gent
— bank
— brib'er·y
— court
— es·tab'lish·ment
— frus·tra'tion
— law
— let'ter of cred'it
— mo'tor ve'hi·cle
— pa'per
— trav'el·er
— u'nit
com·min'gle
com·min'gling of funds
com'mi·nute'
com'mi·nu'tion
com'mis·sar'y
com'mis·sar'i·at
com·mis'sion
— mer'chant
— of an·tic'i·pa'tion
— of ap·praise'ment and
   sale
— of ar·ray'

— of as·size'
— to ex·am'ine wit'ness·
  es
com·mis'sioned of'fi·
  cers
com·mis'sion·er
  coun'ty —
  — of bail
  — of deeds
  — of high'ways'
Com·mis'sion·er of
  Pat'ents and Trade'-
  marks
com·mis'sions
com·mit'
com·mit'ment
  civ'il —
com·mit'tal
com·mit'tee
com·mit'ti·tur
com·mo·da'tum
com·mod'i·ties
com·mod'i·ty
  — fu'tures
  — pa'per
com'mon
  — ap·pen'dant
  — ap·pur'te·nant
  — ar'e·a
  — at large
  — bench
  — car'ri·er
  — de·fense'
  — en'e·my doc'trine
  — en'ter·prise'
  — good
  — hu·man'i·ty doc'trine
  — in gross
  — law
  — mar'ket
  — nui'sance
  — of dig'ging
  — of es·to'vers
  — of pis·ca·ry
  — of shack
  — of tur'ba·ry
  — pleas
  — prop'er·ty
  — re·cov'er·y
  — sans nom·bre'
  — sense

— weal
com'mon·a·ble
com'mon·al·ty
com'mon·ance
com'mon·ers
com'mon-law'
  — ac'tion
  — as·sign'ments
  — cheat
  — con·tempt'
  — cop'y·right'
  — courts
  — crime
  — ex·tor'tion
  — ju'ris·dic'tion
  — lar'ce·ny
  — lien
  — mar'riage
  — mort'gage
  — pro·ce'dure acts
  — rem'e·dy
  — trade'mark'
  — wife
com'mons
Com'mons
  — House of
com'mon·wealth'
com'mo·ran·cy
com'mo·rant
com'mo·ri·en'tes'
com'morth' *or* com'orth'
com'mote'
com·mo'tion
com·mune'
com·mu'ne'
  — con·cil'i·um
  — concilium reg'ni'
  — for'um
  — pla'ci·tum
  — vin'cu·lum
com·mu'ni·a
  — pla'ci·ta
com·mu'ni·bus an'nis
com·mu'ni·cate'
com·mu'ni·ca'tion
  con'fi·den'tial —
  priv'i·leged —
com·mu'ni' cus·to'di·a
com·mu'nis
  — rix'a·trix'
  — scrip'tur·a

— sti'pes'
com'mu·nism
com'mu·nist
Com'mu·nist
com·mu'ni·tas reg'ni'
  Ang'li·ae'
com·mu'ni·ty
  — prop'er·ty
com·mu·ta'tion
  — of sen'tence
  — of tax'es
com'mu·ta'tive
  — jus'tice
com·pact' *n.*
com·pact' *adj.*
com·pan'age
Com·pan'ion of the
  Gar'ter
com·pan'ions
com·pa·ny
  joint'-stock' —
  lim'it·ed —
  pub'lic —
com·par'a·tive
  — ju'ris·pru'dence
  — neg'li·gence
  — rec'ti·tude'
com'pass·ing
com·pat'i·bil'i·ty
com·pel'
com·pel'ling state in'-
  ter·est
com·pen'di·um
com·pen'sa·ble
  — in'ju·ry
com·pen·sa'ti·o' crim'i·
  nis
com·pen·sa'tion
com·pen·sa·to'ry dam'-
  ag·es
com·pe'ru·it ad di'em
com·pete'
com·pe·ten·cy
com·pe·tent
  — au·thor'i·ty
  — ev'i·dence
  — court
  — to stand tri'al
  — wit'ness
com·pe·ti'tion
com·pet'i·tive

— bid'ding
com·pet'i·tors
com'pi·la'tion
com·pile'
com·piled' stat'utes
com·plain'ant
com·plaint'
com·plete'
com·plet'ed
com·ple'tion
com'pli·cat'ed
com'plice
com·plic'i·ty
com·ply'
com'pos men'tis
com'pos su'i'
com·pos'ite work
com·po·si'tion
  — deed
  — in bank'rupt'cy
  — of mat'ter
  — with cred'i·tors
com·pound' *v.*
com·pound' *n.*
com·pound' *adj.*
  — in'ter·est
  — lar'ce·ny
com·pound'er
com·pound'ing a fel'o·
ny
com'pre·hen'sive
  — zon'ing plan
com'print'
com·prise'
com'pro·mise'
  — ver'dict
of'fer of —
comp·trol'ler
  — gen'er·al
  — of cur'ren·cy
com·pul'sa
com·pul'sion
com·pul'so·ry *n.*
com·pul'so·ry *adj.*
  — ar'bi·tra'tion
  — at·ten'dance
  — coun'ter·claim'
  — dis·clo'sure
  — in·sur'ance
  — non·suit'
  — proc'ess'

— sale or pur'chase
— self'-in·crim'i·na'tion
com'pur·ga·tor
com'pu·ta'tion
com'pu·tus
con·ceal'
con·cealed'
con·ceal'ers
con·ceal'ment
con·cep'tion
con·cern'
con·cerned'
con·cern'ing
con'cert'
con·cert'ed ac'tion
con·ces'si'
con·ces'si·o'
con·ces'sion
con·ces'sit sol·ve·re'
con·ces'sor
con·ces'sum
con·ces'sus
con·cil'i·ab'u·lum
con·cil'i·a'tion
con·cil'i·um
  — re'gis
con·ci·o·na'tor
con·clude'
con·clud'ed
con·clu'sion
  — of fact
  — of law
con·clu'sive
  — ev'idence
  — pre·sump'tion
con'cord'
con·cor'dat'
con·cor'di·a
con·cu·bar'i·a
con·cu'be·ant
con·cu'bi·nage
con·cu·bine'
con·cur'
con·cur'rence
con·cur'rent
  — caus'es
  — ju'ris·dic'tion
  — liens
  — pow'er
  — sen'tenc·es
con·cur'ring o·pin'ion

con·cur'so'
con·cus'sion
con·demn'
con'dem·na'tion
con·dem'na·to'ry
con·dic'ti·o'
  — cer'ti'
  — ex le'ge'
  — in deb'i·ta'ti'
  — re'i' fur·ti'vae'
  — si'ne' cau'sa
con·di'ti·o'
con·di'tion
  af·fir'ma·tive —
  cas'u·al —
  con·sis'tent —
  cop'u·la'tive —
  de·pend'ent —
  dis·junc'tive —
  dis·solv'ing —
  — en fait
  es·tate' on —
  ex·press' —
  im·plied' —
  im·pos'si·ble —
  — in deed
  in'de·pend'ent —
  — in fact
  — in law
  mixed —
  mu'tu·al —
  neg'a·tive —
  — of em·ploy'ment
  — of sale
  pos'si·ble —
  po'tes·ta'tive —
  prec'e·dent —
  re·pug'nant —
  res'o·lu·to'ry —
  sin'gle —
  sub'se·quent —
  sus·pen'sive —
con·di'tion·al
  — en·dorse'ment
  — prom'ise
  — sale con'tract'
  — sen'tence
con'do·min'i·um
con'do·na'tion
con·done'
con·duce'

con·duct' *v.*
con'duct' *n.*
  es·top'pel by —
cone and key
con·fec'ti·o'
con·fed'er·a·cy
con·fed'er·a'tion
con·fer·ence
con·fess'
con·fes'si·o'
con·fes'sion
  — and a·void'ance
  — of de·fense'
  — of judg'ment
con·fes'so'
  bill tak'en pro —
con·fes'sor
con'fi·dant'
con·fide'
con'fi·dence
  — game
con'fi·den'tial
  — com·mu'ni·ca'tions
  — re·la'tion
con'fi·den'ti·al'i·ty
con·fine'ment
con·firm'
con·fir·ma'ti·o'
  — char·ta'rum
  — cres'cens'
  — di·min'u·ens'
  — per·fi'ci·ens'
con'fir·ma'tion
  — of sale
con'firm·ee'
con·fir'mor
con·fis'ca·ble
con'fis·ca're'
con'fis·cate'
con'fis·ca'tion
  — acts
  — cas'es
con·fis'ca·to'ry
  — rates
con'fisk'
con·fi'tens' re'us
con'flict'
  — of au·thor'i·ty
  — of in'ter·est
  — of laws
con·flict'ing ev'i·dence

con·formed' cop'y
con·form'ing use
Con·form'i·ty
  — Act
  — stat'ute
con·frai·rie'
con'freres
con'fron·ta'tion
con·fu'sion
con·fute'
con'ge·a·ble
con·gen'i·tal
con·glom'er·ate'
con'gre·gate'
con'gre·ga'tion
con'gress
con·gres'sion·al
  — ap·point'ment
  — com·mit'tee
  — dis'trict
  — im·mu'ni·ty
Con·gres'sion·al Rec'-
ord
con'gress·man
con'jec'ti·o'
con·jec'tur·al
con·jec'ture
con·joint' rob'ber·y
con'joints'
con·ju'dex
con'ju·gal
  — rights
con·junc'tim
  — et di·vi'sim
con·junc'tive
con'ju·ra'ti·o'
con'ju·ra'tion
con'ju·ra'tor
con·nect'
con·nect'ed
con·nect'ing
  — car'ri·er
  — facts
  — up doc'trine
con·nec'tion
con·niv'ance
con·nive'
con'quer·or
con'quest
con'ques·tor
con'qui·si'ti·o'

con'san·guin'e·ous
con'san·guin'i·ty
  — lin'e·al and col·lat'er·
  al
con'science
  — of the court
con'sci·en'tious ob·jec'-
tor
con'scion·a·ble
con·scrip'tion
con·se·crate'
con·sec'u·tive
  — sen'tenc·es
con·sen'su·al
  — con'tract'
  — mar'riage
con·sen'sus ad i'dem
con·sent'
  — de·cree'
  ex·press' —
  im·plied' —
  — judg'ment
  — search
con'se·quence
con·ser'va·tor
con·serve'
con·sid'er
con·sid'er·a·ble
con·si'de·ra'ti·o' cu'ri·
ae'
con·sid'er·a'tion
  con·cur'rent —
  con·tin'u·ing —
  eq'ui·ta·ble —
  ex'e·cut'ed —
  ex·ec'u·to'ry —
  ex·press'—
  fail'ure of —
  fair —
  fair and val'u·a·ble —
  good —
  gra·tu'i·tous —
  il·le'gal —
  im·plied' —
  im·pos'si·ble —
  in·ad'e·quate —
  le'gal —
  mor'al —
  nom'i·nal —
  past —
  pe·cu'ni·ar'y —

suf·fi′cient —
val′u·a·ble —
want of —
con·sid′er·a′tur
con·sid′ered
con·sign′
con′sign·ee′
con·sign′ment
— con′tract′
— sale
con·sig′nor
con·si′li·um
con·si′mi·li′ ca′su′
con·sist′
con·sis′tent
con·sist′ing
con·sis′tor
con·sis′to·ry
— courts
con′so·la′tion
con·sol′i·date′
con·sol′i·dat′ed
— ap·peal′
— bal′ance sheets
— laws
— mort′gage
— se·cu′ri·ties
— tax re′turns
con·sol′i·da′tion
— of ac′tions
— of ben′e·fic·es
con·sol′i·da′tions of
cor′por·a′tions
con·sor′ti·um
con′sort·ship′
con·spic′u·ous
con·spir′a·cy
— in re·straint′ of trade
con′spi·ra′ti·o·ne′
con·spir′a·tors
con·spire′
con′sta·ble
con′sta·ble·wick′
con·stab′u·la′ri·us
con·stab′u·lar′y
con′stant
con′stant·ly
con′stat′
con·state′
con·stit′u·en·cy
con·stit′u·ent

con′sti·tut′ed au·thor′i·ties
con′sti·tu′tion
con′sti·tu′tion·al
— al·cal′de
— con·ven′tion
— court
— law
— of′fi·cer
— right
con·straint′
con·struct′
con·struc′tion
— con′tract′
eq′ui·ta·ble —
strict —
con·struc′tive
— as·sent′
— au·thor′i·ty
— con·di′tion
— con′tract′
— de·ser′tion
— e·vic′tion
— fraud
— in·tent′
— no′tice
— pos·ses′sion
strict and lib′er·al —
— tak′ing
— trust
— trust ex de·lic′to′
con·strue′
con′stu·prate′
con·sue·tu′di·nes
con·sue·tu·din′i·bus et
ser·vi′ci·is
con·su·e·tu′do
— An′gli·ca′na
— cu′ri·ae′
con′sul
con′su·lar courts
con′su·late
con·sul′tar·y re·sponse′
con·sul·ta′tion
con·su′mer
— ad′vo·cate
— cred′it trans·ac′tion
— goods
— re·port′
Con·su′mer
— Cred′it Code

— Credit Pro·tec′tion Act
— Price In′dex
— Prod′uct Safe′ty Com·mis′sion
con·sum′mate adj.
— lien
con′sum·mate′ v.
con′sum·ma′tion
con·sump′tion
con′tam·i·na′tion
con·tan′go′
con·temn′er
con′tem·plate
con′tem·pla′tion
— of bank′rupt′cy
— of death
— of in·sol′ven·cy
con·tempt′
— of court
— pow′er
— pro·ceed′ing
con·ten′tious
con·tent′ment
con′tents
con·ter′mi·nous
con·test′ v.
con′test′ n.
con·test′ed e·lec′tion
con′text′
con·tex′tu·al
con·tig′u·ous
con′ti·gu′i·ty
Con′ti·nen′tal Con′gress
con·tin′gen·cy
— with dou′ble as′pect′
con·tin′gent
— claim
— debt
— es·tate′, in′ter·est, or right
— fee
— fund
— li′a·bil′i·ty
— re·main′der
con·tin′u·ance
con·tin′u·an′do′
con·tin′u·ing
— con′tract′
— of·fense′

con·tin'u·ous
— ad·verse' use
con·tin'u·ous·ly
con'tra
— bo'nos mo'res'
— for'mam col·la'ti·o'nis
— formam do'ni'
— formam fe·of'fa·
men'ti'
— formam sta·tu'ti'
— jus com·mu'ne'
— leg'em ter'rae'
— om'nes' gen'tes'
— pa'cem
— pro'fe·ren'tem
— va'di·um et pleg'i·um
— ver'i·ta'tem lex nun'-
quam al'i·quid' per·
mit'tit
con'tra·band'
con'tra·cep'tion
con'tract'
bi·lat'er·al —
con·di'tion·al —
es·top'pel by —
spe'cial —
un·con'scion·a·ble —
— un'der seal
u'ni·lat'er·al —
u·su'ri·ous —
writ'ten —
con·tract'ing par'ties
con·trac'tion
con'trac'tor
gen'er·al —
in'de·pend'ent —
con'tracts'
ex'e·cut'ed and ex·ec'u·
to'ry —
ex·press' and im·plied' —
joint and sev'er·al —
qua'si' —
con·trac'tu·al ob'li·ga'-
tion
con'tra·dict'
con'tra·dic'tion in
terms
con'tra·fac'ti·o'
con'tra·li·ga'ti·o'
con'tra·man·da'ti·o'
con'tra·man·da'tum

con'tra·pla'ci·tum
con'tra·pos·i'ti·o'
con'tra'ry
— to the ev'i·dence
— to law
con'tra·vene'
con'tra·ven'ing eq'ui·ty
con'tra·ven'tion
con'trec·ta'ti·o'
con·trib'ute
con·trib'u·ting cause
con·tri·bu'tion
con·trib'u·to'ry n.
con·trib'u·to'ry adj.
— neg'li·gence
con·trive'
con·tri'vance
con·trol'
con·trolled'
— sub'stance
con·trol'ler
con·trol'ment
con·tro'ver
con·tro·ver'sial
con·tro·ver'sy
con·tro·vert'
con·tu·ma'ce' cap'i·en'-
do
con·tu·ma'cious con'-
duct'
con'tu·ma·cy
con'tu·max'
con'tu·me·ly
con·tuse'
con·tu'sion
con·u·sance
con'u·sant
con'u·see'
con'u·sor'
con·va·les'cence
con·ven'a·ble
con·vene'
con·ven'ience and ne·
ces'si·ty
con·ven'ient
con'vent
con·ven'ti·cle
con·ven'tion
con·ven'tion·al
con·ven·ti·o'ne'
con·ven'tions

con·ven'tu·als
con·ver'sant
con·ver·san'tes
con·ver·sa'tion
con·verse' n.
con·verse' v. & adj.
con·ver'sion
con·struc'tive —
di·rect' —
eq'ui·ta·ble —
fraud'u·lent —
con·vert'i·ble
— debt
— se·cu'ri·ties
con·vey'
con·vey'ance
ab'so·lute' —
con·di'tion·al —
fraud'u·lent —
mesne —
con·vey'anc·er
con·vey'anc·ing
con·vict' v.
con'vict' n.
con·vict'ed
con·vic'tion
con·vinc'ing proof
clear and —
con·viv'i·um
con·vo·ca'tion
con'voy'
co-ob'li·gor'
cool'ing-off' pe'ri·od
co'-op'
co·op'er·ate'
co·op'er·a'tion
co·op'er·a·tive
— a·part'ment
— as·so'ci·a'tion
— hous'ing
co'op·er·ti·o'
co'op·er'tus
co'-op·ta'tion
co·or'di·nate
— ju'ris·dic'tion
co·par'ce·nar'y
co·part'ner
co·part'ner·ship'
cope
cope'man or copes'man
copes'mate'

cop'pa
cop'pice
co·prin'ci·pal
cop'ro·la'li·a
copse
cop'u·la
cop'u·la'tive term
cop'y
cop'y·hold'
cop'y·right'
  com'mon law —
  — no'tice
Cop'y·right' Act
co'ram
  — dom'i·no' reg'e'
  — ip'so' reg'e'
  — no'bis
  — non ju'di·ce'
  — par'i·bus
  — sec'ta·tor'i·bus
  — vo'bis
cord
co're·spon'dent
corn
corn'age
cor'ner
cor·net'
Corn Prod'ucts case
co·ro'di·o' ha·ben'do'
co·ro'di·um
cor'o·dy
cor'ol·lar'y
co·ro'na
  — ma'la
co·ro·na're'
cor'o·nar'y
cor'o·na'tion
cor'o·ner
cor'o·ner's
  — court
  — in'quest'
cor'po·ral
  — pun'ish·ment
cor'po·rate
  — agent
  — al'ter e'go
  — au·thor'i·ties
  — bod'y
  — bonds
  — char'ter
  — cit'i·zen·ship'

  — en'ti·ty
  — fran'chise'
  — name
  — op'por·tu'ni·ty
  — pur'pose
  — trus·tees'
cor'po·ra'tion
  busi'ness —
  char'i·ta·ble —
  — de fac'to'
  — de ju're'
  joint'-stock' —
  mi'gra·to'ry —
  non·prof'it —
  not'-for-prof'it —
  pro·fes'sion·al —
  qua'si' pub'lic —
  Sub·chap'ter S —
cor'po·ra'tions
  ag·gre'gate and sole —
  close and o'pen —
  do·mes'tic and for'-
    eign —
  ec·cle'si·as'ti·cal and
    lay —
  el'ee·mos'y·nar'y and
    civ'il —
  mu·nic'i·pal —
  pub'lic and pri'vate —
  pub'ic-serv'ice —
  qua'si' —
  sub·sid'i·ar'y and par'-
    ent —
cor'po·ra'tor
cor·po're·al
  — her'e·dit'a·ments
  — prop'er·ty
corps dip'lo·ma·tique'
corpse
cor'pus
  — can·o·ni'ci'
  — ci·vil'is
  — cum cau'sa
  — de·lic'ti'
  — ju'ris
  — juris se·cun'dum
cor·rect' at·test'
cor·rec'tion
cor·rec'tion·al in'sti·tu'-
  tions

cor·rec'tor of the sta'-
  ple
cor·rel'a·tive
  — rights
cor're·spon'dence
cor're·spon'dent
  — bank
cor·rob'o·rate'
cor·rob'o·rat'ing ev'i·
  dence'
cor·rob'o·ra'tive ev'i·
  dence
cor·rupt'
cor·rup'tion
  — of blood
cor·rupt'ly
Cor·rupt' Prac'tic·es
  Act
corse'let
corse'-pres'ent
cor'tex'
cor'tis
cor·vée'
cos'en·age *or* cos'in·age
  or cous'in·age
cos'en·ing
cosh'er·ing
cost
  — ac·count'ing
  — and freight
  — ba'sis
  — bond
  im·put'ed —
co-stip'u·la'tor-cost'-
  -plus' con'tract
costs
  bill of —
  bond for —
  cer·tif'i·cate for —
  dou'ble —
  — of col·lec'tion
  se·cu'ri·ty for —
  stat'u·to'ry —
  — to a·bide' e·vent'
co'sur'e·ties
cot·ar'i·us
co·ten'an·cy
co'te·rie
cotes'wold'
cot'land
cot'seth·la

cot'seth·land
cot'se'tus
cot'tage
cot'ti·er ten'an·cy
cot'ton
cot·u'chans
couch'ant
couch'er *or* courch'er
coun'cil
  com'mon —
  priv'y —
coun'cil·or *or* coun'cil·
  lor
coun'cil·man
coun'sel
  — of rec'ord
  right to —
coun'sel·or *or* coun'sel·
  lor
count *v.*
count *n.*
  spe'cial —
coun'te·nance
count'er *n.*
coun'ter *adj.*
coun'ter·claim'
  com·pul'so·ry —
coun'ter·feit'
coun'ter·feit'er
coun'ter·mand'
coun'ter·of'fer
coun'ter·part'
coun'ter-rolls'
coun'ter·sign'
coun'ter·sig'na·ture
coun'ter·vail'
coun'ter·vail'ing eq'ui·
  ty
coun'tors
count'-out
coun'try
counts
  com'mon —
coun'ty
  — com·mis'sion·ers
  — seat
cou'pled with an in'ter·
  est
cou'pons
course
  — of busi'ness

— of deal'ing
— of em·ploy'ment
— of trade
court
— a·bove'
ap·pel'late —
— be·low'
civ'il —
crim'i·nal —
de fac'to' —
— en banc
eq'ui·ty —
full —
— hand
— in bank
in·fe'ri·or —
law —
— of ap·peals'
— of bank'rupt'cy
— of chan'cer·y
— of claims
— of com'mon pleas
— of com'pe·tent ju'ris·
  dic'tion
— of cus'toms and pat'·
  ent ap·peals'
— of eq'ui·ty
— of er'ror
— of ex·cheq'uer
— of first in'stance
— of gen'er·al ju'ris·dic'-
  tion
— of in'quir·y
— of law
— of lim'it·ed ju'ris·dic'-
  tion
— of ni'si' pri'us
— of or'di·nar'y
— of pas'sage
— of pro'bate'
— of rec'ord
— of ses'sions
— of spe'cial ses'sions
— of star cham'ber
— of the cor'o·ner
pro'bate' —
— re·port'er
su·pe'ri·or —
Court
High — of Ad'mi·ral·ty
— of Ad'mi·ral·ty

His Maj'es·ty's — of Ap·
  peal'
Su·preme' Ju·di'cial —
Supreme — of Er'rors
court'-bar'on
court'house'
court'-leet'
court'-mar'tial
courts
— mar'tial
— of ap·peals'
— of as·size' and ni'si'
  pri'us
court'yard'
cous'in
  first —
  quar'ter —
  sec'ond —
cou'ter·fea'sance
cov'en·a·ble
cov'e·nant
  ab'so·lute' —
  af·firm'a·tive —
  — a·gainst' en·cum'-
    branc·es
  aux·il'ia·ry —
  col·lat'er·al —
  con·cur'rent —
  con·di'tion·al —
  con·tin'u·ing —
  de·clar'a·to'ry —
  de·pend'ent —
  dis·junc'tive —
  ex'e·cut'ed —
  ex·ec'u·to'ry —
  ex·press' —
  — for fur'ther as·sur'-
    ance
  — for qui'et as·sur'ance
  — for ti'tle
  full —
  gen'er·al —
  im·plied' —
  in'de·pend'ent —
  — in gross
  in·her'ent —
  in·tran'si·tive —
  joint —
  mu'tu·al —
  neg'a·tive —
  non'com·pe·ti'tion —

— not to com·pete'
— not to sue
o·blig'a·to'ry —
— of non'claim'
— of right to con·vey'
— of sei'sin
— of war'ran·ty
per'son·al —
prin'ci·pal —
real —
— run'ning with land
— run'ning with ti'tle
sep'a·rate —
sev'er·al —
spe·cif'ic —
— to con·vey'
— to re·new'
— to stand seised
trans'si·tive —
u'su·al —
cov'e·nant·ee'
cov'e·nan'tor
cov'er
cov'er·age
cov'ert
cov'er·ture
cov'er-up'
cov'in
cov'i·nous
cow'ard·ice
coz'en or cos'en
craft
cran'age
cra'ni·al
cra'ni·um
cra'ven
cra'zy
cre·ate'
cre·den'tials
cred'i·bil'i·ty
cred'i·ble
— per'son
— wit'ness
cred'it
bill of —
— bu'reau
con·sum'er —
— in·sur'ance
let'ter of —
line of —
per'son·al —

— rat'ing
— re·port'
— sale
— slip
— un'ion
cred'it·a·ble
cred'it·ed
cred'it mo·bil·ier'
cred'i·tor
at·tach'ing —
— ben·e·fi'ci·ar·y
cer·tif'i·cate' —
ex'e·cu'tion —
gen'er·al —
judg'ment —
jun'ior —
lien —
pe·ti'tion·ing —
prin'ci·pal —
se·cured' —
sub'se·quent —
un·se·cured' —
war'rant —
cred'i·tors' bill or suit
cred'its
mu'tu·al —
cre·du'li·ty
cred'u·lous
creed
cre'mate'
cre·ma'tion
cre'ma·to'ri·ums or cre'-
    ma·to'ri·a
cre·pus'cu·lum
crest
cre'tin·ism
cri'er
cri·ez' la peez
crime
com'mon law —
— a·gainst' na'ture
— against the oth'er
cap'i·tal —
high —
in'fa·mous —
— ma'la in se
— ma'la pro·hib'i·ta
— of o·mis'sion
qua'si' —
stat'u·to'ry —
Crime Con·trol' Act

cri'men
— fal'si
— lae'sae' maj'es·ta'tis
crim'i·nal n.
crim'i·nal adj.
— ca·pac'i·ty
— con·spir'a·cy
— con'ver·sa'tion
— in'for·ma'tion
— in·tent'
— mal'ver·sa'tion
— neg'li·gence
— pro·ceed'ing
crim'i·nal·ist
crim'i·nate'
crim'i·nol'o·gy
crimp
crip'pling
crit'i·cism
cro'ci·a
croft
crois'es
croi'teir
crook
crook'ed
crop'per
cross
— ac'tion
— ap·peal'
— claim
— com·plaint'
— de·mand'
— er'rors
— in'ter·rog'a·to·ry
— li'cens·ing
— re·main'der
— sale
crossed check
cross'-ex·am'i·na'tion
cross'ing
crowd
crown
— cas'es
— cases re·served'
— court
— debts
— lands
— law
— of'fice
— office in chan'cer·y
— pa'per

— side
— so·lic'i·tor
croy
cru'ce' sig·na'ti'
cru'el and un·u'su·al
  pun'ish·ment
cru'el·ty
  men'tal —
  — to an'i·mals
  — to chil'dren
cruise
cry de pais *or* cri de pais
cry'er
cryp'ta
cuck'old
cuck'old·ry
cui bo'no'
cul·a'gi·um
cul de sac
cul'mi·nate'
cul'mi·na'tion
cul'pa
cul·pa'bil·is
cul'pa·bil'i·ty
cul'pa·ble
cul'prit
cul'ti·vate'
cul'ti·vat'ed
cul'ti·va'tor
cul·tu'ra
cul'vert·age
cum cop'u·la
cum o'ne·re'
cum tes'ta·men'to' an·
  nex'o'
cum'u·la'tive
  — div'i·dend'
  — ev'i·dence
  — pre·ferred' stock
  — sen'tence
  — vot'ing
cun'ni·lin'gus
cu'ra
cu'rate
cur'a·tive
cu·ra'tor
cu·ra'tor·ship'
cu'ra·trix'
cure
  — by ver'dict
cur'few

cu'ri·a
  — ad'vi·sa'ri' vult
  — ba·ro'nis *or* bar'on·um
  — co'mi·ta'tus
  — cur'sus aq'uae'
  — do'mi·ni'
  — mag'na
  — ma·jo'ris
  — mil'i·tum
  — pa·la'ti·i'
  — pe'dis pul'ver·i·za'ti'
  — pen'ti·ci·a'rum
  — per·so'nae'
  — re'gis
cur'ing ti'tle
cur'nock'
cur'ren·cy
cur'rent
  — ac·count'
  — debt fund ru!e
  — ex·pens'es
  — funds
  — li'a·bil'i·ties
  — main'te·nance
  — mar'ket val'ue
  — mon'ey
  — ob'li·ga'tions
  — price
  — rate of wag'es
  — rev'e·nues
  — val'ue
  — wag'es
  — year
cur·ric'u·lum
cur'rit qua'tu·or pe'di·
  bus
curs'ing
cur'si·tor bar'on
cur'si·tors
cur'so'
cur'sor
cur'so·ry ex·am'i·na'-
  tion
cur·tail'
cur'te·sy
  — con·sum'mate
  — in·i'ti·ate
Cur'teyn'
cur'ti·lage
cur·ti'les' ter'rae'
cur·til'li·um

cur'tis
cus·to'des
cus·to'di·al
  — in·ter'ro·ga'tion
cus·to'di·a le'gis
cus·to'di·am lease
cus'to·dy
cus'tom
  — and us'age
  — du'ties
cus'tom·ar'i·ly
cus'tom·ar'y
  — dis'patch
  — es·tates'
  — free'hold'
  — in·ter'pre·ta'tion
  — serv'ic·es
  — ten'ants
cus'tom·er
cus'tom·house'
  — bro'ker
cus'toms
  — court
cus'tos
  — bre'vi·um
  — fe·ra'rum
  — hor're·i' re'gi·i'
  — ma'ris
  — mo'rum
  — pla'ci·to'rum co·ro'-
    nae'
  — ro'tu·lo'rum
  — ter'rae'
cus·tu'ma
  — an·ti'qua si've' mag'-
    na
  — par'va et no'va
cu·ta'ne·ous
cuth'red
cut'purse'
cut'ter of the tal'lies
cy'cle
cyc'li·cal
cy'ne-bot
cy'ne·bote'
cy'ne-gild'
cy pres
cy·rog'ra·phar'i·us
cy·rog'ra·phum
cyst

cys'tic
czar

D

dac'ty·log'ra·phy
dag'ger
dai'ly
av'er·age — bal'ance
— bal'anc·es
— oc'cu·pa'tion
— rate of pay
dair'y
dale and sale
dam
dam'age
— fea'sant
— to per'son
dam'age-cleer'
dam'aged
dam'ag·es
ac'tu·al —
com·pen'sa·to'ry —
con'se·quen'tial —
ex·em'pla·ry —
ex·pec'tan·cy —
gen'er·al —
in'ci·den'tal —
— ir·rep'a·ra·ble
liq'ui·dat'ed — and pen'-
al·ties
nom'i·nal —
pe·cu'ni·ar'y —
prox'i·mate —
pun'i·tive —
re·mote' —
spe'cial —
spec'u·la·tive —
— ul'tra
un·liq'ui·dat'ed —
dame
damn
dam'na
dam·na'tus
dam'ni·fi·ca'tion
dam'ni·fy'
dam'num
— abs'que' in·ju'ri·a
— fa·ta'le'

Dane'gelt' *or* Dane'geld'
Dane'lage'
dan'ger
dan·ger'i·a
dan'ger·ous
— crim'i·nal
— in'stru·men·tal'i·ty
— oc'cu·pa'tion
— per se
— weap'on
dan'ism
dap'i·fer
dar·raign'
dar·rein'
— con·tin'u·ance
— pre·sent'ment
— sei'sin
Dart'mouth Col'lege
Case
dash
da'ta
date
— of in'ju·ry
— of is'sue
— of ma·tur'i·ty
da'tive
da'tum
daugh'ter
daugh'ter-in-law'
dau·phin'
day
— cer'tain
— in court
day'book'
day'light'
day'rule' *or* day'writ'
days
— in bank
— of grace
days'man
day'time'
day'were'
dea'con
dead
— freight
— let'ter
— let'ters
— pledge
dead'born'
dead'line'
dead'lock'

dead'ly weap'on
as·sault' with a —
— per se
dead'man'
dead man's
— part
— stat'ute
deaf and dumb
deal
deal'er
deal'ers' talk
deal'ings
dean
death
— ben'e·fits
— cer·tif'i·cate
— du'ty
nat'u·ral —
— pen'al·ty
pre·sump'tive —
— sen'tence
— tax'es
— trap
— war'rant
— watch
death'bed'
— deed
Death on High Seas
Act
deaths'man
de ban'co'
de·bas'ing
de·bauch'
de·bauch'er·y
de be'ne' es'se
de·ben'ture
con·vert'i·ble —
convertible sub·or'di·
nat'ed —
— in·den'ture
sink'ing fund —
— stock
sub·or'di·nat'ed —
deb'et
— et det'i·net
— et so'let
— si'ne' bre've'
de bi·en' et de mal
de bi·ens' le mort
deb'it
deb'i·tor

deb'i·trix'
deb'i·tum
  — si'ne' bre'vi'
de bo'nis non ad·min'i·
  stra'tis
de bo'no' et ma'lo'
debt
  an·ces'tral —
  bad —
  — fi·nanc'ing
  float'ing —
  judg'ment —
  le'gal —
  liq'uid —
  — se·cu'ri·ty
  — serv'ice
debt'ee'
debt'or
debt'or's sum'mons
Dec'a·logue'
de'ca·na'tus
de·ca'ni·a
de·ca'nus
de·cap'i·ta'tion
de·cease'
de·ceased'
de·ce'dent
de·ceit
de·ceit'ful
de'cen·cy
de·cen'na
de·cen'na·ry
de·cep'tion
de·cep'tive
  — sales prac'tic·es
de·ces'sus
de·cide'
dec'i·ma'tion
de·cime'
de·ci'sion
  — on mer'its
dec'la·ma'tion
de·clam'a·to'ry
de·clar'ant
dec'la·ra'tion
  — a·gainst' in'ter·est
  dy'ing —
  — in chief
  — of div'i·dend
  — of home'stead'
  — of in·ten'tion

  — of le·git'i·ma·cy
  — of right
  — of trust
  — of war
  self'-serv'ing —
Dec'la·ra'tion
  — of In'de·pend'ence
  — of Lon'don
  — of Par'is
  — of St. Pe'ters·burg'
de·clar'a·tor of trust
de·clar'a·to'ry
  — ac'tion
  — de·cree'
  — judg'ment
  — stat'ute'
de·clare'
de clau'so' frac'to'
dec'li·na'tion
de·clin'a·to'ry
  — ex·cep'tions
  — plea
de·cline'
de·col·la'ti·o'
de co·mon' droit
de'com·posed'
de con·sil'i·o' or con·cil'-
  i·o'
  — cu'ri·ae'
dec'o·rate'
dec'o·ra'tions
dec'o·ra·tive
dec'o·ra'tor
de cor'po·re' com'i·ta'-
  tus
de'coy'
de·cree'
  con·sent' —
  de·fi'cien·cy —
  — ni'si'
  — of dis'tri·bu'tion
  — of in·sol'ven·cy
  — of nul'li·ty
  — pro con·fes'so'
de·crep'it
de·cre'tal
  — or'der
de·crown'ing
de·cry'
de cu'jus
de cur'su'

de'di'
ded'i·cate'
ded'i·ca'tion
de di'e' in di'em
ded'i·mus po'tes·ta'tem
de·di'tion
de do'lo' ma'lo'
de do'nis
de·duct'i·ble
de·duc'tion
  — for new
  i'tem·ized' —
  stan'dard·ized' —
deed
  es·top'pel by —
  — for a nom'i·nal sum
  gra·tu'i·tous —
  — in fee
  — in·dent'ed
  — in·den'ture
  — of cov'e·nant
  — of gift
  — of re·lease'
  — of sep'a·ra'tion
  — of trust
  — poll
  — to lead uses
deem
deemed trans'fer·or'
deem'sters
Deep Rock doc'trine
de·face'
de fac'to'
  — con'tract'
  — cor'po·ra'tion
  — gov'ern·ment
  — in'te·gra'tion
  — mar'riage
  — seg're·ga'tion
de faire é·chelle'
de'fal·ca'tion
de·falk'
de·fam'a·cast'
def'a·ma'tion
de·fam'a·to'ry
  — li'bel
  — per quod
  — per se
de·fame'
de·fault'
  — judg'ment

de·fea′sance
de·fea′si·ble
  — fee
  — ti′tle
de·fea′si·bly vest′ed re·
  main′der
de·fea′sive
de·feat′
de′fect′
  fa′tal —
  la′tent —
  — of par′ties
  — of sub′stance
  pat′ent —
de·fec′tive
  — ti′tle
de·fec′tor
de·fec′tus
de·fend′
de·fen′dant
  — in er′ror
de·fen′da·re′
de·fen′de·mus
de·fend′er
  pub′lic —
de·fen·er·a′tion
de·fen′es·tra′tion
de·fense′
  af·fir′ma·tive —
  eq′ui·ta·ble —
  friv′o·lous —
  in·san′i·ty —
  le′gal —
  pre′ter·mit′ted —
  real —
de′fen·si′va
de·fen′sive
  —al′le·ga′tion
de·fen′so′
de·fer′
def′er·ence
def′er·en′tial
de·fer′ral
  — pe′ri·od
de·ferred′
  — bonds
  — charge
  — claims
  — com′pen·sa′tion
  — in′come′
  — life an·nu′i·ties

  — pay′ments
  — sen′tence
  — stock
de·fi′ance
de·fi′cien·cy
  — as·sess′ment
  — bill
  — judg′ment
  — no′tice
  — suits
def′i·cit
  — spend′ing
de·file′
de·file′ment
de·fine′
def′i·nite
def′i·ni′ti·o′
def′i·ni′tion
de·fin′i·tive
de·flect′
def′lo·ra′tion
de·force′
de·force′ment
de·for′ci·ant
de·form′i·ty
de·fos′sion
de·fraud′
  in·tent′ to —
de·fraud·a′tion
de·fraud′ed
de·funct′
de fur′to′
de·gas′ter′
de·gen′er·ate
deg′ra·da′tion
de·grad′ing
de gra′ti·a
de·gree′
  — of proof
de·hors′
de·hy′drate′
De′i′ gra′ti·a
de in′cre·men′to′
de in·ju′ri·a
de ju′di·ci′is
de ju′re′
de lat′e·re′
de′la′tor
de·la·tu′ra
de·lay′
del bi·en′ es·tre′

del cre′de·re′
de·lec′tus per·so′nae′
del′e·gate′
del′e·gates′
  the high court of —
del′e·ga′tion
  — of pow′ers
de·lete′
del′e·te′ri·ous
de·lib′er·ate′ v.
de·lib′er·ate adj.
  — speed
de·lib′er·ate·ly
de·lib′er·a′tion
del′i·ca·tes′sen
de·lict′
de·lic′tu·al fault
de·lic′tum
de·lim′it
de·lim′i·ta′tion
de·lin′quen·cy
de·lin′quent n.
de·lin′quent adj.
  — child
  — ju′ve·nile′
  — tax′es
de·lir′i·ous
de·lir′i·um
  — fe′bri·le′
  — tre′mens
de·list′
de·liv′er·ance
de·liv′er·y
  ab′so·lute′ and con·di′-
    tion·al —
  ac′tu·al and con·struc′-
    tive —
  — and ac·cep′tance
  — bond
  — in es′crow′
  — order
  sec′ond —
  sym·bol′ic —
de·lu′sion
de·lu′sive
de·lu′so·ry
de·main′
de ma′lo′
de·mand′ v.
de·mand′ n.
  cross —

— de·pos'its
— draft
— in re·con·ven'tion
— note
on —
de·mand'ant
de·man'dress
de·mar·ca'tion
de·mean'or
de·mens'
de·ment'ed
de·men·te·nant' en a·vant'
de·men'ti·a
— prae'cox'
de mer·ca·tor'i·bus
de·mesne'
— lands
— lands of the crown
de·mesn'i·al
dem'i
de min'i·mus
— non cu'rat lex
dem'i-sangue' or dem'-y-sangue'
de·mise' v.
de·mise' n.
— and re'de·mise'
— of the crown
sin'gle —
de·mised' prem'is·es
de·mi'si'
de·mis'si·o'
de·mo'bil·i·za'tion
de·moc'ra·cy
dem'o·crat'ic
de·mol'ish
dem'o·li'tion
de·mon'e·ti·za'tion
de·mon'stra·ble
de·mon'stra·bly
dem'on·strate'
dem'on·stra'ti·o'
dem'on·stra'tion
de·mon'stra·tive
— ev'i·dence
— leg'a·cy
dem'on·stra'tor
de·mo'tion
de·mur'
de·mur'ra·ble

de·mur'rage
de·mur'rant
de·mur'rer
— book
gen'er·al —
— o're' ten'us
pa·rol' —
speak'ing —
spe'cial —
— to ev'i·dence
— to in'ter·rog'a·to'ries
dem'y-sanke'
den and strond
de·nar'i·ate'
de·nar'i·i'
— de ca·ri·ta'te'
— Pe'tri·i'
de·nar'i·us
— de'i'
— ter'tius com'i·ta'tus
de na·tu'ra bre'vi·um
de·ni'al
gen'er·al —
spe·cif'ic —
den·ier'
den'i·za'tion
den·ize'
den'i·zen
de·nom'i·na'tion
de·nom'i·na'tion·al
de·nounce'
de·nounce'ment
de no'vo'
— hear'ing
tri'al —
den·shir'ing of land
den'ti·frice
den'tist
den'tis·try
de·nu'mer·a'tion
de·nun'ci·a'tion
de·nun'ci·a·to'ry
de·nun'ti·a'ti·o'
de·ny'
de'o·dand'
de of·fi'ce'
de·part'
de·part'ment
de'part·men'tal
de'part·men'tal·ize'
de·par'ture

de·pas'ture
de·pec'u·la'tion
de·pend'a·ble
de·pend'ence
de·pend'en·cy
de·pend'ent n.
de·pend'ent adj.
— con·di'tions
— con'tract'
— cov'e·nant
— prom'ise
— rel'a·tive rev'o·ca'tion
de·pend'ing
de·pe'sas
de pla'ci·to'
de·plet'a·ble ec'o·nom'-ic in'ter·est
de·plete'
de·ple'tion
— al·low'ance
— de·duc'tion
— re·serve'
de'po·lym'er·i·za'tion
de·po'nent
de·pop'u·la'ti·o' a·gro'-rum
de·pop'u·la'tion
de'por·ta'tion
de·pose'
de·pos'it v.
de·pos'it n.
— ac·count'
— box
— com'pa·ny
de·mand' —
— in·sur'ance
— of ti'tle deeds
— pre'mi·um
— ra'tio
— slip
time —
de·pos'i·tar'y
dep'o·si'tion
— de be'ne' es'se
— on writ'ten ques'tions
o'ral —
de·pos'i·tor
de·pos'i·to'ry
de·pos'i·tum
de'pot
de prae·sen'ti'

de·prave'
de·praved' mind
de·pre'cia·ble life
de'pre·ci·a'tion
  ac·cel'er·at'ed —
  — re·serve'
dep're·da'tion
de·pres'sion
dep'ri·va'tion
de·prive'
  — per'ma·nent·ly
de qui'bus
de quo
dep'u·tize'
dep'u·ty
de·raign'
de·rail'er
de·rail'ment
de·range'ment
der'e·lict
  qua'si' —
der'e·lic'tion
de ri·en' cul·pa·ble'
de·riv'a·tive
  — ac'tion
  — con·vey'anc·es
de·rive'
de·rived'
der'o·ga'tion
de·rog'a·to'ry clause
de sa vie
de·scend'
de·scen'dant
  lin'e·al —
de·scend'er
de·scend'i·ble
de·scent'
  — cast
  col·lat'er·al line of —
  di·rect' line of —
  line of —
  ma·ter'nal line of —
  pa·ter'nal line of —
de·scribe'
de·scrip'ti·o' per·so'nae'
de·scrip'tion
de·scrip'tive
des'e·crate'
de·seg're·gate'
de·seg're·ga'tion
de·sert'

de·sert'er
de·ser'tion
  con·struc'tive —
de·serv'ing
des'ic·cate'
de·sign'
des'ig·nate'
des'ig·nat'ing pe·ti'tion
des'ig·na'tion
des'ig·na'ti·o' per·so'-
  nae'
de·signed'
de·sign'ed·ly
de·sire'
de·siste'ment
de son tort
des·patch'es
des'per·ate
  — debt
de·spite'
de·spi'tus
de·spoil'
des'pon·sa'tion
des'pot
des'pot·ism
des·ren'a·ble
des'ti·na'tion
  — du père de fa·mille'
des'ti·tute'
de·stroy'
de·struc'ti·bil'i·ty
de·struc'ti·ble
de·struc'tion
de·tail'
de·tain'
de·tain'er
de·tain'ment
de·tec'tion
de·tec'tive
de·tec'tor
de·ten'tion
  pre·ven'tive —
de·ter'
de·te'ri·o·ra'tion
de·ter'min·a·ble
de·ter'mi·nate
  — ob'li·ga'tion
  — sen'tence
de·ter'mi·na'tion
  — let'ter
  — of will

de·ter'mine
de·ter'rence
de·ter'rent
det'i·net'
de·tin'ue
  — of goods in frank
    mar'riage
de·tin'u·it
de'tour'
de·tourne'ment
de·trac'tion
det'ri·ment
  — to prom'is·ee'
det'ri·men'tal
  — re·li'ance
de u'na par'te'
deu'ter·og'a·my
dev'as·ta'tion
de'vas·ta'vit
de·vel'op
de·vel'oped wa'ter
de·vest'
de'vi·a'tion
de·vice'
dev'il·ling
de·vis'a·ble
de·vise'
  con·di'tion·al —
  con·tin'gent —
  ex·ec'u·to'ry —
  gen'er·al —
  lapsed —
  re·sid'u·ar'y —
  spe·cif'ic —
  vest'ed —
de·vi'see'
de·vi'sor
dev'o·lu'tion
dev'o·lu'tive ap·peal'
de·volve'
de·vy'
dex'tras da're'
di·ac'o·nate
di·ac'o·nus
di·ag·no'sis
di·ag'o·nal
di·a·lec'tics
di·al·lage
di·a·nat'ic
di·ar'i·um
di'a·ther'my

di'a·tim
di'ca
dice
di co·lon'na
dic'ta
dic'tate'
dic'ta'tion
dic'ta·tor
dic·ta'tor·ship' of the pro'le·tar'i·at
dic·to'res'
dic'tum
  gra'tis —
  o·bi'ter —
  sim'plex' —
die *n.*
die *v.*
— with·out' is'sue
di'e·i' dic'ti·o'
di'em clau'sit ex·tre'·mum
di'es
— a·mo'ris
— a quo
— ce'dit
— com·mu'nes in ban'co
— Do·min'i·cus
— ex·cres'cens'
— gra'ti·ae'
— in'ter·ci'si'
— ju·rid'i·cus
— le·git'i·mus
— mar'chi·ae'
— non ju·rid'i·cus
— pa'cis
— so·lar'is
— so'lis
— u·til'es'
di'es da'tus
— in ban'co
— par'ti·bus
— pre'ce par'ti·um
di'et
di·e'ta
Dieu son acte
dif·fa'ce·re'
dif'fer·ence
dif'fi·cult'
dif'for·ci·a're'
dif·fuse'
dif·fu'sion

dig'a·ma *or* dig'a·my
di'gest' *n.*
di·ges'ta
Di'gests'
dig'ging
dig'ni·tar'y
dig'ni·ty
di·ju'di·ca'tion
dike
dik'ing
di·lap'i·da'tion
dil'a·to'ry
— de·fense'
— ex·cep'tions
— mo'tion prac'tice
— pleas
dil'i·gence
  due —
  ex·traor'di·nar'y —
  great —
  high —
  low —
  nec'es·sar'y —
  or'di·nar'y —
  rea'son·a·ble —
  slight —
  spe'cial —
dil'i·gent
di·lu'tion doc'trine
dime
di·min'ished re·spon'si·bil'i·ty doc'trine
dim'i·nu'tion
— in val'ue
— of dam'ag·es
di·mi'si'
di·mi'sit
dim'is·so'ry let'ters
din'ar·cy
di·oc'e·san
— courts
— mis'sion
di'o·cese
di·oi'chi·a
dip
di·plo'ma
di·plo'ma·cy
dip'lo·mat'ic
— a'gent
— re·la'tions
dip'lo·mat'ics

dip'so·ma'ni·a
dip'so·ma'ni·ac'
dip'tych
dip'tych'a
di·rect' *v.*
di·rect' *adj.*
— ac'tion
— at·tack'
— cause
— ev'i·dence
— ex'am·i·na'tion
— in'ju·ry
— in'ter·est
— loss
— pay'ment
— tax
di·rect'ed ver'dict
di·rec'tion
di·rect'ly
di·rec'tor
Di·rec'tor of the Mint
di·rec'tors
di·rec'to·ry
— stat'ute
— trust
dirt
dis·a·bil'i·ty
— clause
— com'pen·sa'tion
— in·sur'ance
  par'tial —
  per'ma·nent —
  tem'po·rar'y —
  to'tal —
dis·a'ble
dis·a'bling
— re·straints'
— stat'ute
dis'ad·vo·ca·re'
dis·af·firm'
dis·af·fir'mance
dis·af·for'est
dis·a·gree'ment
dis·al·low'
dis·alt'
dis·ap·pro'pri·a'tion
dis·ap·prove'
di·sas'ter
dis·a·vow'
dis·a·vow'al
dis·bar'

dis·bar′ment
dis′bo·ca′ti·o′
dis·burse′ments
dis·cern′
dis·cern′i·ble
dis·charge′
— in bank′rupt′cy
mil′i·tar′y —
dis·ci·pli·nar′i·an
dis·ci·pli·nar′y
dis·ci·pline
dis·claim′er
— of war′ran·ty
dis·close′
dis·clo′sure
dis·com′mon
dis·con·tin′u·ance
— of an es·tate′
dis·con·tin′u·ous
dis·con·ve′na·ble
dis·cord′
dis·cor′dance
dis·count′
— bond
— bro′ker
— mar′ket
— rate
— shares
dis·cov′er
dis·cov′ert
dis·cov′er·y
dis·cred′it
dis·creet′ly
dis·crep′an·cy
dis·crete′ly
dis·cre′tion
dis·cre′tion·ar′y
— acts
— dam′ag·es
— pow′er
— re·view′
— trusts
dis·crim′i·na′tion
in·vid′i·ous —
price —
re·verse′ —
dis·cus′sion
dis·ease′
dis·en·tail′ing deed
dis·en·tail′ment
dis·fa′vor

dis·fig′ure
dis·fig′ure·ment
dis·fig′ur·ing
dis·fran′chise′
dis·fran′chise′ment
dis·gav′el
dis·grace′
dis·grad′ing
dis·guise′
dis·her′i·tor
dis·hon′es·ty
dis·hon′or
dis·in·car′cer·ate′
dis·in′cli·na′tion
dis·in·clined′
dis·in·fect′ed
dis·in·her′i·tance
dis·in·ter′
dis·in′ter·est·ed
— wit′ness
dis·junc′tive
— al′le·ga′tion
— term
dis·lo·ca′tion
dis·loy′al
dismes
dis·miss′
dis·miss′al
— a·greed′
— com′pen·sa′tion
— for cause
in·vol′un·tar′y —
vol′un·tar′y —
— with prej′u·dice
— with·out′ prej′u·dice
dis·missed′
— for want of eq′ui·ty
dis·mort′gage
dis·o·be′di·ence
dis·o·be′di·ent child
dis·or′der
dis·or′der·ly
— con′duct′
— house
— per′sons
dis·o′ri·en·ta′tion
dis·par′a·ga′ti·o′
dis·par′a·ga′tion
dis·par′age
dis·par′age·ment
— of title

dis·par′i·ty
dis·patch′ or des·patch′
dis·pau′per
dis·pel′
dis·pen′sa·ry
dis·pen·sa′tion
dis·pense′
dis·place′
dis·play′
dis·pos′a·ble
— earn′ings
— por′tion
dis·pos′al
dis·pose′ of
dis·pos′ing
— ca·pac′i·ty
— mind
dis·po·si′tion
dis·pos′i·tive facts
dis′pos·sess′
dis′pos·ses′sion
dis·prove′
dis·pun′ish·a·ble
dis·put′a·ble pre·sump′-
tion
dis·pute′
dis·qual′i·fy′
dis·rate′
dis·re·gard′
dis·re·pair′
dis·rep′u·ta·ble
dis·re·pute′
dis·rup′tive
dis·sec′tion
dis·seise′
dis′sei·see′
dis·sei′sin
dis·sei′si·trix′
dis·sei′si′tus
dis·sei′sor
dis·sei′so·ress
dis·sem′ble
dis·sent′
dis·sent′er
dis·sent′ers
dis·sent′ing o·pin′ion
dis·sig·na′re′
dis·so·lute′
dis·si·pate′
dis·so·lu′tion
— of a cor′po·ra′tion

— of par'lia·ment
— of a part'ner·ship'
dis·solve'
dis·solv'ing bond
dis·suade'
dis'tance
dis·till'
dis·till'er
dis·till'er·y
dis·tinct'
dis·tinc'tive·ly
dis·tin'guish
dis·tort'
dis·tract'ed per'son
dis·trac'tion rule
dis·train'
dis·train'er or dis·trai'-
 nor
dis·traint'
dis·tress'
— and dan'ger
— in'fin·ite
sec'ond —
— war'rant
writ of grand —
dis·tressed'
— goods
— prop'er·ty
— sale
dis·trib'ute
dis·trib'u·tee'
dis'tri·bu'tion
dis·trib'u·tive
— jus'tice
— share
dis'trict
— at·tor'ney
— clerk
con·gres'sion·al —
— court
— judge
— par'ish·es
— reg'is·try
dis'trict·ing
Dis'trict of Co·lum'bi·a
dis·trin'gas
dis·trin'ge·re'
dis·turb'
dis·tur'bance
— of peace
dis·turb'er

ditch
ditch'ing, dik'ing, or
 til'ing
di·verge'
di'vers
di·ver'si·fi·ca'tion
di·ver'si·fy'
di·ver'sion
di·ver'si·ty
— ju'ris·dic'tion
— of cit'i·zen·ship'
di·vert'
di'ves'
di·vest'
di·ves'ti·tive fact
di·vest'i·ture
di·vest'ment
di·vide'
div'i·dend'
— ad·di'tion
cu'mu·la'tive —
ex —
ex·traor'di·nar'y —
liq'ui·da'tion —
pre·ferred' —
scrip —
stock —
div'i·den'da
di·vine' right of kings
di·vis'i·ble
— con'tract'
— of·fense'
di·vi'sion
— of o·pin'ion
di·vi'sion·al courts
di·vi'sive
di·vorce'
— a men'sa et tho'ro'
— a vin·cu'lo' mat'ri·
 mo'ni·i'
for'eign —
lim'it·ed —
no'fault' —
— suit
di·vor·cée'
di·vorce'ment
di·vulge'
dock v.
dock n.
— war'rnat
dock'age

dock'et
dock'mas'ter
doc'tor
doc'tor-pa'tient priv'i·
 lege
doc'tri·nal in·ter'pre·
 ta'tion
doc'trine
doc'u·ment
 for'eign —
 pub'lic —
doc'u·men·ta'tion
doc'u·ments
 an'cient —
 ju·di'cial —
doc'u·men'ta·ry
— ev'i·dence
dog'-draw'
dog'ger
dog'ma
dog·mat'ic
do'ing busi'ness
doit'kin or doit
dole
dol'lar
do'lus
— bo'nus
— ma'lus
do'main
dom'bec' or dom'boc'
dome
Dome'-Book'
Domes'day'
— Book
domes'men
do·mes'tic n.
do·mes'tic adj.
— an'i·mals
— cor'po·ra'tion
— courts
— ex'ports
— pur'pos·es
— re·la'tions
— ser'vant
do·mes'ti·cat'ed
do·mes'ti·cus
dom'i·cile'
 change of —
 com·mer'cial —
 de fac'to' —
 do·mes'tic —

e·lect′ed —
for′eign —
mat′ri·mo′ni·al —
— of choice
— of cor′po·ra′tion
— of or′i·gin
— of suc·ces′sion
dom′i·ciled′
dom′i·cil′i·ar′y
— ad·min′is·tra′tion
dom′i·cil′i·ate′
dom′i·nant
— es·tate′
— ten′e·ment
dom′i·nate′
do·min′i·cum
do·min′ion
do·mi·nus li′tis
do′mus
— pro·ce′rum
Do′mus
— De′i′
do·na·tar′i·us
do·na′ti·o′
— in′ter vi′vos′
— mor′tis cau′sa
— prop′ter nup′ti·as′
do·na′tion
— lands
don′a·tive
— in·tent′
— trust
do′na·tor
don′a·to′ri·us
don′a·to′ry
done
do′nec′
do·nee′
— ben′e·fi′ci·ar′y
do′nis
— stat′ute de
do′nor
doom
Dooms′day Book
dope
dor′mant
— claim
— ex′e·cu′tion
— judg′ment
— part′ner
dor′mi·to′ry

dor′sum
dor′ture
dos·si·er′
dot
do′tage
do′tal
— prop′er·ty
do′tard
do·ta′tion
dote v.
do′te n.
do′tis ad·min′is·tra′ti·o′
do·tis′sa
dou′ble
— as·sess′ment
— a·dul′ter·y
— costs
— cred′i·tor
— dam′ag·es
— ea′gle
— en′try
— fine
— flem′ish bond
— glaz′ing
— house
— in·dem′ni·ty
— in·sur′ance
— jeop′ard·y
— pat′ent·ing
— re·cov′er·y
— rent
— tax·a′tion
— tax rule
— use
— val′ue
— vouch′er
— waste
— will
dou′bles
doubt
doubt′ful ti′tle
doun
dove
dove′tail′ sen·ior′i·ty
dow′a·ble
dow′a·ger
— queen
dow′er
— by com′mon law
— by cus′tom
— de la plus belle

— ex as·sen′su′ pat′ris
— un′de′ ni′hil hab′et
Dow′-Jones′ av′er·age
dowle stones
dow′ment
down′ward course
dow′ress
dow′ry
Doyle rule
doze
doz′en peers
drach′ma
dra·co′ni·an laws
dra′co re′gis
draff
draft
  bank —
  doc′u·men′ta·ry —
  sight —
  time —
drafts′man
drafts′man·ship′
drag
Dra′go doc′trine
drain
drain′age dis′trict
dram
— shop
— shop act
dra′ma
dra·mat′ic
— com′po·si′tion
— work
draught
draw n.
draw v.
draw′back′
draw′ee′
draw′er
draw′ing
draw′latch′es
dray′age
dredge
Dred Scott case
dreit′-dreit′
drench′es or dreng′es
dren′gage
dress′ing
dri′er
drift v.
drift n.

drifts of the for'est
drift'-stuff'
drift'way'
drill and com·plete' a
  well
drilled
drill'ing in
drink'ing shop
drip
drive n.
drive v.
driv'er
driv'er's li'cense
driv'ing
  — while in·tox'i·cat'ed
droit
  — close
  — com'mon
  — cou·tu·mi·er'
  — d'ac·ces·sion'
  — d'ac·crois·se·ment'
  — d'au·baine'
  — de de·trac·tion'
  — de suite
  — in'ter·na'tion·al
  — mar·i·time'
  — mor'al
  — na·tu·rel'
droit'-droit'
droits
  — ci·vils'
  — of ad·mir'al·ty
droi·tu'ral
drop let'ter
drov'er's pass
drown
drug
  — a·buse'
  — ad'dict
drug'gist
drug'store'
drum'mer
drunk
drunk'ard
drunk'en·ness
dry
  — check
  — dock
  — ex·change'
  — mort'gage
  — nat'u·ral gas

— oil
— rent
— trust
du'al
  — cit'i·zen·ship'
  — na'tion·al'i·ty
  — pur'pose doc'trine
du'ar·chy
du'bi·ous
du'bi·tans
du'bi·tan'te'
du'bi·ta'tur'
du'bi·ta'vit
duc'at
du'ces' te'cum'
  — li'cet lan·gui'dus
duch'y
  — court of Lan'cas·ter
duck'ing stool
due
  — and prop'er care
  — and rea·son'a·ble care
  — bill
  — care
  — com'pen·sa'tion
  — con·sid'e·ra'tion
  — course hold'er
  — course of law
  — date
  — dil'i·gence
  — in'flu·ence
  — no'tice
  — post'ing
  — proc'ess' clause
  — process of law
  — proof
  — re·gard'
du'el
du'el·ing
du'el'lum
dues
  un'ion —
Duke of York's laws
du·loc'ra·cy
du'ly
  — qual'i·fied'
dum
  — so'la
dumb-bid'ding
dum·mo'do'
dum'my

— cor'po·ra'tion
— di·rec'tor
dump
dump'ing
dun
dun'geon
dun'nage
du'o·dec'i·ma ma'nus
du'o·de'num
du'plex'
  — house
  — que·re'la
  — val'or mar'i·ta'gi·i'
du'pli·cate' v.
du'pli·cate n.
  — will
du'li·ca'tum jus
du·plic'i·tous
  — ap·peal'
du·plic'i·ty
du'ra·ble lease
du·ran'te'
  — ab·sen'ti·a
  — mi·no're' ae·ta'te'
  — vi·du·i·ta'te'
  — vir'gin·i·ta'te'
  — vi'ta
du·ra'tion
du·ress'
  — of goods
  — of im·pris'on·ment
  — per mi'nas
du·res'sor
Dur'ham rule
dur'ing
  — good be·hav'ior
Dutch lot'ter·y
du'ties
  — of de·trac'tion
  — on im'ports'
du'ty
  ju·di'cial —
  le'gal —
  — of ton'nage
  — of wa'ter
dwell
dwell'ing house or place
dy'ing
  — dec'la·ra'tion
  — with·out' is'sue
dyke reed or reeve

dy′nas•ty
dys′pa•reu′ni•a
dys•pep′si•a

E

each
— and eve′ry
ea′gle
earl
earl′dom
Earl Mar′shal of Eng′-
land
ear′mark′
earn
earned
— in′come′
— income cred′it
— pre′mi•um
— sur′plus
earn′er
ear′nest
— mon′ey
earn′ing
— ca•pac′i•ty
— pow′er
earn′ings
gross —
net —
sur′plus —
earth
ear′wit′ness
ease
ease′ment
af•fir′ma•tive —
ap•par′ent —
ap•pur′te•nant —
— by es•top′pel
— by pre•scrip′tion
con•tin′u•ing —
dis′con•tin′u•ing —
eq′ui•ta•ble —
im•plied′ —
— in gross
in′ter•mit′tent —
neg′a•tive —
— of ac′cess′
— of con•ven′ience
— of nat′u•ral sup•port′

— of ne•ces′si•ty
pri′vate —
pub′lic —
qua′si′ —
re•cip′ro•cal neg′a•tive —
sec′on•dar′y —
east
Eas′ter
— dues
— of′fer•ings
— term
east′er•ly
eat′ing house
eaves
eaves′drop′ping
eb′ba
ebb and flow
e•bri′e•ty
ec′cen•tric′i•ty
ec′chy•mo′sis
ec•cle′si•as′tic
ec•cle′si•as′ti•cal
— au•thor′i•ties
— com•mis′sion•ers
— coun′cil
— courts
— ju′ris•dic′tion
— law
— mat′ter
ech′o•la′li•a
e•clec′tic
— prac′tice
e•col′o•gy
ec′o•nom′ic
— dis•crim′i•na′tion
— ob′so•les′cence
— strike
— waste
e•con′o•miz′er
e•con′o•my
e con′tra
e con•ver′so′
ec′u•men′i•cal
edge
— lease
e′dict′
E′dicts of Jus•tin′i•an
e•di′tion
ed′i•tor
ed′i•tus
ed′u•cate′

ed′u•ca′tion
ed′u•ca′tion•al
— in′sti•tu′tion
— pur′pos•ses
ef•fect′
ef•fect′ing loan
ef•fec′tive
— as•sis′tance of coun′-
sel
— pro•cur′ing cause
ef•fects′
ef•fec′tu•al
ef•fec′tu•ate′
ef•fi′cient
— cause
— in′ter•ven′ing cause
ef′fi•gy
ef′flux′
ef•flux′ion of time
ef′fort
ef•frac′tion
ef•frac′tor
e′go
e′gress′
eire or eyre
eisne
ei′ther
e•ject′
e•jec′ta
e•jec′tion
e•jec′ti•o′ne′
— cus•to′di•ae′
— fir•mae′
e•ject′ment
e•jec′tor
e•jec′tum
e′ju•ra′tion
e•jus′dem gen′e•ris
e•las′tic
eld′est
e•lect′ed
e•lec′tion
— au′di•tors
— con•test′
— dis′trict
es•top′pel by —
— of rem′e•dies
— re•turns′
e•lec′tive
— fran′chise′
— of′fice

— share
e·lec'tor
e·lec'tor·al
— col'lege
— com·mis'sion
— proc'ess'
e·lec'tric'i·ty
e·lec'tro·car·di·og'ra·
phy
e·lec'tro·cute'
e·lec'tro·cu'tion
e·lec·trol'y·sis
e·lec·tron'ic sur·veil'·
lance
el'ee·mos'y·nar'y
— cor'po·ra'tion
el'e·gan'ter
e·le'git
el'e·ment
el'e·ments
el'e·va'tor
E·lev'enth A·mend'·
ment
e·lic'it
el'i·gi·bil'i·ty
el'i·gi·ble
e·lim'i·na'tion
e·lin·gua'tion
e·li'sors
el·lip'ses'
el·lip'sis
e·loign'ment
e·lon·ga'ta
e·lon·ga'tus
e·lon·ga'vit
e·lope'ment
else'where'
e·lu'ci·date'
e·lude'
em'a·nate'
em'a·na'tion
e·man'ci·pa'tion
E·man'ci·pa'tion Proc'·
la·ma'tion
em·bar'go
em·bark'
em·bar·ka'tion
em·bas·sage
em·bas·sy
em·bez'zle·ment
em·bez'zler

em'ble·ments
em·bo·lism
em·bo·lus
em·brac'er·y
e·men'da
e·men'dals
e·merge'
e·mer'gen·cy
em'i·grant
em'i·gra'tion
ém'i·gré'
em'i·nence
em'i·nent do·main'
em'is·sar'y
e·mis'sion
e·mit'
e·mol'u·ment
em·pan'el
em·pan'eled
em·pan'el·ing
em'per·or
em'pha·ses'
em'pha·sis
em'pha·size'
em'phy·se'ma
em'pire'
em·pir'ic
em·pir'i·cal
em·plead'
em·ploy'
em·ployed'
em·ploy'ee
em·ploy'er
em·ploy'ers' li·a·bil'i·ty
acts
em·ploy'ment
em·po'ri·um
em·pow'er
em'pre·sa'ri·os
emp'tor
en·a'ble
en·a'bling
— act
— clause
— pow'er
— stat'ute
en·act'
en·act'ing clause
en·act'ment
en banc
en bloc

en·bre·ver'
en·ceinte'
en·close'
en·clo'sure
en·cour'age
en·croach'
en·croach'ment
en·cum'ber
en·cum'brance
en·cum'branc·er
en·deav'or
en de·meure'
en·den'zie or en·den'i·
zen
en'do·car·di'tis
en·dorse' or in·dorse'
en·dors·ee' or in'dors·ee'
en·dorse'ment or in·
dorse'ment
ac·com'mo·da'tion —
blank —
con·di'tion·al —
full —
ir·reg'u·lar —
prop'er —
qual'i·fied' —
reg'u·lar —
re·stric'tive —
spe'cial —
en·dors'er or in·dors'er
en·dow'
en·dow'ment
— pol'i·cy
end to end
en·dur'ance
en'e·my
— a'li·en
pub'lic —
En'er·gy
De·part'ment of —
en fait
en·feoff'
en·feoff'ment
en·force'
en·force'a·ble
en·fran'chise'
en·fran'chise'ment
— of cop'y·holds'
en·gage'
en·gaged' in com'·
merce

en·gage′ment
en·gen′der
en′gine
en′gi·neer′
en′gi·neer′ing
en·grav′ing
en gros
en·gross′
en·gross′er
en·gross′ing
en·hanced′
en·hér·i·tance′
e·ni′ti·a pars
en·join′
en·joy′
en·joy′ment
  ad·verse′ —
  qui′et —
en·large′
en·larg′er l′es·tate′
en·larg′ing
en·list′ment
en masse
en mort mayne
E′noch Ar′den Doc′-
  trine
e·nor′mous
en o′wel main
en·roll′
en·rolled′ bill
en·roll′ment
  — of ves′sels
en route
en·seal′
en·serv′er
ens le′gis
en·sue′
en·tail′
en·tailed′
en·tail′ment
en·tend′ment
en·ter
en·ter·ceur′
en′ter·ing
  — judg′ments
en′ter·prise′
en′ter·tain′ment
  — ex·pens′es
en·thu′si·asts′
en·tice′
en·tire′

— blood
— con′tract′
en·tire′ty
en·ti′tle
en·ti′tle·ment
en′ti·ty
en′trails′
en′trance
en·trap′
en·trap′ment
en·treat′y
en·tre·bat′
en′tre·pôt
en′tre·pre·neur′
en·trust′
en′try
  — ad com·mu′nem le′-
  gum
  — by court
  for′ci·ble —
  — of judg′ment
  pre-emp′tion —
  right of —
  writ of —
en′try·man
e·nu′mer·at′ed
  — pow′ers
e·nu′mer·a′tors
en·ure′
en·vel′op
en′ve·lope′
en ven′tre sa mère
en vie
en·vi′ron·ment
en·vi′ron·men′tal
  — im′pact′ state′ments
En·vi′ron·men′tal Pro·
  tec′tion A′gen·cy
en′voy′
en′zyme′
e′o′
  — di′e′
  — in·stan′ti′
  — in·tu′i·tu′
  — lo′ci′
  — nom′i·ne′
ep′i·dem′ic
ep′i·lep′sy
e·piph′y·sis
e·pis′co·pa·cy
E·pis′co·pa′li·an

e·pis′co·pate
e·pis′tle
e·pis′to·la
e·pis′to·lae′
e·pis′to·lar′y
e plu′ri·bus u′num
ep′och
e′qual
  — pro·tec′tion of the
  laws
E′qual Em·ploy′ment
  Op′por·tu′ni·ty Com·
  mis′sion
e·qual′i·ty
e·qual′i·za′tion
e′qual·ize′
e′qual·ly di·vid′ed
E′qual Rights A·mend′-
  ment
e′qui·lib′ri·um
e′qui·nox′
e·quip′
e·quip′ment
eq′ui·ta·ble
  — ac′tion
  — ad·just′ment the′o·ry
  — as·sign′ment
  — con·ver′sion
  — de·fense′
  — dis′tri·bu′tion
  — doc′trine of ap·prox′i·
  ma′tion
  — e·lec′tion
  — es·top′pel
  — ex′e·cu′tion
  — in′ter·est
  — liens
  — life es·tate′
  — mort′gage
  — own′er·ship′
  — rate of in′ter·est
  — re·coup′ment
  — re·demp′tion
  — re·scis′sion
  — re·straint′ doc′trine
  — ser′vi·tudes′
  — ti′tle
  — waste
eq·ui·tas′ seq·ui·tur′ le′-
  gem
eq′ui·ty

coun'ter·vail'ing —
courts of —
— fol'lows the law
— ju'ris·dic'tion
— ju'ris·pru'dence
nat'u·ral —
— of re·demp'tion
per'fect —
— ra'tio
— se·cu'ri·ty
— term
e·quiv'a·len·cy
e·quiv'a·lent
e·quiv'a·lents doc'trine
e·quiv'o·cal
e·ra'sure
e·rect'
e·rec'tion
er'got
E'rie v. Tomp'kins
e·ro'sion
er'rant
— wa'ter
er·ra'ta
er·rat'ic
er·ra'tum
er·ro'ne·ous
er'ror
— ap·par'ent of rec'ord
— case
cler'i·cal —
— co'ram' no'bis
— coram vo'bis
harm'ful —
harm'less —
— in fact
— in law
— in vac'u·o'
— no'mi·nis
— of fact
— of law
re·vers'i·ble —
writ of —
er'rors
as·sign'ment of —
cross —
— ex·cept'ed
es·ca·la'tor clause
es·cape'
— clause
— pe'ri·od

— way
es·cheat'
es·cheat'or
Es·co·be'do rule
es'crow'
es'ne·cy
es'pi·o·nage'
es·pous'als
es'quire'
es·sar·ter'
es·sar'tum
es'sence
— of the con'tract'
es·sen'tial
es·sen'tial·ly
es·soin'
es·tab'lish
es·tab'lish·ment
— clause
— of re·lig'ion
es·tate'
ab'so·lute' —
— at suf'fer·ance
— at will
— by e·le'git
— by en·tire'ty
— by pur'chase
— by stat'ute mer'chant
— by statute sta'ple
— by the cur'te·sy
— by the en·tire'ty
con·di'tion·al —
con·tin'gent —
ex·e·cut'ed —
ex·ec·u·to'ry —
executory de·vise' —
executory re·main'der —
fast —
— for life
— for years
— from pe'ri·od to pe'ri·od
— from year to year
— in com'mon
— in co·par'ce·nar'y
— in dow'er
— in ex·pec'tan·cy
— in fee sim'ple
— in fee tail
— in joint ten'an·cy
— in lands

— in re·main'der
— in re·ver'sion
— less than free'hold'
— of freehold
— of in·her'i·tance
— on con·di'tion·al lim'i·ta'tion
— on limitation
— plan'ning
— pur au'tre vie
qual'i·fied' —
qua'si' — tail
real —
— sub'ject to a con·di'tion·al lim'i·ta'tion
— tail
— tax
— up·on' con·di'tion
— upon condition ex·pressed'
— upon condition im·plied'
vest'ed —
es·tates' of the realm
es'ti·mate'
es'ti·mat'ed
— cost
— use'ful life
es·top'
es·top'pel
— a·gainst' —
— by deed
— by judg'ment
— in pais
es·to'vers
es·tray'
es·treat'
es·trepe'
es·trepe'ment
es·tu·ar'y
et
et al'i·i' è con'tra
et al'i·us
et al'lo·ca'tur'
et cet'er·a or caet'er·a
eth'i·cal
eth'ics
et non
et sic
et ux'or'
eu'no·my

eu'nuch
Eu'ro·dol'lars
eu'tha·na'si·a
e·va'si·o'
e·va'sion
e·va'sive
eve
e'ven
eve'ning
e·vent'
eve'ry
e·vict'
e·vic'tion
e·vic'tor
ev'i·dence
  au·top'tic —
  char'ac·ter —
  ex'pert —
  — of debt
  — prop'er
  rules of —
ev'i·dent
ev'i·den'tia·ry
  — facts
ev'i·dent·ly
e'vil
ev'o·ca'tion
ev'o·lu'tion
ev'o·lu'tion·ism
ev'o·lu'tion·ist
e·volved'
ew'age
ex
ex·ac'tion
ex al'ter·a par'te'
ex·am'en
ex·am'i·na'tion
ex·am'in·er
ex·am'in·ers
ex·an'nu·al roll
ex bo'nis
ex ca·the'dra
ex cau'sa
Ex'cel·len·cy
ex·cept'
ex·cept'ing
ex·cep'ti·o'
ex·cep'tion
  — en masse
ex·cep'tion·al cir'cum·
  stanc'es

ex·cess'
  — in·sur'ance
ex·cess'-prof'it tax
ex·cess'es
ex·ces'sive
  — bail
ex·ces'sive·ly
ex·change'
ex·changed'
ex·cheq'uer
ex'cise'
  — law
ex·cit'ed ut'ter·ance
ex·clu'sion
ex·clu'sion·ar'y rule
ex·clu'sive
  — a'gen·cy
  — deal'ing
  — fran'chise'
  — ju'ris·dic'tion
  — li'cense
  — of in'ter·est and costs
  — own'er·ship'
  — pos·ses'sion
  — rem'e·dy
  — right
  — use
ex·clu'sive·ly
ex co·lo're'
ex'com·mu'ni·ca'tion
ex con'trac'tu'
ex'cul·pate'
ex'cul·pa'tion
ex·cul'pa·to'ry
  — clause
  — state'ment
ex cu'ri·a
ex·cus'a·ble
  — as·sault'
  — hom'i·cide'
  — ne·glect'
ex·cus'a·tor'
ex·cuse'
ex de·fec'tu' san'gui·
  nis
ex de·lic'to'
  — trusts
ex div'i·dend'
ex do'lo' ma'lo'
  — non o·ri'tur' ac'ti·o'
ex'e·cute'

ex'e·cut'ed
  — con·sid'er·a'tion
  — con'tract'
  — es·tate'
  — fine
  — gift
  — note
ex'e·cu'tion
  — cred'i·tor
  — lien
  — of in'stru·ment
  — sale
  writ of —
ex'e·cu'ti·o·ne' fa'ci·
  en'da
ex'e·cu'tion·er
ex·ec'u·tive
  — a'gen·cy
  — ca·pac'i·ty
  — clem'en·cy
  — de·part'ment
  — of'fice
  — or'der
  — pow'ers
  — priv'i·lege
  — ses'sion
ex·ec'u·tor
  — by sub'sti·tu'tion
  — named in will
  — trus·tee'
ex·ec'u·to'ri·al
ex·ec'u·tor·ship'
ex·ec'u·to'ry
  — con·sid'er·a'tion
  — con'tract'
  — de·vise'
  — in'ter·ests
  — lim'i·ta'tion
  — proc'ess'
  — trust
ex·ec'u·tress
ex·ec'u·trix'
ex·em'plar'
ex·em'pla·ry
ex·em'pli·fi·ca'tion
ex·em'pli' gra'ti·a
ex·em'plum
ex·empt'
ex·emp'tion
  — laws
  words of —

ex·empts'
ex'er·cise'
— ju·ris·dic'tion
— of judg'ment
— of ju·di'cial dis·cre'-
   tion
ex'er·cised' do·min'ion
ex'er·cis'ing an op'tion
ex fac'to'
ex fic'ti·o'ne ju'ris
ex gra'ti·a
ex·haus'tion
— of ad·min'is·tra'tive
   rem'e·dies
— of state rem'e·dies
ex·hib'e·re'
ex·hib'it
ex·hib'i·tant
ex·hib'it·ed
ex'hi·bi'tion
ex'hu·ma'tion
ex hy·poth'e·si'
ex'i·gence
ex'i·gen·cy
— of a bond
— of a writ
ex'i·gen'da·ry
ex'i·gent
— cir'cum·stanc'es
— list
— search
ex'i·gi·ble
— debt
ex'i·gi' fa'ci·as'
ex'ile'
ex in·dus'tri·a
ex·ist'
ex·is'tence
ex·ist'ing
— claim
— cred'i·tors
— debt
— use
ex'it
— wound
ex le'ge'
ex le'gi·bus
ex lo·ca'to'
ex ma'le·fi'ci·o'
ex ma·li'ti·a
ex me'ro' mo'to'

ex mo'ra
ex mu·tu'o'
ex ni·hi'lo' ni'hil fit
ex of·fi'ci·o'
ex·on'er·ate'
ex·on'er·a'tion
ex·or'bi·tant
ex par'te'
— di·vorce'
— hear'ing
— in·junc'tion
— ma·ter'na
— pa·ter'na
— pro·ceed'ing
ex·pa'tri·a'tion
ex·pect'
ex·pec'tan·cy
— dam'ag·es
— of life
— ta'bles
ex·pec'tant
— es·tates'
— heir
— right
ex'pec·ta'tion of life
ex·pect'ed
ex·pe'di·en·cy
ex·pe'di·ent
ex·ped'i·ment
ex·ped'i·ta'tion
ex'pe·dite'
ex'pe·dit'er
ex'pe·di'tion
ex'pe·di'tious
ex·pel'
ex·pend'
ex·pend'a·ble
ex·pen'de·re'
ex·pen'di·tors
ex·pen'di·ture
ex·pense'
ex·pens'es
  busi'ness —
  op'er·at'ing —
  — of ad·min'is·tra'tion
  out'-of-pock'et —
ex·pe'ri·ence
ex·per'i·ment
ex·per'i·men'tal tes'ti·
  mo'ny
ex'pert' *n.*

ex'pert *adj.*
— ev'i·dence
— wit'ness·es
ex'pi·ra'tion
ex·pi'ra·to'ry
ex·pire'
ex·plic'it
ex·ploi·ta'tion
ex·ploit'a·tive
ex·plo·ra'tion
ex·plo'sion
ex·plo'sive
ex·port' *v.*
ex'port' *n.*
ex'por·ta'tion
ex·pose'
ex'po·si'tion
ex·pos'i·to'ry stat'ute
ex post fac'to'
— law
ex·po'sure
ex·press'
— ab'ro·ga'tion
— ac'tive trust
— as·sump'sit
— au·thor'i·ty
— con'tract'
— dis·sat'is·fac'tion
— mal'ice
— re·pub'li·ca'tion
— trust
ex·pressed'
ex·pres'si·o' u·ni'us est
  ex·clu'si·o' al·ter'i·us
ex·press'ly
ex·pro'pri·a'tion
ex pro'pri·o'
— mo'tu'
— vi·go're'
ex·pul'sion
ex·punge'
ex·pur·ga'tion
ex·pur·ga'tor
ex re·la'ti·o'ne'
ex ri·go're' ju'ris
ex tem'po·re'
ex·tend'
ex·tend'ed
— cov'er·age clause
ex·tend'ing
ex·ten'sion

— of note
ex·ten'sive
ex·tent'
— in aid
— in chief
— of such pay'ment
ex·ten'u·ate'
ex·ten'u·at'ing cir'cum·
  stanc'es
ex·ten'u·a'tion
ex·te'ri·or
ex·ter'nal
— vi'o·lent and ac'ci·
  den'tal means
ex·ter'ri·to'ri·al'i·ty
ex tes'ta·men'to'
ex·tinct'
ex·tin'guish
ex·tin'guish·ment
— of com'mon
— of cop'y·hold'
— of debts
— of leg'a·cy
— of lien
— of rent
— of ways
ex'tir·pate'
ex'tir·pa'tion
ex·tor'sive·ly
ex·tort'
ex·tor'tion
ex·tor'tion·ar'y
ex·tor'tion·ate
ex·tor'tion·ist
ex'tra
— al·low'ance
— com·mer'ci·a
— com'pen·sa'tion
— fe'o·dum
— ju·di'ci·um
— jus
— le'gem
— serv'ic·es
— ter'ri·to'ri·um
— vi'am
— vir'es'
ex·tract' v.
ex'tract' n.
ex'tra·dite'
ex'tra·di'tion
ex'tra·do'tal prop'er·ty

ex'tra·haz'ard·ous
ex'tra·ju·di'cial
ex'tra·ju·di'cial·ly
ex'tra·lat'er·al right
ex'tra·le'gal
ex'tra·mar'i·tal
ex'tra·mu'ral
ex'tra'ne·ous
— ev'i·dence
— of·fense'
ex·traor'di·nar'y
— cir'cum·stanc'es
— div'i·dend'
— rem'e·dies
— risk
— ses'sion
— writs
ex'tra·pa·ro'chi·al
ex'tra·ter'ri·to'ri·al'i·ty
ex·treme'
— and re·peat'ed cru'el·
  ty
— cruelty
ex·tre'mis
ex·trem'i·ty
ex'tri·cate'
ex·trin'sic
— am'bi·gu'i·ty
— ev'i·dence
ex·u·la're'
ex u'na par'te'
ex vol'un·ta'te'
ey
eye'wit'ness
eyre

F

fab'ric
— lands
fab'ri·ca
fab'ri·ca're'
fab'ri·cate'
fab'ri·cat'ed ev'i·dence
fab'ri·cat'ing
fab'ri·ca'tion
face
— a·mount'
— of in'stru·ment

— of pol'i·cy
— val'ue
fa'cial dis·fig'ure·ment
fa'ci·as'
fa'ci·en'do'
fa'cies'
fac'ile
fa·cil'i·tate'
fa·cil'i·ta'tion
fa·cil'i·ties
fa·cil'i·ty
fac'ing
fac·sim'i·le
— pro'bate'
— sig'na·ture
fact
fac'ta
fac'to'
— et an'i·mo'
fac'tor
fac'tor·age
fac'tor·ing
fac'tor·iz'ing proc'ess'
fac'tors' acts
fac'tor·ship'
fac'tor's lien
fac'to·ry
facts
— in'com·plete'
— in is'sue
fac'tum
— ju·rid'i·cum
— pro'bans
fac'ul·ta'tive
— com'pen·sa'tion
— re'in·sur'ance
fac'ul·ties
fac'ul·ty
faed'er-feoh'
fag'got
fail
fail'ure
— of con·sid'er·a'tion
— of ev'i·dence
— of jus'tice
— of is'sue
— of proof
— of ti'tle
— of trust
— to bar'gain col·lec'-
  tive·ly

— to make de·liv'er·y
— to meet ob'li·ga'tions
— to per·form'
— to state cause of ac'-
tion
— to tes'ti·fy'

faint
— ac'tion
— plead'er

fair n.
fair adj.
— a·bridg'ment
— and eq'ui·ta·ble
— and equitable val'ue
— and fea'si·ble
— and full e·quiv'a·lent
for loss
— and im·par'tial ju'ry
— and impartial tri'al
— and prop'er le'gal as·
sess'ment
— and rea'son·a·ble
com'pen·sa'tion
— and reasonable mar'-
ket val'ue
— and reasonable val'ue
— and val'u·a·ble con·
sid'er·a'tion
— cash mar'ket val'ue
— cash val'ue
— com'ment
— com'pe·ti'tion
— con·sid'er·a'tion
— e·quiv'a·lent
— hear'ing
— mar'ket val'ue
— on its face
— play
— plead'er
— pre·pon'der·ance
— price
— re·turn' on in·vest'-
ment
— tri'al
— us'age
— use doc'trine
— val'u·a'tion
— val'ue

Fair Cred'it
— Bill'ing Act
— Re·port'ing Acts

Fair La'bor Stan'dards
Act
fair'ly
fair'ness doc'trine
fair'way'
fait
— ac·com·pli'
— en·rolle'

faith
faith'ful
faith'ful·ly
fai'tours
fake
fak'er
fa·kir'
fal·ca're'
fald'stool'
fall v.
fall n.
— of land
fall'ing
Fal·lo'pi·an tube
fal'low
— land
fal'lum
fal·sa're'
fal·sa'ri·us or fal·ca'ri·
ous
false
— ac'tion
— and fraud'u·lent
— and mis·lead'ing
state'ment
— an'swer
— ar·rest'
— char'ac·ter
— checks
— claim
— dem'on·stra'tion
— en'try
— im·pri'son·ment
— in'stru·ment
— lights and sig'nals
— mak'ing
— oath
— or fraud'u·lent claim
— per'son·a'tion
— pre'tens'es
— rec'ord
— rep're·sen·ta'tion
— re·turn'

— state'ment
— swear'ing
— to'ken
— ver'dict
— weights
— wit'ness
— words

false'hood'
false'ly
— im·per'son·ate'
— make

fal'si·fi·ca'tion
fal'si·fy'
fal'si·fy'ing
— a judg'ment
— a rec'ord
fal'si·ty
fal'so·nar'i·us
fal'sus
— in u'no'
— in om'ni·bus

fa'ma
fam'a·cide'
fa·mil'i·a
fa·mil'iar
fa·mil'iar'i·ty
fam'i·ly
— al·low'ance
— car doc'trine
— court
— ex·pens'es
— part'ner·ship'
— pur'pose doc'trine
— serv'ice rule
— set'tle·ment

fa·nat'ic
fa·nat'i·cism
fan'ci·ful trade name
far'del of land
fard'ing-deal'
fare
far'leu'
far'ley
farm v.
— out
farm n.
— let
— prod'ucts
Farm Cred'it Ad·min'-
is·tra'tion
farm'er

farm'ing
— op'er·a'tion
— prod'ucts
— syn'di·cate
farm'-to'-mar'ket roads
far'o
far'ri·er
far'thing
— of land
far'vand'
fas
fas'cism
fas'cist
fast bill of ex·cep'tions
fa'tal
— er'rors
— in'ju·ry
— var'i·ance
fa'ther
fa'ther-in-law'
fath'om
fa·tu'a mu'li·er'
fa·tu'i·tas'
fa'tum
fat'u·ous
fa·tu'um ju·dic'i·um
fa·tu'us
fau'bourg'
fau'ces' ter'rae'
fault
Faunt'le·roy' doc'trine
fau'tor
faux
fa'vor
fa'vored
— ben'e·fi'ci·ar'y
— na'tion
fa'vor·it·ism
feal
feal'ty
fear
fea'sance
fea'sant
fea·si·bil'i·ty
fea'si·ble
fea'sor
feasts
feath'er·bed'ding
fe'cial law
fed'er·al
— com'mon law

— courts
— gov'ern·ment
— in'stru·men·tal'i·ty
— ju'ris·dic'tion
— ques'tion
— reg'u·la'tions
— re·serve' notes
Fed'er·al
— A'vi·a'tion Ad·min'is·tra'tion
— Bu'reau of In·ves'ti·ga'tion
— Com·mu'ni·ca'tions Com·mis'sion
— De·pos'it In·sur'ance Cor'po·ra'tion
— Em·ploy'er's Li'a·bil'i·ty Act
— Home Loan Mort'gage Cor'po·ra'tion
— Hous'ing Ad·min'is·tra'tion
— In·sur'ance Con'tri·bu'tions Act
— Ju·di'cial Code
— Land Banks
— Mar'i·time' Com·mis'sion
— Me'di·a'tion and Con'cil·i·a'tion Serv'ice
— Pow'er Com·mis'sion
— Reg'is·ter
— Re·port'er
— Re·serve' Act
— Reserve Banks
— Reserve Board of Gov'er·nors
— Reserve Sys'tem
— Rules Act
— Rules De·cis'ions
— Rules of Ap·pel'late Pro·ce'dure
— Rules of Civ'il Pro·ce'dure
— Rules of Crim'i·nal Pro·ce'dure
— Rules of Ev'i·dence
— Sup'ple·ment
— Tort Claims Act
— Trade Com·mis'sion

fed'er·al·ism
Fed'er·al·ist, The
fed'er·ate'
fed'er·at'ed
fed'er·a'tion
fee
— farm
— farm rent
— tail
fee'ble-mind'ed
feed
fee sim'ple
— ab'so·lute'
— con·di'tion·al
— de·fea'si·ble
— de·ter'min·a·ble
fees
at·tor'ney —
con·tin'gent —
feigned
— ac·com'plice
— ac'tion
— dis·eas'es
— is'sue
fe·la'gus
fele
fel·la'ti·o'
fel·la'tion
fel'low
— heir
— rule
— ser'vant
fe'lo de se
fel'on
fe·lo'ni·a
fe·lo'ni·ce'
fe·lo'ni·ous
— as·sault'
— hom'i·cide'
— in·tent'
— tak'ing
fe·lo'ni·ous·ly
fel'o·ny
com·pound'ing of —
mis·pri'sion of —
re·duc'i·ble —
fel'o·ny-mur'der rule
fe'male
feme *or* femme
— cov'ert
— sole

— sole trad'er
fem'i•cide'
fem'i•nine
fem'i•nism
fem'i•nist
femme
  — coul•eur' lib•re'
fe•na'ti•o'
fence v.
fence n.
  — coun'ty
  — month
fenc'ing pat'ents
fend'er
fen'er•a'tion
Fe•ni'an
feod
feod'al
  — ac'tions
feo'da•ry
feo'dum
feoff•ee'
feoff'ment
  — to us'es
feof'for
feo•na'ti•o'
fer'ae'
  — bes'ti•ae'
  — na•tu'rae'
fer•del'la ter'rae'
fer'i•a
ferme
fer'men•ta'tion
fer'ment'ed liq'uors
fer'mo•ry
fer•ra'tor
fer'ri•age
fer'rum
fer'ry
fer'ry•boat'
fer'ry•man
fes'ta in cap'pis
fest'ing•man'
fest'ing•pen'ny
fes'tum
fe'tal
fe'ti•cide'
fet'ters
feud
feu'dal
  — courts

— law
  — sys'tem
feu'dal•ism
feu'dal•ize'
feu'da•ry
feud'bote'
feu'dum
  — an'ti•qu'um
  — a•per'tum
  — fran'cum
  — hau'ber•ti'cum
  — im'pro•pri'um
  — in'di•vi'du•um
  — lai'cum'
  — li•gi'um
  — ma•ter'num
  — mil•i•ta're'
  — no'bi•le'
  — no'vum
  — no'vum ut an'ti•qu'-
    um
  — pa•ter'num
  — pro•pri'um
  — tal'li•a'tum
few
fi•an•cer'
fi'at
  — jus'ti•ti'a
  — justitia, ru'at coe'lum
  — ut pet'i•tur'
fi'aunt'
fic'tion
  — of law
fic•ti'tious
  — ac'tion
  — name
  — pay•ee'
  — per'son
  — plain'tiff
  — prom'ise
fi'de•i'-com'mis•sar'y
fi•del'i•tas'
fi•del'i•ty
  — bond
  — in•sur'ance
fi'des'
  bo'na —
  ma'la —
  u•ber'ri•ma —
fi•du'cial
fi•du'ci•ar'y

— bond
  — ca•pac'i•ty
  — con'tract'
  — heir
  — re•la'tion
fief
  — ten'ant
field
  — book
  — notes
  — of'fice
  — ware'hous'ing
  — work
fi'e•ri' fa'ci•as'
Fifth A•mend'ment
fight
fight'ing words
fig'u•ra•tive•ly
fig'ures
fil'a•cer
fi•la're'
filch'ing
file n.
file v.
  — wrap'per es•top'pel
fil'i•al
fil'i•ate'
fil'i•a'tion
  — pro•ceed'ing
fil'i•bus'ter
fil'i•us
  — nul'li•us
  — pop'u•li'
fill
fil'ly
fi'lum
  — aq'uae'
  — for'est•ae'
  — vi'ae'
fi•na'gle
fi'nal
  — ap•peal'a•ble or'der
  — a•ward'
  — de•ci'sion
  — dis'po•si'tion
  — judg'ment
  — or'der
  — set'tle•ment
fi•nal'i•ty
fi•nance' v.
fi•nance' charge

fi·nanc′es
fi·nan′cial
— in′sti·tu′tions
— re·spon′si·bil′i·ty acts
— state′ment
— worth
fin′an·cier′
fi·nanc′ing
— a′gen·cy
— state′ment
find
find′er
find′er's fee
find′ing
— of fact
fine *v.*
fine *n.*
— for al′ien·a′tion
— for en·dow′ment
— force
fi′nem fa′ce·re′
fines le roy
fin′ger
fin′ger·prints′
fi′nis
fi·ni′ti·o′
fird′fare′
fird′wite′
fire
— dis′trict
— door
— es·cape′
— ex′it
— in·sur′ance
— sale
— wall
fire′arm′
fire′bug′
fire′fight′er
fire′man
fire′proof′
fire′wood′
fire′works′
fir′kin
firm
— name
— of·fer
fir′ma
fir·ma′ri·us
firm′ly
first

— blush
— class
— de·vi′see′
— fruits
— heir
— im·pres′sion
first′-de·gree′
— burn
— mur′der
first in, first out rule
fisc
fis′cal
— a′gent
— of′fi·cers
— pe′ri·od
— year
fish′er·y
fis·tu′ca *or* fes·tu′ca
fit
fix
— up
fixed
— as·set′
— cap′i·tal
— costs
— fee
— in′come′
— in·debt′ed·ness
— li′a·bil′i·ties
— pric′es
— sal′a·ry
fix′ing bail
fix′ture
trade —
fla′co′
flag
— des′e·cra′tion
fla′grans
— bel′lum
fla′grant
— ne·ces′si·ty
fla·gran′te′
— bel′lo′
— de·lic′to′
flash check
flat
— bond
— mon′ey
— rate
flat′ter·y
flee from jus′tice

fleet
Fle′ta
flight
flim′flam′
flip′ping
float
— stock
float′a·ble
float′er pol′i·cy
float′ing
— cap′i·tal
— charge
— debt
— in′ter·est rate
— lien
— pol′i·cy
— zone
flog′ging
flood
floor
— plan
— plan fi·nanc′ing
— plan′ning
— trad′er
floored
flor′in
flo′tag·es
flo·ter′i·al dis′trict
flot′sam *or* flot′san
flour′ish
flow′age
flow′ing
fluc′tu·ate′
fluc′tu·at′ing
— clause
flume
flu′vi·us
flux
flux′us
fly′ma
foal
fod′der
foe′ner·a′tion
foe′ti·cide′
foe′tus
fold′age
fol′ge·re′
fol′gers
fo′li·o′
fol′low
fol′lows the prop′er·ty

fo·ment'
Food and Drug Ad·
  min·is·tra'tion
Food, Drug, and Cos·
  met'ic Act
foot
— a'cre
— front'age rule
foot'geld'
foot'prints'
for ac·count' of
For'a·ker act
for·bar·rer'
for·bear'ance
for cause
force
— ma·jes·ture'
— ma·jeure'
forced
— heirs
— sale
forc'es
for'ci·ble
— de·tain'er
— en'try
— tres'pass
for col·lec'tion
fore·close'
fore·clo'sure
— sale
fore·go'
fore'hand' rent
for'eign
— a'gent
— ap·pos'er
— bill of ex·change'
— com'merce
— con'su·late
— cor'po·ra'tion
— ex·change'
— im·mu'ni·ty
— judg'ment
— ju'ris·dic'tion
— rep're·sen'ta·tive
— serv'ice
— trade zone
for'eign·er
fore'man
fo·ren'sic
— med'i·cine
— pa·thol'o·gy

fore·see'a·bil'i·ty
fore·see'a·ble
fore'shore'
fore'sight'
for'est
for'est·age
fore·stall'
fore·stall'er
fore·stall'ing
for'es·tar'i·us
for'est·er
fore·warned'
for'feit
for'feit·a·ble
for'fei·ture'
forge
for'ger·y
for hire or re·ward'
fo'ris
fo'ris·fac·tu'ra
fo'ris·fa'mi·li·a're'
fo'ris·fa·mil'i·at'ed
fo'ris·fa·mil'i·a'tus
fo'ris·ju'di·ca'ti·o'
fo'ris·ju'di·ca'tus
for·ju·rer'
form
for'ma
— pau'per·is
for'mal
for·mal'i·ties
for·mal'i·ty
for·ma'ta bre'vi·a
formed
— ac'tion
— de·sign'
for'me·don'
for'mer
— ad·ju'di·ca'tion
— pro·ceed'ings
— test'ti·mo'ny
forms of ac'tion
for'mu·la
for'mu·lae'
for'ni·ca'tion
for'nix
for·swear'
for·taxed'
forth·com'ing
forth'with'
for'ti·o'ri'

for·tuit'
for·tu'i·tous
— e·vent'
for·tu'i·ty
for'tune
fo'rum
— ac'tus
— con'sci·en'ti·ae'
— con·ten·ti·o'sum
— con·trac'tus
— con·ven'i·ens'
— do·mes'ti·cum
— do·mi·cil'i·i'
— ec'cle·si·as'ti·cum
— li'ge·an'ti·ae' re'i'
— non con·ven'i·ens'
— o·rig'i·nis
— re'gi·um
— re'i'
— rei gest'ae'
— rei sit'ae'
— sec'u·la're'
— shop'ping
for val'ue re·ceived'
for'ward
for'ward·er
for'ward·ing
for'wards
fos·sa'tum
fosse way or fosse
fos'ter
— child
— home
— par'ent
fos'ter·age
fos'ter·ing
fos'ter·land'
found
foun·da'tion
found'ed
found'er
found'ers' shares
found'ling
four cor'ners
Four·teenth' A·mend'·
  ment
Fourth A·mend'ment
fourth es·tate'
foy
frac'ti·o'
frac'tion

frac'tion·al
frac'tion·al·lize'
frag·men'ta
frame'-up'
framed
franc
fran'chise'
— ap·pur'te·nant to land
— clause
— tax
fran'chised' deal'er
fran'cus
— ban'cus
— ten'ens'
frank
— al·moigne'
— chase
— fee
— ferm
— fold
— mar'riage
— pledge
— ten'ant
— ten'e·ment
fra·ter'nal
— ben'e·fit as·so'ci·a'tion
— in·sur'ance
fra·ter'ni·ty
frat'ri·age
frat'ri·cide'
fraud
ac'tu·al —
con·struc'tive —
ex·trin'sic —
— in fact
— in law
— in the in·duce'ment
— in trea'ty
in·trin'sic —
tax —
fraud'u·lent
— al'ien·a'tion
— con·ceal'ment
— con·ver'sion
— con·vey'ance
— con·vey'anc·es
— in·tent'
— pref'er·enc·es
— rep're·sen·ta'tion
— trans'fers
stat'utes of or a·

gainst — con·vey'anc·es
fray
frec'tum
free
— and clear
— and e'qual
— bench
— bord
— e·lec'tion
— en'ter·prise'
— en'try, e'gress, and re'gress
— ex'er·cise' clause
— on board
freed'man
free'dom
— of as·so'ci·a'tion
— of choice
— of ex·pres'sion
— of re·lig'ion
— of speech and of the press
Free'dom of In'for·ma'tion Act
free'hold'
free'hold'er
free'man
free'man's roll
freeze'-out'
freight
— book'ing
— car
dead —
— for'ward·er
— mile
— train
freight'er
French'man
frend'wite'
fre·net'i·cus
freo'ling
fre'quent adj.
fre·quent' v.
fre·quent'er
fres'ca
fresh
— dis·sei'sin
— pur·suit'
fresh'-start' ad·just'-ment

fresh'et
fre'tum
fri'ars
friend
— of the court
friend'ly
— fire
— suit
fri·gid'i·ty
fringe ben'e·fits
frisk
friv'o·lous
from time to time
front'-foot' rule
front'age
front'ag·er
fron·tier'
front'ing and a·but'-ting
fro'zen
— ac·count'
— as'sets
fruc'tus
— in·dus'tri·a'les'
fruit
— and the tree doc'trine
— of crime
— of the poi'son·ous tree
frus·tra'tion
— of con'tract'
— of pur'pose doc'trine
fu'gam fe'cit
fu·ga'tor
fu'gi·ta'tion
fu'gi·tive
— from jus'tice
— of·fend'ers
— slave law
full
— age
— an'swer
— blood
— court
— cous'in
— cov'e·nants
— cov'er·age
— de·fense'
— dis·clo'sure
— faith and cred'it
paid in —

— proof
func'tion
func'tion·al
  — de·pre'ci·a'tion
  — ob'so·les'cence
func'tion·ar'y
fund *v.*
fund *n.*
  re·volv'ing —
  sink'ing —
fun'da·men'tal
  — er'ror
  — fair'ness doc'trine
  — law
  — rights
fun'da·men'tal·ist
fun·da'mus
fun·da'tor
fund'ed
  — debt
  — pen'sion plan
fun'di' pub'li·ci'
fu·ner'al
fun'gi·ble
fur
fu·ran'di' an'i·mus
fu'ri·o'sus
fur'long'
fur'lough
fur'nish
fur'ni·ture
fu'ror' bre'vis
fur'ther
  — con·sid'er·a'tion
  — in·struc'tions
fur'ther·ance
fur'tive
fur'tum
  — man'i·fes'tum
fus'tis
fu'ture
  — ac·quired' prop'er·ty
  — ad·vance' clause
  — ad·vanc'es
  — earn'ings
  — es·tate'
  — in'ter·ests
  — per·form'ance
fu'tures
  — con'tract'

— trad'ing
fu·tu'ri'

G

ga·bel' *or* ga·belle'
gaf'ol
gage
gain
gain'age
gain'er·y
gain'ful
  — em·ploy'ment
  — oc'cu·pa'tion
gale
gal'lon
gal'lows
gam'ble
gam'bler
gam'bling
  — de·vice'
  — pol'i·cy
game
  — laws
  — of chance
game'keep'er
gam'ing
  — con'tracts'
  — house
gang
gang'ster
gante'lope *or* gant'lope
gaol
gaol'er
ga·rage'
gar'ble
gar'dein
gar'den
gar'di·a'nus
ga·rene'
gar'nish
gar'nish·ee'
gar'nish·er
gar'nish·ment
gar'ri·son
gar·rot'ing
gar'ter
garth
gas

— cham'ber
gas'o·line'
gassed
gast
gas·tine'
gate
gauge
gau·ge'a·tor
gaug'er
Gault doctrine
gav'el
gav'el·kind'
gav'el·ler
gav'el·man
ga·zette'
ge·boc'ced
geld
geld'a·ble
geld'ing
gelt
ge·mot'
ge'ne·al'o·gy
gene'arch'
gen'er·a
gen'er·al
  — a'gen·cy busi'ness
  — ap·pear'ance
  — as·sem'bly
  — as·sign'ment for ben'-
    e·fit of cred'i·tors
  — as·sump'sit
  — av'er·age
  — be·quest'
  — cir'cu·la'tion
  — con·trac'tor
  — court
  — es·tate'
  — ex·cep'tion
  — ex·ec'u·tor
  — fee con·di'tion·al
  — ju'ris·dic'tion
  — law
  — lien
  — man'a·ger
  — part'ner
  — plea
  — pow'er of ap·point'-
    ment
  — rep'u·ta'tion
  — wel'fare'
Gen'er·al

— Ac·count'ing Of'fice
— As·sem'bly
— Court
— Serv'ic·es Ad·min'is·tra'tion
gen'er·al'i·ty
gen'er·al·ly ac·cept'ed
— ac·count'ing prin'ci·ples
— au'dit·ing stan'dards
gen'er·a'tion
gen'er·a'tion-skip'ping
— tax
— trust
Ge·ne'va Con·ven'tion
gen'i·tals
gen'i·ta'li·a
gen'o·cide'
genre
gens
gen'tes'
gen·ti'les'
gen'tle·man
gen'tle·men's a·gree'·ment
gen'tle·wom'an
gen'u·ine
ge'nus
ge'rens
ger'i·at'rics
Ger'man
ger·mane'
ger·ma'nus
ger'ry·man'der
ger'sume
ges·ta'tion
ges'tum
gib'bet
gift
— cau'sa mor'tis
— in'ter vi'vos'
— in trust
— o'ver
— split'ting
— tax
— to a class
gif'ta aq'uae'
Gift to Mi'nors Act
gild
gilt'-edged'
gin men

gi·ran'te
girth
gise'ment
gis'er
gise'tak'er
gist
— tak'ers
give
— and be·queath'
— bail
— no'tice
— way
give'-and-take'
giv'er
glean'ing
gle'ba
glid'ing
globe doc'trine
gloss
glos'sa
gob
go'ing
— and com'ing rule
— con'cern
— price
— pri'vate
— pub'lic
— through the bar
— val'ue
gold
— bond
— stan'dard
gold'smiths' notes
gon'or·rhe'a
good
— and law'ful men
— and val'id
— and work'man·like' man'ner
— be·hav'ior
— cause
— char'ac·ter
— con'duct'
— con·sid'er·a'tion
— faith
— faith pur'chas·er
— or'der
— rec'ord ti'tle
— re·pute'
— Sa·mar'i·tan doc'trine
— ti'tle

— will
goods
— and chat'tels
— sold and de·liv'ered
goods, wares, and mer'chan·dise'
gov'ern
gov'ern·ment
— de fac'to'
— de ju're'
fed'er·al —
lo'cal —
— of laws
gov'ern·ment'al
— a'gen·cy
— im·mu'ni·ty
— sur'vey'
gov'er·nor
grace
days of —
— pe'ri·od
grade v.
grade n.
— cross'ing
grad'ed of·fense'
grad'u·ate' v.
grad'u·ate n.
grad'u·at'ed
— lease
— tax
gra'dus
graft
grain
— rent
grain'age
gram
gram'mar school
grand n.
grand adj.
— days
— ju'ry
— re·mon'strance
grand'child'
grand'fa'ther
— clause
grand'moth'er
grand'stand' play
grange
— cas'es
gran'ge·ar'i·us
grant v.

— and to freight let

grant *n.*
  — and de·mise'
  land —
  — of per'son·al prop'er·ty
  pri'vate land —
  pub'lic —
  — to us'es
grant, bar'gain, and sell
gran·tee'
grant'-in-aid'
gran'tor
  — trusts
gran'tor-gran·tee' in'dex'
gran'tor's lien
grass hearth
grat'i·fi·ca'tion
gra'tis
  — dic'tum
gra·tu'i·tous
  — al·low'ance
  — bail·ee'
  — guest
  — li'cen·see'
  — pas'sen·ger
  — prom'ise
gra·tu'i·ty
gra·va'men
grave
grav'el pit
grav'en dock
grave'yard'
gra'vis
Gray's Inn
great
Great Char'ter
great'-grand'chil'dren
green'back'
Green Riv'er or'di·nance
Gre·gor'i·an code
gre'mi·um
gres'sume
greve
griev'ance
grieve
grieved
griev'ous

griff
groat
gro'cer
grog'shop'
gross *adj.*
  — earn'ings
  — es·tate'
  — in·ad'e·qua·cy
  — in'come'
  — na'tion·al prod'uct
  — pre'mi·um
  — prof'it
  — re·ceipts'
  — rev'e·nue
  — sales
  — spread
  — weight
gross *v.*
  — up
grosse·ment'
ground
  — land'lord'
  — lease
  — of ac'tion
  — rent
  — wa'ter
group
  — an·nu'i·ty
  — boy'cott'
  — in·sur'ance
  — li'bel
growth stock
grub'stake'
guar'an·tee'
  — clause
  — stock
guar'an·tor'
guar'an·ty *v.*
guar'an·ty *n.*
  — fund
  — in·sur'ance
guard'age
guard'i·an
  — ad li'tem
  — by es·top'pel
  — de son tort
  do·mes'tic —
  — for nur'ture
  gen'er·al —
  — in soc'age
  nat'u·ral —

tes'ta·men'ta·ry —
guard'i·an·ship'
gu'ber·na·to'ri·al
guer·pi' *or* guer·py'
guest
  — stat'ute
gui·don' de la mer
guild
guild'hall'
  — sit'tings
guile
guile'ful
guil'lo·tine'
guilt
guilt'less
guilt'y
guin'ea
gun
gunned
gun'shot'
gun'pow'der
gun'run'ner
gut'ter
gyn'ar·chy
gyn'e·coc'ra·cy
gy'ne·col'o·gist
gy'ne·col'o·gy
gy·ra'tion
gyves

H

ha'be·as cor'pus
  — ad de·lib'er·an'dum et re·cip'i·en'dum
  — ad fac'i·en'dum et re·cip'i·en'dum
  — ad pro'se·quen'dum
  — ad re'spon·den'dum
  — ad sat'is·fac'i·en'dum
  — ad sub'jic·i·en'dum
  — ad tes'ti·fi·can'dum
  — cum cau'sa
ha·ben'dum
  — clause
  — et ten·en'dum
ha·ben'tes' hom'i·nes'
hab'il·is
hab'it

— and re·pute′
hab′it·a·bil′i·ty
  war′ran·ty of —
hab′it·a·ble
  — re·pair′
hab′i·tan·cy
ha′bi·tant *or* ha·bi·tan′
hab′i·ta′tion
ha·bit′u·al
  — crim′i·nal
  — drunk′ard
ha·bit′u·al·ly
ha′ble
ha′ci·en′da
hack stand
hack′ney
  — car′riag·es
haec
  — est con·ven′ti·o′
  — est fi·na′lis con·cor′
    di·a
  — ver′ba
hae′res′
  — as·tra′ri·us
  — de fac′to′
  — in′sti·tu′tus
  — le·git′i·mus
  — na′tus
  — rec′tus
  — su′us
hae′re·ta′re′
haf′ne′
half
  — blood
  — broth′er
  — dol′lar
  — ea′gle
  — sec′tion
  — sis′ter
  — year
half′-tim′er
half′way′ house
ha′li·mas
hall
hall′mark′
hall′age
hal·lu′ci·na′tion
hal·lu′cin·o·gen′ic
ham′let
ham′mer
  sold un′der the —

Ham′mu·ra′bi
  Code of —
han′a·per-of′fice
hand *n.*
  — mon′ey
hand *v.*
  — down
hand′bill′
hand′bor′ow
hand′cuffs′
han′dle
hand′sale′
hand′sel
hand′writ′ing
  — ex·emp′lars′
han′dy·man′
hang
hanged, drawn, and
  quar′tered
hang′ing
hang′man
hanse
Han′se·at′ic
Hanse Towns
hap
hap′pi·ness
ha·rass′
ha·rass′ment
har′bin·ger
har′bor
hard
  — cas′es
  — la′bor
  — of hear′ing
hard′pan′
hard′ship′
har′i·ot
harm′ful
harm′less
  — er′ror
har·mon′ic plane
har′mo·nize′
har′mo·ny
har′ness
har′vest·ing
has′pa
hatch
Hatch Act
hatch′way′
haugh
haul

haul′age
haut
  — che·min′
  — es·tret′
have and hold
ha′ven
hawk′er
hawk′ing
hay in stack
hay′bote′
haz′ard
haz′ard·ous
head
  — mon′ey
  — of a fam′i·ly
  — of wa′ter
head′land′
head′note′
head′right′
heal′er
health
  bill of —
  board of —
  pub′lic —
health′y
hear′ing
  ad′ver·sar′y —
  — de no′vo′
  — ex·am′i·ner
  fair —
  fi′nal —
  — of′fi·cer
  pre·lim′i·nar′y —
  un·fair′ —
hear′say′
heart balm stat′utes
hearth
heat
  — of pas′sion
  — pros·tra′tion
  — stroke
heave to
He′brew
hedge
hedge′bote′
hedge′priest′
hedg′ing
heed′less
heel′er
he·gem′o·ny
heif′er

heir
— ap·par'ent
— at law
— ben'e·fi'ci·ar'y
— by a·dop'tion
— by cus'tom
— by de·vise'
— col·lat'er·al
— con·ven'tion·al
— ex·pec'tant
forced —
— gen'er·al
ir·reg'u·lar —
le'gal —
lin'e·al —
male —
— of the blood
— of the bod'y
— pre·sump'tive
pre'ter·mit'ted —
right —
— spe'cial
— tes'ta·men'ta·ry
— un'con·di'tion·al
heir'dom
heir'ess
heir'looms'
heirs
— and as·signs'
bod'i·ly —
joint —
law'ful —
le·git'i·mate —
nat'u·ral —
heir'ship'
— mov'a·bles
held
helm
hem'i·ple'gi·a
hence'forth'
hench'man
Hep'burn Act
hep'tar'chy
her'ald
her'ald·ry
herb'age
herd
herd'er
here·af'ter
her'e·dit'a·ments
corpo·re·al —

in'cor·po're·al —
he·red'i·tar'y
— dis·ease'
— suc·ces'sion
he·red'i·ty
her'e·sy
here'to·fore'
her'i·ot
her'is·cin'di·um
her'i·ta·ble
— bond
— ju'ris·dic'tions
— ob'li·ga'tion
— se·cu'ri·ty
her·maph'ro·dite'
her'me·neu'tics
Her·mo·ge'ni·an Code
her'ni·a
her'o·in
her'us
he who seeks eq'ui·ty
  must do eq'ui·ty
hi·dal'go
hid'den
— as'set'
— de'fect'
hide and gain
hi'er·ar'chy
high
— de·gree' of care and
  dil'i·gence
— wa'ter·mark' or water
  line
high'bind'er
high'er and low'er
  scale
high'est
— and best use
— de·gree' of care
— proved val'ue
High'ness
high'way'
pub'lic —
— rob'ber·y
high'way'man
hig'ler
hi'jack'er or high'jack'er
Hil'ton doc'trine
hin'der and de·lay'
hire
hir'er

hir'ing
— hall
His Ex'cel·len·cy
His Hon'or
his·tor'ic site
hit'-and-run' ac'ci·dent
hith'er·to'
hoard'ing
hoc
— in·tu'i·tu
— lo'co
— no'mi·ne'
— ti'tu·lo
— vo'ce
hog
hogs'head'
hold
— harm'less
hold'er
— for val'ue
— in due course
hold'ing
— com'pa·ny
— pe'ri·od
hold'o'ver ten'ant
hol'i·day'
le'gal —
stat'u·to'ry —
holm
hol'o·graph'
hom'age
— an·ces'tral
— ju'ry
— liege
hom'ag·er
ho'ma·gi'um
— lig'i·um
— red'de·re'
home
— loan banks
— of'fice
— port
— rule
home'own'er's as·so'ci·
  a'tion
home'own'ers pol'i·cy
home'stall'
home'stead'
— ex·emp'tion laws
hom'i·ci'dal
hom'i·cide'

— by mis'ad·ven'ture
— by ne·ces'si·ty
cul'pa·ble —
ex·cus'a·ble —
fe·lo'ni·ous —
jus'ti·fi'a·ble —
neg'li·gent —
— per in'for·tu'ni·um
reck'less —
— se de'fen·den'do'
ve·hic'u·lar —
ho'mi·cid'i·um
ho'mi·na'ti·o'
homme
ho'mo'
— li'ber
— Ro·ma'nus
ho'mo·sex'u·al
hon'es·te' vi'vе·re'
hon'es·tus
hon'or v.
hon'or n.
— courts
of'fice of —
hon'or·a·ble
— dis'charge'
hon'o·rar'i·um
hon'or·ar'y
hook'land'
hope
ho'ra
hor'i·zon'tal
— merger
— price'-fix'ing con'-
tracts'
— prop'er·ty acts
horn'book'
hors
— pris
horse
— guards
horse'pow'er
hos'pi·tal
base —
field —
hos'pi·ta·li·za'tion
Hos'pi'tal·er or Hos'pi'-
tal·lers
hos'pi·ta'tor
hos·pit'i·a
hos·pit'i·cide'

hos·pit'i·um
host
hos'tage
hos'ti·cide'
hos'tile
— em·bar'go
— fire
— pos·ses'sion
— wit'ness
hos·til'i·ty
hos'tler
hot
— blood
— car'go
hotch'pot'
ho·tel'
hough
hour
house
bawd'y —
board'ing —
— burn'ing
— coun'sel
du'plex' —
dwell'ing —
man'sion —
— of cor·rec'tion
— of ill fame
— of pros'ti·tu'tion
— of ref'uge
— of wor'ship
pub'lic —
tip'pling —
House
In'ner —
— of Com'mons
— of Del'e·gates'
— of Keys
— of Lords
— of Rep're·sen'ta·tives
Out'er —
house'age
house'bote'
house'break'ing
house'hold'
— stuff
house'hold'er
house'keep'er
hous'ing
— code
— courts

hov'el
hoy
hoy'man
huck'ster
hue and cry
hu'i'
huis
huis·se'ri·um
huis·si·ers'
hulks
hull
hu·man'i·tar'i·an doc'-
trine
hun'dred
— court
hun'dred·ors
hun'dred·weight'
hung ju'ry
hun'ger
hunt'ing
hur'dle
hur'ri·cane'
hurt
hus'band
— and wife
hus'band·man
hus'band·ry
hus'band-wife'
— priv'i·lege
— tort ac'tions
hush mon'ey
hust'ings
hy'brid
— class ac'tion
— se·cu'ri·ty
hy'giene'
hyp·not'ic drugs
hyp'no·tism
hy·pos'ta·sis
hy·poth'e·ca
hy·poth'e·car'y ac'tion
hy·poth'e·cate'
hy·poth'e·ca'tion
— bond
hy·poth'e·sis
hy'po·thet'i·cal ques'-
tion
hys'ter·ec'to·my
hys·ter'i·a
hys'ter·ot'o·my

I

i'bi·dem'
i·de'a
i·dée fixe'
i'dem'
— per —
— per·so'na
— so'nans
i·den'tic
i·den'ti·cal
i·den'ti·fi'a·ble
i·den'ti·fi·ca'tion
— of goods
i·den'ti·fy'
i·den'ti·ty
— of in'ter·ests
— of par'ties
id'e·o'
i'de·o·log'i·cal
id'e·ol'o·gy
id·e·o·logue'
ides
id est
id'i·o·cy
id'i·o·path'ic
— dis·ease'
— in·san'i·ty
id'i·o·syn'cra·sy
id'i·ot
id·o'ne·us
if
ig'no·min'y
ig'no·ra'mus
ig'no·rance
ac'ci·den·tal —
cul'pa·ble —
es·sen'tial —
in·vol'un·tar'y —
non'es·sen'tial —
vol'un·tar'y —
ig'no·rant
ig'no·ran'ti·a
— fac'ti' ex·cu'sat
— ju'ris su'i' non prae·
ju'di·cat ju'ri'
— le'gis est la'ta cul'pa
— legis nem'i·nem excu-
sat
ig'no·ra'ti·o' e·len'chi'

ig·nore'
ik'bal'
— da'wa'
ik'rah'
ik'rar'
— na'ma'
ill
— fame
— re·pute'
— will
ill'-ad·vised'
ill'-dis·posed'
ill'-do'ing
il·le'gal
— en'try
— in'ter·est
— per se
— trade
il·le·gal'i·ty
il·le·gal·ly
— ob·tained' ev'i·dence
il·leg'i·ble
il'le·git'i·ma·cy
il'le·git'i·mate
— child
il·lev'i·a·ble
ill'-got'ten
ill'-gov'erned
il·li'cit
— co·hab'i·ta'tion
— con·nec'tion
— dis·till'er·y
— re·la'tions
— trade
il·lic'i·te'
il·lic'i·tum col·le'gi·um
Il'li·nois' land trust
il·lit'er·a·cy
il·lit'er·ate
ill'ness
il·loc'a·ble
il'lud
ill'-us'age
ill'-used'
il·lu'sion
il·lu'sive
il·lu'so·ry
— ap·point'ment
— prom'ise
— trust
il·lus'tri·ous

i·mag'i·nar'y
i·mag'ine
im·bal'ance
im·bar'go
im·be·cile
im'be·cil'i·ty
im·bibe'
im·bro'glio
im'i·tate'
im'i·ta'tion
im'i·ta·tive
im'i·ta'tor
im'ma·nent
im·ma·te'ri·al
— a·ver'ment
— ev'i·dence
— facts
— is'sue
— var'i·ance
im'ma·te·ri·al'i·ty
im'ma·ture'
im·ma·tur'i·ty
im·me'di·a·cy
im·me'di·ate
— cause
— con·trol'
— dan'ger
— de·scent'
— no'tice
im·me'di·ate·ly
im'me·mo'ri·al
— pos·ses'sion
time —
— us'age
im'mi·grant
im'mi·grate'
im'mi·gra'tion
Im'mi·gra'tion
— and Na'tion·al'i·ty Act
— and Nat'u·ral·i·za'tion
Serv'ice
— Ap·peals' Board
im'mi·nent
— dan'ger
— per'il
im'mi·nent·ly dan'ger·
ous ar'ti·cle
im·mo·bi·lis
im'mo·bil'i·ty
im'mo·bi·lize'
im·mod'er·ate

im·mod'est
im·mor'al
— act
— con'duct'
— con·sid'er·a'tion
— con'tracts'
im'mor·al'i·ty
im·mov'a·bles
im·mu'ni·ty
— from pro'se·cu'tion
gov'ern·men'tal tort —
in'ter·spou'sal —
sov'er·eign —
im'mu·ni·za'tion
im'mu·nol'o·gy
im·pact'ed area
im'pact' rule
im·pair'
im·paired' cap'i·tal
im·pair'ing the ob'li·
ga'tion of con'tracts'
im·pan'el
im·par'i·ty
im·parl'
im·par'lance
gen'er·al —
general spec'ial —
special —
im·part'
im·par'tial
— ju'ry
im·part'i·ble feud
im·pass'a·ble
im·peach'
im·peach'ment
ar'ti·cles of —
col·lat'er·al —
— of an·nu'i·ty
— of ver'dict
— of waste
— of wit'ness
im·pec'ca·ble
im·pech'i·a're'
im·pe·cu'ni·ous
im·pe·cu'ni·os'i·ty
im·pede'
im·pe'di·ens'
im·ped'i·ments
im·ped'i·ment to mar'-
riage
im·pel'

im·pend'ing
im·per'a·tive
im·per·cep'ti·ble
im·per'fect
im·per'il
im·pe'ri·ous
im·pe'ri·um
im·per'son·a'tion
false —
im·per'ti·nence
im·per'ti·nent
im·pig'no·ra'ta
im·pig'no·ra'tion
im·pla·ci·ta're'
im·plant'
im·plead'
im·plead'ed
im·plead'er
im'ple·ments
im'pli·cate'
im'pli·ca'tion
im·plic'it
im·plied'
— as·ser'tions
— au·thor'i·ty
— con·sent'
— in·tent'
— prom'ise
— res'er·va'tion
— reservation of wa'ter
doc'trine
— war'ran·ty
im·pli'ed·ly
im'port'
— quo'ta
im'por·ta'tion
im·port'ed
im'port'-ex'port' clause
im'ports'
— clause
im'por·tune'
im'por·tu'ni·ty
im·pose'
im'po·si'tion
im·pos·si·bil'i·ty
ab'so·lute' —
le'gal —
log'i·cal —
— of per·form'ance of
con'tract'
phys'i·cal —

prac'ti·cal —
im·pos'tor
im'posts'
im·pos'ture
im'po·tence
im·po·ten'ti·a ex·cu'sat
le'gem
im·pound'
— ac·count'
im·prac'ti·ca·bil'i·ty
im·prac'ti·ca·ble
im·prac'ti·cal
im·preg'nate'
im'pre·scrip'ti·bil'i·ty
im'pre·scrip'ti·ble
rights
im·pres'sion
case of first —
im·press'ment
im·prest'
— fund
— mon'ey
im·pre'ti·a'bil·is
im'pri·ma'tur
im·pri'mis
im·pris'on
im·pris'on·ment
false —
im·pru'dence
im·pru'dent
im·pris'ti'
im·prob'a·ble
im·prop'er
— cu'mu·la'tion of ac'-
tions
— in'flu·ence
im·prop'er·ly ob·tained'
ev'i·dence
im·prove'
im·proved'
— land
— val'ue
im·prove'ment
— bonds
im·prove'ments
im·prov'i·dence
im·prov'i·dent·ly
im·pru'dence
im·pru'dent
im·pugn'
im·pugn'a·ble

im·pugn'ments
im·pulse'
im·pul'sive
im·pu'ni·ty
im·pu'ta·bil'i·ty
im'pu·ta'tion
— of pay'ment
im·put'ed
— cost
— in'come'
— in'ter·est
— knowl'edge
— neg'li·gence
— no'tice
in'a·bil'i·ty
in ab·sen'tia
in'ac·ces'si·ble
in ac'tion
in·ac'tive
in·ad'e·qute
— con·sid'er·a'tion
— dam'ag·es
— price
— rem'e·dy at law
in'ad·mis'si·ble
in ad·ver'sum
in'ad·ver'tence
in'ad·ver'tent·ly
in·al'ien·a·ble
— in'ter·ests
— rights
in a'li·e'no so'lo
in a'li·o' lo'co'
in am·big'u·o'
in a·per'ta lu'ce'
in a·pic'i·bus ju'ris
in ar·bi'tri·um ju'ris
in arc'ta et sal'va cus·
   to'di·a
in'ar·tic'u·late
in ar·tic'u·lo'
— mor'tis
in'as·much' as
in·au'gu·ra'tion
in au'tre droit
in ban'co'
in be'ing
   life or lives —
in blank
in'board'
in bo'nis

— de·func'ti'
in'bound' com'mon
in bulk
in ca·hoots'
in cam'er·a
— in·spec'tion
— pro·ceed'ings
in·ca'pa·ble
in·ca·pac'i·tat'ed per'-
son
in'ca·pac'i·ty
   le'gal —
   to'tal —
in cap'i·ta
in cap'i·te'
in·car'cer·ate'
in·car'cer·a'tion
in ca'su pro·vi'so'
in cau'sa
in·cau'tious
in·cen'di·a·rist
in·cen'di·ar'y
in·cen'tive
— stock'-op'tion plan
in·cep'tion
in·cert'ae' per·so'nae'
in'cest'
in·ces'tu·o'si'
in·ces'tu·ous
— a·dul'ter·y
— bas'tards
inch
in charge of
in'char·ta're'
in chief
   case —
inch'ma·ree' clause
in·cho'ate
— crimes
— dow'er
— in'stru·ment
— in'ter·est
— lien
— right
in'ci·dence
in'ci·dent
— of own'er·ship'
in'ci·den'tal
— ben'e·fi'ci·ar·y
— dam'ag·es
— pow'ers

— to ar·rest'
— to em·ploy'ment
— use
in·cin'er·a'tion
in·cip'i·ent
in·cip'i·tur
in·cite'
in·cite'ment
in·cit'er
in·ci'vi·le
in·civ'ism
in'cli·na'tion
in·close'
in·closed' lands
in·clo'sure
— acts
in·clude'
in·clud'ed of·fense'
in·clu'si·o' u'ni·us est
   ex·clu'si·o' al·ter'i·us
in·clu'sive
— sur'vey'
in'cog·ni'to
in'co·her'ent
in·co'las dom'i·cil'i·um
   fa'cit
in·com·bus'ti·ble
in'come'
   ac·crued' —
— av'er·ag·ing
— ba'sis
— ben'e·fi'ci·ar·y
   de·ferred' —
   earned —
   fixed —
   gross —
— in re·spect' of de·ce'-
   dent
   net (busi'ness) —
   non·op'er·at'ing —
   op'er·at'ing —
   or'di·nar'y —
   per'son·al —
— prop'er·ty
— state'ment
— tax
— un·earned'
in'come'less
in'come'-tax'
— de·fi'cien·cy
— re·turn'

in'com'ing
in com·men'dam'
in com'mon
in com·mu'ni'
in'com·mu'ni·ca'do
in'com·mu'ni·ca'tion
in'com·mut'a·ble
in'com·pat'i·bil'i·ty
in'com·pat'i·ble
in·com'pe·tence
in·com'pe·ten·cy
in·com'pe·tent ev'i·
  dence
in'com·plete' trans'fer
in'con·clu'sive
in'con·gru'i·ty
in con·junc'tion with
in·con'se·quen'tial
in'con·sid'er·a·ble
in con·sid'e·ra·ti·o·ne
  — in'de
  — le'gis
  — prae'mis·so'rum
in con·sim'i·li' ca'su
in'con·sis'ten·cy
in'con·sis'tent
in con'tem·pla'tion of
  death
in·con·tes·ta·bil'i·ty
  — clause
in'con·ti·nence
in'con·ti·nen'ti'
in con·trac'ti·bus
in'con·tro·vert'i·ble
in'con·ven'ience
in·co'po·li'tus
in·cor'po·ra'mus
in·cor'po·rate'
in·cor'po·ra'tion
  — by ref'er·ence
in·cor'po·rat'ed law so·
  ci'e·ty
in·cor'po·ra'tor
in cor'po·re'
in'cor'po·re'al
  — chat'tels
  — her'e·dit'a·ments
  — prop'er·ty
  — rights
  — things
in·cor'ri·gi·ble

in'cor·rupt'i·ble
in'crease'
  af'fi·da'vit of —
  costs of —
in·cred'i·ble
in'cre·ment
in'cre·men'tal
  — cost
in'cre·men'tum
in·crim'i·nate'
in·crim'i·nat'ing
  — ad·mis'sion
  — cir'cum·stance'
  — ev'i·dence
in·crim'i·na'tion
in·crim'i·na·to'ry
  state'ment
in·croach'ment
in·cul'pate'
in·cul'pa·to'ry
in·cum'ben·cy
in·cum'bent
in·cum'ber
in·cum'branc·es
  cov'e·nant a·gainst' —
in·cum'branc·er
in·cur'
in·cur'a·ble dis·ease'
in'cu'ri·a
in·cur'ra·ble
in·cur'ra·men'tum
in·cur'sion
in cus·to'di·a le'gis
in'de'
in·deb'i·ta'tus
  as·sump'sit —
in·debt'ed·ness
in·de'cen·cy
  pub'lic —
in·de'cent
  — as·sault'
  — ex'hi·bi'tion
  — ex·po'sure
  — lib'er·ties
  — pub'li·ca'tions
in'de·fea'si·ble
in·def'i·nite
  — fail'ure of is'sue
  — leg'a·cy
  — num'ber
in de·lic'to'

in·dem'ni·fi·ca'tion
in'dem·nif'i·ca·to'ry
in·dem'ni·fy'
in·dem'ni·tee'
in·dem'ni·tor
in·dem'ni·ty
  — a·gainst' li'a·bil'i·ty
  — bond
  — con'tract'
  — in·sur'ance
  — lands
  — pol'i·cy
in·den'i·za'tion
in·dent'
in·den'tor
in·den'ture
  — of a fine
  — of trust
  — trus·tee'
in'de·pend'ence
in'de·pend'ent
  — ad·just'er
  — ad·vice'
  — con'tract'
  — con'trac'tor
  — cov'e·nant
  — sig·nif'i·cance
  — source rule
in'de·struc'ti·ble
  — trust
in'de·ter'min·a·ble
in'de·ter'mi·nate
  — con·di'tion·al re·lease'
  — ob'li·ga'tion
  — sen'tence
in'dex'
  — an'i·mi' ser'mo'
  — of·fens'es
In'di·an
  — Claims Com·mis'sion
  — coun'try
  — dep're·da'tions acts
  — lands
  — res'er·va'tion
  — ti'tle
  — tri'bal prop'er·ty
  — tribe
in·di·ca'tion
in·dic'a·tive ev'i·dence
in'di·ca'vit
in·di'ci·a

— of ti'tle
in·di'ci·um
in·dict'
in·dict'a·ble
— of·fense'
in·dict'ed
in'dict·ee'
in·dic'ti·o'
in·dict'ment
joint —
in·dic'tor
in di'em
in·dif'fer·ent
in'di·gent
— de·fen'dant
— in·sane' per'son
in·dig'ni·ty
in'di·rect'
— at·tack'
— ev'i·dence
— tax
in'dis·creet'
in'dis·cre'tion
in'dis·crim'i·nate
in'dis·pen'sa·ble
— ev'i·dence
— par'ties
in·dis·po·si'tion
in'dis·sol'u·ble
in'dis·tan'ter
in·dite'
in'di·vid'u·al
— as'sets'
— debts
— pro·pri'e·tor·ship'
— re·tire'ment ac·count'
— sys'tem of lo·ca'tion
in'di·vid'u·al·ly
in'di·vis'i·ble
in'di·vi'sum
in'do·lence
in do·min'i·co'
in·dorse'
in'dors·ee'
— in due course
in·dorse'ment
ac·com'mo·da'tion —
blank —
con·di'tion·al —
full —
ir·reg'u·lar —

prop'er —
qual'i·fied' —
reg'u·lar —
re·stric'tive —
spe'cial —
special — of writ
un·au'thor·ized' —
— with·out' re'course'
in·dors'er
in dor'so'
in du'bi·o'
in·du'bi·ta·ble proof
in·duce'
in·duce'ment
in·du'ci·ae'
in·duct'
in·duc'ti·o'
in·duc'tion
in·dul'gence
in·du'ment
in du'plo'
in·dus'tri·al
— dis·ease'
— goods
— re·la'tions
in·dus'tri·am
per —
in'dus·try
in e·a'dem cau'sa
in·e'bri·ate
in'e·bri'e·ty
in·ed'u·ca·ble
in'ef·fec'tu·al
in'ef·fi'cien·cy
in·el'i·gi·bil'i·ty
in·el'i·gi·ble
in em'u·la·ti·o'nem vi·
ci'ni'
in·eq'ua·ble
in'e·qual'i·ty
in·eq'ui·ta·ble
in·eq'ui·ty
in eq'ui·ty
in'es·cap'a·ble
— per'il
in es'se
in est de ju're
in ev'i·dence
in·ev'i·ta·ble
— ac'ci·dent
in ex·cam'bi·o'

in'ex·cus'a·ble ne·glect'
in·ex·e·cu'ta·ble
in ex'e·cu'tion and pur·
su'ance of
in ex'i·tu'
in ex·ten'so'
in ex·tre'mis
in fa'ci·e' cu'ri·ae'
in fa'ci·en'do'
in fact
in fac'to'
in fa'mi·a
in·fa·mous
— crime
— pun'ish·ment
in'fa·my
in'fan·cy
in'fans
in'fant
in·fan'ti·cide'
in fa·vo'rem
— lib'er·ta'tus
— vi'tae'
in·fec'tion
in feo'do'
in·feoff'ment
in·fer'a·ble
in'fer·ence
— on —
rea'son·a·ble — rule
in'fer·en'tial
— facts
in·fe'ri·or
— court
in'feu·da'tion
in fic'ti·o'ne ju'ris
sem'per ae'qui·tas ex·
is'tit
in'fi·del
in'fi·de'lis
in'fi·del'i·ty
in fi'e·ri'
in fi'ne'
in·fin'i·tum
in·firm'
in·fir'ma·tive
— con·sid'er·a'tion
— fact
— hy·poth'e·sis
in·fir'mi·ty
in fla·gran'te de·lic'to

in·flam′ma·ble
in·flam′ma·to′ry
in·fla′tion
in·fla′tion·ar′y
in·flict′
in·flu·ence
in·for′mal
— con′tract′
— pro·ceed′ings
in′for·mal′i·ty
in·form′ant
in for′ma pau′per·is
in′for·ma′tion
— and be·lief′
crim′i·nal—
— in the na′ture of a
   quo war′ran·to′
— of in·tru′sion
in′for·ma′tus non sum
in·formed′ con·sent′
in·form′er
in·form′er's priv′i·lege
in fo′ro′
— con′sci·en′ti·ae′
— con′ten·ti·o′so′
in′for·tu′ni·um
 hom′i·cide′ per—
in′fra
— ae·ta′tem′
— an′nos′ nu′bi·les′
— an′num
— annum luc′tus
— bra′chi·a
— civ′i·ta·tem
— dig′ni·ta·tem cu′ri·ae′
— fu·ro′rem
— hos·pit′i·um
— ju′ris·dic′ti·o′nem
— me′tas′
— prae·sid′i·a
— qua′tu·or′ ma′ri·a
— quatuor pa·ri′e·tes′
— reg′num
in·frac′tion
in·frac′tor
in·fran′gi·ble
in frau′dem
— cred′i·to′rum
— le′gis
in·fringe′ment
 con·trib′u·to′ry —

crim′i·nal —
di·rect′ —
— of cop′y·right′
— of pat′ent
— of trade′mark′
vi·car′i·ous —
in·fring′er
in′fu·ga′re′
in full
in·fu′sion
in fu·tu′ro′
in gen′e·re′
in·gen′ious
in·ge′ni·um
in′ge·nu′i·tas′
in′ge·nu′i·ty
in·gen′u·ous
in·gen′u·us
in·grat′i·tude′
in gre′mi·o′ le′gis
in′gress′
in gross
in′gros·sa′tor
in·gross′ing
in′gui·nal
in·hab′it
in·hab′i·tant
in hac par′te′
in haec ver′ba
in·here′
in·her′ent
— de′fect
— pow′er
— pow′ers of a court
— right
in·her′ent·ly dan′ger·ous
in·her′e·trix′
in·her′it
in·her′it·a·ble blood
in·her′i·tance
— act
es·tate′ of —
— tax
in·her′i·tor
in·her′i·trix
in′hi·bi′tion
in hoc
in′hu·mane′
in·hu′man treat′ment
in i·is′dem′ ter′mi·nis

in·im′i·ca·ble
in·im′i·cal
in in′di·vid′u·o′
in in′fi·ni′tum
in i·ni′ti·o′
in in·teg′rum
in in·vid′i·um
in in·vi′tum
in·iq′ui·ty
in·i′qu·um est a′li·
 quem re′i′ su′i′ es′se
 ju′di·cem
in·i′tial
— car′ri·er
in·i′ti·ate′
in·i′ti·a′tion fee
in·i′ti·a·tive
In′i·ur′col·leg′ui·a
in ju·di′ci·o′
in·junc′tion
 fi′nal —
 in′ter·loc′u·to′ry —
 man′da·to′ry —
 per′ma·nent —
 per·pet′u·al —
 pre·lim′i·nar′y —
 pre·ven′tive —
 pro·vi′sion·al —
 spe′cial —
 tem′po·rar′y —
in′jure
in ju′re′
— al·ter′i·us
— pro′pri·o′
in·ju′ri·a
— abs′que dam′no′
— non ex·cu′sat in·ju′ri·
 am
— non prae·su′-mi·tur′
— pro′pri·a non ca′det in
 ben′e·fi′ci·um fa′ci·
 en′tis
in′ju·ries
ab′so·lute′ —
pri′vate —
pub′lic —
rel′a·tive —
in·ju′ri·ous
— false′hood′
— words
in′ju·ry

ac′ci·den′tal —
bod′i·ly —
civ′il —
ir·rep′a·ra·ble —
per′ma·nent —
per′son·al —
real —
re·par′a·ble —
ver′bal —
in·jus′tice
in jus vo·ca′re′
in kind
in′la·ga′tion
in′land′ *n.*
in′land *adj.*
— bill of ex·change′
— nav′i·ga′tion
— trade
— wa′ters
in′lan·tal *or* in′lan·ta′le
in·law′
in law
in lec′to′ mor·ta′li′
in lieu of
in lim′i·ne′
  motion —
in li′tem
in lo′co′
  — pa·ren′tis
in ma·jo′rem cau·te′-
  lam
in ma·jo′re sum′ma
  con′ti·ne′tur mi′nor
in ma′lam par′tem
in′mate′
in max′i·ma po·ten′ti·a
  min′i·ma li·cen′ti·a
in me′di·as res
in med′i·co′
in mis′er·i·cor′di·a
in mi′ti·o′ri′ sen′su′
in mo′dum as·si′sae′
in mo′ra′
in mor′tu·a ma′nu′
inn
in·nav′i·ga·bil′i·ty
in·nav′ga·ble
in′ner
  — bar′ris·ter
  — house
inn′ings

inn′keep′er
in′no·cence
in′no·cent
  — a′gent
  — con·vey′anc·es
  — pur′chas·er
  — tres′pass
  — tres′pass·er
in·noc′u·ous
in·nom′i·nate
  —con′tracts′
in no′mi·ne De′i, A·
  men′
in′no·tes′ci·mus
in no′tis
in′no·va′tion
Inns of Chan′cer·y
Inns of Court
in nu′bi·bus
in′nu·en′do
in nul′li·us bo′nis
in nul′lo est er·ra′tum
in ob·scu′ris, quod
  min′i·mum est seq′ui·
  mur
in·oc′u·late′
in o′di·um spo′li·a·to′ris
in′of·fi′cious tes′ta·
  ment
in om′ni·bus
in·op′er·a·tive
in pais
  es·top′pel —
in pa′ri′
  — cau′sa
  — de·lic′to
  — ma·te′ri·a
in pa′ti·en′do′
in pec′to·re′ ju′di·cis
in pe·jo′rem par′tem
in per·pe′tu·am re′i′
  me·mo′ri·am
in per′pe·tu′i·ty
in per·pe′tu·um re′i′
  tes′ti·mo′ni·um
in per′son
in per·so′nam
  — ju′ris·dic′tion
  — not in rem
in ple′na vi′ta
in ple′no′ lu′mi·ne′

in pos′se
in po′tes·ta′te′pa·ren′tis
in prae′mis·so′rum fi′-
  dem
in prae·sen′ti′
in pren′der
in pri′mis
in prin·cip′i·o′
in promp′tu′
in pro′pri·a
  — cau′sa ne′mo′ ju′dex
  — per·so′na
in′quest′
  ar·rest′ of —
  cor′o·ner′s —
  — ju′ry
  — of lu′na·cy
  — of of′fice
  — of sher′iffs
in·quir′y
  court of —
  writ of —
in′qui·si′tion
  — af′ter death
  — of lu′na·cy
in·quis′i·tor
in re
in re′bus
in re·gard′ to
in rem
  judg′ment —
  — ju′ris·dic′tion
  — mort′gage
  qua′si′ —
in ren′der
in re·pub′li·ca max′i·
  me′ con·ser·van′da
  sunt ju′ra bel′li′
in re′rum na·tu′ra
in re·spect′ of
in·sane′
  — de·lu′sion
  — per′son
in·san′i·ty
  cho·re′ic —
  con·gen′i·tal —
  — de·fense′
  id′i·o·path′ic —
  le′gal —
  man′ic-de·pres′sive —
  pel·lag′rous —

pol′y·neu·rit′ic —
pu·er′per·al —
syph′i·lit′ic —
trau·mat′ic —
in sat′is·fac′tion
in·scribed′
in·scrip′tion
in′se·cure′
in′se·cu′ri·ty clause
in·sem′i·nate′
in·sem′i·na′tion
 ar′ti·fi′cial —
in·sen′si·ble
in sep·a·ra′li′
in·sert′ v.
in′sert′ n.
in·sid′er
— in′for·ma′tion
— re·ports′
— trad′ing
in·sid′i·ous
in′sight′
in·sig′ni·a
in sim′i·li′ ma·te′ri·a
in′si·mul
in·sin′u·a′tion
in′so·far′
 — as
 — that
in′so·la′tion
in sol′i·do′
in so′li·dum
in so′lo′
in·sol′ven·cy
in·sol′vent
in spe′cie
in·spect′
in·spec′ta·tor
in·spec′tion
 in cam′er·a —
 — laws
 — of doc′u·ments
 rea′son·a·ble —
 — rights
 — search′es
in·spec′tor
in·spec′tor·ship′, deed
 of
in′sta·bil′i·ty
in·stall′
in·stal·la′tion

in·stall′ment
— con′tract′
— cred′it
— land con′tract′
— loan
— meth′od
— plan
re′tail — sale
— sale
in′stance
— court
in′stant
in′stan·ta′ne·ous
— crime
— death
in′stan·ter
in′stant·ly
in′star
in sta′tu′ quo
in′sti·gate′
in′sti·ga′tion
in′sti·ga′tor
in′stir·pa′re′
in stir′pes′
in′sti·tute′
in′sti·tut′ed ex·ec′u·tor
In′sti·tutes′
— of Gai′us
— of Jus·tin′i·an
— of Lord Coke
The·oph′i·lus′ —
in′sti·tu′tion
in′sti·tu′ti·o′nes′
in·struct′
in·struc′tion
 per·emp′to·ry —
in·struc′tions
— to ju′ry
in′stru·ment
— of ap·peal′
— of ev′i·dence
in′stru·men′ta
in′stru·men′tal
in′stru·men·tal′i·ty rule
in′sub·or′di·na′tion
in sub·sid′i·um
in′suf·fi′cien·cy
— of ev′i·dence to sup·
 port′ ver′dict
in′suf·fi′cient
in′su·la

in′su·lar
— courts
— pos·ses′sions
in′su·late′
in′su·la′tion pe′ri·od
in′sult′
in·su′per
in·su′per·a·ble
in′sup·port′a·ble
in·sur′a·ble
— in′ter·est
— val′ue
in·sur′ance
 ac′ci·dent—
 ac·counts′ re·ceiv′a·
  ble —
 — ad·just′er
 — a′gent
 air trav′el —
 all′-risk′ —
 an·nu′i·ty —
 as·sess′ment life — pol′i·
  cy
 au′to·mo·bile′ —
 — bro′ker
 bur′gla·ry —
 busi′ness —
 business in′ter·rup′-
  tion —
 cas′u·al·ty —
 col·li′sion —
 com·mer′cial —
 — com·mis′sion·er
 — com′pa·ny
 com′pre·hen′sive —
 con·cur′rent—
 con·vert′i·ble col·li′-
  sion —
 convertible life —
 co·op′er·a·tive —
 cred′it —
 crime —
 crop —
 de·creas′ing term —
 de·pos′it —
 dou′ble —
 em·ploy′ers′ —
 em·ploy′er's li′a·bil′i·
  ty —
 en·dow′ment —

er'rors and o·mis'-
  sions —
ex·cess' —
ex·tend'ed term —
fam'i·ly in'come' —
fi·del'i·ty —
fire —
first par'ty —
fleet pol'i·cy —
float'er —
fra·ter'nal —
gov'ern·ment —
group —
group'-term' life —
guar'an·ty —
hail —
health —
home'own'ers —
in·dem'ni·ty —
in·dus'tri·al —
in'land ma·rine' —
joint life —
key man life —
lev'el pre'mi·um —
li'a·bil'i·ty —
life —
lim'it·ed pay'ment life —
limited pol'i·cy —
live'stock' —
maj'or med'i·cal —
mal·prac'tice —
man'u·al rat'ing —
ma·rine' —
mort'gage —
mo'tor ve'hi·cle —
mu'tu·al —
na'tion·al serv'ice life —
no'-fault' au'to —
non·as·sess'a·ble —
old line life —
or'di·nar'y life —
paid'-up' —
par·tic'i·pat'ing —
part'ner·ship' —
plate glass —
— pol'i·cy
— pre'mi·um
prod'uct li'a·bil'i·ty —
pub'lic li'a·bil'i·ty —
— rat'ing
re·cip'ro·cal —

re·new'a·ble term —
re·tire'ment in'come' —
sin'gle pre'mi·um —
so'cial —
split dol'lar —
steam boil'er —
step'-rate' pre'mi·um —
straight life —
sur'e·ty and fi·del'i·ty —
term —
ti'tle —
tor·na'do —
— trust
trust —
un·em·ploy'ment —
war risk —
whole life —
in·sure'
in·sured'
  ad·di'tion·al —
in·sur'er
in·sur'gent
in'sur·rec'tion
in·tact'
in'takes'
in·tan'gi·ble
  — as'set'
  — prop'er·ty
in·tan'gi·bles
  — tax
in tan'tum
in'te·ger
in'te·grat'ed
  — bar
  — con'tract'
  — prop'er·ty set'tle·
    ments
  — writ'ing
in'te·gra'tion
  de fac'to' —
  de ju're' —
  hor'i·zon'tal —
  ver'ti·cal —
in·teg'ri·ty
in'tel·lec'tu·al
in·tel'li·gence
in·tel'li·gi·bil'i·ty
in·tem'per·ance
in·tend'
in·ten'dant
in·tend'ed

— to be re·cord'ed
— use doc'trine
— wife
in·tend'ment of law
in·tent'
  com'mon —
  crim'i·nal —
  gen'er·al —
  spe·cif'ic —
  — to kill
  trans·ferred' —
in·ten'ti·o' cae'ca' ma'-
  la'
in·ten'tion
in·ten'tion·al
in'ter
in'ter·a'gen·cy
in'ter a'li·a
in'ter a'li·os'
in'ter a'pi·ces' ju'ris
in'ter·bank'
in'ter·bor'ough
in'ter·bourse'
in'ter bra'chi·a
in'ter·cede'
in'ter·ces'sion
in'ter·cep'tion
in'ter·change'a·bly
in'ter·com'mon
in'ter·com·mun'ing
in'ter con'ju·ges'
in'ter con·junc'tas per·
  so'nas
in'ter·course'
in'ter·dict'
in'ter·dic'tion
  — of fire and wa'ter
in'ter·es'se
  pro — su'o'
  — ter'mi·ni'
in'ter·est
  ab'so·lute' —
  ac·crued' —
  ac·cu'mu·lat'ed —
  Bos'ton —
  com'pound —
  con·ven'tion·al —
  — e'qual·i·za'tion tax
  ex·ces'sive —
  gross —
  im·put'ed —

joint —
le'gal —
New York —
nom'i·nal —
or'di·nar'y —
— rate
sim'ple —
— up·on' —
in·ter·est·ed
in·ter·fere'
in·ter·fer'ence
in·ter·gov'ern·men'tal
in·ter·im
— com·mit'ti·tur
— cu·ra'tor
— fi·nanc'ing
— of'fi·cer
— or'der
— re·ceipt'
— state'ments
in·ter·in·sur'ance
— ex·change'
In·te'ri·or De·part'-
ment
in·ter·lin'e·a'tion
in·ter·lin'ing
in·ter·lock'
in·ter·lock'ing di·rec'-
tor·ate
in·ter·loc'u·tor
in·ter·loc'u·to'ry
— ap·peal'
In·ter·loc'u·to'ry Ap·
peals' Act
in·ter·lop'ers
in·ter·mar'riage
in·ter·med'dle
in·ter·me'di·ar'y
— bank
in·ter·me'di·ate
— ac·count'
— courts
— or'der
in·ter·me'di·a'tor
in·ter·ment
in ter'mi·nis ter'mi·
nan'ti·bus
in·ter·mit'tent
— ease'ment
— stream
in·ter·mix'ture

— of goods
in'tern'
in·ter'nal
— act
— af·fairs' doc'trine
— affairs of cor'po·ra'-
tion
— com'merce
— im·prove'ments
— po·lice'
— rev'e·nue
— se·cu'ri·ty acts
— wa'ters
In·ter'nal Rev'e·nue
— Code
— Serv'ice
in'ter·na'tion·al
— a·gree'ments
— com'merce
— court of jus'tice
— ju'ris·dic'tion
— law
In'ter·na'tion·al
— Mon'e·tar'y Fund
— Shoe Case
in·tern'ment
in'ter pa'res'
in'ter par'tes'
in'ter·pel'late'
in'ter·plea'
in'ter·plead'er
stat'u·to'ry —
In'ter·pol'
in·ter·po·late'
in·ter·po·lat'ed ter'mi·
nal re·serve'
in·ter·po·la'tion
in·ter·pose'
in·ter·po·si'tion
in·ter'pret
in·ter'pre·ta'tion
— clause
close —
ex·ten'sive —
ex·trav'a·gant —
free —
lib'er·al —
lim'it·ed —
pre·des'tined —
re·stric'tive —
strict —

in·ter'pret·er
in'ter·ra'cial
in'ter re·ga'lia
in'ter·reg'num
in·ter'ro·ga'tion
cus·to'di·al —
in·ter·rog'a·to'ries
in·ter'ro·gee'
in ter·ro'rem
— clause
— pop'u·li'
in'ter·rup'tion
in'ter·sec'tion
in'ter se, in'ter se'se'
in'ter·spou'sal
in'ter·state'
— a·gree'ments
— com'merce
— com'pact'
— ex'tra·di'tion
— law
— ren·di'tion
In'ter·state'
— Com'merce Act
— Commerce Com·mis'-
sion
— Land Sales Full Dis·
clo'sure Act
in'ter·sti·ces'
in'ter·sti'tial
in'ter·ur'ban
in'ter·ven'ing
— act
— a'gen·cy
— cause
— dam'ag·es
— force
in'ter·ve'nor
in'ter·ven'tion
in'ter·view'
in'ter·view·ee'
in'ter·view'er
in'ter vi'rum et ux'o·
rem
in'ter vi'vos
— gift
— trans'fer
— trust
in·tes'ta·ble
in·tes'ta·cy
in·tes'tate'

— suc·ces'sion
in tes'ti·mo'ni·um
in the course of em·
   ploy'ment
in'ti·ma·cy
in'ti·mate *adj.*
in'ti·mate' *v.*
in'ti·ma'tion
in·tim'i·date'
in·tim'i·da'tion
in'to
in'tol and ut'tol
in·tol'er·a·ble
in·tol'er·ance
in to'to'
in·tox'i·cant
in·tox'i·cat'ed
in·tox'i·cat'ing liq'uor
in·tox'i·ca'tion
 pub'lic —
in'tox·im'e·ter
in'tra
in'tra an'ni' spa'ti·um
in·trac'ta·ble
in'tra fi'dem
in tra·jec'tu'
in'tra·lim'i·nal
in'tra luc'tus tem'pus
in'tra·mu'ral
in'tra qua'tu·or ma'ri·a
in tran'si·tu'
in'tra pa·ri·e'tes'
in'tra·state'
   — com'merce
in'tra vi'res'
in'tri·cate
in·trin'sic
   — ev'i·dence
   — fraud
   — val'ue
in'tro·duc'tion
in'tro·mis'sion
in'tro·ver'sion
in·trud'er
in·tru'sion
in·trust'
in'un·da'tion
in·ure'
in·ure'ment
in u'te·ro'
in ut·ro·que' ju're

in vac'u·o'
in vad'i·o'
in vain
in val'id
in·val'i·da'tion
in·va'sion
   — of cor'pus prin'ci·pal
   — of pri'va·cy
in·vec'tive
in·vei'gle
in·vent'
in·ven'tion
in·ven'tor
in'ven·to'ry
in ven'tre sa mère
in·ven'tus
in·verse'
   — con'dem·na'tion
   — or'der of al'ien·a'tion
     doc'trine
in'vert'
in·vest'
in·ves'ti·ga'tion
in·ves'ti·ga'to'ry pow'-
   ers
in·ves'ti·tive fact
in·ves'ti·ture'
in·vest'ment
   — ad·vis'er
   — bank'er
   — bill
   — com'pa·ny
   — con'tract'
   — cred'it
   — prop'er·ty
   — se·cu'ri·ty
   — tax cred'it
   — trust
In·vest'ment
   — Ad·vis'ers Act
   — Com'pa·ny Act
in·ves'tor
in vin'cu·lis
in·vi'o·la·bil'i·ty
in·vi'o·la·ble
in'vi·ta'tion
   — to bid
in·vite'
in·vit'ed er'ror
in·vit'ee'
in'vo·ca'tion

in'voice'
   — book
in·voke'
in·vol'un·tar'y
   — al'ien·a'tion
   — con·fes'sion
   — con·ver'sion
   — con·vey'ance
   — de·pos'it
   — dis·con·tin'u·ance
   — lien
   — man'slaugh'ter
   — pay'ment
   — ser'vi·tude'
   — trans'fer
   — trust
in wit'ness where·of'
i·o'ta
i'ron-safe' clause
ip'se'
ip'se' dix'it
   — fac'to'
ip'so' ju're
ir·ra'tion·al
ir're·but'ta·ble
   — pre·sump'tion
ir·rec'on·cil'a·ble dif'-
   fer·enc·es
ir're·cov'er·a·ble
ir're·cu'sa·ble
ir're·deem'a·ble
ir're·duc'i·ble
ir·ref'u·ta·ble
ir·reg'u·lar
   — judg'ment
ir·reg'u·lar'i·ty
ir·rel'e·van'cy
ir·rel'e·vant
   — al'le·ga'tion
   — an'swer
ir're·me'di·a·ble
ir're·mis'si·ble
ir're·mov'a·bil'i·ty
ir·rep'a·ra·ble
   — dam'ag·es
   — harm
   — in'ju·ry
ir're·peal'a·ble
ir're·plev'i·a·ble
ir're·sis'ti·ble
   — force

— im′pulse′
ir′re·spec′tive
ir′re·spon′si·ble
ir′re·triev′a·ble
— break′down′ of mar′-
riage
ir′re·vers′i·ble
ir·rev′o·ca·ble
— let′ter of cred′it
ir′ri·ga′tion
— com′pa·ny
— dis′trict
ir′ri·tant
is′land
i′so·late′
i′so·lat′ed sale
is′su·a·ble
— de·fense′
— plea
— terms
is′su·ance
is′sue *v.*
is′sue *n.*
  col·lat′er·al —
  feigned —
  hot —
  — in fact
  — in law
  new —
  — pre·clu′sion
  real —
  — roll
  ul′ti·mate —
is′su·er
is′sues and prof′its
i′tem
i′tem·ize′
i′tem·ized′ de·duc′tions
i·tin′er·ant
— ped′dling
— ven′dor
its
it's

J

jac′ti·ta′tion
jac·ti′vus
jac′tus

jail
jail′er *or* jail′or
jail′house′ law′yer
jan′i·tor
Ja′nus-faced′
Ja′son clause
jay′walk′ing
Jencks Act *or* Rule
jeop′ard·y
— as·sess′ment
jerk
jet′sam
jet′ti·son
jet′ty
jeux de bourse
jew′el
jew′el·ry
jit′ney
job′ber
John Doe
join
join′der
  col·lu′sive —
  com·pul′so·ry —
  — in de·mur′rer
  — in is′sue
  — in plead′ing
  — of ac′tions
  — of claims
  — of de·fen′dants
  — of er′ror
  — of is′sue
  — of of′fens·es
  — of par′ties
  — of rem′e·dies
  per·mis′sive —
joint
— ac·count′
— ac′tion
— and sev′er·al
— au′thor·ship′
— bank ac·count′
— cause of ac′tion
— debt′ors
— de·fen′dants
— en′ter·prise′
— es·tate′
— ex·ec′u·tors
— fea′sors in pa·ri′ de·
lic′to′
— in·dict′ment

— li′a·bil′i·ty
— lives
— neg′li·gence
— of·fense′
— pol′i·cy
— stock in·sur′ance
com′pa·ny
— tax re·turn′
— ten′an·cy
— tort
— tort′-fea′sors
— tri′al
— ven′ture
— ver′dict
— will
joint′ist
joint′ly
— ac·quired′ prop′er·ty
— and sev′er·al·ly
— owned prop′er·ty
joint′ress *or* join′tu·ress
join′ture
jok′er
Jones Act
jos′tle
jou·ir′
jour
— en banc
jour′nal
— en′try rule
jour′nal·ist
jour′ney
jour′ney·man
jour′neys ac·count′
joy′rid′ing
ju′dex′
judge
— ad′vo·cate
— advocate gen′er·al
— de fac′to′
— or′di·nar′y
— pro tem′po·re′
— tri′al
judge′-made′ law
judg′ment *or* judge′ment
— ar·rest′ of
— con·fes′sion of
— cred′i·tor
— debt
— debt′or
de·clar′a·to·ry —

de·fault' —
de·fi'cien·cy —
dor'mant —
es·top'pel by —
fi'nal —
— in per·so'nam
— in rem
— in re·trax'it
in'ter·loc'u·to'ry —
— in'ter par'tes'
— lien
mon'ey —
— not'with·stand'ing
ver'dict
of'fer of —
— on de·mur'rer
— on mer'its
— on the plead'ings
— pa'per
per'son·al —
— proof
— qua'si' in rem
— re·cov'ered
sum'ma·ry —
— void on its face
ju'di·ca're
ju'di·ca'ti·o'
ju'di·ca·to'ries
ju'di·ca·ture'
— acts
ju'di·ces'
ju·di'cial
— act
— ac'tion
— ac'tiv·ism
— au·thor'i·ty
— bonds
— branch
— busi'ness
— cir'cuit
— cog'ni·zance
— com'i·ty
— coun'cil
— cy pres
— de·ci'sion
— dec'la·ra'tion of law
— de·part'ment
— dic'tum
— dis·cre'tion
— dis'trict
— er'rors

— es·top'pel
— ev'i·dence
— func'tion
— im·mu'ni·ty
— in·quir'y
— knowl'edge
— leg'is·la'tion
— lien
— no'tice
— oath
— of'fi·cer
— o·pin'ion
— pow'er
— pro·ceed'ing
— rec'ords
— rem'e·dy
— re·prieve'
— re·view'
— sale
— self'-re·straint'
— sep'a·ra'tion
— sys'tem
Ju·di'cial
— Ar'ti·cle
— Re·view' Act
ju·di'ci·ar'y
— act
ju·di'cious
ju·di'cious·ly
ju·dic'i·um
— cap·i·ta'le'
— De'i'
juge de paix
jump bail
jun'ior
— cred'i·tor
— ex'e·cu'tion
— lien
— lien'or
— mort'gage
— right
— se·cured' par'ty
jun'ket
junk'shop'
jun'ta
jun'to
ju'ra
ju'ral
— cause
ju'ra·men'tum
ju·ra're'

ju'rat
ju·ra'tion
ju·ra'tor
ju'rats
ju're
— bel'li'
— ci·vil'i'
— gen'ti·um
— ux·or'is
ju·rid'i·cal
— day
ju'ris
— doc'tor
— pos·i·ti'vi'
— pri·va'ti'
— ut'rum'
ju'ris·con·sult'
ju'ris·con·sul'tus
ju'ris·dic'tion
— in per·so'nam
— in rem
— of the sub'ject mat'-
   ter
— o'ver the per'son
— qua'si' in rem
ju'ris·dic'tion·al
— a·mount'
— dis·pute'
— facts
— lim'its
— state'ment
ju'ris·pru'dence
ju'rist
ju·ris'tic
ju'ror
al'ter·nate —
— des'ig·nate
ju'ry
ad·vi'so·ry —
— box
— chal'lenge
— com·mis'sion·er
dead'locked' —
fair and im·par'tial —
grand —
hung —
im·pan'el·ing of —
— in·struc'tions
— list
— of good and law'ful
   men

— pan'el
pet'it —
poll'ing of —
— proc'ess'
— se·lec'tion
se'ques·tra'tion of —
spe'cial —
tri'al —
— wheel
ju·ry·man
ju'ry·wom'an
jus
— ab'sti·nen'di'
— ab'u·ten'di'
— ac'cres·cen'di'
— bel'li'
— ca'no'ni·cum
— ci'vi·le'
— com·mu'ne'
— co·ro'nae'
— cu'ri·a'li·ta'tis
— da're'
— di'ce·re
— dis'po·nen'di'
— dis'tra·hen'di'
— div'i·den'di'
— du'pli·ca'tum
— fal·can'di'
— gen'ti·um
— glad'i·i'
— hab·en'di'
— hae·re'di·ta'tis
— in'cog·ni'tum
— in'di·vid'u·um
— in per·so'nam
— in re
— in re a'li·e'na
— in re prop'ri·a
— le·gi·ti'mum
— mar'i·ti'
— na·tu'rae'
— na'tu·ra'le'
— nav'i·gan'di'
— non scrip'tum
— per·so·na'rum
— pos'ses·si·o'nis
— pos'si·den'di'
— pri·va'tum
— pro·pri'e·ta'tis
— pub'li·cum
— quae·si'tum

— re'cu·per·an'di'
— re'rum
— san'gui·nis
— scrip'tum
— so'li'
— spa'ti·an'di'
— stric'tum
— ter'ti·i'
— u·ten'di'
just
— cause
— cause of prov'o·ca'-
  tion
— com'pen·sa'tion
— ti'tle
jus'tice v.
jus'tice n.
— in eyre
— of the peace
— seat
Justice Department
jus'tic·es
— of as·size'
— of gaol de·liv'er·y
— of la'bor·ers
— of ni'si' pri'us
— of o'yer and ter'min·
  er
— of the bench
— of the hun'dred
— of the pa·vil'ion
— of the quo'rum
— of trail'-bas'ton
jus'tice·ship'
jus·ti'ci·a·ble
— con'tro·ver'sy
jus·ti'ci·ar'y
jus'ti·cies'
jus'ti·fi'a·ble
— cause
jus'ti·fi·ca'tion
jus'ti·fi·ca'tors
jus'ti·fied'
Jus·tin'i·an's In'sti·
  tutes'
jus·ti'ti·a
just'ness
ju've·nile'
— courts
— de·lin'quent
— of·fend'ers

jux'ta
— ra'tam'
jux'ta·po·si'tion

K

ka'ha·wa'i
Kahn re·ac'tion or test
kai'a
kan'ga·roo' court
keel'age
Kee'ler pol'y·graph'
keep n.
keep v.
— house
— in re·pair'
— rec'ords
keep'er
— of a bawd'y house
— of a gam'bling house
— of the for'est
— of the great seal
— of the king's con'-
  science
— of the priv'y seal
keep'ing
— a look'out'
— books
— term
— the peace
kelp'-shore'
Ken'ny meth'od or
  treat'ment
kent'ledge
Ken·tuck'y rule
Ke'ogh plan
kept
— wom'an
kerf
kernes
ker'o·sene'
key'age
key man in·sur'ance
key'note' ad·dress'
key'us
kick'back'
kid'der
kid'nap·ing or kid'nap·
  ping

Kil'berg' doc'trine
kil'der·kin
kil'keth
kill
killed in'stant·ly
kill'er
kill'ing by mis'ad·ven'-
  ture
kin
kind
kin'dred
king'dom
king'-geld'
king's
  — ad'vo·cate
  — bench
  — cham'bers
  — cor'o·ner and at·tor'-
    ney
  — coun'sel
  — ev'i·dence
  — proc'tor
  — re·mem'branc·er
kings'-at-arms'
kins'folk'
kins'man
kins'wom'an
kin'tal or kin'tle
kint'lidge
kiss'ing the book
kit'ing
kith and kin
kit'ty
klep'to·ma'ni·a
knack'er
knave
knav'er·y
knave'ship'
knee
  — jerk
knife
knif'ing
knight
  — mar'shal
knight'hood'
knights
  — bach'e·lors
  — ban'ner·et
  — of St. Mi'chael and
    St. George
  — of St. Pat'rick

— of the Bath
— of the Cham'ber
— of the Gar'ter
— of the post
— of the shire
— of the this'tle
— serv'ice
knock
  — and an·nounce' rule
  — down
knock'out' drops
know all men
know'-how'
know'ing·ly
  — and will'ful·ly
knowl'edge
  — and be·lief'
knowl'edge·a·ble
known
  — heirs
Ko'ran
ko·shu·ba'
Ku Klux Klan
ku'le·a'na
kyth

L

la'bel
la'bi·al
la'bor
  — con'tract'
  — dis·pute'
  — or'gan·i·za'tion
  — pick'et·ing
  — sep'a·ra'tion
  — un'ion
lab'o·ra·to'ry
la'bor·er
la'bor·ers
  — stat'utes of
la'bor-man'age·ment
  — re·la'tions
Labor-Management
  Relations Act
lab'y·rin'thine
lac'er·ate'
La'cey Act
lach'es

es·top'pel by —
lack of ju'ris·dic'tion
lac'ta
lac'tate'
lac·ta'tion
la·cu'na
la'cus
lad'en in bulk
lad'ing, bill of
la'dy court
La'e·trile'
lag
lage
  — day
lage'-man
la·ge'na
lahl'slit'
lais'sez faire'
la'i·ty
Lam'beth de·gree'
lame duck
  — ses'sion
Lame Duck A·mend'-
  ment
land
  — bank
  — cer·tif'i·cate
  — cop
  — court
  — de·part'ment
  — farm
  — ga'bel
gen'er·al — of'fice
  — grant
  — man'age·ment
  — meas'ure
  — of'fic·es
  — pat'ent
  — rev'e·nues
seat'ed —
  — tax
  — ten'ant
  — trust
  — use plan·ning
  — wait'er
  — war'rant
land'ed
  — es·tate' or prop'er·ty
  — es·tates' court
  — pro·pri'e·tor
  — se·cu'ri·ties

land'grave'
land'ing
land'locked'
land'lord'
land'lord's' war'rant
land'lord'-ten'ant law
land'mark'
land'-poor'
land'reeve'
— and ten'ant
lands
  ac·com'mo·da'tion —
  boun'ty —
  cer·tif'i·cate —
  — claus'es con'sol·i·da'-
    tion acts
  crown —
  de·mesne' —
  do·na'tion —
  fab'ric —
  farm —
  min'er·al —
  place —
  pub'lic —
  swamp —
lands, ten'e·ments, and
  her'e·dit'a·ments
lan'guage
Lan'ham Act
lap'i·da'tion
lap'page
lapse v.
lapse n.
  — pat'ent
  — stat'utes
lapsed
  — de·vise'
  — leg'a·cy
  — pol'i·cy
lar'board
lar'ce·nous
  — in·tent'
lar'ce·ny
  — by bail·ee'
  — by ex·tor'tion
  — by fraud or de·cep'-
    tion
  — by trick
com'mon-law' —
com'pound —
con·struc'tive —

— from the per'son
grand —
mixed —
pet'it —
sim'ple —
larg'er par'cel
las·civ'i·ous
  — car'riage
  — co·hab'i·ta'tion
last
  — an'te·ce'dent rule
  — clear chance
  — re·sort'
  — will
la'tent
  — am'bi·gu'i·ty
  — deed
  — de'fect'
  — eq'ui·ty
lat'er·al
  — rail'road'
  — sup·port'
lat'er·al·ly
lat'ro·ci·na'tion
lat'ro·cin·y
lau'da·num
lau'dum
launch
lau're·ate
lau'rels
law
  — ar'bi·trar'y
  — charg'es
  — court of ap·peals'
  — en·force'ment of'fi·cer
  — French
  — Lat'in
  — list
  — lords
  — mar'tial
  — mer'chant
  — of arms
  — of cap'ture
  — of ev'i·dence
  — of na'tions
  — of na'ture
  — of the case
  — of the land
  — of the road
  — of the sta'ple
  — re·ports'

  — re·view'
  — school
law'-a·bid'ing
law'book'
law'break'er
Law Day
law'ful
  — age
  — ar·rest'
  — au·thor'i·ties
  — cause
  — dam'ag·es
  — de·pend'ents
  — dis'charge'
  — en'try
  — goods
  — heirs
  — is'sue
  — rep're·sen'ta·tives
law'less
  — man
law'mak'er
laws
  — of the sev'er·al states
  — of war
Law School Ad·mis'-
  sion Test
law'suit'
law'yer
lay n.
  — days
  — sys'tem
lay adj.
  — cor'po·ra'tion
  — fee
  — judge
  — peo'ple
  — wit'ness
lay v.
  dam'ag·es
  — off
  — out
lay'a·way'
laye
lay'ing
  — foun·da'tion
  — the ven'ue
lay'man
lay'off'
lay'out'
lay'stall'

lea or ley
lead'ing
— a use
— a wit'ness
— case
— coun'sel
— ques'tion
league
leak'age
leal
leal'te
lean
leap year
learn
learn'ed *adj.*
lease
— and re·lease'
con·cur'rent —
gross —
long'-term' —
mas'ter —
min'er·al —
net —
oil and gas —
per·cent·age —
per·pet'u·al —
lease'back'
sale and —
lease'hold'
— im·prove'ments
— in'ter·est
lé·au·te'
leave *v.*
— no is'sue
leave *n.*
— and li'cense
— of ab'sence
— of court
— to de·fend'
lec'tur·er
ledg'er
— book
leet
leets
— and law days
leg'a·cy
ab'so·lute' —
ac·cu·mu·la'tive —
ad·di'tion·al —
al'ter·nate —
con·di'tion·al —

con·tin'gent —
cu'mu·la'tive —
de·mon'stra·tive —
— du'ty
gen'er·al —
in·def'i·nite —
lapsed —
mo'dal —
pe·cu'ni·ar'y —
re·sid'u·ar'y —
spe'cial —
spe·cif'ic —
— tax
trust —
u'ni·ver'sal —
void —
le'gal
— a·cu'men
— age
— aid
— as'sets'
— ca·pac'i·ty to sue
— cap'i·tal
— cause
— con·clu'sion
— cru'el·ty
— cus'to·dy
— de·pend'ent
— det'ri·ment
— dis·trib'u·tees'
— du'ty
— en'ti·ty
— es·top'pel
— eth'ics
— ev'i·dence
— ex·cuse'
— fic'tion
— fraud
— heirs
— hol'i·day
— im·pos'si·bil'i·ty
— in'ju·ry
— in·san'i·ty
— in'ter·est
— in·vest'ment
— is'sue
— jeop'ard·y
— li'a·bil'i·ty
— list
— mal'ice
— name

— neg'li·gence
— no'tice
— ob'li·ga'tion
— per'son·al rep're·sen'-
  ta·tive
— pos·ses'sor
— prej'u·dice
— pre·sump'tion
— priv'i·ty
— pro·ceed'ing
— rate of in'ter·est
— rep're·sen'ta·tive
— re·scis'sion
— re·serve'
— res'i·dence
— right
— sep'a·ra'tion
— serv'ic·es
— strike
— sub'di·vi'sions
— sub'ro·ga'tion
— ten'der
— ti'tle
— u'su·fruct'
— vot'er
— will'ful·ness
le'gal·ese'
le·ga'lis ho'mo'
le'gal·ism
le'gal·is'tic
le'gal'i·ty
le'gal·i·za'tion
le'gal·ize'
le'gal·ized' nui'sance
le'gal·ly
— a·dopt'ed
— com·mit'ted
— com'pe·tent
— con'sit·tut'ed court
— li'a·ble
— suf·fi'cient ev'i·dence
— sufficient ten'der
le'gal·ness
Le'gal Serv'ic·es Cor'-
  po·ra'tion
le·ga're'
leg'a·tar'y
leg'a·tee'
le·ga'tion
le·ga'tor
leg'a·to'ry

le·ga′tum
le′gem
leg′is·late′
leg′is·la′tion
leg′is·la′tive
— act
— ap·por′tion·ment
— coun′cil
— coun′sel
— courts
— de·part′ment
— dis′trict·ing
— ex·pens′es
— func′tion
— his′to·ry
— im·mu′ni·ty
— in·tent′
— in·ves′ti·ga′tions
— ju′ris·dic′tion
— of′fi·cer
— pow′er
leg′is·la′tor
leg′is·la′ture
le·git′i·ma·cy
le·git′i·mate′ v.
le·git′i·mate adj.
le·git′i·ma′tion
le·git′i·me′
le·git′i·mus
le′git vel non?
lend
lend′er
lend′ing mon′ey or cred′it
lese′ maj′es·ty
les′ing or leas′ing
le′sion
les′sa
les·see′
less′er of·fense′
les′sor
— of the plain′tiff
lest
let n.
let v.
— in
le′thal
— weap′on
let′ter
— book
— car′ri·er

— mis′sive
— of ad·vice′
— of at·torn′ment
— of com′ment′
— of cre′dence
— of cred′it
— of ex·change′
— of in·tent′
— of li′cense
— of marque
— of re·call′
— of re′cre·den′tials
— rul′ing
let′ters
— of ab′so·lu′tion
— of ad·min′is·tra′tion
— of guard′i·an·ship′
— of re·quest′
— of safe con′duct′
— pat′ent
— ro′ga·to′ry
— tes′ta·men′ta·ry
let′ting
— out
le·vant′ et cou·chant′
lev′ee
— dis′trict
lev′er·age
lev′i·a·ble
Le·vit′i·cal de·grees′
lev′i·ty
lev′y
eq′ui·ta·ble —
lev′y·ing war
lewd
— and las·civ′i·ous co·hab′i·ta′tion
— house
lewd′ness
lex
— a·grar′i·a
— a·mis′sa
— Ang′li·æ′
— a′pos·ta′ta
— ap·par′ens′
— a·quil′i·a
— bar′ba·ra
— bre·ho′ni·a
— com′mis·so′ri·a
— com·mu′nis
— do′mi·cil′i·i′

— fo′ri′
— ju·di′ci·a′lis
— lo′ci′
— loci ac′tus
— loci ce′le·bra′ti·o′nis
— loci con·trac′tus
— loci de·lic′tus
— loci do′mi·cil′i·i′
— loci re′i′ si′tae′
— loci so·lu′ti·o′nis
— ma′ni·fes′ta
— mer′ca·to′ri·a
— na′tu·ra′le′
— non co′git ad im′pos·si·bil′i·a
— non cu′rat de min′i·mis
— Ro·ma′na
— sac′ra·men·ta′lis
— si′tus
— ta′li·o′nis
— ter′rae′
ley
li′a·bil′i·ty
— bond
— cre·at′ed by stat′ute
— for dam′ag·es
— im·posed′ by law
— in·sur′ance
joint and sev′er·al —
lim′it·ed —
per′son·al —
sec′on·dar′y —
strict —
li′a·ble
li′bel v.
li′bel n.
— of re·view′
li′bel·ant
li′bel·ee′
li′bel·ous
— per quod
— per se
li′ber
lib′er·al
strict and — construc′tion in·ter′pre·ta′tion
lib′er·ate′
lib′er·a′tion
li·ber′ti·cide′
lib′er·ties

lib'er·ty
  civ'il —
  nat'u·ral —
  — of a port
  — of con'science
  — of con'tract'
  — of speech
  — of the globe
  — of the press
  — of the rules
  per'son·al —
  po·lit'i·cal —
  re·lig'ious —
  — to hold pleas
li'bra
  — pen'sa
li'brar'y
li'cense
  — cas'es
  driv'er's —
  ex·clu'sive —
  ex'e·cut'ed —
  ex·ec'u·to'ry —
  ex·press' —
  — fee or tax
  im·plied' —
  — in am'or·ti·za'tion
li'censed vict'ual
li'cens·ee'
  — by in'vi·ta'tion
  — by per·mis'sion
  ex·clu'sive —
li'cens·ing
  — acts
  — pow'er
li'cen·sor'
li·cen'ti·ate
li·cen'tious·ness
li'cet
lic'it
lick'ing of thumbs
lie n.
  — de·tec'tor
lie v.
  — in fran'chise'
  — in grant
  — in liv'er·y
  — in wait
  — to
liege
  — hom'age

— lord
liege'man
lien
  — ac·count'
  — cred'i·tor
  — of a cov'e·nant
  — of fac'tor at com'mon
    law
lien·ee'
lien'or
lieu
  in — of
  — lands
  — tax
lieu·ten'an·cy
lieu·ten'ant
  — colo'nel
  — com·mand'er
  — gen'er·al
  — gov'er·nor
life
  — an·nu'i·ty
  — ben'e·fi'ci·ar'y
  — es·tate'
  — ex·pec'tan·cy
  — in be'ing
  — in·sur'ance
  — or limb
  — peer'age
  — sen'tence
  — ta'bles
  — ten'ant
  — ten'an·cy
life'hold'
life'land'
li·ga're'
li'geance
light'house'
  — board
light'ship'
light'er·age
light'er·man
lights
lig'i·us
light
  — ben'e·fits
  — char'ac·ter
like'-kind' ex·change'
like'li·hood'
like'ly
like'ness

like'wise'
limb
lim'it
lim'i·ta'tion
  col·lat'er·al —
  con·di'tion·al —
  con·tin'gent —
  — in law
  — o'ver
  spe'cial —
  — ti'tle
  ti'tle by —
  words of —
Lim'i·ta'tion of Li'a·
    bil'i·ty Act
lim'i·ted
  — ad·min'is·tra'tion
  — ad·mis'si·bil'i·ty
  — ap·peal'
  — di·vorce'
  — en'tre·pre·neur'
  — ex·ec'u·tor
  — guar'an·ty
  — ju'ris·dic'tion
  — li'a·bil'i·ty
  — own'er
  — part'ner
  — part'ner·ship'
  — pay'ment plan
  — pow'er of ap·point'-
    ment
  — pub'li·ca'tion
Lin'coln's Inn
Lind'bergh Act
lin'e·a
  — ob·li'qua
  — rec'ta
lin'e·age
lin'e·al
  — con'san·guin'i·ty
  — de·scent'
  — heir
  — war'ran·ty
lin'e·a·ments
lines and cor'ners
line'-up'
lin'gual
link
liq'uid
  — as'sets'
  — debt

liq'ui·date'
liq'ui·dat'ed
— ac·count'
— claim
— dam'ag·es
— debt
— de·mand'
liq'ui·dat'ing
— dis'tri·bu'tion
— part'ner
— trust
liq'ui·da'tion
— div'i·dend
— tax'a·ble
liq'ui·da'tor
li·quid'i·ty
liq'uor
— deal'er
— shop
lis
— al'i·bi' pen'dens'
— mo'ta
— pen'dens'
list
— of cred'i·tors
— price
list'ed
— se·cu'ri·ties
list'ing n.
bro'ker·age —
ex·clu'sive a'gen·cy —
exclusive au·thor'i·za'-
tion to sell —
gen'er·al —
mul'ti·ple —
net —
o'pen —
li'te pen·den'te'
li'ter or li'tre
lit'e·ra
lit'e·rae'
— hu·ma'ni·o'res'
— mor'tu·ae'
lit'er·al
— con'tract'
— con·struc'tion
— proof
lit'er·ar'y
— com'po·si'tion
— prop'er·ty
— work

lit'er·ate
lit'i·gant
lit'i·gate'
lit'i·ga'tion
li·ti'gious
lit'mus test
lit'ter·ing
lit'to·ral
— land
— rights
Lit'vi·nov as·sign'ment
live'li·hood'
liv'er·y
— con·vey'ance
— of sei'sin
— of'fice
— sta'ble
liv'er·y·man
lives in be'ing
live'stock'
— in·sur'ance
live stor'age
liv'id
li·vid'i·ty
liv'ing
— a·part'
— in a·dul'ter·y
— in o'pen and no·to'ri·
ous a·dul'ter·y
— is'sue
— sep'a·rate and a·part'
— to·geth'er
— with hus'band
Lloyd's
— bonds
— in·sur'ance
— of Lon'don
— un'der·writ'ers
load'ing
load line
load'man'age
loaf
loan
am'or·tized' —
— as·so'ci·a'tion
call —
— cer·tif'i·cates
com·mer'cial —
com·mod'i·ty —
con·sum'er —
day —

de·mand' —
— for ex·change'
— for use
gra·tu'i·tous —
in·stall'ment —
non'-re'course' —
per'son·al —
se·cured' —
short'-term' —
— so·ci'e·ties
time —
loaned
— em·ploy'ee
— ser'vant doc'trine
loan'shark'ing
lob'by·ing
lob'by·ist
lo·bot'o·mize'
lo·bot'o·my
lo'cal
— ac'tions
— af·fairs'
— a'gent
— and spe'cial leg'is·la'-
tion
— as·sess'ment
— chat'tel
— con·cern'
— gov'ern·ment
— im·prove'ment
— law
— op'tion
— prej'u·dice
— rules
— stat'ute
— us'age
lo·cal'i·ty
lo'cal·i·za'tion
lo'cate'
lo'cat'ed
lo·ca'tion
loc'a·tive calls
lo'ca'tor
locked
lock'out'
lock'up' house
lo'co·mo'tive
lo'co' pa·ren'tis
lo'cum' te'nens'
lo'cus
— clas'si·cus

— con·trac'tus
— crim'i·nis
— de·lic'ti'
— in quo
— par·ti'tus
— paen'i·ten'ti·ae'
— pub'li·cus
— re'git ac'tum
— re'i' si'tae'
— si·gil'li'
— stan'di'
lode
lode'man or loads'man
lodg'er
lodg'ing house
lodg'ings
log'book'
log'ging
log'ic
log'i·cal
— rel'e·van·cy
log'roll'ing
loi'ter
Lom'bards'
long
— ac·count'
— and short haul clause
— arm stat'utes
— arm ju'ris·dic'tion
— po·si'tion
— robe
— ton
lon·gev'i·ty pay
Long Par'lia·ment
long'shore'man
Long·shore'men's and
  Har'bor Work'ers'
  Com'pen·sa'tion Act
long'-term'
— cap'i·tal gain
— capital loss
— fi·nanc'ing
look and lis'ten
look'out'
loop'hole'
  tax —
loot
loot'ér
lord
— ad'vo·cate
— and vas'sal

— chief bar'on
— chief jus'tice
— high chan'cel·lor
— high stew'ard
— high treas'ur·er
— in gross
— jus'tice clerk
— keep'er
— lieu·ten'ant
— may'or
— may'or's court
— of a man'or
— or'di·nar'y
— par'a·mount'
— priv'y seal
— war'den of Cinque
  Ports
Lord Mans'field's' Rule
lords
— ap·pel'lants
— com·mis'sion·ers
— jus'tic·es of ap·peal'
— march'ers
— of ap·peal'
— of appeal in or'di·nar'-
  y
— of e·rec'tion
— of par'lia·ment
— or·dain'ers
— spir'i·tu·al
— tem'po·ral
lord'ship'
lose
loss
ac'tu·al —
ca'su·al·ty —
con·struc'tive —
dead —
hob'by —
— lead'er
net op'er·at'ing —
— of con·sor'ti·um
par'tial —
— pay'a·ble clause
— pay·ee'
proof of —
— ra'tio
— re·serve'
sal'vage —
to'tal —
lost adj.

— cor'ner
— or not lost
— pa'pers
— prop'er·ty
— will
lost n.
— and scot
odd —
round —
lot'ter·y
love and af·fec'tion
love'-day'
low'er of cost or mar'-
  ket
low'est re·spon'si·ble
  bid'der
low wa'ter
low'-wa'ter mark
loy'al
loy'al·ty
— oath
lu'cid
— in'ter·val
lu'cra·tive
— bail'ment
— of'fice
lu'cre
lug'gage
lum'ber
lu'men
lu'mi·na
lu'mi·na're'
lump'ing sale
lump sum
lump'-sum'
— al'i·mo'my
— dis'tri·bu'tion
— pay'ment
— set'tle·ment
lu'na·cy
lu'nar
— month
lu'na·tic
lust
lust'ful
lux'u·ry tax
ly'ing
— by
— in fran'chise'
— in grant
— in wait

lynch law
ly·ser'gic ac'id di'eth·
yl·am'ide (LSD)

M

mace
— bear'er
mace'-proof'
Mach'i·a·vel'li·an
mach'i·na'tion
ma·chine'
ma·chine'a·ble
ma·chin'er·y
ma·chin'ist
mac'ro·ec'o·nom'ics
mac'ro·scop'ic
mac'ro·struc'ture
mac'u·late'
mad'am or ma·dame'
made known
made'-to-or'der
mad'man'
mad'ness
Mad Par'lia·ment
mad'wom'an
Ma'fi·a
ma·gis'ter
— li'tis
— na'vis
— re'rum u'sus
— so·ci'e·ta'tis
mag'is·te'ri·al
— pre'cinct'
mag'is·tra·cy
mag'is·trate'
mag'is·trate's' court
Mag'na Char'ta or Car'-
ta
mag'na cul'pa
mag'nate'
mag'ni·fi·ca'tion
mag'ni·fy'
mag'num o'pus
Mag'nu·son-Moss'
War'ran·ty Act
maid'en
— as·size'
— rents

maid'en·head'
mail
— fraud
— mat'ter
mail'a·ble
mail'-or'der
— di·vorce'
— house
maim
main
— chan'nel
— pur'pose doc'trine
— sea
main-à-main'
main'line'
main'ly
main'per·na·ble
main'prise'
main'-rent'
main·tain'
main·tained'
main·tain'or
main'te·nance
— as·sess'ment
— and cure
— of mem'ber·ship'
clause
maî'tre
maj'es·ty
ma'jor
— and mi'nor fault rule
— dis·pute'
— gen'er·al
ma·jo'ra re·ga'li·a
ma·jor'i·ty
— of qual'i·fied' e·lec'-
tors
— of stock'hold'ers
— o·pin'ion
— rule
— vote
make
— a con'tract'
— an as·sign'ment
— an a·ward'
— de·fault'
mak'er
mak'ing law
ma·la'
— fi'des'
— in se

— mens
— prax'is
— pro·hib'i·ta
mal'a·dies
mal'ad·just'ed
mal'ad·just'ment
mal'ad·min'is·tra'tion
mal'a·dy
mal·aise'
ma·lar'i·a
ma·lar'i·al
mal'con'duct'
mal de mer
mal'e·dic'tion
mal'e·dic'to·ry
mal'e·fac'tion
mal'e·fac'tor
mal'e·fac'tress
ma·lef'i·cence
ma·lef'i·cent
ma·lev'o·lence
ma·lev'o·lent
mal·fea'sance
mal·formed'
mal·func'tion
mal grée
mal'ice
ac'tu·al —
— a·fore'thought'
con·struc'tive —
ex·press' —
gen'er·al —
im·plied' —
— in fact
— in law
le'gal —
par·tic'u·lar —
pre'con·ceived' —
pre·med'i·tat'ed —
— pre·pense'
spe'cial —
u'ni·ver'sal —
ma·li'cious
— a·ban'don·ment
— a·buse' of le'gal proc'-
ess'
— ac·cu·sa'tion
— act
— ar·rest'
— in'ju·ry
— kill'ing

— mis'chief
— mo'tive
— pros'e·cu'tion
— tres'pass
— use of proc'ess'
ma·li'cious·ly
ma·li'cious·ness
ma·lign'
ma·lig'nan·cy or ma·lig'-
  nance
ma·lig'ni·ty
ma·lin'ger
ma·lin'ger·er
mal'le·a·bil'i·ty
mal'le·a·ble
Mal'lo·ry Rule
mal·nour'ished
mal·nu·tri'tion
ma'lo
— a'ni·mo'
— gra'to'
— sen'su'
mal·prac'tice
  le'gal —
  med'i·cal —
mal·treat'ment
ma'lum
— in se
— pro·hib'i·tum
mam'ma·ry
man'a·cles
man'age
man'age·a·bil'i·ty
man'age·a·ble
man'age·ment
man'ag·er
man'ag·ing a'gent
man'bote'
manche pre·sent'
man'ci·pate'
man·da'mus
man·da·tar'y
man'date'
man·da·to'ry
— in·junc'tion
— sen'tenc·ing
— stat'utes
man·da'vi' bal'li·vo'
ma·neu'ver
ma·neuv'er·a·ble
man'gle

man'han'dle
man'hole'
man'hood'
man'-hour'
man·hunt'
ma'ni·a
— a po'tu'
— fa·nat'i·ca
fit of —
  hom'i·ci'dal —
— trans·i·to'ri·a
ma'ni·ac'
ma·ni'a·cal·ly
man'ic
man'ic-de·pres'sive
man'i·fest'
— des'ti·ny
— law
— ne·ces'si·ty
man'i·fes·ta'tion
— of in·ten'tion
man'i·fes'to
ma·nip'u·la'tion
man'kind'
man'made'
Mann Act
man'ner
— and form
man'ning
man of straw
man'or
ma·no'ri·al
manse
man'sion
— house
man'slaugh'ter
  in·vol'un·ta'ry —
  mis'de·mean'or —
  vol'un·tar'y —
man'steal'ing
man'su·e'tae' na·tu'rae'
man·tic'u·late'
man'-traps'
man'u·al
— de·liv'er·y
— gift
— la'bor
— rates
man'u·fac'to'ry
man'u·fac'ture
man'u·fac'tur·er

man'u·fac'tur·er's
— li'a·bil'i·ty doc'trine
man'u·fac'tur·ing
— cor'po·ra'tion
— es·tab'lish·ment
man'u·mis'sion
man'u·mit'
ma'nu' o'pe·ra
ma·nure'
man'u·script'
Mapp v. O·hi'o
mar'a·thon'
ma·raud'er
Mar'bur·y v. Mad'i·son
march'es
mar'chio·ness
ma're'
— clau'sum
— li'be·rum'
mar'e·schal'
ma·ret'tum
mar'gin
— ac·count'
buy'ing on —
— call
— list
— of prof'it
— trad'ing
— trans·ac'tion
mar'gin·al
— note
— street
mar'i·jua'na
ma·ri'na
ma·ri·na'ri·us
ma·rine'
— belt
— car'ri·er
— con'tract'
— in·sur'ance
— in'ter·est
— league
— risk
Ma·rine' Corps
mar'i·ner
mar'i·tal
— a·gree'ments
— co·er'cion
— com·mu'ni·ca'tions
  priv'i·lege
— de·duc'tion

— por'tion
— priv'i·leg·es
— prop'er·ty
— rights and du'ties
mar'i·time'
— belt
— cause
— con'tract'
— court
— in'ter·est
— ju'ris·dic'tion
— law
— lien
— loan
— prof'it
— serv'ice
— state
— tort
Mar'i·time'
— Ad·min'is·tra'tion
— Com·mis'sion
mar'i·tus
mark
marked mon·ey
mar'ket
— geld
ge'o·graph'ic —
list'ed — se·cu'ri·ties
— mak'ing
— or'der
o'pen —
— o·vert'
— price
prod'uct —
rel'e·vant —
— share
— struc'ture
— val'ue
mar'ket·a·ble
— se·cu'ri·ties
— ti'tle
mar'ket·ing
— con'tract'
mark'ing up
marks'man
marks'man·ship'
mark'up'
Mar'kush' doc'trine
marque
law of —

— and re·pri'sal, let'ters
of
mar'quis or mar'quess
mar'riage
— ar'ti·cles
— bro'ker·age
— cer'e·mo'ny
— cer·tif'i·cate'
com'mon-law' —
— con·sid'er·a'tion
— li'cense
mor'ga·nat'ic —
— no'tice book
— per ver'ba de prae·
sen'ti'
— por'tion
— prom'ise
prox'y —
pu'ta·tive —
— set'tle·ment
mar'shal
— of the queen's bench
mar'shal·ing
— as'sets'
— liens
— rem'e·dies
— se·cu'ri·ties
Mar'shal·sea
mar'tial law
Mar'tin·mas'
mar'tyr
Marx'ism
Marx'ist
Mar'y Car'ter a·gree'-
ment
mas'o·chism
ma'son
Ma'son-Dix'on line
ma'son·ry
mas'quer·ade'
mass
— pick'et·ing
— strike
mas'sa
Mas'sa·chu'setts
— rule
— trust
mas'sa·cre
mas·sage'
— par'lor
Mass'es

mas·seur'
mas·seuse'
mass'-pro·duced'
mast
— sell'ing
mas·tec'to·my
mas'ter
— a·gree'ment
— and ser'vant
— at com'mon law
— build'er
— in chan'cer·y
— in lu'na·cy
— of a ship
— of the crown of'fice
— of the fac'ul·ties
— of the horse
— of the mint
— of the ord'nance
— of the rolls
— plan
— pol'i·cy
spe'cial —
tax'ing —
mas'ter's re·port'
mate
ma·te'ri·a
ma·te'ri·al
— al'le·ga'tion
— al'ter·a'tion
— ev'i·dence
— fact
— rep're·sen·ta'tion
— wit'ness
ma·te'ri·al·man
ma·te'ri·el' or ma·té'ri·el'
ma·ter'nal
— line
— prop'er·ty
ma·ter'na ma·ter'nis
ma·ter'ni·ty
math'e·mat'i·cal ev'i·
dence
mat'i·ma
mat'ri·cide'
ma·tric'u·la
ma·tric'u·late'
mat'ri·mo'ni·al
— ac'tion
— caus'es
— co·hab'i·ta'tion

— dom′i·cile′
— res
mat′ri·mo′ny
ma′trix
ma′tron
mat′ter
— in con′tro·ver′sy
— in deed
— in is′sue
— in pais
— of course
— of fact
— of form
— of law
— of rec′ord
— of sub′stance
mat′u·ra′tion
ma·ture′
ma·tured′
— claim
ma·tur′i·ty
max′im
max′i·mize′
max′i·mum
may′hem′
may′he·ma′vit
mayn
mayn·o′ver
may′or
may′or·al′ty
may′or·ess
may′or′s court
Mc·Nabb′-Mal′lo·ry
  Rule
mead′ow
mean
— high tide
— low′er low tide
— low tide
— re·serve′
me·an′der
— lines
mean′ing
means
meas′ure
— of dam′ag·es
— of val′ue
meas′ur·er
meas′ur·ing mon′ey
me·chan′ic
me·chan′i·cal

— arm
— e·quiv′a·lent
— move′ment
— proc′ess′
— skill
me·chan′ic's lien
med′dle
me′di·a con′clu·den·di′
me′di·an
me′di·ate′
— da′tum
— de·scent′
— pow′ers
— tes′ti·mo′ny
me′di·a′tion
Me′di·a′tion and Con·
  cil′i·a′tion Serv′ice
me′di·a′tor
me′di·a′tors of ques′-
  tions
Med′i·caid′
med′i·cal
— de·duc′tion
— ev′i·dence
— ex·am′in·er
— ex·pens′es
— ju′ris·pru′dence
— serv′ic·es
Med′i·care′
med′i·ca′tion
me·dic′i·nal
med′i·cine
— chest
fo·ren′sic —
med′i·co·le′gal
Med′i·ter·ra′ne·an
  pass′port′
me′di·um of ex·change′
med·le′tum
med′ley
meet′ing
— of cred′i·tors
— of minds
meg′a·lo·ma′ni·a
mei′lic·ke sys′tem
mein′dre age
mel′an·cho′li·a
me′li·or′
mel′io·ra′tions
mem′ber
— bank

— firm
— of Con′gress
— of par′lia·ment
mem′ber·ship′ cor′po·
  ra′tion
mem′brum
mem′o·ran′da
mem′o·ran′dum
— ar′ti·cles
— check
— clause
— de·ci′sion
— in er′ror
— of al′ter·a′tion
— of as·so′ci·a′tion
— sale
me·mo′ri·al
me·mo′ri·al·ize′
me·mor′i·ter
mem′o·ri·za′tion
mem′o·ry
 le′gal —
man′ace
mé·nage′ à trois
men·da′cious
men·dac′i·ty
men′di·can·cy
men′di·cant
me′ni·al
men of straw
mens
— le′gis
— leg′is·la·to′ris
— re′a
— tes′ta·to′ris in tes′ta·
  men′tis spec·tan′da
  est
men′sa
— et tho′ro′
men·sa′li·a
men′sis
men′sor
men′tal
— al′ien·a′tion
— an′guish
— ca·pac′i·ty
— com′pe·tence
— cru′el·ty
— de′fect
— in′ca·pac′i·ty
— in·com′pe·ten·cy

— res'er·va'tion
— state
— suf'fer·ing
men·tal'i·ty
men'te' cap'tus
men·ti'ri'
men·ti'tion
mer'ca·ble
mer'can·tant
mer'can·tile'
— a·gen·cies
— law
— pa'per
— part'ner·ship'
mer'can·til'ism
mer'cat
mer'ca·tive
mer·ca'tum
mer·ca·ture
mer'ce·dar'y
mer'ce·nar'y
Mer'cen-lage'
mer'chan·dise'
— bro'ker
mer'chant
— ap·prais'er
com·mis'sion —
law —
— sea'man
stat'ute —
mer'chant·a·bil'i·ty
mer'chant·a·ble
— ti'tle
mer'chant·man
mer'ci·a·ment
Mer'ci·an law
mer'ci·ful
mer'ci·less
mer'cy
mere
— ev'i·dence
— li'cens·ee'
— mo'tion
— right
mère
mere'ly
mere'stone'
mer'e·tri'cious
merg'er
— clause
con·glom'er·ate —

hor'i·zon'tal —
short'-term' —
ver'ti·cal —
mer'i·to'ri·ous
— cause of ac'tion
— con·sid'er·a'tion
— de·fense'
mer'its
mer'it sys'tem
mese
mes·nal'ty or mes·nal'i·ty
mesne
— as·sign'ment
— con·vey'ance
— en·cum'brance
— lord
— prof'its
writ of —
mes'sage
mes'sen·ger
mes'suage
mes·ti'zo
me'ta
me·tab'o·lism
me·tach'ro·nism
met'a·law'
me·tal'lic
met'al·lur'gi·cal
met'a·phys'i·cal
mete
me'ter or me'tre
— rate
metes and bounds
meth'od
meth'o·ma'ni·a
met'ric sys'tem
me·trop'o·lis
met'ro·pol'i·tan
— coun'cil
— dis'trict
me'tus
Mex'i·can di·vorce'
Mich'ael·mas
— term
mich'el-ge·mote'
mich'el-syn'oth or mich'el-syn'od
mi'cro·ec'o·nom'ics
mi'cro·struc'ture
mid'-chan'nel

mid'dle
— line of main chan'nel
— of the riv'er
— term
— thread
mid'dle·man'
mid'night dead'line'
mid'ship'man
Mid'sum'mer Day
mid'way'
mid'wife'
mid'wife'ry
might
mi'grant
mi·gra'tion
mi'gra·to'ry
— di·vorce'
— game
mile
mile'age
— tax
mile'stones'
mil'i·tant
mil'i·tan·cy
mil'i·tar'y
— ap·peals'
— base
— boards
— boun'ty land
— com·mis'sion
— courts
— forc'es
— gov'ern·ment
— ju'ris·dic'tion
— jus'tice
— law
— of·fens'es
— serv'ice
— ten'ures
— tes'ta·ment
mi·li'tia
mi·li'tia·men
mill
— pow'er
— priv'i·lege
— run
—site
milled mon'ey
Mil'ler-Tyd'ings Act
mill'ing in tran'sit
min'a·ble

mind
— and mem'o·ry
mind'ful
mine
min'er
min'er·al
— deed
— dis'trict
— lands
— lease
— lode
— right
— roy'al·ty
— ser'vi·tude'
min'i·mal
min'i·mum
— con'tacts'
— fee sched'ules
— roy'al·ty clause
— sen'tence
— wage
min'ing
— claim
— com'pan·ies
— dis'trict
— lease
— lo·ca'tion
— part'ner·ship'
— rent
min'is·ter
min'is·te'ri·al
— act
— du'ty
— func'tion
— of'fice
— of'fi·cer
— pow'er
— trust
min'is·ters plen'i·po·
ten'ti·ar'y
min'is·try
mi'nor
— de'vi·a'tion rule
— dis·pute'
— fact
— of·fens'es
mi·nor'i·ty
— o·pin'ion
— stock'hold'er
mint
— mark

— mas'ter
mint'age
mi'nus
min'ute
— book
min'utes
Mi·ran'da rule
mir'ror
mis'ad·ven'ture
mis'al·lege'
mis'al·li'ance
mis'ap·pli·ca'tion
mis'ap·pre·hen'sion
mis'ap·pro'pri·a'tion
mis'be·got'ten
mis'be·hav'ior
mis'brand'ing
mis'cal'cu·late'
mis·car'riage
— of jus'tice
mis·car'ry
mis·cast'ing
mis·ceg'e·na'tion
mis'cel·la'ne·ous
mis'cel·la'ny
mis·charge'
mis·chief
mis·chie'vous
mis·cog'ni·zant
mis·con'duct
—in of'fice
mis'con·strue'
mis'con·tin'u·ance
mis'cre·ant
mis·date'
mis·deed'
mis'de·liv'er·y
mis'de·mean'ant
mis'de·mean'or
mis'de·scrip'tion
mis'di·rec'tion
mise
— mon'ey
mis'e·re·re'
mis'er·i·cor'di·a
mis·fea'sance
mis·fea'sor
mis·for'tune
mis·giv'ing
mis·guid'ed
mis·han'dle

mis'in·form'
mis'in·ter'pret
mis·join'der
mis·judge'
mis·laid'
mis·lead'ing
mis·man'age
mis·name'
mis·no'mer
mis·place'
mis·plead'ing
mis·pri'sion
neg'a·tive —
— of fel'o·ny
— of trea'son
pos'i·tive —
mis·read'ing
mis're·cit'al
mis're·port'
mis·rep're·sen·ta'tion
false —
fraud'u·lent —
in'no·cent —
ma·te'ri·al —
neg'li·gent —
miss'ing ship
mis'sion·ar'ies
mis'sion·ar'y
mis'sions
mis'sives
mis·state'ment
mis·take'
mu'tu·al —
— of fact
— of law
Mis'ter
mis'trans·late'
mis·treat'
mis·treat'ment
Mis'tress or mis'tress
mis·tri'al
mis·trust'
mis·un'der·stand'
mis·us'er
mit'i·gat'ing cir'cum·
stanc'es
mit'i·ga'tion
— of dam'ag·es
— of pun'ish·ment
mit·ter'
mit'ti·mus

mixed
— es·tate'
— in·sur'ance com'pa·ny
— laws
— ques'tion of law and fact
— ques'tions
— sub'jects of prop'er·ty
mix'tion
M'Nagh'ten rule
mob
mob'bing and ri'ot·ing
mo·bil'i·a
mob'ster
mock
mo'dal leg'a·cy
mode
mod'el
— act
— ju'ry in·struc'tions
mod'er·ate *adj.*
mod'er·ate' *v.*
mod'er·a'tor
mod'i·fi·ca'tion
mod'i·fy'
mo'do' et for'ma
mo'dus
— hab'i·lis
— op'er·an'di'
— te·nen'di'
— trans'fer·ren'di'
— va·can'di'
moe'ble
moer·da
moi'e·ty
mo'les·ta'tion
mol'li·fy'
mo·men'tum
mon'a·chism
mon'ar·chy
mon·e'ta
mon'e·ta'gi·um
mon'e·tar'y
mon'ey
— bill
— chang'es
— claims
— de·mand'
— had and re·ceived'
— judg'ment
— land

— lent
— made
— mar'ket
— of a·dieu'
— or'der
— paid
mon'ey·chang'er
mon'ey·lend'er
mon'ey-or'der of'fice
mon'ey-pur'chase plan
mon'ger
mon'go·loid'
mon'i·ment
mo·ni'tion
mon'i·to'ry
— let'ters
mo·noc'ra·cy
mon'o·crat'
mo·nog'a·mous
mo·nog'a·my
mon'o·gram'
mon'o·graph'
mo·nom'a·chy
mon'o·ma'ni·a
mon'o·po'li·um
mo·nop'o·ly
— pow'er
mo·nop'so·ny
mon'ster
mon·strans' de droit
month
mon'u·ment
moon'shine'
moor
moor'age
moor'ing
moot *n.*
moot *adj.*
— court
— hall
— hill
— man
— point
— ques'tion
moot'ing
mor'al
— ac'tions
— cer'tain·ty
— con·sid'er·a'tion
— du·ress'
— ev'i·dence

— fraud
— haz'ard
— in·san'i·ty
— law
— ob'li·ga'tion
— tur'pi·tude'
mor'a·to'ri·um
mor'a·tur' in le'ge
more
— fav'or·a·ble terms clause
— or less
more·o'ver
morgue
mor'i·bund'
Mor'mon
mo'ron'
mor'phine'
mor'phi·no·ma'ni·a *or* mor'phin·ism
Mor'ris plan com'pa·ny
mors
mort
mor'tal
mor·tal'i·ty
— ta'bles
mort'gage
am'or·tized' —
— bank'er
blan'ket —
— bond
— bro'ker
— cer·tif'i·cate
chat'tel —
— clause
closed'-end' —
con·sol'i·dat'ed —
con·struc'tion draw —
con·ven'tion·al —
eq'ui·ta·ble —
first —
first — bonds
gen'er·al —
grad'u·at'ed pay'ment —
— guar'an·tee' in·sur'ance
joint —
ju·di'cial —
jun'ior —
lease'hold' —
le'gal —

— lien
— loan
— of goods
o'pen-end' —
pack'age —
pur'chase-mon'ey —
sec'ond —
sen'ior —
straight —
tac'it —
var'i·a·ble rate —
Welsh —
wrap'a·round' —
mort'ga·gee'
— in pos·ses'sion
mort'gag·ing out
mort'ga·gor'
mor'ti·fi·ca'tion
mor'tis cau'sa
mort'main'
— acts
mor'tu·ar'y
— ta'bles
mor'tu·us
most fa'vored na'tion clause
most suit'a·ble use val'u·a'tion
mote
moth'er-in-law'
motion
— for judg'ment not'-with·stand'ing ver'-dict
— for judgment on the plead'ings
— for more def'i·nite state'ment
— for new tri'al
— in bar
— in lim'i·ne'
— to dis·miss'
— to strike
— to sup·press'
mo'tive
Mo'tor Car'ri·er Act
mo'tor·cy'cle
mo'tor ve'hi·cle
mount'ings
mourn'ing
mouth of riv'er

mov'a·ble
— es·tate'
— free'hold'
mov'a·bles
move
move'ment
mov'ent *or* mov'ant
mov'ing pa'pers
muf'fler
mug'ger
mug'shot'
mu·lat'to
mulct
mule
mu·li·er'
—puis·né'
mu'li·er·a'tus
mul'ta
mul'ti·craft' un'ion
mul'ti·dis'trict lit'i·ga'-tion
mul'ti·far'i·ous
— is'sue
— leg'is·la'tion
— lit'i·ga'tion
mul'ti·far'i·ous·ness
mul'ti·lat'er·al
— a·gree'ment
mul'ti·na'tion·al
— cor'po·ra'tion
mul'ti·par'tite'
mul'ti·ple
— ac'cess'
— counts
— ev'i·dence
— list'ing
— of·fens'es
— sen'tenc·es
mul'ti·ple-par'ty ac·counts'
mul'ti·plic'i·ty
— ac'tions
— of suits
mul'ti·tude'
mum'mi·fi·ca'tion
mu·nic'i·pal
— ac'tion
— af·fairs'
— aid
— au·thor'i·ties
— bonds

— char'ter
— claims
— cor'po·ra'tion
— corporation de fac'to'
— courts
— dom'i·cile'
— e·lec'tion
— func'tion
— gov'ern·ment
— law
— lien
— of'fi·cer
— or'di·nance
— pur'pos·es
qua'si' —
— se·cu'ri·ties
— tax·a'tion
— war'rants
mu·nic'i·pal'i·ty
mu'ni·ments
mu·ni'tions
mu'ral mon'u·ments
mur'der
de·praved' heart —
fel'o·ny —
first'-de·gree' —
— in the first de·gree'
— in the sec'ond degree
sec'ond-de·gree' —
— with mal'ice a·fore'-thought'
mur'der·er
mur'der·ess
mur'der·ous
mur'drum
mu·se'um
mus'ter
— mas'ter
— book
— roll
mu·ta'tion
— of li'bel
mu·ta'tis mu·tan'dis
mute
mu'ti·la'tion
mu'ti·nous
mu'ti·ny
mu'tu·al
— af·fray'
— ben'e·fit as·so'ci·a'tion
— benefit in·sur'ance

— fund
— in·sur′ance com′pa·ny
— mis·take′
— re·lief′ as·so′ci·a′tion
— re·serve′ com′pa·ny
— sav′ings bank
— wills
mu·tu·al′i·ty
— of ob′li·ga′tion
— of rem′e·dy
mu·tu·ar′y
mu·tu′um
mys·te′ri·ous dis·ap·
pear′ance
mys′te·ry

N

na·if′
na′ked
name
— and arms clause
named in·sur′ed
name′ly
Na·po′le·on′ic Code
nar′co·a·nal′y·sis
nar·cot′ics
narr and cog·no′vit
law
nar′ra·tive
— ev′i·dence
nar′ra·tor
nar′row seas
na′tion
na′tion·al
— bank
— cur′ren·cy
— debt
— de·fense′
— e·mer′gen·cy
— or′i·gin
Na′tion·al
— En·vi′ron·men′tal
Pol′i·cy Act
— Guard
— La′bor Re·la′tions Act
— Labor Relations
Board
— Me′di·a′tion Board

— Serv′ice Life In·sur′-
ance
na′tion·al′i·ty
Na′tion·al′i·ty Act
na′tion·al·i·za′tion
na′tive
na·tu′ra bre·vi′um
nat′u·ral
— af·fec′tion
— and prob′a·ble con′se·
quenc′es
— flood chan′nel
— law
— life
— mon′u·ment
— ob′ject of tes′ta·tor′s
boun′ty
— pre′mi·um
— re′sourc′es
— rights
nat′u·ral-born′ sub′ject
nat′u·ral·i·za′tion
nat′u·ral·ize′
nat′u·ral·ized′ cit′i·zen
nau·fra′gi·um
naught
nau′ti·cal
— as·ses′sors
— mile
na′val
— base
— courts
— courts′-mar′tial
— law
— of′fi·cer
nav′i·ga′ble
— in fact
— riv′er or stream
— wa′ters
— waters of the U·nit′ed
States
nav′i·gate′
nav′i·ga′tion
— ser′vi·tude′
nav′i·ga′tion·al vis′i·
bil′i·ty
na′vy
— bills
— de·part′ment
neap tide
near

— mon′ey
neat cat′tle
ne·ca′tion
nec′es·sa′ries
nec′es·sar′i·ly in·clud′-
ed of·fense′
nec′es·sar′y
— and prop′er clause
— in′fer·ence
— par′ties
ne·ces′si·tous cir′cum·
stanc′es
ne·ces′si·ty
ne·croph′i·lism
need′ful
need′less
need′y
ne′er′-do-well′
ne ex′e·at′
— bond
— re·pub′li·ca
ne·far′i·ous
ne·gate′
ne·ga′tion
neg′a·tive
— a·ver′ment
— con·di′tion
— preg′nant
neg′a·tiv′ism
ne·glect′
ne·glect′ed
— child
— mi′nor
neg′li·gence
ac′tion·a·ble —
ac′tive —
col·lat′er·al —
com·par′a·tive —
con·cur′rent —
con·trib′u·to′ry —
crim′i·nal —
cul′pa·ble —
de·grees′ of —
es·top′pel by —
gross —
haz′ard·ous —
im·put′ed —
— in law
le′gal —
or′di·nar′y —
pas′sive —

— per se
slight —
sub'se·quent —
wan'ton —
will'ful —
neg'li·gent
— es·cape'
— hom'i·cide'
— man'slaugh'ter
— of·fense'
neg'li·gent·ly
— done
ne·go'tia·bil'i·ty
ne·go'tia·ble
— bond
— doc'u·ment of ti'tle
— in·stru'ments
— words
ne·go'ti·ate'
ne·go'ti·a'tion
Ne'gro
neigh'bor
neigh'bor·hood'
nei'ther par'ty
ne'mo'
ne'o·phyte'
neph'ew
nep'o·tism
ner'vous·ness
net
— as'sets'
— bal'ance
— earn'ings
— es·tate'
— in'come'
— in'ter·est
— lease
— lev'el an'nu·al pre'mi·
  um
— list'ing
— loss
— na'tion·al prod'uct
— op'er·at'ing as'sets'
— operating in'come'
— po·si'tion
— pre'mi·um
— price
— pro'ceeds'
— prof'its
— re·turn'
— rev'e·nues

— sale con'tract'
— sales
— sin'gle pre'mi·um
— ton'nage
— val'ue
— weight
— worth
— yield
neu'tral
neu·tral'i·ty
— laws
— proc'la·ma'tion
neu'tral·i·za'tion
nev'er in·debt'ed, plea
  of
new
— ac'qui·si'tion
— and use'ful
— as'sets'
— as·sign'ment
— cause of ac'tion
— for old
— mat'ter
— style
— tri'al
New'gate'
New Inn
new'ly dis·cov'ered ev'-
  i·dence
news'pa'per
New York
— in'ter·est
— Stock Ex·change'
New York Times v.
  Sul'li·van
next
— de·vi·see'
— e·ven'tu·al es·tate'
— friend
— in, first out
— of kin
— pres'en·ta'tion
nick'name'
niece
night
— de·pos'it
— mag'is·trate'
night'time'
night'walk'ers
ni'hil
— dic'it

— est
— ha'bet
ni'hil·ist
nil
— de'bet
nim'mer
nine'ty (90) day let'ter
ni'si'
— de·cree'
— fe'ce·ris
— pri'us
no
— ar·riv'al, — sale
— a·ward'
— bill
— bo'nus clause
— con'test' clause
— ev'i·dence
— eye'wit'ness rule
— funds
— goods
— lim'it or'der
— pro'test
no'-ac'tion
— clause
— let'ter
no·bil'i·ty
no'cent
no'-fault'
— di·vorce'
— in·sur'ance
nol'le pro·se'qui'
no'lo' con·ten'de·re'
no'men
— ju'ris
nom'i·nal
— ac·count'
— cap'i·tal
— con·sid'er·a'tion
— dam'ag·es
— de·fen'dant
— in'ter·est rate
— part'ner
— par'ty
— plain'tiff
— trust
nom'i·nate' *v.*
nom'i·nate *adj.*
— con'tracts'
nom'i·nat'ing and re·
  duc'ing

nom'i·na'tion
— pa'per
— to a liv'ing
nom'i·nee'
— trust
non
— as·sump'sit
— ce'pit
— com'pos men'tis
— con·ces'sit
— con'stat'
— est fac'tum
— ob·stan'te'
— obstante ve·re·dic'to'
— o·mit'tas
— pros
— se'qui·tur
non·a·bil'i·ty
non·ac·cep'tance
non·ac·cess'
non·ac·qui·es'cence
non·ad·mis'sion
non'age
non·an·ces'tral es·tate'
non·ap·par'ent ease'-
   ment
non·ap·pear'ance
non·as·sess'a·ble
non·bail'a·ble
non·can·cel·a·ble
non·claim'
non'com·bat'ant
non'com·mis'sioned
non'com·pet'i·tive
   traf'fic
non'con·form'ing uses
non'con·form'ist
non'con·test'a·ble
non'con·tin'u·ous
   ease'ment
non'con·tri·bu'tion
   clause
non·cu'mu·la'tive div'i·
   dends'
non·de·liv'er·y
non·de·script'
non·de·tach'a·ble fa·
   cil'i·ties
non·di·rec'tion
non·dis·clo'sure
non·e·nu'mer·at'ed day

non·fea'sance
non·for'feit·a·ble
non·func'tion·al
non'in·sur'a·ble risk
non·in'ter·course'
non·in'ter·ven'tion will
non·is'su·a·ble pleas
non·join'der
non·ju'rors
non·lev'i·a·ble
non·mail'a·ble
non·med'i·cal pol'i·cy
non·mer'chant·a·ble ti'-
   tle
non·nav'i·ga·ble
non·ne·go'tia·ble
non·oc'cu·pa'tion·al
non·pay'ment
non·per·form'ance
non·prof'it
— as·so'ci·a'tion
— cor'po·ra'tion
non·re'course'
— loan
— note
non·res'i·dence
non·res'i·dent
non·sane'
— mem'o·ry
non'sense'
non'-stock' cor'po·ra'-
   tion
non·suit'
non'sup·port'
non'ten'ure
non·us'er
non·waiv'er a·gree'-
   ment
nor'mal
— law
— mind
— school
nor'mal·ly
Nor'man French
no'-strike' clause
nos'trum
no'ta
no·tar'i·al
— acts
— will
no'ta·ry pub'lic

no·ta'tion
— cred'it
note *v.*
note *n.*
— of hand
— of pro'test'
notes
— pay'a·ble
— re·ceiv'a·ble
not ex·ceed'ing
not found
not guilt'y
no'tice
ac'tu·al —
a·ver'ment of —
con·struc'tive —
ex·press' —
im·me'di·ate —
im·plied' —
— in lieu of serv'ice
ju·di'cial —
— of ac'tion
— of ap·peal'
— of ap·pear'ance
— of dis·hon'or
— of judg'ment
— of lis pen'dens'
— of mo'tion
— of or'ders *or* judg'-
   ments
— of pro'test'
— of tri'al
per'son·al —
pre·sump'tive —
pub'lic —
— race stat'utes
rea'son·a·ble —
— re·cord'ing stat'utes
— to ad·mit'
— to ap·pear'
— to cred'i·tors
— to plead
— to quit
no'ti·fy'
not'ing
not lat'er than
not less than
no'to·ri'e·ty
no·to'ri·ous
— co·hab'i·ta'tion
— in·sol'ven·cy

— pos·ses'sion
not pos·sessed'
not prov'en
not sat'is·fied'
not to be per·formed'
  with·in' one year
not trans·fer'a·ble
no·va'tion
nov'el
  — as·sign'ment
  — dis·sei'sin
No·vel'lae' Con'sti·tu'-
  ti·o'nes'
Nov'els
nov'el·ty
no'vus ho'mo'
nox'ious
nu'cle·us
nu'da
  — pa'ti·en'ti·a
  — pos·ses'si·o'
nude
  — con'tract'
  — mat'ter
  — pact
nu'dum pac'tum
nu'ga·to'ry
nui'sance
  a·bate'ment of a —
  ac'tion·a·ble —
  — at law
  com'mon —
  con·tin'u·ing —
  — in fact
  — per ac·ci'dens'
  per'ma·nent —
  — per se
nul
  — ti'el rec'ord
  — tort
null
nul'la bo'na
nul'li·fi·ca'tion
nul'li·fy'
nul'li·ty
  — of mar'riage
nul'li·us fil'i·us
num'bers game
nun'ci·o'
nunc pro tunc
nun'cu·pate'

nun'cu·pa'tive will
nup'tial
nur'ture
nyc·them'er·on'
nym'pho·ma'ni·a

O

oath
  af'fir·ma'tion in lieu
    of —
  — a·gainst' brib'er·y
  as·ser'to·ry —
  cor'po·ral —
  de·ci'sive or de·ci'so·
    ry —
  — ex of·fi'ci·o'
  ex'tra·ju·di'cial —
  false —
  — in li'tem
  ju·di'cial —
  loy'al·ty —
  — of al·le'giance
  — of cal'um·ny
  of·fi'cial —
  poor debt'or's —
  prom'is·so'ry —
  pur'ga·to'ry —
  qual'i·fied' —
  sol'emn —
  sup'ple·to'ry —
  vol'un·tar'y —
ob'du·ra·cy
ob'du·rate
o·be'di·ence
o·be'di·en'tial
o·bese'
o·be'si·ty
o·bey'
ob'fus·cate'
ob'fus·ca'tion
ob'fus·ca·to'ry
o'bit
  — si'ne' pro'le'
o'bit·er
  — dic'tum
o·bit'u·ar'y
ob·ject' v.
ob'ject n.

  — of an ac'tion
  — of a stat'ute
ob·jec'tion
ob·jec'tion·a·ble
ob'jec·tiv'i·ty
ob'jects of a pow'er
ob'late'
  — rolls
ob·la'ti'
ob·la'tion
ob'li·gate'
ob'li·ga'ti·o'
ob'li·ga'tion
  ab'so·lute' —
  ac·ces'so·ry —
  al·ter'na·tive —
  civ'il —
  con·di'tion·al —
  con·junc'tive —
  con·trac'tu·al —
  de·ter'mi·nate —
  di·vis'i·ble —
  ex·press' —
  fail'ure to meet —
  her'i·ta·ble —
  im·per'fect —
  im·plied' —
  in'de·ter'mi·nate —
  in'di·vis'i·ble —
  joint —
  mor'al —
  nat'u·ral —
  o'be·di·en'tial —
  — of a con'tract'
  pe'nal —
  per'fect —
  per'son·al —
  pri'mar'y —
  prim'i·tive —
  prin'ci·pal —
  pure —
  real —
  sec'on·dar'y —
  sev'er·al —
  sim'ple —
  sin'gle —
  sol'i·dar'y —
o·blig'a·to'ry
  — pact
  — rights
  — writ'ing

ob′li·gee′
ob′li·gor′
o·blique′
o·blit′er·a′tion
o·bliv′i·on
o·bliv′i·ous
ob′lo·quy
ob·nox′ious
ob·rep′tion
ob′ro·ga′tion
ob·scene′
— li′bel
ob·scen′i·ty
ob·scur′ant·ism
ob·scure′
ob·scu′ri·ty
ob·ser′vant
ob·serve′
ob·ses′sion
ob·ses′sive
ob·sig′na·to′ry
ob′so·les′cence
ob′so·les′cent
ob′so·lete′
ob′sta·cle
ob·stan′te′
ob·stet′rics
ob′sti·nate
— de·ser′tion
ob·strep′er·ous
ob·stric′tion
ob·struct′
ob·struct′ing
— an of′fi·cer
— jus′tice
— pro·ceed′ings of the leg′is·la′ture
— proc′ess′
— the mails
ob·struc′tion
— to nav′i·ga′tion
ob·struc′tion·ist
ob·tain′
ob·tain′ment
ob·ten′tion
ob·ven′tion
ob′vi·ous
— dan′ger
— risk
oc·ca′sion
oc·clude′

oc·clu′sion
oc·cult′
oc′cu·pan·cy
oc′cu·pant
com′mon —
gen′er·al —
spe′cial —
oc′cu·pa′tion
— tax
oc′cu·pa′tion·al
— dis·ease′
— haz′ard
Oc′cu·pa′tion·al Safe′ty and Health Ad·min′is·tra′tion
oc′cu·pa′tive
oc′cu·pi′er
oc′cu·py′
oc′cu·py′ing
— claim′ant
oc·cur′
oc·cur′rence
o′cean
oc′tave
oc′to·ge·nar′i·an
oc′to·roon′
oc′u·lar
oc′u·list
odd′-job′
odd lot
— doc′trine
— or′der
o′di·ous
o′di·um
oed′i·pal
Oed′i·pus com′plex′
of age
of coun′sel
of course
off′al
off′-board′
off′-col′or
off′-cut′
of·fend′er
of·fense′
con·tin′u·ing —
crim′i·nal —
qua′si′ —
same —
sec′ond —
of·fen′sive

— and de·fen′sive league
— lan′guage
— weap′on
of′fer v.
of′fer n.
— and ac·cep′tance
ir·rev′o·ca·ble —
— of com′pro·mise′
— of judg′ment
— of proof
of′fer·ee′
of′fer·ing
— cir′cu·lar
— state′ment
of′fer·ings
in′ter·state′ —
in′tra·state′ —
pri′vate —
pub′lic —
of′fer·or
off′-grade′
off hire
of′fice
— cop′y
— hours
ju·di′cial —
lu′cra′tive —
min′is·te′ri·al—
— of hon′or
po·lit′i·cal —
prin′ci·pal —
pub′lic —
state —
of′fice-block′ bal′lot
of′fice·hold′er
of′fi·cer
civ′il—
— de fac′to′
— de ju′re
mil′i·tar′y —
— of jus′tice
— of the U·nit′ed States
pub′lic —
war′rant —
of·fi′cial n.
of·fi′cial adj.
— act
— bond
— im·mu′ni·ty doc′trine
— map
— mis·con′duct

— rec'ord
— re·ports' or re·port'ers
Of·fi'cial
— Ga·zette'
— Rec'ords Act
of·fi'cial·ly
of·fi'cial·ty
of·fi'ci·ate'
of·fi'cious will
off'-li'cense
off-lim'its
of force
off'-peak'
off'set'
— ac·count'
— well
off'spring'
of grace
of rec'ord
of right
of the blood
Old Age, Sur·vi'vors' and Dis'a·bil'i·ty In·sur'ance
O'le·ron', laws of
ol·fac'tion
ol·fac'to·ry
ol'i·gar'chy
ol'i·gop'o·ly
ol'o·graph'
ol'o·graph'ic tes'ta·ment
O·lym'pi·ad'
om'buds'man
o·mis'sion
o·mit'tance
om'ni·bus'
— bill
— clause
— hear'ing
om'ni·com'pe·tent
om'ni·um
on ac·count'
— of whom it may con·cern'
on all fours
o'nan·ism
on call
on de·fault'
on de·mand'
one per'son, one vote

on'er·ous
— cause
— con'tract'
— deed
— gift
— ti'tle
one'-sid'ed
one'-to-one'
on file
on or a·bout'
on or be·fore'
on pain of
on'set' date
on'shore'
on stand
on the per'son
o'nus
— pro·ban'di'
o'pen
— a case
— ac·count'
— a judg'ment
— and no·to'ri·ous
— a rule
— bid
— bulk
— court
— cred'it
— let'ter of cred'it
— list'ing
— mar'ket
— mort'gage clause
— or'der
— price term
— sea
— sea'son
— shop
— space
— the plead'ings
— un'ion
o'pen-and-shut'
o'pen-door'
o'pen-end'
— a·gree'ment
— con'tract'
— cred'it
— in·vest'ment com'pa·ny
— investment trust
— mort'gage
— trans·ac'tion

o'pen·ing
— state'ment of coun'sel
o'pen·tide'
op'er·a n.
o'pe·ra pl.n.
op'er·ate'
op'er·at'ing
— ex·pens'es
— mar'gin
— prof'it
op'er·a'tion
— of law
op'er·a'tion·al
op'er·a·tive
— part
— words
op'er·a'tor
ope'tide'
oph'thal·mol'o·gist
o'pi·ate
o·pine'
o·pin'ion
con·cur'ring —
dis·sent'ing —
— ev'i·dence
per cu'ri·am —
— tes'ti·mo'ny
o'pi·um
op·po'nent
op'por·tun'ism
op·pos'er
op'po·site
— par'ty
op'po·si'tion
op·pres'sion
op·pres'sor
op·pro'bri·um
op·ti'cian
op'ti·ma·cy
op'tion
na'ked —
stock —
— to pur'chase
op'tion·al writ
op'tion·ee'
op·tom'e·trist
op·tom'e·try
o'pus
o'ral
— ar'gu·ment
— con·fes'sion

— con'tract'
— ev'i·dence
— plead'ing
— trust
— will
Or'ange·men
or'a·tor
or'a·trix
or·ba'tion
or'bit
or·dain'
or·dain'ers
or·deal'
or'der
 a·greed' —
 — bill of lad'ing
 charg'ing —
 day —
 de·cre'tal —
 dis·cre'tion·ar'y —
 fi'nal —
 in'ter·loc'u·to'ry —
 mar'ket —
 mon'ey —
 — ni'si'
 — of dis·charge'
 — of fil'i·a'tion
 — of re·vi'vor
 per·cent'age —
 re·strain'ing —
 speak'ing —
 stop —
 stop pay'ment —
 — to show cause
or'der·ly
or'ders
 — of the day
or'di·nance
or'di·nar'y *n.*
or'di·nar'y *adj.*
 — care
 — course of busi'ness
 — dan'gers in'ci·dent to
   em·ploy'ment
 — ex·pens'es
 — in'come'
 — loss
 — neg'li·gence
 — per'sons
 — pro·ceed'ing
 — re·pairs'

— risks
— sea'man
— serv'ic·es
— skill
or'di·na'tion
ore'-leave'
or'gan
or·gan'ic
 — act
 — law
or'gan·i·za'tion
or'gan·ize'
or'gan·ized' la'bor
or'gi·as'tic
or'i·fice
o·rig'i·nal
 — bill
 — con'trac·tor
 — con·vey'anc·es
 — doc'u·ment rule
 — en'try
 — es·tates'
 — ev'i·dence
 — grade doc'trine
 — in·ven'tor
 — is'sue
 — ju'ris·dic'tion
 — pack'age doc'trine
 — writ
or'phan
or'phan·age
 — part
or'phans' court
or'tho·pe'dics
or'tho·pe'dist
os·ten'si·ble
 — a'gen·cy
 — au·thor'i·ty
 — own'er·ship'
 — part'ner
os'te·o·path'
os'te·op'a·thy
os'tra·cism
os'tra·cize'
Os'wald's law
oth'er·wise'
ought
oust
oust'er
 — of ju'ris·dic'tion
ou·ster'

— le main
— le mer
out'age
out'-bound'a·ries
out'build'ing
out'cast'
out'come'-de·ter'mi·
 na'tive
out'crop'
out'er
 — bar
 — con'ti·nen'tal shelf
 — door
out'fit'
out'go'
out'house'
out'land'
out'law'
out'lawed'
out'law'ry
out'lay'
out'let'
out'line'
out'lot'
out of ben'e·fit
out of court
 — set'tle·ment
out'-of-pock'et
 — ex·pens'es
 — loss
 — rule
out of term
out of the state
out of time
out'pa'tient
out'put'
 — con'tract'
out'rage'
out'rid'ers
out'right'
out'set'
out·side'
 — di·rec'tor
 — sales·man
out·stand'ing
 — and o'pen ac·count'
o·var'i·an
o'ver·as·sess'ment
o'ver·breadth' doc'trine
o'ver·bur'den
o'ver·charge'

o'ver·come'
o'ver·com'pen·sate'
o'ver·dose' *v.*
o'ver·dose' *n.*
o'ver·draft'
o'ver·draw'
o'ver·due'
o'ver·ex·er'tion
o'ver·ex·tend'
o'ver·flow'
o'ver·flowed' lands
o'ver·freight'
o'ver·haul' *v.*
o'ver·haul' *n.*
o'ver·head' *adj. & n.*
o'ver·head' *adv.*
o'ver·in·sur'ance
o'ver·lap'
o'ver·lease'
o'ver·load' *v.*
o'ver·load' *n.*
o'ver·look'
o'ver·ly·ing right
o'ver·plus'
o'ver·rate'
o'ver·reach'ing clause
o'ver·reg'u·late'
o'ver·ride'
o'ver·rid'ing roy'al·ty
o'ver·rule'
o'ver·run' *v.*
o'ver·run' *n.*
o'vers
over sea
o'ver·see'
o'ver·se'ers
  — of high'ways'
o'ver·sight'
o'ver·sub·scrip'tion
o·vert'
  — act
  — word
o'ver·take'
o'ver-the-coun'ter
  — mar'ket
o'ver-the-road'
o'ver·throw'
o'ver·time'
  — wage
o'ver·ture
owe

ow'el·ty
  — of ex·change'
  — of par·ti'tion
  — of serv'ic·es
ow'ing
own
owned by
own'er
  eq'ui·ta·ble —
  gen'er·al and ben'e·fi'-
    cial —
  joint —
  le'gal —
  part —
  pro haec vi'ce —
  real —
  rec'ord —
  re·put'ed —
  ri·par'i·an —
  sole and un'con·di'tion·
    al —
  spe'cial —
own'er·ship'
  ex·clu'sive —
  in'ci·dent of —
  in'ter·val —
  os·ten'si·ble —
ox'y·gen·ize'
o'yer
  — and ter'mi·ner
  — de rec'ord
o'yez'

P

pa·ca're'
pace
pac'i·fi·ca'tion
pac'i·fism
pac'i·fist
pack'age
packed par'cels
pack'er
pack'ing list
pact
  — de non a·li·en·an'do
  nude —
  o·blig'a·to'ry —
pac'tum

  —de non a·li·en·an'do
  nu'dum —
pad'dock
pa·go'da
paid'-in'
  — cap'i·tal
  — sur'plus
paid'-up'
  — in·sur'ance
  — stock
pain
  — and suf'fer·ing
pains and pen'al·ties
  bill of —
pair'ing-off'
pais *or* pays
  as·sur'ance by mat'ter
    in —
  con·vey'anc·es in —
  es·top'pel in—
  mat'ter in —
pa·la'gi·um
pal'i·mo'ny
pal'li·ate'
pal'li·a'tion
palm'ing off doc'trine
palm'is·try
palm off
pal'pa·ble
pal'pate'
Pals'graf' doc'trine
pam'phlet
pan·dem'ic
pan'der
pan'der·er
pan'der·ing
  — of ob·scen'i·ty
pan'el
pan'nel·la'tion
pan'to·mime'
pa'pal
  — su·prem'a·cy
pa'per
  ac·com'mo·da'tion —
  — block·ade'
  com·mer'cial —
  — hang'ings
  — mon'ey
  — pat'ent
  — prof'it
  — stan'dard

Pap smear
par
— i'tems
— of ex·change'
— val'ue
pa·rab'o·la
par'age *or* pa·ra'gi·um
par'a·graph'
par'a·le'gal
par'al·lel'
— ci·ta'tion
pa·ral'y·sis
par'a·mount'
— eq'ui·ty
— ti'tle
par'a·mour'
par'a·noi'a
par'a·noid'
par'aph
par'a·pher·na'lia
par'a·pro·fes'sion·al
pa·ra'tum ha'be·o'
par'cel
par'cels
  bill of —
par'ce·nar'y
par'cen·er
parch'ment
par'don
  ab'so·lute' —
  — at·tor'ney
  con·di'tion·al —
  ex·ec'u·tive —
  full —
  gen'er·al —
  par'tial —
  un'con·di'tion·al —
par'don·ers
par'ens'
— pa'tri·ae'
par'ent
—com'pa·ny
par'ent·age
pa·ren'tal
— li'a·bil'i·ty
— rights
par'ent-child' im·mu'ni·
  ty
par'en·te'la
pa·ren'the·sis
par'en·thet'i·cal

par'ent·hood'
pa·ren'ti·cide'
pa'res'
pa'ri'
— cau'sa
— de·lic'to
— ma·te'ri·a
— pas'su
— ra'ti·o'ne
par'i-mu'tu·el bet'ting
par'ish
pa·rish'ion·ers
par'i·ty
— ra'tion
par'i·um ju·di'ci·um
park *n.*
park *v.*
park'ing
park'way'
par'lia·ment
par'lia·men'ta·ry
— a'gents
— com·mit'tee
— law
— tax'es
pa·ro'chi·al
pa·rol'
— a·gree'ment
— con'tract'
— ev'i·dence
— evidence rule
pa·role'
— board
— of'fi·cers
pa·rols' de ley
par'ri·cide'
pars
— re'a
par'son
par'son·age
part
— per·form'ance
par'tial
— ac·count'
— av'er·age
— de·pend'en·cy
— e·vic'tion
— ev'i·dence
— in'ca·pac'i·ty
— in·san'i·ty
— lim'i·ta'tion

— loss
— pay'ment
— re·lease'
— ver'dict
par'ti·al'i·ty
par'ti·ble lands
par·tic'i·pant
par·tic'i·pate'
par·tic'i·pa'tion
— loan
— mort'gage
par·tic'u·lar
— lien
— ten'ant
par·tic'u·lar'i·ty
par·tic'u·lars
  bill of —
— of crim'i·nal charg'es
— of sale
par'ties
— and priv'ies
— in in'ter·est
  nec'es·sar'y —
  prop'er —
— to crime
par'ti·san
par·ti'tion
  deed of —
— of a suc·ces'sion
  ow'el·ty of —
part'ner
  dor'mant —
  full —
  gen'er·al —
  jun'ior —
  lim'it·ed —
  liq'ui·dat'ing —
  nom'i·nal —
  os·ten'si·ble —
  qua'si' —
  se'cret —
  si'lent —
  sleep'ing —
  sol'vent —
  spe'cial —
  sur·viv'ing —
part'ner·ship'
— a·gree'ment
— ar'ti·cles
— as'sets'
— as·so'ci·a'tion

— at will
— cer·tif'i·cate
col·laps'i·ble —
com·mer'cial —
— debt
fam'i·ly —
gen'er·al —
— in com'men·dam
— in·sur'ance
lim'it·ed —
min'ing —
par·tic'u·lar —
se'cret —
spe'cial —
stat'u·tor'y —
trad'ing —
u'ni·ver'sal —
par'ty n.
ag·grieved' —
in'jured —
po·lit'i·cal —
real—
real — in in'ter·est
— to be charged
—wall
par'ty adj.
— ju'ry
— struc'ture
— wall
pass n.
pass v.
pass'a·ble
pas'sage
pas'sage·way'
pass'book'
pass'sen·ger
— mile
pas'sim
pass'ing tick'et
pas'sion
pas'sive
pass'port'
past
— con·sid'er·a'tion
— rec'ol·lec'tion re·
   cord'ed
pas'teur·ize'
pas'tur·age
pas'ture
pat'ent adj.
— am'bi·gu'i·ty

— de'fect'
let'ters —
— writ
pat'ent n.
— ap·peals'
— bill of'fice
de·sign' —
— in·fringe'ment
land —
— med'i·cine
— of'fice
— of prec'e·dence
pi'o·neer'—
plant —
— pool'ing
re·is'sued —
— right
— right deal'er
— rolls
— suit
pat'ent·a·ble
Pat'ent and Trade'-
   mark' Of'fice
pat'ent·ee'
pa'ter
— pa'tri·ae'
pa'ter·fa·mil'i·as
pa·ter'nal
— line
— pow'er
— prop'er·ty
pa·ter'nal·ism
pa·ter'ni·ty
— suit
pa·thol'o·gist
pa·thol'o·gy
pa·tib'u·lar'y
pa·tib'u·lat'ed
pa'ti·ens'
pa'tient
pa'tri·a
pa'tri·arch'
pat'ri·cide'
pat'ri·mo'ny
pa·trol'man
pa'tron
pa'tron·age
pa'tron·ize'
pat'tern
pau'per
pau'per's oath

pawn
pawn'bro'ker
pawn·ee'
paw'nor
pax re'gis
pay n.
pay v.
pay'a·ble
— af'ter sight
— on de·mand'
— to bear'er
— to or'der
pay'-as-you-go'
pay·ee'
pay'er or pay'or
pay'ing quan'ti·ties
pay'mas'ter
pay'ment
bal·loon' —
— guar'an·teed'
— in'to court
— on de·mand'
part—
par'tial —
vol'un·tar'y —
pay'off'
pay'roll'
— tax
peace
— and qui'e·tude'
ar'ti·cles of the —
bill of —
— bond
breach of —
con·ser'va·tor of the —
jus'tice of the —
— of'fi·cers
pub'lic —
peace'a·ble
peace'ful
pec'u·la'tion
pe·cu'liar
pe·cu'ni·a
pe·cu'ni·ar'y
— ben'e·fits
— be·quest'
— caus'es
— con·di'tion
— con·sid'er·a'tion
— dam'ag·es
— in'ju·ry

— in'ter·est
— leg'a·cy
— loss
ped'dler
ped'er·as'ty
pe·des'tri·an
pe·di·a·tri'cian
pe'di·at'rics
ped'i·gree'
peep'ing Tom
peer'age
peer'ess
peers
  ju'ry of one's —
peg
peine forte et dure
pelfe
pe'nal
— ac'tion
— bill
— bond
— clause
— code
— in'sti·tu'tion
— laws
— ser'vi·tude'
— stat'utes
— sum
pe'nal·ize'
pen'al·ty
— clause
pen'ance
pen'den·cy
pen'dens'
pen'dent ju'ris·dic'tion
pen·den'te' li'te'
pend'ing
pen'e·tra'tion
pe'nis
pen'i·ten'tia·ry
Pen·noy'er Rule
Penn'syl·va'ni·a Rule
pen'ny stocks
pen'ny·weight'
pe·nol'o·gy
pen reg'is·ter
pen'sion
  de·fined' — plan
  fund'ed — plan
  non·con·trib'u·to'ry —
    plan

qual'i·fied' — plan
— trust
Pen'sion Ben'e·fit
  Guar'an·ty Cor'po·ra'-
  tion
pen'sion·a·ble
pen'sion·er
pe·num'bra doc'trine
pe'on·age
peo'ple
pep'per·corn'
per
per ac'ci·dens'
per·am'bu·la'tion
per and post
per an'num
per au'tre vie
per a·ver·si·o'nem
per cap'i·ta
per·ceiv'a·ble risk
per cent or per·cent'
per·cent'age
— lease
— of com·ple'tion
  meth'od
— or'der
per·cep'tion
perch
per'co·late'
per'co·lat'ing wa'ters
per con'se·quens'
per con'tra
per cu'ri·am
per·di'da
per di'em
per·du'ra·ble
per·emp'tion
per·emp'to·ry
— chal'lenge
— day
— ex·cep'tions
— pa'per
— rule
— un'der·tak'ing
per·en'ni·al
per'fect
— at'tes·ta'tion clause
— in'stru·ment
— trust
per·fect'ed
per·fect'ing bail

per·fec'tion
— of se·cu'ri·ty in'ter·est
per·fid'i·ous
per'fi·dy
per'fo·rate'
per·form'
per for'mam do'ni'
per·form'ance
—bond
part —
pub'lic —
spe·cif'ic —
per frau'dem
per'il
per'ils
— of the lakes
— of the sea
per in·cu'ri·am
per in·dus'tri·um
per in·for·tu'ni·um
pe'ri·od
pe'ri·od'ic
— al'i·mo'ny
— ten'an·cy
pe'ri·od'i·cal
pe·riph'er·al rights
pe·riph'ra·sis
per'ish
per'ish·a·ble
— com·mod'i·ty
— goods
per'jure
per·ju'ri·ous
per'ju·ry
perks
per le'gem ter'rae'
per'ma·nent
— a·bode'
— al'i·mo'ny
— dis'a·bil'i·ty
— em·ploy'ment
— in'ju·ry
— law
per mis'ad·ven'ture
per·mis'sion
per·mis'sions
per·mis'sive
— coun'ter·claim'
— join'der
— use
— waste

per·mit′ v.
per′mit n.
per′mit·tee′
per mit·ter′
— le droit
— l′es·tate′
per′mu·ta′tion
per my et per tout
per′nan·cy
per·ni′cious
per os
per pais
tri′al —
per′pe·trate′
per′pe·tra′tor
per·pet′u·al
— e′dict′
— suc·ces′sion
per·pet′u·at′ing tes′ti·
mo′ny
per′pe·tu′i·ties
rule a·gainst′ —
per′pe·tu′i·ty
— of the king
per proc′u·ra′tion
per′qui·sites
per quod
per rec′tuum
per sal′tum
per sam′ple
per se
— vi′o·la′tions
per′se·cute′
per·sist′ence
per′son
— ag·grieved′
fic·ti′tious —
pro·tect′ed —
— in lo′co pa·ren′tis
— un′der dis′a·bil′i·ty
per·so′na
— des′ig·na′ta
— gra′ta
— non gra′ta
per′son·a·ble
per′son·al
— ef·fects′
— hold′ing com′pa·ny
tax
— in′come′
— ju′ris·dic′tion

— law
— li′a·bil′i·ty
— prop′er·ty tax
— re·cog′ni·zance
per′son·al·ty
per′son·ate′
per′spi·ca′cious
per·spic′u·ous
per stir′pes′
per·suade′
per·sua′sion
per·sua′sive·ness
per·tain′
per′ti·nent
per to′tam cu′ri·am
per tout et non per my
per′tur·ba′tion
per ver′ba
— de fu·tu′ro′
— de prae·sen′ti′
per·verse′
— ver′dict
per·ver′sion
per·vert′ n.
per·vert′ v.
per vi′vam vo′cem
per year
pes′su·ra·ble wares
pes′ti·cide′
Pe′ter′s pence
pet′it
pe·tite′ as·size′
pe·ti′tion
— de droit
— in bank′rupt′cy
pe·ti′tion·ee′
pe·ti′tion·er
pe·ti′tion·ing cred′i·tor
pe·ti′ti·o′ prin·cip′i·i′
pet′i·to·ry ac′tion
pet′ti·fog′ger
pet′ty
— bag of′fice
— cash
— of′fi·cers
pe·yo′te
pha·lanx′
phal′lic
phar′ma·ceu′ti·cal
phar′ma·cist
phar′ma·col′o·gy

phar′ma·cy
phe·nom′e·non
phi·lan′thro·py
phle·bi′tis
pho′bi·a
pho·tog′ra·pher
pho·tog′ra·phy
phy′la·sist
phys′i·cal
— cru′el·ty
— de·pre′ci·a′tion
— dis′a·bil′i·ty
— fact
— force
— harm
— im·pos′si·bil′i·ty
— in′ca·pac′i·ty
— in′ju·ry
— ne·ces′si·ty
phy·si′cian
phy·si′cian-pa′tient
priv′i·lege
phys′i·o·ther′a·py
pi′a·cle
pick′et
pick′et·ing
peace′a·ble —
un·law′ful —
pick′pock′et
piece′work′
pie′pou′dre or pie′pow′-
der
pier
pierc′ing cor′po·rate
veil
pil′fer
pil′fer·age
pil′fer·er
pil′lage
pil′lo·ry
pi′lot
pi′lot·age
— au·thor′i·ties
pimp
pin mon′ey
pi′o·neer′ pat′ent
pi′ous uses
pi′ra·cy
pi′rate
pi·rat′i·cal·ly
pis′ca·ry

pis'tol
pit'fall'
pit'tance
plac'ard'
place
  — lands
  — of a·bode'
  — of busi'ness
  — of con'tract'
  — of de·liv'er·y
  — of em·ploy'ment
  — where
place'ment
plac'er
  — claim
  — lo·ca'tion
pla'cit
plac'i·ta ju'ris
plac'i·tum
pla'gia·rism
pla'gia·rist
pla'gia·ry
plague
plain'clothes' man
plaint
plain'tiff
  — in er'ror
use —
plain view doctrine
plan
  — er'ror rule
planned u'nit de·vel'-
  op·ment
plan·ta'tion
plat
  — map
plat'form'
play'-debt'
plea
af·firm'a·tive —
  — a·gree'ments
a·nom'a·lous —
bad —
  — bar'gain·ing
com'mon —
crim'i·nal —
dil'a·to'ry —
dou'ble —
false —
for'eign —
  — in a·bate'ment

  — in bar
  — in dis·charge'
  — in re'con·ven'tion
neg'a·tive —
  — ne·go'ti·a'tions
  — of con·fes'sion and
    a·void'ance
  — of guilt'y
  — of no'lo' con·ten'de·re
  — of priv'i·lege
  — of re·lease'
per·emp'to·ry —
sham —
  — side
spe'cial —
special — in bar
plead
  — is'su·a·bly
  — o'ver
  — to the mer'its
plead'ed
plead'er
spe'cial —
plead'ing
ar·tic'u·lat'ed —
com'mon law —
dou'ble —
spe'cial —
plead'ings
ple·be'ian
ple·be'i·ty
pleb'i·scite'
pledge
pledg·ee'
pledg'er·y
pledg'es
pledg'or
ple'na·ry
  — ac'tion
  — con·fes'sion
  — ju'ris·dic'tion
  — pow'ers
  — ses'sion
  — suit
ple'ne'
plen'i·po·ten'ti·ar'y
plev'in
plight
plot
plot'tage
plow back

plumb'er
plun'der
plun'der·age
plu'ral
  — mar'riage
plu·ral'i·ty
poach
poach'ing
pock'et ve'to
point
  — re·served'
  — sys'tem
poi'son
poi'son·ous tree doc'-
  trine
pok'er
po'lar star rule
po·lice'
  — court
  — ju'ry
  — jus'tice
  — mag'is·trate'
  — of'fi·cer
  — pow'er
  — reg'u·la'tions
  — su'per·vi'sion
po·lice'man
po·lice'wom'an
pol'i·cy
as·sess'a·ble —
blan'ket —
en·dow'ment —
ex·tend'ed —
float'ing —
in'con·test'a·ble —
in'ter·est —
  — loan
mas'ter —
mixed —
  — of in·sur'ance
o'pen —
paid'-up' —
pub'lic —
term —
time —
  — val'ue
val'ued —
voy'age —
wa'ger —
  — year
po·lit'i·cal

— cor'po·ra'tion
— crime
— law
— lib'er·ty
— of·fens'es
— of'fice
— par'ty
— ques'tions
— rights
— sub'di·vi'sion
— tri'al
pol'i·tics
pol'i·ty
poll
  — mon'ey
  — tax
poll'ing the ju'ry
polls
pol·lute'
pol·lu'tion
pol'y·an'dry
po·lyg'a·my
pol'y·graph'
pol'y·op'so·ny
pol'y·pol'y
pond
  great —
  pri'vate —
  pub'lic —
pool'ing
  — as'sets'
  — con'tracts'
  — of in'ter·ests
poor
  — law
  — rate
poor'-law' board
pop'er·y
pop'u·lace
pop'u·la'tion
pop'u·lar sense
por'no·graph'ic
por·rect'ing
port
  — au·thor'i·ty
  — charg'es
  — dues
  for'eign —
  home —
  — of call
  — of de·liv'er·y

— of de·par'ture
— of des'ti·na'tion
— of dis·charge'
— of en'try
— risk
— toll
— war'den
port'a·ble
Por'tal-to-Por'tal Act
por'ter
por'ter·age
por'tion
  — dis·pos'i·ble
port'reeve'
port'sale'
pos'i·tive
  — ev'i·dence
  — law
  — wrong
po·si·ti'vi' ju'ris
pos'se
pos·sess'
pos·sessed'
pos·ses'sion
  ac'tu·al —
  ad·verse' —
  chose in —
  civ'il —
  con·struc'tive —
  cor·po're·al —
  de·riv'a·tive —
  es'tate' in —
  ex·clu'sive —
  hos'tile —
  — is nine'-tenths' of the
    law
  na'ked —
  nat'u·ral —
  o'pen —
  peace'a·ble —
  ped'al —
  qua'si' —
  scram'bling —
  u'ni·ty of —
  va'cant —
pos·ses'sor
  bo'na fide
  ma'la fide
pos·ses'so·ry
  — ac'tion
  — claim

— in'ter·est
— judg'ment
— lien
— war'rant
pos'si·bil'i·ty
  bare —
  — cou'pled with an in'-
    ter·est
  na'ked —
  — of re·vert'er
  — on a —
pos'si·ble
post
  — di'em
  — dis·sei'sin
  — ex·change'
  — fac'to'
  — fac'tum
  — hac
  — hoc
  — na'tus
  — notes
  — o'bit
  — of'fice
  — rem
  — roads
  — ter'mi·num
post'act'
post'age
  — stamp
post'al
  — cur'ren·cy
  — or'der
  — sav'ings de·pos'i·to'-
    ries
Post'al Serv'ice
post'-con·vic'tion rem'-
  e·dies
post'date'
post'dat'ed check
post'ed
  — wa'ters
pos·te'ri·or'i·ty
pos·ter'i·ty
post'hu·mous
  — child
  — word
post'ing
post li'tem mo'tam
post'man
post'mark'

post′mas′ter
— gen′er·al
post′mor′tem
post·nup′tial
— a·gree′ment
— set′tle·ment
post·pone′
post-ter′mi·nal sit′tings
post-tri′al
— dis·cov′er·y
— mo′tions
— rem′e·dies
po′ta·ble
po′ten·tate′
po·ten′ti·a
po·ten′tial
Po·to′mac mort′gag·es
pound
— breach
pound′age fees
pour′-o′ver
— trust
— will
pov′er·ty
— af′fi·da·vit
pow′er
ap·pen′dant —
ap·pur′te·nant —
— cou′pled with an in′-
ter·est
ex·clu′sive —
ex·ec′u·tive —
— in gross
na′ked —
— of al′ien·a′tion
— of ap·point′ment
— of at·tor′ney
— of dis·po·si′tion
— of rev′o·ca′tion
— of sale
— of ter′mi·na′tion
— of vis′i·ta′tion
spend′ing —
tax′ing —
pow′ers
col·lat′er·al —
con′sti·tu′tion·al —
com′merce —
cor′po·rate —
en·force′ment —
e·nu′mer·at′ed —

ex·press′ —
gen′er·al and spe′cial —
general and special — in
trust
im·plied′ —
— in gross
in·her′ent —
min′is·te′ri·al —
nec′es·sar′y and prop′-
er —
pre-emp′tive —
re·served′ or re·sid′u·al
state —
re·sult′ing —
prac′ti·ca·ble
prac′ti·ca·bly
prac′ti·cal
prac′tice
— of law
— of med′i·cine
prac′tic·es
prac·ti′tion·er
prae′ci·pe′
prae′di·al
prae·to′ri·an law
prae·var′i·ca·tor′
prag·mat′ic
prai′rie
prax′is
pray
prayer
— for re·lief′
— of proc′ess′
pre′am·ble
pre′ap·point′ed ev′i·
dence
pre·au′di·ence
pre·car′i·ous
— cir′cum·stanc′es
— loan
— pos·ses′sion
— right
— trade
prec′a·to′ry
— trust
— words
pre·cau′tion
prec′e·dence
pat′ent of —
prec′e·den·cy
prec′e·dent

— con·di′tion
prec′e·dents sub si·len′-
ti·o′
pre·ced′ing
pre′ce par′ti·um
pre·cept′
— of at·tach′ment
pre·cinct′
prec′i·pe′
pre·cip′i·ta′tion
pre·cise′
pre·clude′
pre·clu′sion or′der
pre·cog′ni·tion
pre′co·ni·za′tion
pre·con′tract′
pre·date′
pred′a·to′ry in·tent′
pred′e·ces′sor
pre′di·al
— ser′vi·tude′
pred′i·cate′ v.
pred′i·cate n. & adj.
pre·dis·pose′
pre·dom′i·nant
pre-emp′tion
— claim′ant
— doc′trine
— en′try
— right
pre-emp′tion·er
pre-emp′tive
— right
pre′fect′
pre·fer′
pref′er·ence
— share
pref′er·en′tial
— as·sign′ment
— claim
— debts
— div′i·dend′
— shop
— tar′iff
— trans′fer
pre·ferred′
— cred′i·tors
— debt
— div′i·dend′
— dock′ets
— stock

— stock bail'out'
preg'nan·cy
  plea of —
preg'nant neg'a·tive
pre·judge'
prej'u·dice
  without —
prej'u·di'cial
  — er'ror
  — pub·lic'i·ty
prel'ate
pre·lim'i·nar'y
  — com·plaint'
  — ev'i·dence
  — ex·am'i·na'tion
  — hear'ing
  — in·junc'tion
  — proof
  — war'rant
pre·mar'i·tal
pre'ma·ture'
pre·med'i·tate'
pre·med'i·tat'ed de·
  sign'
pre·med'i·tat'ed·ly
pre·med'i·ta'tion
pre·mier'
  — ser'jeant
prem'is·es
pre'mi·um
  — loan
  — note
  — tax
  un·earned' —
pre·mon'i·to'ry
pre·na'tal
  — in'ju·ries
pren·der' or pren'dre
pre·nup'tial a·gree'-
  ment
pre·paid'
  — ex·pense'
  — in'come'
  — le'gal serv'ic·es
prep'a·ra'tion
pre·pare'
pre·pay'ment
  — pen'al·ty
pre·pense'
pre·pon'der·ance
  — of the ev'i·dence

pre·req'ui·site
pre·rog'a·tive
  — court
  — law
  — writs
pres
pres'by·ter
Pres'by·te'ri·an·ism
pre·scrib'a·ble
pre·scribe'
pre·scrip'tion
  cor'po·ra'tions by —
pre·scrip'tive
  — ease'ment
pres'ence
  — of an of'fic·er
  — of de·fen'dant
  — of the court
  — of the tes'ta'tor
pre·sent' v.
pres'ent n.
pres'ent adj.
  — a·bil'i·ty
  — con·vey'ance
  — dan'ger test
  — en·joy'ment
  — es·tate'
  — in'ter·est
  — rec'ol·lec'tion re·
    cord'ed
  — recollection re·vived'
  — sale
  — time
  — use
pres'en·ta'tion
pre·sen'ta·tive ad·vow'-
  son
pre·sen'tence
  — hear'ing
  — in·ves'ti·ga'tion
  — re·port'
pre·sent'er
pre·sent'ing bank
pres'ent·ly
pre·sent'ment
pres'ents
pres'er·va'tion
pre·serve'
pre·side'
pres'i·dent
  — judge

  — of the coun'cil
pres'i·den'tial
  — e·lec'tors
  — pow'ers
Pres'i·dent of the
  U·nit'ed States
pre·sid'ing judge
press
press'ing sea'men
pre·sum'a·bly
pre·sume'
pre·sumed' in·tent'
pre·sump'ti·o'
pre·sump'tion
  con·clu'sive —
  dis·put'a·ble —
  ir're·but'ta·ble —
  — of death
  — of in'no·cence
  — of le·git'i·ma·cy
  — of sur·vi'vor·ship'
  re·but'ta·ble —
  stat'u·to'ry —
pre·sump'tions
  con·flict'ing —
  — of fact
  — of law
pre·sump'tive
  — ev'i·dence
  — trust
pre'sup·pose'
pre·tend'
prête-nom'
pre·tens'es
  false —
pre'ter le'gal
pre·ter'mi·nal
pre·ter·mis'sion
  — stat'ute
pre·ter·mit'
pre·ter·mit'ted heir
pre'text'
pre·tex'tu·al
pre'ti·um
  — af'fec·ti·o'nis
  — pe·ric'u·li'
  — se·pul'chri'
pre·tri'al
  — con'fer·ence
  — dis·cov'er·y
  — di·ver'sion

— hear'ing
— or'der
pre·vail'
pre·vail'ing
  — par'ty
  — pric'es
pre·var'i·ca'tion
pre·vent'
pre·vent'a·ble
pre·ven'ta·tive
pre·ven'tion
pre·ven'tive
  — de·ten'tion
  — jus'tice
pre'view'
pre'vi·ous
  — ques'tion
pre'vi·ous·ly
  — taxed in'come'
pri'a·pism
price
  ask'ing —
  — cur'rent
  — dis·crim'i·na'tion
  — ex·pect'an·cy
  — in'dex'
  — lead'er·ship'
  sup·port' —
  — sup·ports'
  tar'get —
price'-earn'ings ra'tio
price'-fix'ing
priest'-pen'i·tent priv'i·
  lege
pri'ma fa'cie'
  — case
  — ev'i·dence
  — tort
pri'mage
pri'mar'y
  — ac·tiv'i·ty
  — al'le·ga'tion
  — ben'e·fi'ci·ar'y
  — boy'cott'
  — dis·pos'al of the soil
  — e·lec'tion
  — ev'i·dence
  — ju'ris·dic'tion
  — mar'ket
  — ob'li·ga'tion
  — pow'ers

— pur'pose
pri'mate'
prime
  — con'trac'tor
  — cost
  — mak'er
  — min'is·ter
  — rate
  — ser'jeant
pri·mer'
prim'er
  — fine
  — sei'sin
prim'i·tive ob'li·ga'tion
pri'mo·gen'i·ture
prince
Prince of Wales
prin'cess roy'al
prin'ci·pal *adj.*
prin'ci·pal *n.*
  — and sur'e·ty
  — in the first de·gree'
  — in the sec'ond de·
    gree'
  — of the house
  un'dis·closed' —
  vice —
prin'ci·ple
print
Print'ers Ink Stat'ute
print'ing
pir'or *n.*
  — pe'tens'
  — tem·po're' po'ti·or'
pri'or *adj.*
  — art
  — cred'i·tor
  — in'con·sis'tent state'-
    ments
  — jeop'ard·y
  — lien
  — re·straint'
  — use doc'trine
pri'o·ri' pe·ten'ti'
pri·or'i·ty
prise
pris'on
  — bounds
  — breach
  — break'ing
pris'on·er

— at the bar
— of war
pri'va·cy, right of
pri'vate
  — bank
  — bill of'fice
  — ex·am'i·na'tion
  — foun·da'tions
  — in'ter·na'tion·al law
  — law
  — let'ter rul'ing
  — nui'sance
  — of'fer·ing
  — per'son
  — place'ment
  — rul'ing
  — street
pri'va·teer'
pri·va'tion
pri'vat·ize'
priv'ies
priv'i·lege
  — ab'so·lute'
  —a·gainst' self'-in·crim'i·
    na'tion
  ex·clu'sive —
  ex·ec'u·tive —
  — from ar·rest'
  jour'nal·ist's —
  — of tran'sit
  qual'i·fied' —
  real —
  spe'cial —
  — tax
  writ of —
priv'i·leged
  — com·mu'ni·ca'tions
  — cop'y·holds'
  — debts
  — ev'i·dence
  — ves'sel
priv'i·leg·es and im·
  mu'ni·ties
priv'i·ty
  — of blood
  — of con'tract'
  — of es·tate'
  — of pos·ses'sion
  — or knowl'edge
priv'y
  — coun'cil

— coun'cil·or
— purse
— seal
— sig'net
— to'ken
— ver'dict
prize
— courts
— goods
— law
— mon'ey
pro
— and con
prob'a·bil'i·ty
high — rule
prob'a·ble
— cause
— con'se·quence
— ev'i·dence
— fu'ture pay'ments
— ground
prob'a·bly
pro'bate'
— bond
— code
— court
— du'ty
— home'stead'
— judge
— ju'ris·dic'tion
— pro·ceed'ing
pro·ba'ti·o'
— mor'tu·a
— ple'na
— sem'i-ple'na
— vi'va
pro·ba'tion
— of'fi·cer
pro·ba'tion·er
pro'ba·tive
— ev'i·dence
— facts
pro'bi·ty
pro bo'no'
— et ma'lo'
— pub'li·co'
pro'ce·den'do'
— on aid prayer
pro·ce'dur'al
— due proc'ess'
— law

pro·ce'dure
— acts
pro·ceed'
pro·ceed'ing
col·lat'er·al —
ex·ec'u·to'ry —
— in er'ror
spe'cial —
sum'ma·ry —
sup'ple·men'ta·ry —
pro·ceed'ings
— in bank'rupt'cy
le'gal —
or'di·nar'y —
pro'ceeds'
proc'ess'
a·buse' of —
— a'gent
a'li·as —
com·pul'so·ry —
crim'i·nal —
ex·ec'u·to'ry —
fi'nal —
ir·reg'u·lar —
ju·di'cial —
le'gal —
me·chan'i·cal —
mesne —
— of in'ter·plead'er
— of law
o·rig'i·nal —
— pat'ent
reg'u·lar —
— serv'er
serv'ice of —
sum'ma·ry —
trus·tee' —
void —
pro·ces'sion
pro·ces'sion·ing
pro·cès'-ver·bal'
pro·chein'
— a·mi' or a·my'
— a·void'ance
pro'chro·nism
pro·claim'
proc'la·ma'tion
proc'la·ma'tor
pro con·fes'so'
pro con·sil'i·o
pro·con'sul

pro cor'po·re reg'ni
pro'cre·a'tion
proc'tor
proc'u·ra·cy
proc'u·ra'tion
proc'u·ra'tor
proc'u·ra'trix
pro·cure'
pro·cure'ment
— con'tract'
pro·cur'er
pro·cur'ing cause
prod'i·gal
pro·di'tion
pro·di'tor
pro'duce n.
pro·duce' v.
pro·duc'er
pro·duc'ing
— cause
prod'uct
— li'a·bil'i·ty
pro·duc'tion
—for com'merce
— of suit
pro emp·to're
pro e'o' quod
pro fac'to'
pro·fane'
pro·fane'ly
pro·fan'i·ty
pro·fess'
pro·fes'si·o ju'ris
pro·fes'sion
pro·fes'sion·al
— as·so'ci·a'tion
— cor'po·ra'tion
— re·spon'si·bil'i·ty
pro·fes'sor
prof'fer
prof'fered ev'i·dence
pro'file'
prof'it
— and loss
— and loss ac·count'
— and loss state'ment
— à pren'dre
— à ren'dre
gross —
— mar'gin
net —

op'er·at'ing —
prof'it·a·ble
prof'i·teer'ing
prof'its
  mesne —
  net —
  pa'per —
  sur'plus —
  un'dis·trib'ut·ed —
  un'di·vid'ed —
prof'it-shar'ing plan
pro for'ma
pro·gres'sion
pro·gres'sive tax
pro hac vi'ce
pro·hib'it
pro·hib'it·ed de·grees'
pro·hi·bi'tion
pro·hib'i·tive im·ped'i·ments
pro·hib'i·to'ry
pro il'la vi'ce
pro in'de·fen'so'
pro in'di·vi'so'
pro in'ter·es'se su'o'
pro lae'si·o'ne fi·de'i'
pro·lapse'
pro le·ga'to'
pro'les'
pro'le·tar'i·at *or* pro'le·tar'i·ate
pro'le·ta'ri·us
pro'li·cide'
pro·lif'er·ate'
pro·lix'i·ty
pro'lon·ga'tion
pro ma·jo'ri' cau·te'la
prom'is·cu'i·ty
pro·mis'cu·ous
prom'ise
  fic·ti'tious —
  il·lu'so·ry —
  — im·plied' in fact
  — implied in law
  na'ked —
  new —
  — of mar'riage
  pa·rol' —
  — to pay the debt of an·oth'er
prom'is·ee'

prom'i·sor'
prom'is·so'ry
  — es·top'pel
  — fraud
  — note
  — war'ran·ty
pro·mote'
pro·mo'tion
pro·mot'er
prompt
  — de·liv'er·y
  — ship'ment
prompt'ly
prom'ul·gate'
prom'ul·ga'tion
pro non scrip'to'
pro·no'ta·ry
pro·nounce'
pro·nun'ci·a'tion
proof
  af·fir'ma·tive —
  — be·yond' a rea'son·a·ble doubt
  de·gree' of —
  — ev'i·dent or pre·sump'tion great
  full —
  half —
  neg'a·tive —
  — of claim
  — of debt
  — of loss
  — of serv'ice
  — of will
  pos'i·tive —
  pre·lim'i·nar'y —
  stan'dard of —
pro o'pe·re et la·bo're
prop'a·gan'da
prop'a·gan'dist
prop'a·gate'
pro par'ti·bus lib'er·an'dis
prop'er
  — care
  — ev'i·dence
  — feuds
  — in'de·pend'ent ad·vice'
  — look'out'
  — par'ty
prop'er·ly

prop'er·ty
  ab'so·lute' —
  com'mon —
  com·mu'ni·ty —
  in·tan'gi·ble —
  mis·laid' —
  mixed —
  mov'a·ble —
  — of an·oth'er
  per'son·al —
  pri'vate —
  real —
  — right
  sep'a·rate —
  — set'tle·ment
  spe'cial —
  state —
  tan'gi·ble —
  — tax
  — torts
  un·claimed' —
pro'phy·lac'tic
pro·pin'qui·ty
pro·po'nent
pro·por'tion·ate
pro·pos'al
pro·pose'
prop'o·si'tion
pro pos·ses'si·o'ne
  prae·sum'i·tur' de ju're
pro pos'ses·so're
pro pos'se su'o'
pro·pound'
pro·pri'e·tar'y
  — ar'ti·cles
  — ca·pac'i·ty
  — cap'i·tal
  — du'ties
  — func'tions
  — gov'ern·ments
  — in'ter·est
  — lease
  — rights
pro·pri'e·tas'
pro·pri'e·tor
pro·pri'e·to'ri·al
pro·pri'e·tor·ship'
pro·pri'e·ty
pro'pri·o' vi·go're
prop'ter

— af·fec'tum
— de·fec'tum
— defectum san·gui'nis
— de·lic'tum
— hoc
— hon·o'ris re·spec'tum
— im'po·ten'ti·am
— pri'vi·le'gi·um
pro que·ren'te
pro ra'ta
— clause
— dis'tri·bu'tion clause
pro·rate'
pro re na'ta
pro'ro·ga'tion
pro·rogue'
pro sa·lu'te an'i·mae'
pro·scribed'
pro se
pros'e·cute'
pros'e·cut'ing
— at·tor'ney
— wit'ness
pros'e·cu'tion
pros'e·cu'tor
— of the pleas
pri'vate —
pub'lic —
pros'e·cu'trix
pro'se·qui'
pro·se'qui·tur'
pro so'ci·o
pro so'li·do'
pro·spec'tive
— dam'ag·es
— law
pros'pec·tor
pro·spec'tus
pros·the'sis
pros'ti·tu'tion
pros'ti·tute'
pro tan'to'
pro·tec'tion
pro·tec'tive
— com·mit'tee
— cus'to·dy
— or'der
— tar'iff
— trust
pro·tec'tor·ate
pro tem

pro tem'po·re
pro'test'
— fee
no'tice of —
su'pra —
waiv'er of —
pro'tes·tan'do'
Prot'es·tant
prot'es·ta'tion
pro·thon'o·tar'y
pro'to·col'
prov'a·ble
prove
pro·vide'
pro·vid'ed
— by law
prov'ince
pro·vi'sion
pro·vi'sion·al
— com·mit'tee
— court
— gov'ern·ment
— in·junc'tion
— rem'e·dy
— sei·zure
pro·vi'sions
pro·vi'so
tri'al by —
pro·vi'sor
prov'o·ca'tion
pro·voke'
pro'vost'
— mar'shal
prowl'er
prox'i·mate
— cause
— con'se·quence' or re·
sult'
— dam'ag·es
prox'i·mate·ly
prox·im'i·ty
prox'y
— mar'riage
— state'ment
pru'dence
pru'dent
— man rule
pru·den'tial
pru'ri·ent in'ter·est
pseu'do
pseu'do·cy·e'sis

pseu'do·graph'
pseu'do·nym'
psy·chi'a·trist
psy·chi'a·try
psy'cho·a·nal'y·sis
psy'cho·an'a·lyst
psy'cho·di'ag·no'sis
psy'cho·log'i·cal
psy·chol'o·gist
psy'cho·neu·ro'sis
psy'cho·path'
psy'cho·pa·thol'o·gy
psy·cho'sis
psy·cho·ther'a·py
psy·chot'ic
pto'maine'
pu'ber·ty
pub'lic *n.*
pub'lic *adj.*
— ad'vo·cate
— a'gen·cy
— ap·point'ments
— au·thor'i·ty
— build'ing
— char'ac·ter
— con'tract'
— con·ven'ience
— cor'po·ra'tions
— de·fen'der
— en'ti·ty
— fig'ure
— funds
— in'ter·est
— in'vi·tee'
— lands
— land sys'tem
— law
— li'a·bil'i·ty in·sur'ance
— nui'sance
— of'fense
— of'fer·ing
— of'fice
— of·fi'cial
— pas'sage
— place
— pur'pose
— rec'ord
— safe'ty
— sale
— serv'ice
— service com·mis'sion

— service cor'po·ra'tion
— tri'al
— trust
— trus·tee'
— use
— u·til'i·ty
— ves'sel
— ways
— wel'fare'
Pub'lic
— U·til'i·ty Hold'ing
Com'pa·ny Act
— Ves'sels Act
pub'li·can
pub'li·ca'tion
pub'li·ci' ju'ris
pub'li·cist
pub·lic'i·ty
pub'lic·ly
pub'lish
pub'lish·er
pu·dic'i·ty
pueb'lo
pu'er·il'i·ty
puff'er
puff'ing
pu'gi·list
puis
— dar·rein' con·tin'u·
ance
puis'ne
pull'ing
pul'mo·nar'y
pul'sa'tor
punc'tu·a'tion
punc'tum tem'po·ris
pun'dit
pun'ish·a·ble
pun'ish·ment
cru'el and un·u'su·al —
cu'mu·la·tive —
in'fa·mous —
pu'ni·tive
— dam'ag·es
— pow'er
— stat'ute
pu'ni·to'ry
pu'pil
pur
— au'tre vie
— cause de vi·ci·nage'

pur'chase
— a·gree'ment
— meth'od of ac·count'-
ing
— mon'ey
— or'der
— price
qua·si' —
words of —
pur'chase-mon'ey
— mort'gage
— re·sult'ing trust
— se·cur'i·ty in'ter·est
pur'chas·er
bo'na fide —
first —
— for val'ue
in'no·cent —
— of a note *or* bill
pure
— ac'ci·dent
— race stat'ute
pur·ga'tion
purge
purg'ing con·tempt'
pur'lieu
pur·loin'
pur'part
pur'par·ty
pur'port' *n.*
pur·port' *v.*
pur'pose
pur'pose·ly
pur·pres'ture
pur·prise'
purse
purs'er
pur·su'ant
pur·sue'
pur·su'er
pur·suit'
— of hap'pi·ness
pur tant que
pu'rus id'i·o'ta
pur·vey'ance
pur·vey'or
pur'view
push mon'ey
push'er
put
— in

— off
pu'ta·tive
— fa'ther
— mar'riage
— spouse
puts and calls
put'ting in fear
pyr'a·mid·ing
pyr'a·mid sales scheme
py'ro·ma'ni·a
Pyx, trial of the

Q

qua
quack
quack'er·y
quad'ran·gle
quad'rant
quad·ren'ni·um
quad'ri·par'tite'
quad'ri·par·ti'tus
quad'ri·ple'gi·a
quad'ri·ple'gic
quad·roon'
quad'rum·vi·rate
quad·ru'plet
quad·ru'pli·ca'tion
quae
— co'ram no'bis re·si'-
dant
— est e·a'dem
— ni'hil frus'tra
quae're'
quae'rens'
— ni'hil cap'i·at per bil'-
lam
— non in·ve'nit ple'gi·
um
quaes'ti·o'
ca'dit —
— vex·a'ta
quaes'tus
Quak'er
qual'i·fi·ca'tion
qual'i·fied'
— ac·cep'tance
— e·lec'tor
— en·dorse'ment

— es·tate'
— fee
— pen'sions
— priv'i·lege
— prop'er·ty
— vot'er
qual'i·fy'
qual'i·ty
— of es·tate'
quam·di'u'
— se be'ne ges'se·rit
quan'do' ac·cid'er·int
quan'ti' mi·no'ris
quan'ti·ty
quan'tum
— dam·nif'i·ca'tus
— mer'u·it
— va·le'bant
quar'an·tine'
qua're'
— clau'sum fre'git
— e'je·cit in'fra ter'mi·
    num
— im'pe·dit
— in'cum·bra'vit
— in·tru'sit
— non per·mit'tit
— ob·strux'it
quar'en·te'na ter'rae'
quar'rel
quar'ry
quart
quar'ter
— day
— ea'gle
— seal
— sec'tion
— ses'sion
— session courts
quar'ter·ing
— of sol'diers
quar'ter·i·za'tion
quar'ter·ly
— courts
quar'ters of cov'er·age
quar'to di'e post
quash
qua'si
— ad·mis'sion
— con·trac'tus
— de·lict'

— es·top'pel
— ex con·trac'tu
— in rem
— ju·di'cial
— post'hu'mous child
qua'si-char'i·ta·ble
qua'si-leg'is·la'tive
qua'si-pub'lic
qua'si-tra·di'ti·o
quat'er cous'in
qua'tu·or pe'di·bus
  cur'rit
quay
quay'age
queen reg'nant
queen's
— bench
— coun'sel
— ev'i·dence
— pris'on
— proc'tor
que es·tate'
que est le mesme
que·re'la
quer'u·lous
ques'ta
ques'tion
  cat'e·gor'i·cal —
  fed'er·al —
  hy'po·thet'i·cal —
  ju·di'cial —
  lead'ing —
  po·lit'i·cal —
ques'tus est no'bis
qui'a
— emp·to'res'
— ti'met
quib'ble
quick
— as'set' ra'tio
— as'sets'
— child
— with child
quick'en·ing
quick'lime'
quick'sil'ver
quid pro quo
qui·es'cence
qui·es'cent
qui'et v.
qui'et adj.

— en·joy'ment
— ti'tle ac'tion
qui·e'ta non mo·ve're'
qui·e'ta·re'
qui·e'tus
quin'troon'
quin·tu'plet
quis'ling
quit
  no'tice to —
qui tam
quit'claim'
— deed
quit'rent'
quit'tance
quo'ad hoc
quo an'i·mo'
quod
— com'pu·tet
— cum
— no'ta
— par'tes' re·pla'ci·tent
— par·ti'ti·o fi'at
— re·cu'per·et
— vi'de'
quo'rum
quo'ta
quo·ta'tion
quo·tid'i·an
quo'tient ver'dict
quo war·ran'to'

R

rab·bin'i·cal di·vorce'
rab'id
ra'bies
race
—re·cord'ing stat'ute
race'-no'tice re·cord'-
  ing stat'utes
ra'cial
ra'cial·ly mo'ti·vat'ed
ra'cism
ra'cist
rack
rack'et
rack'et·eer'
rack'et·eer'ing

rack'-rent'
ra'dar
ra'di·al
ra'di·a'tion
rad'i·cals
ra'di·ol'o·gy
ra'di·us
raf'fle
raft'age
raid
raid'er
rail'age
rail'head'
rail'road'
rail'side'
rail'-wa'ter
rail'way'
Rail'way' La'bor Act
raise
— a pre·sump'tion
— an is'sue
— rev'e·nue
raised check
rais'ing
— a prom'ise
— a use
— por'tions
rake'-off'
ram'i·fy'
ram'i·fi·ca'tion
ramp
ran'cel·man
ran·cid'i·ty
ran'cor
ran'cor·ous
ran'dom
range
rang'er
rank
rank'ing of cred'i·tors
ran'sack'
ran'som
— bill
rap
rape
stat'u·to'ry —
rap'ine
rap'ist
rap·port' à suc·ces'sion
rap·proche·ment'
rar'e·fied'

rase
ra'sure
rat'a·ble
— es·tate'
— prop'er·ty
ratch'et
one'-way' —
rate
class —
com·mod'i·ty —
dis'count' —
le'gal —
— of ex·change'
— of in'ter·est
— of re·turn'
prime —
— tar'iff
rat'i·fi·ca'tion
rat'i·fy'
rat'ing
cred'it —
ra'tio
— de·ci·den'di'
— le'gis
ra'tion·al
— ba'sis test
— doubt
— pur'pose test
ra'tion·ale'
ra'ti·o·nal'i·bus de·vi'sis
ra'tion·al·i·za'tion
ra'ti·o'ne
— dom'i·cil'i·i'
— im'po·ten'ti·ae'
— ma·te'ri·ae'
— per·so'nae'
— priv'i·le'gi·i'
— re'i si'tae'
— so'li'
— ten'u·rae'
rat'ten·ing
ra·vine'
rav'ish
rav'ished
rav'ish·er
rev'ish·ment
raw
— land
— ma·te'ri·als
raze
re

reach
— and ap·ply'
reach'a·ble
re'acq·uired' stock
re'ac·qui·si'tion
re·ac'tion
re·ac'tion·ar'y
read'ers
read'i·ly
re'ad·journ'
re'ad·just'ment
re'ad·mit'tance
read'y and will'ing
re'af·firm'
re'af·fir·ma'tion
re'af·for'est·ed
re'al
— chy'min
— ev'i·dence
— in'ju·ry
— law
— things
re'al es·tate'
— bro'ker
— in·vest'ment trust
— syn'di·cate
Re'al Es'tate' Set'tle·ment Pro·ce'dures Act
re·al'i·ty
re'al·ize'
re'al·ized' gain or loss
re'al·lege'
re'al·lo·cate'
re'al·lot'
realm
re'al·tor
re'al·ty
re'ap·ply'
re'ap·por'tion·ment
re'ap·prais'er
re'ap·pre·hend'
rear
re·ar'gu·ment
rea'son
rea'son·a·ble
— act
— and prob'a·ble cause
— be·lief'
— care
— crea'ture

— doubt
— force
— ground
— in'fer·ence rule
— man doc'trine *or*
    stan'dard
— no'tice
— part
— rule of cer'tain·ty
— sus·pi'cion
— time
— use the'o·ry
re'as·sert'
re'as·sess'ment
re'as·sign'
re'as·sur'ance
re'at·tach'ment
re'bate'
reb'el *n.*
re·bel' *v.*
re·bel'lion
re·bel'lious as·sem'bly
re·build'
re'bus sic stan'ti·bus
re·but'
— an eq'ui·ty
re·but'ta·ble pre·sump'-
    tion
re·but'tal
re·but'ter
re·but'ting ev'i·dence
re·cal'ci·trant
re·call'
— a judg'ment
re·call'ment
re·cant'
re·cap'i·tal·i·za'tion
re·cap'tion
re·cap'ture
— clause
— of de·pre'ci·a'tion
re·ceipt'
re·ceipt'or
re·ceiv'a·ble
re·ceive'
re·ceiv'er
— pen·den'le li'te
re·ceiv'er's cer·tif'i·cate
re·ceiv'er·ship'
re·ceiv'ing sto'len
    goods *or* prop'er·ty

re'cent·ly
re·cep'tion
re·cep'tor
re·cess'
re·ces'sion
Recht
re·cid'i·vism
re·cid'i·vist
re·cip'ro·cal
— con'tract'
— laws
— or in'ter·in·sur'ance
    ex·change'
— prom'is·es
— trade a·gree'ments
— trusts
— wills
Re·cip'ro·cal En·force'-
    ment of Sup·port' Act
re·cip'ro·cate'
rec'i·proc'i·ty
re·cit'al
re·cite'
reck
reck'less
— dis're·gard' of rights
    of oth'ers
— driv'ing
— hom'i·cide'
— mis·con'duct
reck'less·ly
reck'less·ness
reck'on
reck'on·ing
re·claim'
re·claim'ant
rec'la·ma'tion
— dis'trict
Rec'la·ma'tion
— Act
— Bu'reau
re·clu'sion
re'cod·i·fi·ca'tion
re'cod'i·fy'
rec'og·ni'tion
re·cog'ni·tors
re·cog'ni·zance
rec'og·nize
rec'og·nized'
— gain or loss
re·cog'ni·zee'

re·cog'ni·zor
rec'ol·lec'tion
re'com·mence'
rec'om·mend'
rec'om·men·da'tion
    let'ter of—
rec'om·men'da·to'ry
re'com·mit'
re'com·mit'ment
rec'om·pen'sa·ble
rec'om·pense'
— of re·cov'er·y in val'-
    ue
rec'on·cil'a·ble
rec'on·cile'
rec'on·cil'i·a'tion
— state'ment
re'con·duc'tion
re'con·firm'
re'con·fir·ma'tion
re'con·fis'cate'
re'con·fis·ca'tion
re'con·sid'er
re'con·sid'er·a'tion
re'con·sign'
re'con·sign'ment
re'con·struct'
re'con·struc'tion
re'con·tin'u·ance
re'con·trol'
re'con·ven'tion
re'con·ven'tion·al
    de·mand'
re'con·ver'sion
re'con·vey'ance
re'con·vict'
re'con·vic'tion
re·cord' *v.*
rec'ord *n.*
    ar·rest' —
— com·mis'sion
    courts of —
    crim'i·nal —
— date
    debts of —
    dim'i·nu'tion of —
    es·top'pel by —
    face of —
    ju·di'cial —
    leg'is·la'tive —
    mat'ter of —

— no'tice
nul ti'el —
— of ni'si' pri'us
— on ap·peal'
pub'lic —
ti'tle of —
tri'al by —
rec'or·da'tion
re·cord'er
re·cord'ing acts
re·cor'dum
re'-count'
re·coup' or re·coupe'
re·coup'ment
re'course'
— note
with —
with·out' —
re·cov'er
re·cov'er·a·ble
re·cov'er·ee'
re·cov'er·er
re·cov'er·y
com'mon —
fi'nal —
rec're·ant
re·crim'i·na'tion
re'cru·des'cence
re·cruit'
re·cruit'ing
rec'tal
rec'ti·fi·ca'tion
— of bound'a·ries
— of reg'is·ter
rec'ti·fi'er
rec'ti·fy'
rec'tor
rec'to·ry
rec'tum
— es'se
— ro·ga're
sta're ad —
rec'tus in cu'ri·a
re·cu'per·ate'
re·cu·pe·ra'ti·o'
re·cu'per·a'tion
re·cur'
re·cur'rence
re·cus'al
rec'u·sants
rec'u·sa'tion

re·cu'sa·tor
re·cuse'
red·den'dum
red·di'tion
re·deem'
re·deem'a·ble
— bond
— rights
— stock
re'de·liv'er·y
— bond
re'de·mise'
re·demp'tion
equity of —
— pe'ri·od
— price
tax —
the right of —
re'de·ter'mine
re'de·ter'mi·na'tion
red'-green' blind'ness
red'-hand'ed
red her'ring
red'hi·bi'tion
red·hib'i·to'ry
— ac'tion
— de'fect' or vice
re·dis'count'
— rate
re'dis·sei'sin
re·dis·tri·bu'tion
red'i·tus
— al'bi'
— as·sis'sus
— cap·i·ta'les'
— nig'ri'
— qui·e'ti'
— sic'cus
red lights a·head' doc'-
trine
red'lin'ing
red'out'
re'draft'
re·dress'
re·dress'er
re·dress'ment
red tape
re·dub'bers
re·duce'
re·duc'i·ble

re·duc'ti·o' ad ab·sur'-
dum
re·duc'tion
— of cap'i·tal
— to pos·ses'sion
— to prac'tice
re·dun'dan·cy
re'-e·lect'
re'-em·ploy'
re'-en·act'
re'-en·act'ment rule
re-en'try
re'-es·tab'lish
reeve
re'-ex·am'i·na'tion
re'-ex·change'
re'-ex·port'
re·fer'
ref'e·ree'
court of —
— in bank'rupt'cy
ref'er·ence
— in case of need
— stat'utes
ref'er·en'dum
re·fi'nance'
re·fine'ment
re·flex'ive
re·form'
ref'or·ma'tion
re·for'ma·to·ry
re·frac'tion
re·fresh'ing
— the mem'o·ry
— the rec'ol·lec'tion
ref'uge
re·fund' v.
re·fund' n.
— an·nu'i·ty con'tract'
— claim
re·fund'ing bond
re'funds'
re·fus'al
right of first —
re·fuse' v.
ref'use n.
re·fute'
ref'u·ta'tion
re·ga'lia
re·gard'
re'gen·cy

re′gent
re′gi·a vi′a
reg′i·cide′
re·gime′
re·gi′na
re′gion·al
reg′is·ter
  — in bank′rupt′cy
  — of deeds
  — of land of′fice
  — of pat′ents
  — of ships
  — of the treas′ur·y
  — of wills
reg′is·tered
  — bond
  — check
  — mail
  — rep′re·sen′ta·tive
  — ton′nage
  — trade′mark′
  — vot′ers
reg′is·ter's court
reg′is·trant
reg′is·trar′
reg′is·tra′tion
  — of stock
  — state′ment
reg′is·try
  — of deeds
reg′nal years
reg′nant
re·grant′
re·gress′
re·gres′sive
  — tax
reg′u·la
reg′u·la·ble
reg′u·lar
  — army
  — course of busi′ness
  — en′tries
  — on its face
  — rate
reg′u·lar′i·ty
reg′u·lar·ize′
reg′u·lar·ly
reg′u·lars
reg′u·late′
reg′u·la′tion
  — charge

— of an ex·ec′u·tive de·
  part′ment
Reg′u·la′tion
  — A
  — Z
re·gur′gi·tate′
re′ha·bil′i·tate′
  — a wit′ness
re′ha·bil′i·ta′tion
re′ha·bil′i·ta′tor
re′ha·bil·i·tee′
re·hear′ing
re′hy·poth′e·ca′tion
reif
re′i′ in·ter·ven′tus
re·im·burse′
re·in·cor′po·rate′
re·in·cor′po·ra′tion
re·in·state′
  — a case
re·in·state′ment
re·in·sur′ance
re·in·sured′
re·in·sur′er
re·in·te·gra′tion
re·in·vest′
re·in·ves′ti·ture
re·in·vest′ment
re·is′sue
re·is′su·a·ble notes
re·ject′
re·jec′tion
re·join′
re·join′der
re·join′ing grat′is
re·lapse′ *v.*
re′lapse *n.*
re·late′
re·lat′ed
  — claim
  — par′ty trans·ac′tions
re·la′tion
  — back
re·la′tions
re·la′tion·ship′
rel′a·tive *adj.*
  — con·fes′sion
  — con·ven′ience doc′-
    trine
  — fact
  — pow′ers

  — rights
re·la′tor
re·la′trix
re·lax′ant
re·lax·a′re
re·lax·a′ti·o′
re·lease′ *v.*
re·lease′ *n.*
  — by op′er·a′tion of law
  — by way of en·larg′ing
    an es′tate′
  — by way of en′try and
    feoff′ment
  — by way of ex·tin′-
    guish·ment
  — by way of pass′ing an
    es·tate′
  — by way of passing a
    right
con·di′tion·al —
deed of —
ex·press′ —
im·plied′ —
  — of dow′er
  — of mort′gage
  — to us′es
re-lease′
re·leas′ee′
re·leas′er *or* re·lea′sor
rel′e·gate′
rel′e·ga′tion
rel′e·van·cy
rel′e·vant
  — ev′i·dence
  — mar′ket
re·li′a·ble
re·li′ance
  — dam′ag·es
  — on prom′ise
rel′ict
re·lic′tion
re·lief′
re·lieve′
re·lig′ion
re·lig′ious
  — cor′po·ra′tion
  — free′dom
  — lib′er·ty
  — use
re·lin′quish
re·lin′quish·ment

re·lo′cate′
re′lo·ca′tion
re·ly′
re·main′der
  char′i·ta·ble —
  con·tin′gent —
  cross —
  ex′e·cut′ed —
  ex·ec′u·to′ry —
  vest′ed —
  — vested sub′ject to be′-
    ing di·vest′ed
re·main′der·man
re·mand′
re·mar′gin·ing
re·mar′riage
re·mar′ry
re·me′di·al
  — ac′tion
  — stat′ute
rem′e·dies
  join′der of —
rem′e·di·less
rem′e·dy
  civ′il —
  cu′mu·la′tive —
  eq′ui·ta·ble —
  ex·traor′di·nar′y —
  le′gal —
  — over
re·mise′
re·miss′
re·mis′sion
re·miss′ness
re·mit′
re·mit′ment
re·mit′tance
re·mit·tee′
re·mit′ter
re·mit′ting bank
re·mit′tit dam′na
re·mit′ti·tur′
  — dam′na
  — of rec′ord
re·mit′tor
rem′nant rule
re·mod′el
re·mon′e·ti·za′tion
re·mon′strance
re·mote′
  — cause

  — dam′age
  — pos′si·bil′i·ty
re·mote′ness
  — of ev′i·dence
re·mov′al
  — bond
  — from of′fice
  — of caus′es
  or′der of —
  — to a·void′ tax
  — with·out′ prop′er
    cause
re·mov′er
re·mov′ing cloud from
  ti′tle
re·mu′ner·a′tion
ren·coun′ter
ren′der
  — an ac·count′
  — judg′ment
  — ver′dict
ren′dez·vous′
ren·di′tion
  — of judg′ment
  — of ver′dict
ren′e·gade′
re′ne·go′ti·a·ble
re′ne·go′ti·a′tion
Re′ne·go′ti·a′tion
  — Act
  — Board
re·new′
re·new′al
  — of note
re·nounce′
re′no·va′re
rent
  — charge
  — con·trol′
  fee farm —
  — roll
  — seck
  — serv′ice
  — strike
rent′age
rent′al
  — val′ue
rent′-roll′
rents
  — is′sues, and prof′its
  — of as·size′

  — res′o·lute′
re·nun′ci·a′tion
ren·voi′
re′o ab·sen′te
re·o′pen·ing a case
re·or′gan·i·za′tion
  tax free —
  Type A, B, or C —
re·pair′
re·pairs′
  ex·traor′di·nar′y —
rep′a·ra′tion
re·pa′tri·a′tion
re·pay′
re·peal′
re·peat′ers
rep′e·ti′tion
re·place′
re·place′ment in·sur′-
  ance
re·plead′
re·plead′er
re·pledge′
re′pleg·i·a′re
re·plev′i·a·ble or re·
  plev′i·sa·ble
re·plev′in
  — bond
  per′son·al —
re·plev′i·sor
re·plev′y
re·pli′ant or rep′li·cant
rep′li·cate′
rep′li·ca′tion
re·ply′
re·port′
  — of leg′is·la′tive com·
    mit′tee
re·port′er
re·po·si′tion
re·pos·ses′sion
rep′re·sent′
rep′re·sen·ta′tion
  es·top′pel by —
  false —
  ma·te′ri·al —
  — of per′sons
  prom′is·so′ry —
rep′re·sen·ta·tive
  per′son·al —
rep′re·sen·tee′

rep're·sen'tor
re·prieve'
rep'ri·mand'
re·pri'sals
  gen'er·al —
  neg'a·tive —
  pos'i·tive —
  spe'cial —
re·pris'es
rep'ro·bate'
rep'ro·ba'tion
re'pro·duce'
re'pro·duc'tion
re·pub'lic
re·pub'li·can
re'pub'li·ca'tion
re·pub'lish
re·pu'di·ate'
re·pu'di·a'tion
re·pu'di·a'tor
re·pug'nan·cy
re·pug'nant
re·pur'chase
rep'u·ta·ble
  — cit'i·zen
rep'u·ta'tion
re·pute'
  ill —
re·put'ed
  — own'er
re·quest'
  — for ad·mis'sions
  — for in·struc'tions
re·quire'
re·quire'ment con'-
  tract'
req'ui·si'tion
re·quit'al
res
  — der·e·lic'ta
  — ges'tae'
  — in'te·gra
  — in'ter a'li·os ac'ta
  — ip'sa lo'qui·tur'
  — ju'di·ca'ta
  — no'va
  — nul'li·us
  — per'i·it do'mi·no'
  — pub'li·cae'
  — quo·tid'i·a'nae'
  — re·lig'i·o'sae'

re·sal'a·ble
re'sale'
  — price main'te·nance
re·scind'
re·scis'sion of con'-
  tract'
re·script'
  — o·pin'ion
res'cue
  — doc'trine
re·scyt'
res'er·va'tion
  — of claim
re·serve' *v.*
re·serve' *n.*
  bad debt —
  con·tin'gen·cy —
  de·ple'tion —
  de·pre'ci·a'tion —
  le'gal —
  re·place'ment —
  sink'ing fund —
re·served' land
re·set'
re·set'tle·ment
res'i·ance
res'i·ant
re·side'
res'i·dence
  le'gal —
res'i·den·cy re·quire'-
  ments
res'i·dent
  — a'gent
  — a'li·en
  — free'hold'er
res'i·den'tial
  — clus'ter
  — den'si·ty
re·sid'u·al
re·sid'u·ar'y
  — be·quest'
  — clause
  — de·vise' and de·vi'see'
  — es·tate'
  — gift
  — leg'a·cy
  — leg'a·tee'
res'i·due'
re·sid'u·um
  — rule

res'ig·na'tion
re·sign·ee'
re·sil'ien·cy
re·sist'
re·sis'tance
re·sist'ing an of'fi·cer
res'o·lu'tion
  con·cur'rent —
  joint —
re·sol'u·to'ry con·di'-
  tion
re·sort'
re·sourc'es
re·spec'tive
re·spec'tive·ly
res'pite
  — of ap·peal'
  — of hom'age
re·spond'
re·spon'de·at
  — oust'er
  — su·pe'ri·or
re·spon'dent
re'spon·den'ti·a
re·spon'si·bil'i·ty
  — of e·vic'tion
re·spon'si·ble
  — bid'der
  — cause
  — gov'ern·ment
re·spon'sive
  — plead'ing
res·sei'ser
rest
Re·state'ment of Law
res'tau·rant
res'ti·tu'tion
  — of con·ju·gal rights
  writ of —
re·stor'a·tive
re·store'
re·strain'
re·strain'ing
  — or'der
  — pow'ers
re·straint'
  — of mar'riage
  — of trade
  — on al'ien·a'tion
re·strict'
re·strict'ed

re·stric'tion
re·stric'tive
— cov'e·nant
— en·dorse'ment
rests
re·sult'
re·sult'ing
— pow'er
— trust
— use
re·sum'mons
re·sump'tion
re·sur·ren'der
re'tail'
— in·stall'ment ac·count'
— installment con'tract'
— sale
re'tail'er
re·tain'
re·tained' earn'ings
re·tain'er
right to —
— pay
re·tain'ing
— fee
— lien
re·tak'ing
re·tal'i·a'tion
re·tal'i·a·to'ry
— e·vic'tion
— law
re·tar'date'
re'tar·da'tion
re·ten'tion
re·tire'
re·tire'ment an·nu'i·ty
re·tor'sion
re·tract'
re'trac·ta'tion
re·trax'it
re·treat' n.
re·treat' v.
— to the wall
re·tri'al
ret'ri·bu'tion
re·trib'u·tive
ret'ro'
ret'ro·ac'tive
— in'ter·fer'ence
— law
— stat'ute

ret'ro·ces'sion
ret'ro·spec'tive
rette
re·try'
re·turn'
— book
fair —
false —
— of proc'ess'
— of pre'mi·um
— of serv'ice
re·turn'a·ble
re·turn' day
gen'er·al —
re·un'ion
re'u·nite'
re'us
re·val'i·date'
re·val'or·ize'
re·val'u·a'tion
reve
rev'el
re·ven'di·ca'tion
re·venge'
rev'e·nue
— bills
— bonds
— law or meas'ure
— stamps
Rev'e·nue
— Pro·ce'dure
— Rul'ing
rev'e·nues
land —
pub'lic —
re·ver'i·fy'
re·ver'i·fi·ca'tion
re·ver'sal
re·verse'
— dis·crim'i·na'tion
— stock split
re·vers'i·ble er'ror
re·ver'sion
re·ver'sion·ar'y
— in'ter·est
— lease
re·ver'sion·er
re·vert'
re·vert'er
re·vest'
re·view'

bill of —
re·view'a·ble
re·vin'di·cate'
re·vin'di·ca'tion
re·vise'
re·vised' stat'utes
re·vi'sion
re·vi'sor
re·viv'al
— of ac'tion
— of will
— stat'utes
re·vive'
re·vi'vor
bill of —
writ of —
rev'o·ca·ble
— cred'it
— let'ter of credit
— trans'fer
— trust
rev'o·ca'tion
— of pro'bate'
— of will
re·voke'
re·volt'
rev'o·lu'tion
rev'o·lu'tion·ar'y
re·volv'ing
— charge ac·count'
— cred'it
— fund
— let'ter of cred'it
— loan
re·ward'
rex
Rho'di·an Laws
ri·baud'
Rich'ard Roe
ric'tus
rid'er
— roll
ridge'ling or ridg'ling
rid'i·cule'
ri·en'
— culp
— dit
rig
rig'ging the mar'ket
right
— and wrong test

— of ac'tion
— of en'try
— of hab'i·ta'tion
— of lo'cal self'-gov'ern·ment
— of pos·ses'sion
— of pri'va·cy
— of prop'er·ty
— of re·demp'tion
— of rep'resen·ta'tion and per·form'ance
— of search
— of sur·vi'vor·ship'
— of way
— pat'ent
— to at·tor'ney
— to be·gin'
— to re·deem'
— to trav'el
right'eous
right'ful
— own'er
right'-hand'ed
rights
— of per'sons
— of things
pe·ti'tion of —
pri'vate —
vest'ed —
right'-to-work' laws
rig'or
— ju'ris
— mor'tis
rig'or·ous
ring
ring'ing
— the change'es
— up
ri'ot
in·cite'ment to —
ri'ot·er
ri'ot·ous as·sem'bly
ri'ot·ous·ly
ri'pa
ri·pa'ri·a
ri·par'i·an
— na'tions
— own'er
— pro·pri'e·tor
— rights
— wa'ter

ripe for judg'ment
ripe'ness doc'trine
ris'ing of court
risk
as·sump'tion of —
— cap'i·tal
— in'ci·dent to em·ploy'ment
ob'vi·ous —
— of nav'i·ga'tion
or'di·nar'y —
per·ceiv'a·ble —
— pre'mi·um
rite
riv'er
road
— dis'tricts
road'bed'
road'stead'
road'way'
rob
rob'ber
rob'ber·y
ag'gra·vat'ed —
robes
Rob'in·son-Pat'man Act
rod
ro·ga're
ro·ga'ti·o'
ro'ga·to'ry let'ters
rogue
rogu'er·y
roll n.
as·sess'ment —
judg'ment —
tax —
roll v.
rolled'-up'
roll'ing
— o'ver
— stock
— stock pro·tec'tion act
roll'-o'ver pa'per
rolls
mas'ter of the —
ob'late' —
— of par'lia·ment
— of the Ex'cheq'uer
— of the Tem'ple

— of'fice of the Chan'cer·y
Ro'man Cath'o·lic
— Church
Ro'man law
rood of land
room'er
root
— of de·scent'
— of ti'tle
Ror'schach' test
ros'ter
ro'ta
ro'tate'
rot'ten clause
rou·lette'
round
— lot
— rob'in
rout
route
rou'tous'ly
roy
roy'al
— as·sent'
— pre·rog'a·tive
roy'al·ties
roy'al·ty
— a'cres
— bo'nus
ru·bel'la
rub'ber check
ru'bric
rude'ness
rule v.
rule n.
—ab'so·lute'
— a·gainst' per'pe·tu'i·ties
— day
— dis·charged'
— in Shel'ley's Case
— ni'si'
— of ap·por'tion·ment
— of four
— of Kent
— of law
— of len'i·ty
— of ne·ces'si·ty
— of pre·sump'tion
— of prop'er·ty

— of rea′son
— of 1756
— of 78
— of the road
special —
— to plead
— to show cause
rules
  cross —
  — of course
  — of court
  — of nav′i·ga′tion
  — of prac′tice
  — of pro·ce′dure
rul′ing
rum′mage
rum′mag·er
ru′mor
rum′run′ning
run
run′a·way′ shop
run′ner
run′ning
  — ac·count′
  — at large
  — days
  — pol′i·cy
  — with the land
  — with the re·ver′sion
run′-off′
rup′ture
ruse de guerre
rus′ti·cum fo′rum
rus′tler
Ry′lands v. Fletch′er
  case

S

Sab′bath
Sab′bath-break′ing
sab·bat′i·cal
sab′o·tage′
sab′o·teur′
sac·cade′
sac·cad′ic
sac′cha·rin
sac′cus
sac′ra·men′tum

sa′cred
sac′ri·fice′
sac′ri·lege
sa′dism
sa′do·mas′o·chism
sa′do·mas′o·chist
sae·vi′ti·a
safe
  — lim′it of speed
  — place to work
safe′-con′duct
safe′crack′er
safe′-de·pos′it
  — box
  — com′pa·ny
safe′guard′
safe′keep′ing
safe′ty
Safe′ty Ap·pli′ance Act
sa′ga·man
sages de la ley
said
sail
sail′ing
  — in·struc′tions
sail′ors
sail′ors′ will
Sail′ors′ Re·lief′ Act
sake
sal′a·ble
  — val′ue
sa·la′cious
sal′a·ry
  fixed —
sale
  ab′so·lute′ —
  — a·gainst′ the box
  — and lease′back′
  — and re·turn′
  bill of —
  — by sam′ple
  cash —
  con·di′tion·al —
  con·sign′ment —
  ex·clu′sive —
  ex′e·cut′ed —
  ex′e·cu′tion —
  ex·ec′u·to′ry —
  fair —
  forced —
  fore·clo′sure —

fraud′u·lent —
gross —
  — in gross
in·stall′ment —
ju·di′cial —
mem′o·ran′dum —
net —
  — on ap·prov′al
  — on cred′it
  — or re·turn′
  — per a·ver′si·o′nem
pri′vate —
pub′ic —
re′tail′ in·stall′ment —
sher′iff′s —
tax —
vol′un·tar′y —
wash —
  — with all faults
  — with right of re·
    demp′tion
sales
  — a′gent
  — a·gree′ment
  — fi·nance′ com′pa·ny
  — in′voice′
  — tax
sales′man
Sa′lic Law
sa′line′
  — land
sa·loon′
sa·loon′keep′er
sa·lu′bri·ous
sal′us
sa·lute′
sal′vage
  — charg′es
  eq′ui·ta·ble —
  — loss
  — serv′ice
  — val′ue
salve
sal′vo
sal′vor
sal′vus ple′gi·us
Sa·mar′i·tan
same
  — ev′i·dence test
  — in·ven′tion
  — of·fense′

sam'ple
  sale by —
sam'pler
san'a·to'ri·um
sanc'tion
sanc'tu·ar'y
sand'bag'
sand'wich lease
sane
san'guine
san'i·tar'i·um
san'i·tar'y
  — code
san'i·ta'tion
san'i·ty
  — hear'ing
  — tri'al
sans
  — ce·o' que
  — frais
  — im·peach'ment de
    wast
  — jour
  — re·cours'
sap
sat'is·fac'tion
  ac·cord' and —
  con'tracts' to —
  — of judg'ment
  — of lien
  — of mort'gage
  — piece
sat'is·fac'to·ry
  — ev'i·dence
sat'is·fied' term
sat'is·fy'
saunke'fin'
sau'va·gine
save
  — harm'less clause
sav'er de·fault'
sav'ing
  — clause
  — to suit'ors clause
sav'ings
  — ac·count'
  — account trust
  — and loan as·so'ci·a'-
    tion
  — bank
  — bank trust

— bond
— notes
sa'vour
Sax'on lage
say a·bout'
scab
scab'rous
scaf'fold
scald
scale
  — or'der
  — tol'er·ance
scal'ing laws
scalp'er
scamp
scan'dal
scan'dal·ous mat'ter
scape'goat'
scar
scarp'er
scat'o·log'i·cal
scav'en·ger
sched'ule
sched'uled
  — in'ju·ries
  — prop'er·ty
scheme
schism
Schism Bill
schiz'o·phre'ni·a
schol'ar
schol'ar·ship'
school
  — board
  — com·mit'tee
  — di·rec'tors
  — dis'trict
  dis'trict —
  grade —
  high —
  — lands
  normal —
  pri'vate —
  — pur'pos·es
school'house'
school'mas'ter
school'room'
schools
  com'mon —
  pub'lic —
school'teach'er

sci·en'ter
scil'i·cet'
scin·til'la
  — ju'ris
  — of ev'i·dence
sci'on
sci're fa'ci·as
  — ad au'di·en'dum er·
    ro'res'
  — ad dis'pro·ban'dum
    deb'i·tum
  — ad re'ha·ben'dam ter'-
    ram
  — qua're res'ti·tu'ti·o'-
    nem non
  — sur mort'gage
  — sur mu·nic'i·pal claim
sci're fe'ci'
scite
scoff'law'
scold
scope
  — of a pat'ent
  — of au·thor'i·ty
  — of em·ploy'ment
sco'po·phil'i·ac'
score
scorn
scot
  — and lot
  — and lot vot'ers
scot'-free'
scoun'drel
scram'bling
  — pos·ses'sion
scratch'ing the tick'et
scrawl
scri'ba
scrip
  — div'i·dend'
script
scrip'tum
scriv'en·er
  mon'ey —
scroll
scru'ple
scru'pu·lous
scru'ti·nize'
scru'ti·ny
  strict —
scur·ril'i·ty

scur′ri·lous
sea
— brief
— laws
— let′ter
main —
— rov′ers
sea′bed′
seal
com′mon —
cor′po·rate —
— days
great —
— of′fice
— pa′per
pri′vate —
priv′y —
pub′lic —
quar′ter —
sealed
— and de·liv′ered
— bid
— in′stru·ment
— ver′dict
seal′ing
— of rec′ords
— up
seals
sea′men
sé′ance′
search
— and sei′zure
— in′ci·dent to ar·rest′
un·law′ful —
un·rea′son·a·ble —
— war′rant
search′er
sea′-reeve′
seas
high —
sea′shore′
sea′son·al
— em·ploy′ment
seat′ed land
seat of gov′ern·ment
sea′ward
sea′wor·thi·ness
sea′wor′thy
se·bas′to·ma′ni·a
se·cede′
se·ces′sion

seck
se·clude′
se·clu′sion
sec′ond
— lien
— mort′gage
sec′ond·ar′y n.
sec′ond·ar′y adj.
— boy′cott′
— dis′tri·bu′tion
— ease′ment
— ev′i·dence
— li′a·bil′i·ty
— mean′ing
— of′fer·ing
— par′ties
— pick′et·ing
sec′ond-de·gree′
— crime
— mur′der
sec′ond-hand′
— ev′i·dence
sec′onds
se′cre·cy
se′cret
— lien
— serv′ice
sec′re·tar′y
— gen′er·al
— of em·bas·sy
— of le·ga′tion
— of state
se·crete′
se′crets of state
sect
sec′ta
sec·tar′i·an
sec′tion
— of land
sec′u·lar
— busi′ness
sec′u·lar·ism
se·cun′dum
— ae′qu·um et bo′num
— al′le·ga′ta et pro·ba′ta
— ar′tem
— bo′nos mo′res′
— for′man char′tae′
— formam do′ni′
— formam sta·tu′ti′
— le′gem com·mu′nem

— nor′mam le′gis
— reg′u·lam
— sub·jec′tam ma·te′ri·am
se·cure′
se·cured′
— cred′i·tor
— loan
— par′ty
— trans·ac′tion
se·cu′ri·ties
— bro′ker
mar′shal·ing —
— of′fer·ing
pub′lic —
treas′ur·y —
Se·cu′ri·ties
— Act of 1933
— and Ex·change′ Com·mis′sion
— Ex·change′ Act of 1934
— In·ves′tor Pro·tec′tion Act
se·cu′ri·ty
— a·gree′ment
as·sess′a·ble —
col·lat′er·al —
con·vert′i·ble —
— coun′cil
coun′ter —
— de·pos′it
eq′ui·ty —
ex·empt′ed —
— for costs
— for good be·hav′ior
— fund
gov′ern·ment —
hy′brid —
— in′ter·est
list′ed —
mar′ket·a·ble —
non·mar′ket·a·ble —
out·stand′ing —
per′son·al —
real —
re·deem′a·ble —
un·list′ed —
vot′ing —
se′cus
sed′a·tive

se·da'to' an'i·mo'
sed'en·tar'y
sedge flat
sed'i·men·ta'tion
se·di'tion
se·di'tious
— li'bel
— speech
sed
— per cu'ri·am
— quae're'
— vi'de'
se·duce'
se·duc'tion
see
seen
seep'age
seg're·ga'tion
seign'ior
seign'ior·age
seign'ior·ess
seign'ior·y
sei'si'
sei'sin or sei'zin
ac'tu·al —
con·struc'tive —
cov'e·nant of —
eq'ui·ta·ble —
— in deed
— in fact
— in law
liv'er·y of —
prim'er —
qua'si' —
sei·si'na
seize
seized or seised
seiz'ing of her'i·ots
sei'zure
se·lect'
— coun'cil
se·lect'men
self'-ac'cu·sa'tion
self'-con'tra·dic'to·ry
self'-deal'ing
self'-de·fense'
self'-de·struc'tion
self'-em·ploy'ment tax
self'-ev'i·dent
self'-ex'e·cut'ing
self'-help'

self'-i·den'ti·fi·ca'tion
self'-in·crim'i·na'tion
self'-in·flict'ed
self'-in·sur'ance
self'-in·sur'er
self'-liq'ui·dat'ing
self'-serv'ing dec'la·ra'-
  tion
sell
sell'er
sell'ing stocks short
sem·ble'
sem'i·an'nu·al
sem'i·com'a·tose'
sem'i·con'scious
sem'i·ju·di'cial
sem'i·le'gal
sem'i·month'ly
sem'i·nal
sem'i·nar'y
sem'i·na'tion
sem'i·of·fi'cial
sem'i·pri'vate
sem'i·pub'lic
sem'i·skilled'
sem'i·week'ly
sem'per pa·ra'tus
sen'age
sen'ate
sen'a·tor
send
se·nes'cence
se'nile' de·men'ti·a
se·nil'i·ty
sen'ior
— coun'sel
— in'ter·est
— judge
— lien
— mort'gage
sen·ior'i·ty
sen'si·ble
sen'so·ry
sen'su·al
sen'sus
sen'tence
con·cur'rent —
con·sec'u·tive —
de·ferred' —
de·ter'mi·nate —
fi'nal —

fixed —
im'po·si'tion of —
— in ab·sten'ti·a
in'de·ter'mi·nate —
in'ter·loc'u·to'ry —
life —
man'da·to'ry —
max'i·mum —
min'i·mum —
pre·sump'tive —
split —
straight or flat —
sus·pen'sion of —
with·held' —
sen'ten·ces
cu'mu·la'tive —
merg'er of —
— to run con·cur'rent·ly
sen'tenc·ing
— coun'cil
— stat'utes
sen·ten'ti·a
sen'ti·nel
sen'try
sep'a·ra·ble
sep'a·rate' v.
sep'a·rate adj.
— ac'tion
— but e'qual doc'trine
— con'tro·ver·sy
— de·mise' in e·ject'-
  ment
— es·tate'
— ex·am'i·na'tion
— main'te·nance
— of·fens'es
— prop'er·ty
— re·turn'
— tri'al
sep'a·ra'tion
— a·gree'ment
— a men'sa et tho'ro'
— from bed and board
— of ju'ry
— of pat'ri·mo'ny
— of pow'ers
— of spous'es
— of wit'ness·es
— or'der
sep'a·ra·tists
sep'tum

sep′ul·cher
se·quel′a
se·quel′ae′
se′quels
se·ques′ter
se·ques′tered ac·count′
se′ques·tra′tion
se′ques·tra′tor
serf
ser′geant or ser′jeant
— at arms
— at law
se′ri·al
— bonds
— note
— right
se′ri·ate′ly
se′ri·a′tim
se′ries
se′ri·ous
— and will′ful mis·con-
   duct
— crime
— ill′ness
ser′jeant·y
ser′ment
se′ro·log′i·cal test
ser′rat′ed
ser′vant
serve
serv′ice
— by pub′li·ca′tion
— charge
civ′il —
con·struc′tive —
— con′tract′
— es·tab′lish·ment
— life
— mark
— oc′cu·pa′tion tax
— of proc′ess
per′son·al —
proof of —
sal′vage —
sub′sti·tut′ed —
serv′ice·a·ble
ser′vi·ent
— ten′e·ment
ser′vil′i·ty
ser·vi′ti·um
ser′vi·tude′

eq′ui·ta·ble —
in·vol′un·tar′y —
pe′nal —
ser′vi·tus
ser′vus
sess
ses′si·o′
ses′sion
bi·en′ni·al —
joint —
— laws
reg′u·lar —
ses′sions
quar′ter —
spe′cial —
set n.
— of ex·change′
set v.
— a·side′
— down
— out
— up
set′back′
set′off′
set′tle
— up
set′tle·ment
eq′ui·ty of —
fam′i·ly —
fi′nal —
— op′tion
— state′ment
vol′un·tar′y —
set′tler
set′tlor
sev′er
sev′er·a·bil′i·ty
— clause
— doc′trine
sev′er·a·ble
— con′tract′
— stat′ute
sev′er·al
— ac′tions
— in·her′i·tance
— li′a·bil′i·ty
sev′er·al·ly
sev′er·al·ty
es·tate′ in —
sev′er·ance
— dam′age

— of ac′tions
— pay
— tax
se·vere′
se·ver′i·ty
sew′age
se′ward or sea′ward
sew′er
sex
sex′u·al
— in′ter·course′
shaft
shake′down′
shall
sham
— plead′ing
shape′up′
share v.
— and share a·like′
share n.
— cer·tif′i·cate
— of cor′po·rate stock
share′crop′per
share′crop′ping
share′hold′er
share′own′er
share′-rent′er
share′-ten′ant
share′-war′rant to
   bear′er
shark
sharp
shave
sheep
sheep′skin′
Shel′ley′s Case
shel′ter
sher′iff
dep′u·ty —
high —
pock′et —
sher′iff′s
— court
— court in Lon′don
— deed
— ju′ry
— sale
sher′iff·wick′
Sher′man An′ti·trust′
   Act
shield laws

shift'ing
— clause
— in'come'
— risk
— sev'er·al·ty
— stock of mer'chan·
dise'
— the bur'den of proof
— use
shil'ling
ship v.
ship n.
— bro'ker
— chan'dler·y
— chan'nel
gen'er·al —
— mas'ter
— mon'ey
ship'ment
Ship Mort'gage Act
ship'per
ship'ping
— ar'ti·cles
— doc'u·ment
— or'der
— pa'pers
ship's
— bill
— com'pa·ny
— hus'band
— pa'pers
ship'wreck'
shire
shock
shoot
shop
— right
— stew'ard
shop'book' rule
shop'books'
shop'keep'er
shop'lift'ing
shore
— lands
short
— cov'er·ing
— in'ter·est
— lease
— no'tice
— po·si'tion
— sale

— sum'mons
short'change'
short'ly af'ter
short'-swing' prof'its
short'-term'
— debt
— pa'per
— se·cu'ri·ty
shot
should
show n.
show v.
— cause
show'er
show'up'
shrub
shut down
shut'-in' roy'al·ty
shy'ster
sic
sick
sick'ness
side
— lines
— re·ports'
side'-bar' rules
side'walk'
sight
— draft
sign
sig'nal
sig'na·to'ry
sig'na·ture
— card
un·au'thor·ized' —
signed
sig'net
sig'ni·fi·ca'tion
sig'ni·fy'
si i'ta est
si'lence
es·top'pel by —
— of ac·cused'
si'lent part'ner
silk
sil'ver
— cer·tif'i·cates
— plat'ter doc'trine
sim'i·lar
— hap'pen·ings
— sales

si·mil'i·ter
si'mo·ny
sim'ple
— kid'nap'ping
— neg'li·gence
— rob'ber·y
sim'plex'
sim·plic'i·ter
si'mul cum
sim'u·late'
sim'u·lat'ed
— con'tract'
— fact
— judg'ment
— sale
sim'u·la'tion
si'mul·ta·ne·ous
— death clause
Si'mul·ta·ne·ous Death
Act
since
si'ne'
— di'e'
— hoc quod
— nu'me·ro'
— pro'le
— qua non
si'ne·cure'
sin'gle
— cred'i·tor
— ju'ror charge
— pub'li·ca'tion rule
sin'gu·lar
sink'ing fund
— de·ben'ture
— meth'od of de·pre'ci·
a'tion
si pri'us
sis'ter
— cor'po·ra'tion
sis'ter-in-law'
sit
sit'-down' strike
site
sit'ting
sit'tings
— in bank or en banc
— in cam'er·a
sit'u·ate'
sit'u·a'tion
— of dan'ger

si'tus
six'-day' li'cense
six'ty-day' no'tice
skel'e·ton bill
skid
skill
skilled wit'ness·es
skill'ful
skip'trac'ing
slack'er
slains
  let'ter of —
slan'der
  — of ti'tle
slan'der·er
slan'der·ous per se
slate
slave
slav'er·y
slave trade
slay
sledge
slice
slick
slid'ing scale
slight
slip
  — law
  — law print
  — o·pin'ion
slip'per·y slope
slope
slot ma·chine'
slough
slow'down'
sluice'way'
slum
slum'lord'
slur
slush fund
small
  — busi'ness cor'po·ra'-
    tion
  — claims courts
  — es·tate' pro'bate'
  — loan acts
Small Busi'ness
  — Ad·min'is·tra'tion
  — In·vest'ment Act
smart mon'ey
smear

smelt'ing
Smith Act
smug'gling
smut
snatch'er
sneak thief
snip'er
soak'age
so'ber
so·bri'e·ty
so'bri·quet'
soc'ag·er
so'-called'
so'cial
  — clubs
  — con'tract' or com'-
    pact'
  — guest
  — in·sur'ance
so'cial'ism
So'cial Se·cu'ri·ty
  — Act
  — Ad·min'is·tra'tion
so·ci·é·té'
  — an·o·nyme'
  — d'ac·quets'
  — en com'man·dite'
  — en nom col·lec'tif
  — en par·tic'i·pa'tion
  — par ac'tions'
so·ci'e·ty
so'ci·o·path'ic per'son·
  al'i·ty
sod'o·mite'
sod'o·my
soft'-core'
so help you God
soil
  — bank
soit
so'journ'ing
so'lar
  — day
  — month
so·la'ti·um
sold
  — note
sol'dier
Sol'diers' and Sail'ors'
  Civ'il Re·lief' Act
sol'dier's will

sole
  — ac'tor doc'trine
  — and un'con·di'tion·al
    own'er
  — cause
  — pro·pri'e·tor·ship'
sol'emn
so·lem'ni·ty
sol'em·nize'
so·lic'it
so·lic'i·ta'tion
  — of bribe
so·lic'i·tor
  — gen'er·al
sol'i·dar'i·ty
sol'i·dar'y
sol'i·dum
sol'i·tar'y con·fine'-
  ment
sol'ven·cy
sol'vent
sol'vit
  — ad di'em
  — an'te di'em
  — post diem
Som'er·sett's Case
som·nam'bu·lism
som'no·lence
son
son as·sault' de·mesne'
son'-in-law'
soon
so·phis'ti·ca'tion
sop'o·rif'ic
so·ror'i·cide'
sors
sough
sound v.
sound adj.
  — and dis·pos'ing mind
    and mem'o·ry
  — health
  — ju·di'cial dis·cre'tion
  — mind
  — val'ue
sound'ing
  — in dam'ag·es
sound'ness
source
  — of in'come'
sourc'es of the law

sous
— seing pri·vé'
sov'er·eign
— im·mu'ni·ty
— peo'ple
— pow'er
— pre·rog'a·tive
— right
— states
sov'er·eign·ty
spank
spas·mod'ic
speak
speak'er
speak'ing
— de·mur'rer
— mo'tion
— or'der
— with pros'e·cu'tor
spe'cial
— act
— dis'trict
— er'rors
— ex·am'in·er
— ex·cep'tion
— ex'e·cu'tion
— ex·ec'u·tor
— facts rule
— grand ju'ry
— in'ter·est groups
— in'ter·rog'a·to'ries
— ju'ris·dic'tion
— law
— lien
— mat'ter
— pa'per
— per'mit
— place
— reg'is·tra'tion
— ses'sion
— use per'mit
— use val'u·a'tion
— ver'dict
— war'ran·ty
— warranty deed
spe'cial·ist
spe'cial·ty
— debt
spe'cie
spe'cies
spe'cif'ic

— be·quest'
— in·tent'
spe·cif'i·cal·ly
spec'i·fi·ca'tion
spec'i·fy'
spec'i·men
spec'tro·graph'
spec'u·la'tion
spec'u·la'tive dam'ag·
es
spec'u·lum
speech
— or de·bate' clause
speed'y
— ex'e·cu'tion
— rem'e·dy
— tri'al
Speed'y Tri'al Act
spell'ing
spend
spend'thrift'
— trust
spe·ra'te'
spin'-off'
spin'ster
spir'i·tu·al
spir'i·tu·ous liq'uors
spit'al or spit'tle
spite fence
split
— gift
— in'come'
— or'der
— sen'tence
split'-off'
split'ting a cause of
ac'tion
spoil
spoil'a·ble
spo'li·a'tion
spo'li·a'tor
spon'de·o
spon'sions
spon'sor
spon'sor·ship'
spon·ta'ne·ous
— com·bus'tion
— dec'la·ra'tion
— ex'cla·ma'tion
sport'ing house
spot

— price
— trad'ing
— zon'ing
spou'sals
spouse
spread
spring branch
spring'ing use
sprin'kling trust
spu'ri·ous
— bank bill
— class ac'tion
spur track
spy
square
squat'ter
squat'ter's rights
squeeze'-out'
squire
stab
sta·bil'i·ty
sta'bil·ize'
— pric'es
sta'ble
stag'num
stake
stake'hold'er
stake'out'
stale
— check
— claim
— de·mand'
stall'age
stamp
— acts
— du'ties
— tax
stance
stand
stan'dard n.
— es·tab'lished by law
— of care
— of need
— of proof
— of weights and meas'-
ures
stan'dard adj.
— de·duc'tion
— mort'gage
stan'dard·ize'
stand'ing

— a·side′ ju′rors
— by
— in lo′co′ pa·ren′tis
— mas′ter
— mute
— or′ders
— seized to us′es
— to be sued
— to sue doc′trine
sta′ple ar′ti·cle of com′merce
Staple Inn
star′board′
star′-cham′ber
sta′re de·ci′sis
star page
stash
state v.
state n.
— of facts
— of mind
— of mind ex·cep′tion
— of the case
state adj.
— ac′tion
— au′di·tor
— banks
— courts
— pa′per of′fice
— po·lice′ pow′er
— seal
— sov′er·eign·ty
stat′ed
— ac·count′
— cap′i·tal
— meet′ing
— term
State De·part′ment
state′hood′
state′house′
state′ment
— of ac·count′
— of af·fairs′
— of claim
— of con·fes′sion
— of con·di′tion
— of de·fense′
— of in′come′
— of par·tic′u·lars
state′s
— at·tor′ney

— ev′i·dence
— rights
stat′ing
— an ac·count′
— part of bill
sta′tion adj.
— house
Sta′tion·er′s Com′pa·ny
sta′tion·er′y
sta′tist
sta·tis′tics
stat′us
— of ir′re·mov′a·bil′i·ty
— quo
stat′ute
af·fir′ma·tive —
crim′i·nal —
de·clar′a·to′ry —
en·a′bling —
ex·pos′i·to′ry —
gen′er·al —
lo′cal —
neg′a·tive —
— of dis′tri·bu′tions
— of frauds
— of la′bor·ers
— of lim′i·ta′tions
— of us′es
— of wills
pe′nal —
per·pet′u·al —
pri′vate —
pub′lic —
pu′ni·tive —
ref′er·ence —
re·me′di·al —
re·vised′ —
Stat′ute
— of E·liz′a·beth
— of Wills
stat′utes at large
stat′u·to′ry
— bond
— con·struc′tion
— crime
— ded′i·ca′tion
— ex·cep′tion
— ex′po·si′tion
— ex·tor′tion
— fore·clo′sure
— in′stru·ments

— law
— lien
— ob′li·ga′tion
— part′ner·ship′ as·so′ci·a′tion
— pen′al·ty
— rape
— re·lease′
— sta′ple
— suc·ces′sor
sta·tu′tum
stay v.
stay n.
— laws
— of ex′e·cu′tion
— of pro·ceed′ings
— or′der
stead′y
— course
steal
steal′ing chil′dren
stealth
steam′ship′
steer′age
steer′er
ste·nog′ra·pher
ste·nog′ra·phy
step
step′child′
step′-down′ in ba′sis
step′fa′ther
step′-in-the-dark′ rule
step′moth′er
step′son′
step′-up′ in ba′sis
ste·ril′i·ty
ster′il·ize′
ster·il·i·za′tion
ster′ling
stet pro·ces′sus
ste′ve·dore′
stew′ard
stick′er
stick′ler
sti′fling a pros′e·cu′tion
stig′ma
stig′ma·tize′
still
still′born′
stim′u·lant

stint
sti'pend'
sti·pen'di·ar'y
  — es·tates'
sti'pes'
stip'u·late'
stip'u·lat'ed
  — dam'ag·es
stip'u·la'tion
stir'pes'
stock
  as·sent'ed —
  — as·so'ci·a'tion
  — at'tri·bu'tion
  au'thor·ized' —
  — bail'out'
  blue'-chip' —
  bo'nus —
  — bro'ker
  call'a·ble pre·ferred' —
  cap'i·tal —
  — cer·tif'i·cate
  com'mon —
  con·trol' —
  con·vert'i·ble —
  — cor'po·ra'tion
  cu'mu·la'tive —
  — div'i·dend'
  do'nat·ed —
  — ex·change'
  float'ing —
  growth —
  guar'an·teed' —
  guar'an·ty —
  — in·sur'ance com'pa·ny
  — in trade
  is'sued —
  — job'ber
  — law dis'trict
  let'ter —
  — life in·sur'ance com'-
    pa·ny
  list'ed —
  — mar'ket
  non·as·sess'a·ble —
  non·cu'mu·la'tive —
  non·vot'ing —
  — note
  no par —
  — op'tions
  out·stand'ing —

paid'-up' —
par·tic'i·pa'tion —
par val'ue —
pen'ny —
pre·ferred' —
pre'mi·um —
  — pur'chase plan
re·deem'a·ble —
reg'is·tered —
re·strict'ed —
  — rights
  — split
sub·scribed' —
  — sub·scrip'tion
  — swap
  — trans'fer tax
treas'ur·y —
un·is'sued —
un·list'ed —
vot'ing —
  — war'rant
wa'tered —
stock'hold'er
stock'hold'er's
  — de·riv'a·tive suit
  — eq'ui·ty
  — li'a·bil'i·ty
  — suit
stock'hold'ers' rep're·
  sen'ta·tive ac'tion
stocks
stop *v.*
  — and frisk
stop *n.*
  — or'der
  — pay'ment or'der
  — sign
stop'gap'
stop'-lim'it or'der
stop'-loss' or'der
stop'page
  —in tran'si·tu'
  — of work
stor'age
store
store'house'
store'room'
storm
stow'age
stow'a·way'
stowe

strad'dle
strag'gler
straight line
straight'-line' de·pre'ci·
  a'tion
stra·min'e·us ho'mo'
strand
strand'ing
stran'ger
  — in blood
stran'gle
stran'gu·la'tion
strat'a·gem
strat'e·gy
stra·toc'ra·cy
straw
  — bail
  — man or par'ty
stray
stream
  — of com'merce
street
  — name
  — rail'way'
street'walk'er
strict
  — con·struc'tion
  — fore·clo'sure
  — in·ter'pre·ta'tion
  — li'a·bil'i·ty
stric'ti' ju'ris
stric·tis'si·mi' ju'ris
strict'ly
  — con·strued'
  — min'is·te'ri·al du'ty
stric'to' ju're'
stric'tum jus
stric'ture
strike *n.*
  ec'o·nom'ic —
  gen'er·al —
  ju'ris·dic'tion·al —
  sec'ond·ar'y —
  sit'-down' —
  sym'pa·thy —
  wild'cat' —
strike *adj.*
  — suits
strike'break'er
strik'ing
  — a ju'ry

— off the roll
— price
strin'gent
strip
— mine
strip'-min'ing
strong
— hand
strong'-arm'
strong'box'
strong'ly cor·rob'o·rat'-
ed
struck
— ju'ry
— work
struc'tur·al al'ter·a'tion
or change
struc'ture
strum'pet
strych'nine'
stul'ti·fy'
stump
stump'age
stu'pe·fa'cient
stu'pe·fac'tion
stu'por
stu'prum
stur'geon
style
su'a·ble
su'a spon'te
sub
sub·a'gent
sub·al'tern
Sub'chap'ter S cor'po·
ra'tion
sub co·lo're ju'ris
sub'com·mis'sion
sub'com·mit'tee
sub con·di'ti·o'ne'
sub'con'scious
sub'con'tract'
sub'con'trac'tor
sub cu'ri·a
sub dis·junc'ti·o'ne
sub'di·vide'
sub'di·vi'sion
sub·duct'
sub·flow'
sub'ir'ri·gate'
sub·ja'cent sup'port

sub'ject
— mat'ter
— to
sub·jec'tion
sub·jec'tive
sub'ject-mat'ter ju'ris·
dic'tion
sub ju'di·ce'
sub'lease'
sub·let'ting
sub·li'cense
sub·mer'gence
sub·mis'sion
— bond
— to ju'ry
sub·mit'
sub·mit'tal
sub mo'do'
sub·mort'gage
sub nom
sub nom'i·ne'
sub·nor'mal
sub'no·ta'tions
sub·or'di·nate'
— of'fer
sub·or'di·nat'ed bonds
or de·ben'tures
sub·or'di·na'tion
— a·gree'ment
sub·orn'
sub'or·na'tion of per'-
ju·ry
sub·orn'er
sub·part'ner
sub·poe'na
— ad tes'ti·fi·can'dum
— du'ces' te'cum
sub po'tes·ta'te
sub·ro·ga'tion
sub·ro·gee'
sub·ro·gor'
sub ro'sa
sub·scribe'
sub·scribed'
— cap'i·tal
— stock
sub·scrib'er
sub·scrib'ing wit'ness
sub·scrip'tion
— con'tract'
— list

— rights
sub'se·quent
— con·di'tion
— cred'i·tor
sub'ser'vant
sub·ser'vi·ent
sub·sid'i·ar'y
sub'si·dize'
sub'si·dy
sub si·len'ti·o'
sub·sist'
sub·sis'tence
sub'soil'
sub'stance
sub'stan'dard
sub·stan'tial
— ca·pac'i·ty
— com·pli'ance rule
— dam'ag·es
— e·quiv'a·lent of pat'-
ent·ed de·vice'
— ev'i·dence
— jus'tice
— per·form'ance
sub·stan'tial·ly
sub·stan'ti·ate'
sub'stan·tive
— due proc'ess'
— ev'i·dence
— fel'o·ny
— law
— of·fense'
— rights
sub'sti·tute' v.
sub'sti·tute' n.
— de·fen'dant
— fa'ther
sub'sti·tut'ed
— ba'sis
— ex·ec'u·tor
— serv'ice
sub·sti·tu'tion
— of judg'ment doc'-
trine
— of par'ties
sub·sti·tu'tion·al
sub·sti·tu'tion·ar'y
— ev'i·dence
— ex·ec'u·tor
sub·strac'tion
sub·ten'ant

sub'ter·fuge'
sub'ter·ra'ne·an wa'-
  ters
sub·trac'tion
  — of con'ju·gal rights
sub·ver'sion
sub·ver'sive ac·tiv'i·ties
suc·ces'sion
  ar'ti·fi'cial —
  — du'ty
  he·red'i·tar'y —
  in·tes'tate' —
  ir·reg'u·lar —
  le'gal —
  nat'u·ral —
  — tax
  tes'ta·men'ta·ry —
  va'cant —
suc·ces'sive
suc·ces'sor
  — in in'ter·est
  sin'gu·lar —
  — trus·tee'
suc·cinct'
such
sud'den
  — af·fray'
  — e·mer'gen·cy doc'trine
  — heat of pas'sion
  — or vi'o·lent in'ju·ry
  — per'il rule
sue
  — out
suf'fer
suf'fer·ance
suf'fer·ing a re·cov'er·y
suf·fi'cien·cy of ev'i·
  dence
suf·fi'cient
  — cause
  — ev'i·dence
suf'fo·cate'
suf'frage
sug·gest'
sug·ges'tion
  — of er'ror
sug·ges'tive
  — in·ter'ro·ga'tion
su'i·cid'al
su'i·cide'
su'i

— gen'e·ris
— ju'ris
su'ing and la'bor·ing
  clause
suit
  — a·gainst' state
  class —
  de·riv'a·tive —
  — mon'ey
  — of a civ'il na'ture
  — or pro·ceed'ings at
    law or in chan'cer·y
suit'a·ble
suite
suit'or
suit'ors'
  — de·pos'it ac·count'
  — fee fund
Suits in Ad'mi·ral·ty
  Act
sum
  — cer'tain
  — in gross
  — pay'a·ble
  — re·ceiv'a·ble
sum·mar'i·ly
sum·ma'ry n.
sum'ma·ry adj.
  — con·vic'tion
  — courts mar'tial
  — e·ject'ment
  — e·vic'tion
  — judg'ment
  — ju'ris·dic'tion
  — pro·ceed'ing
  — proc·ess'
sum·ma'tion
sum'ming up
sum'mon
sum'mons
  — ad re'spon·den'dum
  — and or'der
sum'mum jus
sump'tu·ar'y laws
Sun'day
  — clos'ing laws
sun'dries
sun'dry
sun'set' law
sun'shine' law
sun'stroke'

su'o
  — nom'i·ne'
  — pe·ric'u·lo'
su'per·an'nu·ate'
su'per·car'go
su·per'flu·ous
su'per·in'sti·tu'tion
su'per·in·tend'
su'per·in·ten'dent
su·pe'ri·or n.
su·pe'ri·or adj.
  — courts
  — fel'low ser'vant
  — force
su·pe'ri·or'i·ty
su'per·nu'mer·ar'ies
su'per·sede'
su'per·se'de·as
  — bond
su'per·sed'ing cause
su'per·sen·ior'i·ty
su'per·ses'sion
su'per·sti'tious use
su'per·ven'ing
  — cause
  — neg'li·gence
su'per·ven'tion
su'per·vise'
su'per·vi'sion
su'per·vi'sor
su'per·vi'so·ry
  — con·trol'
su'per vi'sum cor'po·ris
sup·plant'
sup'ple·ment
sup'ple·men'tal
  — act
  — af'fi·da'vit
  — an'swer
  — bill
  — bill in na'ture of bill
    of re·view'
  — claim
  — com·plaint'
  — plead'ing
sup'ple·men'ta·ry
  — pro·ceed'ings
sup'pli·ant
sup'pli·er
sup·plies'
sup·ply'

sup·port'
sup·port'a·ble
sup'po·si'tion
sup·press'
sup·pres'sion
— hear'ing
— of ev'i·dence
su'pra
— pro'test'
sup'ra·ri·par'i·an
su·prem'a·cy
— clause
su·preme'
— law of the land
— pow'er
Su·preme' Court
— of Ju'di·ca·ture
— of the U·nit'ed States
Su·preme' Ju·di'cial Court
sur'charge' n.
sur'charge' v.
— and fal'si·fy'
sur dis·claim'er
sur'e·ty
— bond
— com'pa·ny
— in·sur'ance
— of the peace
sur'e·ty·ship'
con'tract' of —
— de·fens'es
sur'face
— wa'ters
sur'geon
Sur'geon Gen'er·al
sur'ger·y
sur·mise'
sur mort'gage
sur'name'
sur'plus
ac·cu'mu·lat'ed —
ac·quired' —
ap·pre'ci·a'tion —
ap·pro'pri·at'ed —
cap'i·tal —
earned —
in·i'tial —
op'er·at'ing —
paid'-in' —
re·served' —

re·val'u·a'tion —
un·earned' —
sur'plus·age
sur·prise'
sur·re·but'ter
sur·re·join'der
sur·ren'der
— by bail
— by op'er·a'tion of law
— of a pref'er·ence
— of char'ter
— of cop'y·hold'
— of crim'i·nals
— to us'es of will
— val'ue
sur·ren'der·ee'
sur·ren'der·or
sur'rep·ti'tious
sur'ro·ga·cy
sur'ro·gate
— par'ent
sur'ro·gate's court
sur·round'
sur·round'ing cir'cum·stanc'es
sur·sise'
sur·tax'
sur·veil'lance
sur·vey' v.
sur'vey' n.
— of a ves'sel
sur·vey'or
sur·viv'al
— ac'tions
— stat'utes
sur·vive'
sur·viv'ing
— spouse
sur·vi'vor
sur·vi'vor·ship'
— an·nu'i·ty
sus·cep'ti·ble
sus·pect' v.
sus·pect' n.
sus·pect' adj.
— clas'si·fi·ca'tions
sus·pend'
sus·pend'ed sen'tence
sus·pense'
sus·pen'sion
— of a right

— of arms
— of a stat'ute
— of busi'ness
sus·pen'sive
sus·pen'so·ry
sus·pi'cion
sus·pi'cious char'ac·ter
sus·tain'
su'ze·rain·ty
swamp
— and o'ver·flowed' land
swear
swear'ing
— in
— the peace
sweat eq'ui·ty
sweat'ing
sweat'shop'
sweep'ing
sweep'stakes'
sweet'en·ers
sweet'heart' con'tract'
swell
Swift v. Ty'son Case
swift wit'ness
swin'dler
swin'dling
switch
switch'yard' doc'trine
sworn
— state'ment
syl'la·bus
syl'lo·gism
sym·bol'ic
— de·liv'er·y
— speech
sym'me·try
Sy·mond's Inn
sym'pa·thet'ic strike
symp'to·mat'ic
syn'al·lag·mat'ic con'tract'
syn'chro·nism
syn'chro·ni·za'tion
syn'dic
syn'di·cal·ism
syn'di·cate n.
syn'di·cate' v.
syn'di·cat'ing
syn'drome'
syn'graph'

syn′od
syn·on′y·mous
syn·op′sis
syn·thet′ic
syph′i·lis
sys′tem
sys′tem·at′ic
sys·tem′ic

T

tab′er·na′cle
ta·bet′ic de·men′ti·a
ta′ble
— of cas′es
— rents
tab·leau′ of dis′tri·bu′-
tion
ta·boo′
tab′u·la
— ra′sa
tab′u·lar
T′-ac·count′
tac′it
— ac·cep′tance
— ad·mis′sions
— ded′i·ca′tion
— hy·poth′e·ca′tion
— law
— mort′gage
— re′lo·ca′tion
tac′i·te′
tack
tack′ing
Taft′-Hart′ley Act
tail
— after pos′si·bil′i·ty of
is′sue ex·tinct′
es·tate′ in —
— fe′male′
— gen′er·al
— male
sev′er·al —
— spe′cial
taint
take
— a·way′
— back
— by stealth

— care of
— ef·fect′
— up
take′-home′ pay
take′o′ver
— bid
tak′er
tak′ing
ta′les′
tales′man
tal′lage or tail′age
tal·la′gi·um
tal′ley or tal′ly
Tal′mud′
tal′weg′
tame
tam′per
tam′per·ing with ju′ry
tam′pon′
tam quam
tan′gi·ble
— ev′i·dence
— per′son·al prop′er·ty
— property
tank
tank′age
tan′ta·mount′
tan′trum
tape
tape′-re·cord′
tape re·cord′er
tap′ping
tar′dy
tare
tar′get
— com′pa·ny
— of·fense′
— wit′ness
tar′iff
an′ti·dump′ing —
au·ton′o·mous —
joint —
pref′er·en′tial —
pro·tec′tive —
rev′e·nue —
tar′nish
task
task′mas′ter
task′set′ter
task′work′
tat′too′

taunt
tau·tol′o·gous
tau·tol′o·gy
tav′ern
— keep′er
tav′ern·er
tax v.
tax n.
ad va·lo′rem —
a·muse′ment —
— an′tic′i·pa′tion war′-
rants
— as·sess′ment
— as·ses′sor
— au′dit
— a·void′ance
— ben′e·fit rule
cap′i·tal gains —
capital stock —
cap′i·ta′tion —
— cer·tif′i·cate
col·lat′er·al in·her′i·
tance —
con·sump′tion —
— court
— cred′it
— de·duc′tion
— deed
di·rect′ —
es·tate′ —
— e·va′sion
ex·cess′ prof′its —
ex′cise′ —
— ex·emp′tion
— fer′rets
floor —
— fore·clo′sure
fran′chise′ —
— fraud
— free
gift —
grad′u·at′ed —
gross re·ceipts′ —
head —
— home
in′come′ —
in·her′i·tance —
land —
— laws
— lease
— lev′y

li'cense —
— lien
lo'cal —
— loss
lux'u·ry —
nor'mal —
oc'cu·pa'tion —
pay'roll' —
per'son·al —
personal prop'er·ty —
poll —
pro·por'tion·al —
pub'lic —
— pur'chas·er
real es·tate' —
re·gres'sive —
— roll
— sale
sales —
sev'er·ance —
sink'ing fund —
spe·cif'ic —
stamp —
stock trans'fer —
suc·ces'sion —
— ti'tle
ton'nage —
un'dis·trib'ut·ed prof'-
    its —
use —
with·hold'ing —
tax'a·ble
— es·tate'
— gift
— in'come'
— year
tax·a'tion
dou'ble —
— of costs
pro·gres'sive —
pro·por'tion·al —
re·gres'sive —
tax'es
in'di·rect' —
lo'cal —
par'lia·men'ta·ry —
pro·por'tion·al —
tax'-ex·empt'
tax'i·cab'
tax'ing
— dis'trict pow'er

— mas'ter
— pow'er
tax'less
tax'pay'er
tax'pay'ers' lists
teach
teach'er
tea chest
team
team'ster
team'work'
tear
tear gas
tear'ing of will
tech'ni·cal
— er'rors
— mort'gage
tech'ni·cal'i·ty
tech'ni·cal·ly
tech·ni'cian
tech·nique'
teen'-ag'er
tel'e·gram'
— rack'et
tel'e·graph'
tel'e·phone'
Tel'e·type'
tel'e·vi'sion
tell'er
tell'ers in par'lia·ment
tell'tales'
tem'per·ance
tem'pest
Tem'plars
tem'po·ra'lis
tem'po·ral'i·ties
tem'po·ral'i·ty
tem'po·ral lords
tem'po·rar'i·ly
tem'po·rar'y
— al'i·mo'ny
— de·ten'tion
— dis'a·bil'i·ty
— in·junc'tion
— re·strain'ing or'der
Tem'po·rar'y E·mer'-
gen·cy Court of Ap·
peals'
tem'po·re
tem'po·rize'
tempt

temp·ta'tion
tem'pus
— con·tin'u·um
— se·mes'tre
— u'ti·le'
ten'a·ble
te·na'cious
ten'an·cy
— by the en·tire'ty
— for a pe'ri·od
gen'er·al —
— in com'mon
— in co·par'ce·nar'y
— in part'ner·ship'
joint —
sev'er·al —
ten'ant
— at suf'fer·ance
— at will
— a vo·lun'te
— by cop'y of court roll
— by the cur'te·sy
— by the man'ner
— for life
— for years
— from month to month
— from pe'ri·od to pe'ri·
od
— from year to year
— in cap'i·te
— in com'mon
— in dow'er
— in fee
— in fee sim'ple
— in sev'er·al·ty
— in tail
— in tail ex pro'vi·si·o'-
ne' vi'ri'
land —
— of the de·mesne'
— par'a·vaile'
qua'si' — at suf'fer·ance
sole —
ten'ant·a·ble re·pair'
ten'ants
— by the verge
joint —
ten'ant's fix'tures
ten'ant·ship'
ten·con'
tend

ten'den·cy
tender
  le'gal —
  — of'fer
  — of is'sue
  — of per·form'ance
ten'e·ment
  dom'i·nant —
  — house
  ser'vi·ent —
ten'e·men'tal land
te·ne're
ten'et
Ten'nes·see' Val'ley
  Au·thor'i·ty
ten'or
ten'-per·cent'er
Tenth A·mend'ment
ten'u·it
ten'u·ra
ten'ure
  — in of'fice
ten'ured fac'ul·ty
term
  — bonds
  — for de·lib'er·at'ing
  — for years
  gen'er·al —
  — in gross
  — in·sur'ance
  — loan
  — of court
  — of lease
  — of of'fice
  — pro'ba·to'ry
  reg'u·lar —
termes de la ley
ter'mi·na·ble
  — in'ter·est
  — prop'er·ty
ter'mi·nate'
ter'mi·na'tion
  — of con·di'tion·al con'-
    tract'
  — of em·ploy'ment
ter'min·er
ter'mi·ni'
ter'mi·nol'o·gy
ter'mi·nus
term'less
term'or

terms
  at·ten'dant —
  — of trust
  spe'cial —
  — to be un'der
  un'der —
ter'ra
  — af'fir·ma'ta
  — bos·ca'lis
  — cul'ta
  — de'bil·is
  — do·min'i·ca
  — ex'cul·ta'bil·is
  — ex'ten·den'da
  — frus'ca or fris'ca
  — hy·da'ta
  — lu·cra'bil·is
  — ma'nens vac'u·a oc·
    cu·pan'ti con·ce'di·
    tur'
  — no'va
  — pu·tu'ra
  — sab'u·lo'sa
  — tes'ta·men·ta'lis
  — trans'it cum o'ne·re
  — ves·ti'ta
  — wai·na'bil·is
terre'-ten'ant
ter'ri·er
ter'ri·to'ri·al
  — courts
  — ju'ris·dic'tion
  — prop'er·ty
  — wa'ters
ter'ri·to·ri·al'i·ty
ter'ri·to'ry
  — of a judge
ter'ror
ter'ror·ism
ter'ror·ist
ter'ror·is'tic threats
ter'ti·ar'y
ter'ti·um quid
test
  — case
  — oath
  — pa'per
test'a·ble
tes'ta·cy
tes'ta de nev'il
tes'ta·ment

mil'i·tar'y —
mu'tu·al —
mys'tic —
tes'ta·men'ta·ry
  — ca·pac'i·ty
  — caus'es
  — char'ac·ter
  — class
  — dis'po·si'tion
  — guard'i·an
  let'ters —
  — pa'per or in'stru·ment
  — pow'er
  — suc·ces'sion
  — trust
  — trus·tee'
tes'tate'
  — suc·ces'sion
tes·ta'tion
tes·ta'tor
tes·ta'trix
tes·ta'tum
  — writ
tes'te' of a writ
test'ed
tes'tes
  tri'al per —
tes'ti·fy'
tes'ti·mo'ni·al
  — ev'i·dence
  — proof
tes'ti·mo'ni·um
  — clause
tes'ti·mo'ny
  ex'pert' —
  neg'a·tive —
  pos'i·tive —
tes'tis
test'-tube'
Tex'as Rang'er
text
text'book'
tex'tu·al
thane
thane'lands'
thane'ship'
Tha'vies Inn
the'a·ter or the'a·tre
theft
  — bote
  — by false pre'text'

theme
then
— and there
thence
— down the riv'er
thence·forth'
the·oc'ra·cy
the'o·ret'i·cal
the'o·rize'
the'o·ry
— of case
— of law
— of plead'ing doc'trine
ther'a·pist
ther'a·py
there'a·bout'
there·af'ter
there'a·mong'
there·at'
there·by'
there·for'
there'fore'
there·from'
there·in'
there'in·af'ter
there'in·be·fore'
there·of'
there·on'
there·to'
there'to·fore'
there·un'der
there·un·til'
there·un·to'
there·up·on'
there·with'
there'with·al'
the·sau'rus
thief
thieve
thiev'er·y
thin
— cap'i·tal·i·za'tion
— cor'po·ra'tion
things
— in ac'tion
— of val'ue
— per'son·al
— real
think
third
— con·vic'tion

— de·gree'
— mar'ket
third par'ty
— ben'e·fi'ci·ar'y
— claim pro·ceed'ing
— com·plaint'
— prac'tice
thirds
Thir·teenth' A·mend'-
  ment
thir'ty-day' let'ter
thir'ty-nine' ar'ti·cles
this day six months
thor'ough·fare'
thor'ough·ly
thought'less
thread
threat
threat'en·ing
— let'ters
three'-judge' courts
three'-mile' lim'it
thrift'less
thrift'y
throt'tle
through
— bill of lad'ing
— lot
through·out'
through'put'
through'way'
Throw'back' Rule
thrown from au'to·mo·
  bile'
throw out
thrust'ing
thug
thumb'print'
thus
tick
tick'et
— of leave
— spec'u·la'tor
tick'et-of-leave' man
tid'al
tide
  neap —
tide'land'
tides'men'
tide'wa'ter
tide'way'

tie
tied prod'uct
tie'-in' ar·range'ment
ti·el'
ti·erce'
tight
till'a·ble
till'age
till'-tap'ping
tim'ber
— lease
tim'ber·lode'
time
— bar'gain
— bill
— char'ter
— check
cool'ing —
— de·pos'it
— draft
— im'me·mo'ri·al
— is of the es'sence
— of mem'o·ry
— or'der
— out of mem'o·ry
— pol'i·cy
rea'son·a·ble —
time'keep'er
time'ly
time'-price' dif'fer·en'-
  tial
time'serv'er
time'work'
ti·moc'ra·cy
tine'wald'
tin'ker·men
tin'-pen'ny
tip
tip'-off'
tip·pees'
tip'per
tip'pler
tip'pling house
tip'staff'
tip'ster
tithe'-free'
ti'ther
tithes
  great —
  mi·nute' —
  mixed —

per′son·al —
pre′di·al —
— rent charge
tith′ing
— man
— pen′ny
tit′il·late′
ti′tle
ab′so·lute′ —
ab′stract′ of —
ad·verse′ —
bond for —
— by ac·ces′sion
— by ac·cre′tion
— by ad·verse′ pos·ses′-
  sion
— by de·scent′
— by pre·scrip′tion
chain of —
clear —
clear rec′ord —
col′or of —
cov′e·nants for —
— deeds
— de·fec′tive in form
doc′u·ment of —
doubt′ful —
eq′ui·ta·ble —
ex·am′i·na′tion of —
good —
— guar′an·ty com′pa·ny
im·per′fect —
— in·sur′ance
le′gal —
lu′cra·tive —
mar′ket·a·ble —
mer′chant·a·ble —
— of a cause
— of an act
— of cler′gy·men
— of dec′la·ra′tion
— of en′try
on′er·ous —
pa′per —
pas′sive —
per′fect —
pre·sump′tive —
rec′ord —
re·ten′tion —
root of —
— search

sin′gu·lar —
— stan′dards
tax —
— to or′ders
— trans·ac′tion
un·mar′ket·a·ble —
war′ran·ty of —
ti′tle·hold′er
tit′u·lar
to·geth′er
to have and to hold
to wit
to·bac′co·nist
to′ken
— in′te·gra′tion
— mon′ey
tol′er·ate′
tol′er·a′tion
toll v.
toll n.
— and team
— bridge
— gath′er·er
— road
— thor′ough
— trav′erse
— turn
toll′age
toll′booth′
toll′er
tolls
tomb
tomb′stone′
— ad
ton
— mile
ton′nage
— du′ty
— rent
ton′sure
ton′tine′
took and car′ried a·
  way′
tool
top lease
top′-se′cret
tor·ment′
tor·pe′do doc′trine
Tor′rens ti′tle sys′tem
tort
— claims acts

con′sti·tu′tion·al —
in·ten′tion·al —
mar′i·time′ —
per′son·al —
prop′er·ty —
qua′si′ —
will′ful —
tort′-fea′sor
tor′tious
tor′tu·ous
tor′ture
To′ry
to′tal
— de·pend′en·cy
— dis′a·bil′i·ty
— e·vic′tion
— loss
to·tal′i·tar′i·an
to·tal′i·ty
— of the cir′cum·stanc′-
  es
to′tal·ize′
Tot′ten Trust
tot′ting up
touch and stay
tour d′e·chelle′
tourn
tout
— temps prist
— un sound
tow′a·ble
tow′age
— serv′ice
to·ward′
to·wards′
to wit
town
— clerk
— col·lec′tor
— com·mis′sion·er
— cri′er
— hall
— meet′ing
— or′der or war′rant
— pound
— pur′pose
— reeve
— tax
— treas′ur·er
town′ship′
— trus′tee′

town'site'
tox·e'mi·a
tox'ic
tox'i·cal
tox'i·cant
tox'i·cate'
tox'i·col'o·gy
tox'i·co·ma'ni·a
tox'i·co'sis
tox'i·fy'
tox'in
trac'ing
tracks
tract
trac'tor
trade v.
trade n.
— ac·cep'tance
— and com'merce
— a·gree'ment
— as·so'ci·a'tion
— com·mis'sion
— dis·pute'
— dol'lar
— fix'tures
— li'bel
— name
— se'cret
— un'ion
— us'age
trade'mark'
trad'er
trades'man
trad'ing
— cor'po·ra'tion
— part'ner·ship'
— stamps
— voy'age
— with the en'e·my
tra·di'ti·o'
tra·di'tion
tra·di'tion·ar'y ev'i·
  dence
tra·duce'
tra·duc'tion
traf'fic
— reg'u·la'tions
traf'fick·ing
— in drugs
traf'fick·er
trail'er

train
— wreck
train'bands'
train'load'
trai'tor
trai'tor·ous·ly
trai'tress
tra·jec·ti'ti·a pe·cu'ni·a
tram'mer
tramp
— steam'er
tram'road'
tram'way'
tran'quil·iz'er
trans·act'
trans·act'ing busi'ness
trans·ac'tion
— or oc·cur'rence test
trans·ac'tion·al im·mu'-
  ni·ty
tran'script'
— of rec'ord
trans·fer' v.
trans·fer n.
— a'gent
— in con'tem·pla'tion of
  death
— of a cause
— pay'ments
— tax
— tick'et
trans·fer'a·ble
trans'fer·ee'
— li'a·bil'i·ty
trans·fer'ence
trans·fer'or'
trans·ferred' in·tent'
trans·gres'sion
trans·gres'sive trust
trans·gres'sor
tran'sient n.
tran'sient adj.
— for'eign·er
— mer'chant
— per'son
tran·si're'
tran'sit
— in rem ju'di·ca'tam
— ter'ra cum o'ne·re
tran'si·tive
— cov'e·nant

tran'si·to'ry
— ac'tion
trans·la'tion
trans·la'tive fact
trans·mis'sion
trans·mit'tal
tran·spire'
trans·port' n.
trans·port' v.
trans·por·ta'tion
trans·ship'ment
trans·ves'tism
trans·ves'tite
trap
tras·sans'
tras·sa'tus
trau'ma
trau·mat'ic
trau'ma·tism
tra·vail'
trav'el
— ex·pense'
Trav'el Act
trav'eled or trav'elled
— part of high'way'
— place
— way
trav'el·er or trav'el·ler
trav'el·er's
— check
— let'ter of cred'it
trav'el·ing sales'man
trav'erse
com'mon —
crim'i·nal —
gen'er·al —
— ju'ry
— of in·dict'ment or pre·
  sent'ment
spe'cial —
— up·on' a —
tra·vers'er
tra·vers'ing note
trav'es·ty
treach'er·ous
treach'er·y
tread'mill'
tread'wheel'
trea'son
con·struc'tive —
— fel'o·ny

high —
mis·pri′sion of —
pet′it —
trea′son·a·ble
treas′ure
treas′ur·er
Treas′ur·er of the U·
  nit′ed States
treas′ure-trove′
treas′ur·y
  — bill
  — bond
  — cer·tif′i·cate
  — note
  — se·cu′ri·ties
  — shares
  — stock
  — war′rant
Treas′ur·y
  — De·part′ment
  — Reg′u·la′tions
treat′ment
trea′ty
  — clause
  — of peace
  — pow′er
treb′le
  — costs
  — dam′ag·es
tres′pass
  — ab i·ni′ti·o′
con·tin′u·ing —
crim′i·nal —
  — de bo′nis as′por·ta′tis
  — for mesne prof′its
joint —
  — on the case
per′ma·nent —
  — qua′re′ clau′sum fre′-
    git
  — to chat′tels
  — to land
  — to try ti′tle
  — vi et ar′mis
tres′pass·er
  — ab i·ni′ti·o′
in′no·cent —
tri′al
  — a·mend′ment
  — at bar
  — at ni·si′ pri′us

— bal′ance
  — by cer·tif′i·cate
  — by court or judge
  — by fire
  — by grand as·size′
  — by ju′ry
  — by news me′di·a
  — by pro·vi′so
  — by the rec′ord
  — by wa′ger of bat′tel
  — by wager of law
  — by wit′ness
  — court
  — de no′vo′
fair and im·par′tial —
  — list
new —
  — on the mer′its
  — per pais
pub′lic —
sep′a·rate —
speed′y —
tri′fur·cat′ed —
  — with as·ses′sors
tri·an′gu·lat′ed
trib′a·dism
trib′al
  — lands
tribe
tri·bu′nal
trib′u·tar′y
trib′ute′
trick′er·y
tri′er of fact
Trin′i·ty Term
trin′kets
tri′ors
trip
tri·par′tite′
trip′li·cate
tri·um′vi·rate
triv′i·al
tron′age
troops
tro′phy
trou′ble
tro′ver
troy weight
tru′an·cy
truce
truck

truck′er
truck′load′
true
  — ad·mis′sion
  — bill
  — cop′y
  — val′ue rule
  — ver′dict
trumped′-up′
trunk rail′way′
trust
ac·cu′mu·la′tion —
ac′tive —
al′i·mo′ny —
  — al·lot′ments
an·nu′i·ty —
bond —
busi′ness —
  — cer·tif′i·cate
ces′tui que —
char′i·ta·ble —
Claf′lin —
Clif′ford —
com′mon law —
com·mu′ni·ty —
  — com′pa·ny
com·plete′ vol′un·
    tar′y —
com·plex′ —
con·struc′tive —
con·tin′gent —
cre·a′tion of —
  — deed
de·pos′it —
di·rect′ —
di·rec′to·ry —
dis·cre′tion·ar′y —
dry —
ed′u·ca′tion·al —
e·quip′ment —
  — es·tate′
  — ex de·lic′to′
ex·e·cut′ed —
ex·ec′u·to′ry —
  — ex mal′e·fi′ci·o′
ex·press′ —
express ac′tive —
express pri′vate pas′-
  sive —
fixed —
for′eign si′tus —

— fund
— fund doc'trine
gran'tor —
hon'or·ar'y —
il·lu'so·ry —
im·per'fect —
im·plied' —
— in·den'ture
in'de·struc'ti·ble —
— in in·vi'tum
— in'stru·ment
in'stru·men'tal —
in·sur'ance —
in'ter vi'vos —
in·vol'un·tar'y —
ir·rev'o·ca·ble —
land —
— leg'a·cy
lim'it·ed —
liq'ui·da'tion —
liv'ing —
mar'i·tal de·duc'tion —
Mas'sa·chu'setts —
min'is·te'ri·al —
mixed —
na'ked —
nom'i·nee' —
non'dis·cre'tion·ar'y —
— of'fi·cer
pas'sive —
per·pet'u·al —
per'son·al —
pour'-o'ver —
prec'a·to'ry —
pri'vate —
— prop'er·ty
pub'lic —
— re·ceipt'
re·cip'ro·cal —
— res
re·sult'ing —
rev'o·ca·ble —
sav'ings bank —
se'cret —
shift'ing —
short'-term' —
sim'ple —
spe'cial —
spend'thrift' —
split'-in'ter·est —
sprink'ling —

ten'ta·tive —
— ter'ri·to'ry
tes'ta·men'ta·ry —
trans·gres'sive —
ver'ti·cal —
vol'un·tar'y —
vot'ing —
trust'-bust'ing
trus·tee'
— ad li'tem
— de son tort
— ex mal'e·fi'ci·o'
— in bank'rupt'cy
ju·di'cial —
— proc'ess'
qua'si' —
tes'ta·men'ta·ry —
trus·tee'ship'
Trust In·den'ture Act
trus'tor
trust'wor'thy
truth
truth'ful
Truth'-in-Lend'ing Act
try
tsar *or* czar
tub
Tuck'er Act
tu·i'tion
tu·mul'tu·ous
tun
tun'ing
tun'nage
tur'ba·ry
turf and twig
turn *or* tourn
turn'coat' wit'ness
turn'key'
— con'tract'
turn'out'
turn'pike'
turn'ta'ble doc'trine
tur'pis
— cau'sa
— con·trac'tus
tur'pi·tude'
mor'al —
tur'pi·tu'do'
tu'te·lage
tu'te·lar'y
tu'tor

— al·i·en'us
— pro'pri·us
tu'tor·ship'
— by na'ture
— by will
tu'trix
twelve'-month' bond
twen'ty per cent rule
twice in jeop'ard·y
twist'ing
two is'sue rule
ty'ing
— ar·range'ment
type'writ'ing
ty'phoid' fe'ver
tyr'an·ny
ty'rant
tythe
tyth'ing

U

u'bi jus, i'bi re·me'di·um
u·biq'ui·ty
ul'lage
ul·te'ri·or
ul'ti·ma ra'ti·o'
ul'ti·mate
— facts
ul'ti·ma'tum
ul'tra
dam'ag·es —
— ma're
— re·pris'es
— vi'res'
ul'tra·haz'ard·ous
ul'tra·ism
um·bil'i·cal
um'brage
um'pir'age
um'pire'
un'a·bat'ed
un·a'ble
un'ac·cept'a·ble
un'ac·count'a·ble
un'ac·crued'
un'ac·cused'
un'ac·knowl'edged

un′ad·just′ed
un′a·dul′ter·at′ed
un′af·fil′i·at′ed
un·al′ien·a·ble
un·al′lowed
un·alt′er·a·ble
un·am·big′u·ous
un·am′or·tized′
un′na·nim′i·ty
u·nan′i·mous
un·an′swer·a·ble
un·ap·peal′a·ble
un·ar′gu·a·ble
un·as·cer·tained′
  — du′ties
un·as·sail′a·ble
un·as·signed′
un′at·tached′
un·at·test′ed
un·au′dit·ed
un·au′thor·ized′
  — use
un′a·vail′a·bil′i·ty
u′na vo′ce′
un′a·void′a·ble
  — ac′ci·dent
  — ca′su·al·ty
  — cause
  — dan′gers
un′be·com′ing
  con′duct′ —
un′be·known′
un·bi′ased
un·born′
  — ben′e·fi′ci·ar′ies
  — child
un·break′a·ble
un·bro′ken
un·called′-for′
un·cer′tain·ty
un·chal′lenged
un·changed′
un·char′tered
un·chaste′
un·chas′ti·ty
un·claimed′
un′cle
un·clean′ hands
un·clear′
un·col·lect′ed
un·col·lect′i·ble

un′com·pelled′
un·com′pen·sat′ed
un·com′pli·cat′ed
un·com·ply′ing
un·com′pro·mis′ing
un′con·cealed′
un′con·di′tion·al
  — dis′charge′
un′con·scion·a·bil′i·ty
un·con′scion·a·ble
  — bar′gain
un·con′scious
un′con·sti·tu′tion·al
un′con·strained′
un·con′sum·mat·ed
un′con·tam′i·nat′ed
un′con·tra·dict′ed
un′con·trol′la·ble
  — im′pulse′
un′con′tro·vert′ed
un′con·tro·vert′i·ble
un′con·ven′tion·al
un′co·op′er·a′tive
  — wit′ness
un·couth′
un·cov′ered
un·cuth′
un·dam′aged
un·dat′ed
un′de·cid′ed
un′de·clared′
un′de·fend′ed
un′de·ni′a·ble
un′de·nied′
un′der
un′der·age′
un′der and sub′ject
un′der·as·sess′ment
un′der·cap′i·tal·ized′
un′der col′or of law
un′der con·trol′
un′der·cov′er
un′der·cur′rent of sur′-
  face stream
un′der·cut′
un′der·de·vel′oped
un′der·drawn′
un′der·em·ploy′ment
un′der·es′ti·mate′
un′der·fill′
un′der·flow′

  — of sur′face stream
un′der·grade′
un′der·ground′
  — wa′ters
un′der·growth′
un′der·hand′ed
un′der herd
un′der in·sur′ance
un′der·in·sured′
un′der·lease′
un′der·les·see′
un′der·let′
un′der·ly′ing
un′der·load′
un′der·mine′
un′der·not′ed
un′der·nour′ished
un′der pain of
un′der pro′test′
un′der·paid′
un′der·priced′
un′der·sell′
un′der·sexed′
un′der-sher′iff
un′der·signed′
un′der·sized′
un′der·stand′
un′der·stand′ing
un′der·stat′ed
un′der·state′ment
un′der·stood′
un′der·take′
un′der·tak′er
un′der·tak′ing
un′der·ten′ant
un′der-the-coun′ter
un′der the in′flu·ence
  of in·tox′i·cat′ing liq′-
  uor
un′der-the-ta′ble
un′der·took′
un′der·tu′tor
un′der·val′u·a′tion
un′der·way′
un′der·world′
un′der·write′
un′der·writ′er
un′de·scend′ed
un′de·signed′
un′de·sir′a·ble
un′de·ter′min·a·ble

un'de·ter'mined
un'de·vel'oped
un'de·vised'
un·di'ag·nosed'
un'di·rect'ed
un'dis·bursed'
un·dis'ci·plined
un'dis·closed'
 — a'gen·cy
 — prin'ci·pal
un'dis·put'ed
 — fact
un'dis·trib'ut·ed
 — prof'its tax
un'di·vid'ed
 — prof'its
 — right
un'di·vulged'
un·dock'
un·doc'u·ment'ed
un·dow'ered
un·due'
 — in'flu·ence
un·earned'
 — in'come'
 — in'cre·ment
 — sur'plus
un·earth'
un·ed'it·ed
un·ed'u·cat'ed
un'e·man'ci·pat'ed
un'em·ployed'
un'em·ploy'ment
un'en·closed' place
un'en·cum'bered
un'en·dorsed'
un'en·force'a·ble
un'en·fran'chised
un'en·tailed'
un'en·tered
un'en·ti'tled
un·e'qual
un'e·quiv'o·cal
un·err'ing
un·eth'i·cal
un'ex·cep'tion·a·ble
un'ex·e·cut'ed
un'ex·er'cised'
un'ex·pect'ed
un'ex·pend'ed
un'ex·pired' term

un'ex·plained'
un'ex·pressed'
un'ex·ten'u·at·ed
un·fair'
 — com'pe·ti'tion
 — hear'ing
 — la'bor prac'tice
 — meth'ods of com'pe·
  ti'tion
 — trade prac'tic·es
un·faith'ful
un·fav'or·a·ble
un·fenced'
un·fet'tered
un·fin'ished
un·fit'
un'fore·see'a·ble
un'fore·seen'
un'for·feit·a·ble
un'for·giv'a·ble
un·found'ed
un·freeze'
un·friend'ly
un'ful·filled'
un·fund'ed
un·gov'ern·a·ble
un·grad'ed
un·grant'ed
un'guar·an·teed'
un·guard'ed
un·hab'it·a·ble
un·hal'lowed
un·harmed'
un·haz'ard·ous
un·hin'dered
U'ni·at' Church *or* U'ni·
 ate' Church
un'i·den'ti·fi'a·ble
u'ni·fac'tor·al ob'li·ga'·
 tion
u'ni·fied'
 — cred'it
 — trans'fer tax
u'ni·form'
U'ni·form'
 — Com·mer'cial Code
 — Con·sum'er Cred'it
  Code
 — Con·trolled' Sub'·
  stanc·es Act

 — Di·vorce' Rec'og·ni'·
  tion Act
 — Prin'ci·pal and In'·
  come' Act
 — State laws
u'ni·for'mi·ty
u'ni·fy'
u'ni·gen'i·ture
u'ni·lat'er·al
 — con'tract'
 — mis·take'
 — rec'ord
un'im·paired'
un'im·peach'a·ble wit'·
 ness
un'im·proved' land
un'in·closed' place
un'in·cor'po·rat'ed
 — as·so'ci·a'tion
un'in·fect'ed
un'in·hab'it·a·ble
un'in·spect'ed
un'in·sur'a·ble
un'in·sured'
 — mo'tor·ist cov'er·age
un'in·tel'li·gi·ble
un'in·tend'ed
un'in·ten'tion·al
un'in·ter·rupt'ed
un'ion
 — cer'ti·fi·ca'tion
 closed —
 com'pa·ny —
 — con'tract'
 craft —
 hor'i·zon'tal —
 in'de·pend'ent —
 in·dus'tri·al —
 in'ter·na'tion·al —
 lo'cal —
 — mort'gage clause
 na'tion·al —
 o'pen —
 — rate
 — se·cu'ri·ty clause
 — shop
 trade —
 ver'ti·cal —
un'ion·i·za'tion
un'ion·ize'
Un'ion Jack

u'ni·pa·rent'al
u·nique'
un·is'sued stock
u'nit
  bar'gain·ing —
  — of pro·duc'tion
  — own'er·ship' acts
  — pric'ing
u'ni·tar'y
u·nite'
u·nit'ed in in'ter·est
U·nit'ed Na'tions
U·nit'ed States
  — At·tor'ney
  — bonds
  — Code
  — com·mis'sion·er
  — courts
  — cur'ren·cy
  — Mag'is·trate'
  — notes
  — of'fi·cer
  — Re·ports'
  — Su·preme' Court
u'nit·i·za'tion
u'nit·ize'
u'ni·ty
  — of in'ter·est
  — of pos·ses'sion
  — of sei'sin
  — of time
  — of ti'tle
u'ni·ver'sal
  — a'gent
  — leg'a·cy
  — part'ner·ship'
  — suc·ces'sion
u'ni·ver'si·ty
u'ni·vo'cal
un'ju·di'cious
un·just'
  — en·rich'ment
un·just'i·fi'a·ble
un·known' per'sons
un·la'den
un·law'ful
  — act
  — as·sem'bly
  — bel·lig'er·ent
  — de·tain'er
  — en'try

— pick'et·ing
un·law'ful·ly
un·leash'
un·less'
  — lease
un·li'censed
un·lim'i·ted
un·liq'ui·dat'ed
  — claim
  — dam'ag·es
  — debt
  — de·mand'
un·list'ed
un·liv'a·ble
un·liv'er·y
un·load'ing
un·lo'cat·ed
un·looked'-for' mis'hap
un·man'age·a·ble
un·mar'ket·a·ble ti'tle
un·mar'ried
un'ma·tured'
un·med'i·tat'ed
un·mer'chant·a·ble
un·mo·lest'ed
un·mort'gaged
un·nat'u·ral
  — of·fense'
  — will
un·nec'es·sar'y
  — hard'ship'
un·oc'cu·pied'
un'of·fi'cial
un·or'gan·ized'
un·owned'
un·paid'
un·pat'ent·a·ble
un·pat'ent·ed
un·prec'e·dent'ed
  — rain'fall'
un·prej'u·diced'
un'pre·med'i·tat'ed
un'pro·duc'tive
un'pro·fes'sion·al
  — con'duct
un·prof'it·a·ble
un'pro·test'ed
un·prov'en
un'pro·vid'ed
un·pun'ished
un·qual'i·fied'

un'ques
un·ques'tion·a·ble
un·rea'son·a·ble
  — ap·pre'ci·a'tion
  — com'pen·sa'tion
  — re·fus'al to sub·mit' to op'er·a'tion
  — re·straint' of trade
  — restraint on al'ien·a'tion
  — search
un're·cord'ed
un're·cov'ered
un're·deemed'
un're·dressed'
un·reg'is·tered
un·reg'u·lat'ed
un're·lat'ed
  — of·fens'es
un're·linq'uished
un're·mit'ted
un're·mu'ner·a'tive
un're·pealed'
un're·pent'ing
un'rep·re·sent'ed
un're·quit'a·ble
un're·served'
un're·sist'ing
un're·spon'sive
  — ev'i·dence
un're·strict'ed
un're·view'a·ble
un're·voked'
un·right'ful
un·ru'li·ness
un·ru'ly and dan'ger·ous
un·safe'
un·san'i·tar'y
un·sat'is·fac'to·ry
un·sched'uled
un·sealed'
un·seat'ed land
un·sea'wor'thy
un'se·cured'
un·seem'ly
un·seg're·gat'ed
un·sen'tenced
un·set'tled
  — ques'tion of law
un·signed'

un·skilled'
un·sol'emn
 — war
 — will
un·sound'
 — mind
un'suc·cess'ful
un·suit'a·ble
un·su'per·vised'
un·sworn'
 — state'ment
un·taxed'
un·ten'ant·a·ble
un·tend'ed
un·thrift'
un·til'
un·time'ly
un'to·ward'
un·true'
un·us'a·ble
un·u'su·al
 — cir'cum·stance'
 — pun'ish·ment
un·val'ued
 — pol'i·cy
un·ver'i·fied'
un·vouched'
un·war'rant·ed
un·whole'some
 — food
un·will'ing
un·wor'thy
un·writ'ten
 — law
up·hold'
up'keep'
up'lands'
up·lift'ed hand
up·on' pain of
up'per bench
up'set' price
up'-to-date'
ur'ban
 — home'stead'
 — re·new'al
 — ser'vi·tude'
ur'ban·i·za'tion
ure
ur'gen·cy
ur'gent
u'ri·nal'y·sis

us'a·ble
us'age
 cus'tom and —
 gen'er·al —
 — of trade
us'ance
use v.
use n.
 — and hab'i·ta'tion
 — and oc'cu·pa'tion
 ces'tui que —
 char'i·ta·ble —
 con·tin'gent —
 ex·clu'sive —
 ex'e·cut'ed —
 ex·ec'u·to'ry —
 ex·ist'ing —
 feoff·ee' to —
 — im·mu'ni·ty
 of·fi'cial —
 pas'sive —
 per·mis'sive —
 — plain'tiff
 re·sult'ing —
 sec'on·dar'y —
 shift'ing —
 spring'ing —
 su'per·sti'tious —
 — tax
 — var'i·ance
us·ee'
use'ful
 — life
use'ful·ness
us'er
 ad·verse' —
ush'er
us'ing
 — mail to de·fraud'
 — the serv'ice of an·
   oth'er for pay
us'que
u'su·al
 — course
 — cov'e·nants
 — place of a·bode'
 — terms
u'su·fruct'
 im·per'fect —
 le'gal —
 per'fect —

 qua'si' —
u'su·fruc'tu·ar'y
u·su'ra
 — man'i·fest'a
 — mar'i·ti'ma
u'sur·er
u·su'ri·ous
 — con'tract'
u·surp'
u'sur·pa'tion
 — of ad·vow'son
 — of fran'chise'
 — of of'fice
u·surped' pow'er
u·surp'er
 — of a pub'lic of'fice
u'su·ry
u·ten'sil
u'ter·ine
u'ter·o·ges·ta'tion
u'ter·us
u·til'i·ty
u'til·i·za'tion
u'til·ize'
ut·lage'
ut'most'
 — care
 — re·sis'tance
ut'ter v.
ut'ter adj.
 — bar
 — bar'ris·ter
ut'ter·ance
 ex·cit'ed —
ut'ter·ly
ux'or
ux·o'ri·cide'

V

va'can·cy
va'cant
va'cate'
va·ca'tion
 — of judg'ment
va·ca'tur
vac'ci·na'tion
vac·cine'
va'cu·a pos·ses'si·o'

va·cu'i·ty
vac'u·um
va'di·a're' du·el'lum
va'di·um
— mor'tu·um
— po'ne·re
— vi'vum
vag'a·bond'
vag'a·bond'age
va·gi'na
va'gran·cy
va'grant
— act
vague
vague'ness doc'trine
va·len'ti·a
val'et
val'id
— rea'son
val'i·date'
val'i·dat'ing stat'ute
va·lid'i·ty
— of a stat'ute
— of a trea'ty
— of a will
val'ley
val'or
— ben'e·fi'ci·o'rum
— mar'i·ta'gi·i'
val'or·i·za'tion
val'or·ize'
val'u·a·ble
— con·sid'er·a'tion
— im·prove'ments
— pa'pers
— thing
val'u·ate'
val'u·a'tion
— list
val'ue
ac'tu·al cash —
book —
cash sur·ren'der —
clear —
face —
fair —
fair and eq'ui·ta·ble —
fair and rea'son·a·ble —
fair and reasonable
mar'ket —
fair cash —

fair cash mar'ket —
in·trin'sic —
liq'ui·da'tion —
market —
net —
no par —
— of mat'ter in con'tro·
ver'sy
par —
— re·ceived'
scrap —
stat'ed —
true —
use —
val'ue-ad'ded
val'ued pol'i·cy
val'ue·less
val'u·er
van'dal
van'dal·ism
van'dal·ize'
van·ta'ri·us
var'i·a·ble
— an·nu'i·ty
var'i·ance
ar'e·a —
fa'tal —
var'i·a'tion
var'i·ous
va·sec'to·my
vas'sal
— states
vas'sal·age
vas'tum
vaude'ville'
vav'a·sor' or vav'a·sour'
vec'tor
veg'e·ta·ble
ve'hi·cle
ve·hic'u·lar
— hom'i·cide'
vei'es'
veil'ings
vein
ve'jours
vel non
ve'nal
ve·nal'i·ty
ve·na'ri·a
ve·na'ti·o'
vend

vend·ee'
ven·det'ta
vend'i·ble
ven·di'tion
ven·di'ti·o'ni ex·po'nas
ven'di·tor
ven'di·trix
ven'dor
— and pur'chas·er act
ven'dor's lien
ven'due'
— mas'ter
ve·ne're·al
— dis·ease'
ven'er·y
ven'geance
venge'ful
ve'ni·a
ve'ni·al
ve·ni·re'
— de no'vo'
— fa'ci·as
— facias ad res'pon·den'-
dum
— facias de no'vo'
— facias ju'ra·to'res'
— facias tot ma·tro'nas
ve·ni're·man
ve'nit
— et de·fen'dit
— et di'cit
vent
ven'ter
ven'ti·late'
ven'ti·la'tion
ven'ture
ven'ue
— facts
— ju'ris·dic'tion
ve·ran'dah or ve·ran'da
ve·ray'
ver'ba
— pre·ca'ri·a
ver'bal
— act
— as·saults'
— note
— proc'ess'
ver·ba'tim
ver'bi·age
ver'der·er or ver'de·ror

ver'dict
  ad·verse' —
  — by lot
  chance —
  com'pro·mise' —
  — con'trar'y to law
  di·rect'ed —
  es·top'pel by —
  ex·ces'sive —
  false —
  gen'er·al —
  in·struct'ed —
  — of no cause of ac'tion
  — of not guilt'y
  — of not guilty by rea'-
    son of in·san'i·ty
  o'pen —
  par'tial —
  priv'y —
  pub'lic —
  quo'tient —
  sealed —
  spe'cial —
  stip'u·la'tion on ma·jor'i·
    ty —
  — sub'ject to o·pin'ion
    of court
ve're·dic'tum
verge or virge
ver'i·fi·ca'tion
ver'i·fied'
  — cop'y
  — names
ver'i·fy'
ver'i·ly
ver'i·ty
ver'sus
ver'ti·cal
  — in'te·gra'tion
  — merg'er
  — price'-fix'ing con'-
    tract'
ver·tig'i·nous
ver'ti·go'
ve'rus
ver'y
  — high de·gree' of care
  — lord and — ten'ant
ves'sel
  for'eign —
  pub'lic —

vest
vest'ed
  — de·vise'
  — es·tate'
  — gift
  — in in'ter·est
  — in pos·ses'sion
  — in'ter·est
  — leg'a·cy
  — pen'sion
  — re·main'der
  — rights
ves·tig'i·al words
ves·tig'i·um
vest'ing or'der
ves'try
ves'try·men
ves·tu'ra
  — ter'rae'
ves'ture
  — of land
vet'er·an
ve'te·ra sta·tu'ta
vet'er·i·nar'i·an
ve'to
  i'tem —
  pock'et —
  — pow'er
vex
vex·a'ri
vex·a'ta quaes'ti·o'
vex·a'tion
vex·a'tious
  — ac'tions act
  — de·lay'
  — pro·ceed'ing
  — re·fus'al to pay
vexed ques'tion
vi'a
  — an·ti'qua — est tu'ta
  — ex·ec'u·ti'va
  — or'di·na'ri·a
  — pub'li·ca
  — re'gi·a
vi'a·bil'i·ty
vi'a·ble
  — child
vi'a·duct'
vic'ar
vic'ar·age
vi·car'i·al

  — tithes
vice n.
vice adj.
  — ad'mi·ral
  — chan'cel·lor
  — con'sul
  — crimes
  — mar'shal
  — pres'i·dent
  — prin'ci·pal
vice'roy'
vi'ce ver'sa
vic'i·nage
vi·cin'i·ty
vi'cious
  — pro·pen'si·ty
vi·con'ti·el or vi·coun'ti·
  el
  — ju'ris·dic'tion
vic'tim
vic'tim·ize'
vic'tim·less crimes
vict'ual·er or vict'ual·ler
vict'uals
vic'tus
vi'de'
  — an'te'
  — in'fra
  — post
  — su'pra
vi·del'i·cet'
vi·du'i·ty
vie
vi et ar'mis
view
  — and de·liv'er·y
  de·mand' of —
  — of an in'quest'
view'ers
vig'il
vig'i·lance
vig'i·lant
vig'i·lan'te
vig'i·lan·tism
vig'or
vil'lage
vil'lain
vil'lein
  — in gross
  — re·gar'dant
  — serv'ic·es

— soc'age
vil'lein·age
vil'len·ous judg'ment
vin·a'gi·um
vin'di·ca're'
vin'di·cate'
vin'di·ca'tion
vin'di·ca'tor
vin'di·ca·to'ry parts of law
vin·dic'tive
— dam'ag·es
vi'nous
— liq'uor
vint'ner
vi'o·la·ble
vi'o·la'tion
vi'o·la'tive
vi'o·la'tor
vi'o·lence
vi'o·lent
— death
— of·fens'es
— pre·sump'tion
vi'o·lent·ly
vir
vi·ra'go
vi'res'
vir·ga'ta
vir'gate
virge
ten'ant by —
vir'gin
vir'go in·tac'ta
vir'gin'i·ty
vi'ri·cide'
vi·ril'i·ty
vir'tu·al
— rep're·sen·ta'tion
vir'tue of of'fice
vir'tu·ous
vir·tu'te
— cu'jus
— of·fi'ci·i'
vir'u·lence
vir'u·lent
vi'rus
vis
— ar·ma'ta
— clan'des·ti'na
— com'pul·si'va

— ex'pul·si'va
— im·pres'sa
— in·er'mis
— in·ju'ri·o'sa
— la'i·ca
— leg'i·bus est in'i·mi'ca
— li'ci·ta
— ma'jor
— per·tur'ba·ti'va
— prox'i·ma
— sim'plex'
vi'sa
vis'-à-vis'
vis'count'
vi'sé'
vis'i·ble
— means of sup·port'
vis'it
vis'i·ta'tion
— books
— rights
vis'i·tor
visne
vi'sus
vi'tal
— sta·tis'tics
vi'ta·min
vi'ti·ate'
vit·il'i·gate'
vit're·ous
vi·var'i·um
vi'va·ry
vi'va vo'ce
vi'vum va'di·um
viz
vo·cab'u·la ar'tis
vo·ca'tion
vo·cif'er·ous
vo'co'
voice
— ex·em'plars'
— i·den'ti·fi·ca'tion
voice'print'
void
— ab i·ni'ti·o'
— con'tract'
— for vague'ness
— in part
— in to'to'
— judg'ment
— mar'riage

— on its face
— proc'ess'
void'a·ble
— con'tract'
— judg'ment
— mar'riage
— pref'er·ence
void'ance
voir dire
vo'lens'
vo·len'ti' non fit in·ju'·ri·a
vo·li'tion
vo·li'tion·al
Vol'stead' Act
vo·lu·it sed non dix'it
vol'un·tar'i·ly
vol'un·tar'i·ness
vol'un·tar'y
— a·band'on·ment
— cour'te·sy
— dis'con·tin'u·ance
— ex·po'sure to un·nec'·es·sar'y dan'ger
— ig'no·rance
— ju'ris·dic'tion
vol'un·teer'
vote
cast'ing —
vot'er
votes and pro·ceed'·ings
vot'ing
— by bal'lot
cu'mu·la'tive —
— stock rights
— trust
— tax
Vot'ing Rights Act
vouch
vouch·ee'
vouch'er
— to war'ran·ty
vouch'ing in
vox pop'u·li'
voy'age
— char'ter
for'eign —
vo·yeur'
vo·yeur'ism
vul'gar

W

wab′ble
wa·cre·our′
wa′di·a
wad′set
wage
— and hour laws
— as·sign′ments
— earn′er
— gar′nish·ment
wage′less
wa′ger
— of bat′tel
— of law
— pol′i·cy
wa′ger·ing
— con′tract′
— gain
wag′es
Wag′ner Act
wag′on
wag′on·age
wag′on·way′
waif
wain′a·ble
wain′age
wait and see doc′trine
wait′ing
— clerks
— pe′ri·od
waive
waiv′er
— by e·lec′tion of rem′e·
dies
ex·press′ —
im·plied′ —
lien —
— of ex·emp′tion
— of im·mu′ni·ty
— of pre′mi·um clause
— of pro′test′
— of tort
walk′ers
walk′out′
wall
Walsh′-Hea′ly Act
wam′pum
wan′der
want

— of con·sid′er·a′tion
— of ju′ris·dic′tion
— of re·pair′
want′age
wan′ton
— act
— acts and o·mis′sions
— and fu′ri·ous driv′ing
— and reck′less mis·
con′duct
— con′duct′
— in′ju·ry
— mis·con′duct
— neg′li·gence
wan′ton·ness
wap′en·take′
war
ar′ti·cles of —
civ′il —
— claus′es
— crimes
im·per′fect —
laws of —
per′fect —
— pow′er
ward
— in chan′cer·y
— mote
— pa′tient
— of ad′mi·ral·ty
— of court
war′da
ward′age
war′den
— of the Cinque Ports
war′den·ship′
ward′er
ward′er·ship′
ward′ing
wards
— and liv′er·ies
— of ad′mi·ral·ty
— of court
ward′ship′
— in cop′y·holds′
ware
ware′house′
— book
— re·ceipt′
— sys′tem
ware′house′man

ware′house′men′s lien
war′fare′
war′like′
warn
warn′ing
warp
warp′age
war′rant v.
war′rant n.
bench —
— cred′i·tor
death —
dis·tress′ —
in′ter·est —
land′lord′s′ —
land —
— of ar·rest′
— of at·tor′ney
— of com·mit′ment
— of′fi·cer
— of mer′chant·a·bil′i·ty
out·stand′ing —
search —
— to sue and de·fend′
war′rant·a·ble
war′ran·tee′
war′ran·ties
cu′mu·la′tion and con′-
flict′ of —
war′rant·less
war′ran·tor
war′ran·ty
af·fir′ma·tive —
col·lat′er·al —
con·struc′tion —
con·tin′u·ing —
cov′e·nant of —
— deed
ex·ec′u·to′ry —
ex·press′ —
full —
gen′er·al —
im·plied′ —
lim′i·ted —
lin′e·al —
— of fit′ness
— of fitness for a par·
tic′u·lar pur′pose
— of hab′it·a·bil′i·ty
— of mer′chant·a·bil′i·ty
per′son·al —

prom'is•so'ry —
spe'cial —
vouch'er to —
war'ren
War'saw Con•ven'tion
wash
 — bank
 — sale
 — trans•ac'tion
washed sale
wash'out'
 — sig'nal
wast'age
waste
 a•me'lio•rat'ing —
 — book
 com•mis'sive —
 dou'ble —
 eq'ui•ta•ble —
 im•peach'ment of —
 nul —
 per•mis'sive —
 vol'un•tar'y —
 — wa'ter
waste'ful
wast'ing
 — as'set'
 — prop'er•ty
 — trust
wast'rel
watch n.
watch v.
 — and ward
watch'dog'
watch'ful
watch'man
wa'ter
 de•vel'oped —
 — dis'trict
 — gauge or gage
 — or•deal'
 — pow'er
 — right
 — right claim
 sur'plus —
wa'ter•course'
wa'tered stock
wa'ter•front'
wa'ter•logged'
wa'ter•mark'
wa'ter•proof'

wa'ters
 coast —
 flood —
 for'eign —
 in'land —
 nav'i•ga•ble —
 per'co•lat'ing —
 pri'vate —
 pub'lic —
 sub'ter•ra'ne•an —
 sur'face —
 ter'ri•to'ri•al —
 tide —
 — of the U•nit'ed States
wa'ter•tight'
wa'ter•way'
wa'ter•works'
wa'ter•wor'thy
wa'ver•ing
way
 — of ne•ces'si•ty
 pri'vate —
 right of —
way'bill'
way'far'er
way'far'ing
way'go'ing crop
way'lay'
way'leave'
ways and means
way'ward
way'war'den
weal
wealth
weap'on
wear and tear
wear'ing ap•par'el
wear'-out'
weath'er•ing
Webb'-Pom'er•ene Act
wed
wed'ded
wed'ding
wed'lock'
week
week'day'
week'ly
weigh'age
weigh'ment
weight
 gross —

min'er's —
net —
 — of ev'i•dence
weir
wel'fare'
 — clause
 — of child
well
well'-be'ing
well'-con•di'tioned
well'-de•fined'
well-found'ed
well'head'
well'-know'ing
welsh'er
welsh'ing
Welsh mort'gage
wes'ter•ly
west'ward
wet
 — gas
 — oil
wet'back'
weth'er
wet'proof'
whack
whale
whal'er
wharf
wharf'age
wharf'in•ger
wharf'ing out
wharf'mas'ter
Whar'ton Rule
what•ev'er
what'so•ev'er
wheel
wheel'age
wheel'ers
wheel'wright'
whelps
when
 — and where
whence
whence'so•ev'er
when•ev'er
when is'sued
where
where'a•bouts'
where•af'ter
where•as'

where·at'
where·by'
where'for'
where'fore'
where'from'
where·in'
where'in·so·ev'er
where·of'
where·on'
where'so·ev'er
where'through'
where'to'
where·un'der
where·un'to
where'up·on'
wher·ev'er
where'with'
where'with·al'
wheth'er
which
which·ev'er
which'so·ev'er
Whig
while
whilst
whim
whip'lash'
— in'ju·ry
whip'ping
whip'saw'
whis'key *or* whis'ky
white
— a'cre
— mule
— per'sons
— rents
— slave
— spurs
white'-col'lar crimes
white'wash'
who·ev'er
whole
— blood
— gale
— life in·sur'ance
whole'sale'
— deal'er
— price
whole'sal'er
whole'some
whol'ly

— and per'ma·nent·ly
  dis·a'bled
— de·pend'ent
— de·stroyed'
— dis·a'bled
whom·ev'er
whom'so·ev'er
whore
whore'house'
whore'mas'ter
whose'so·ev'er
who'so·ev'er
wid'get
wid'ow
wid'ow·er
wid'ow·hood'
wid'ow's
— al·low'ance
— e·lec'tion
wife
wife's part
wild
— an'i·mals
— land
wild'cat' strike
wild'cat'ter
Wild's Case
will *v.*
will *n.*
am'bu·la·to'ry —
an'te·nup'tial —
con·di'tion·al —
con·joint' —
— con'test'
coun'ter —
dou'ble —
es·tate' at —
hol'o·graph'ic —
joint —
joint and mu'tu·al —
liv'ing —
mu'tu·al —
mys'tic —
non'in·ter·ven'tion —
nun'cu·pa'tive —
re·cip'ro·cal —
re·nun'ci·a'tion of —
self'-proved' —
stat'ute of —
— sub'sti·tute'
un'of·fi'cious —

will'ful
— and ma·li'cious in'ju·
  ry
— and wan'ton act
— and wanton in'ju·ry
— in·dif'fer·ence to the
  safe'ty of oth'ers
— mis·con'duct
— misconduct of em·
  ploy'ee
— mur'der
— neg'li·gence
— tort
Wil'liams Act
will'ing·ly
wind'fall'
— prof'its tax
wind'ing up
win'dow
—tax
wind'storm'
wind up
wine
win'ner
win'ter
wire'tap'
wire'tap'ping
wit
wit'am
with
— all faults
— con·sent'
— prej'u·dice
— re'course'
— strong hand
with·draw'
with·draw'al
— of charges
with·draw'ing
— a ju'ror
— rec'ord
with·hold'
with·hold'ing
— of ev'i·dence
— tax
with·in'
with·out'
— day
— de·lay'
— giv'ing com'pen·sa'-
  tion there·for'

— her con·sent'
— im·peach'ment of
  waste
— no'tice
— prej'u·dice
— re'course'
— re·serve'
— stint
— this, that
wit'ness *v.*
wit'ness *n.*
  ad·verse' —
  — a·gainst' him·self'
  at·test'ing —
  — box
  com'pe·tent —
  cred'i·ble —
  ex'pert' —
  grand ju'ry —
  hos'tile —
  ma·te'ri·al —
  pros'e·cut'ing —
  sub·scrib'ing —
  swift —
  — to will
wit'ness·ing part
wit'ting
wit'ting·ly
wit'word'
wive
wom'en
wood
  — leave
woods
wood'work'
wood'work'er
words
  — ac'tion·a·ble in them·
    selves'
  — of art
  — of lim'i·ta'tion
  — of pro'cre·a'tion
  — of pur'chase
work
  — and la'bor
  — of art
  — of na'tion·al im·por'-
    tance
  — of ne·ces'si·ty
  — prod'uct
  — re·lease' pro'gram

— re·lief'
— week
work'a·way'
work'day'
work'er
work'hand'
work'house'
work'ing
  — cap'i·tal
  — days
  — in'ter·est
  — pa'pers
work'man
work'man·like'
work'men's
  — com'pen·sa'tion
  — compensation acts
  — compensation board
    courts
  — compensation in·sur'-
    ance
  — compensation loss
work'-out'
work'wom'an
works
  new —
  pub'lic —
work'shop'
world
World Court
world'ly
  — busi'ness
  — em·ploy'ment
wor'ry·ing cat'tle or
  sheep
wor'ship
  pub'lic —
wor'sted
worth
wor'thi·er ti'tle
worth'less
  — check
  — se·cu'ri·ties
wor'thy
would
wound
wound'ed feel'ings
wound'ing
wran'gle
wrap'a·round' mort'-
  gage

wrath
wreck
wreck'age
wreck'er
wreck'-free'
wrench
wres'tling
wring
wrin'kle
wrist'drop'
writ
  a·li·as —
  close —
  con·cur'rent —
  ju·di'cial —
  jun'ior —
  — of as·sis'tance
  — of at·tach'ment
  — of ca'pi·as
  — of cer'ti·o·rar'i
  — of con·spir'a·cy
  — of cov'e·nant
  — of debt
  — of de·ceit'
  — of de·liv'er·y
  — of det'i·nue'
  — of dow'er
  — of e·ject'ment
  — of en'try
  — of er'ror
  — of error co'ram no'bis
  — of error coram vo'bis
  — of ex'e·cu'tion
  — of for'me·don
  — of ha'be·as cor'pus
  — of in'quir'y
  — of main'prize' *or*
    main'prise'
  — of man·da'mus
  — of mesne
  — of pos·ses'sion
  — of pre·ven'tion
  — of prob'a·ble cause
  — of pro·hi·bi'tion
  — of qua're im'pe·dit
  — of quo war'ran'to
  — of re·cap'tion
  — of re·plev'in
  — of res'ti·tu'tion
  — of re·view'
  — of right

— of su'per·se'de·as
— of su'per·vi'so·ry con·trol'
— of waste
o·rig'i·nal —
pat'ent —
per·emp'to·ry —
pre·rog'a·tive —
— pro re·tor'no' ha·ben'-do'
write'-down'
write'-off'
write'-up'
writ'ing
— o·blig'a·to'ry
writ'ten
— con'tract'
— in'stru·ment
— law
wrong
pri'vate —
pub'lic —
wrong'do'er
wrong'do'ing
wrong'ful
— a·buse' of proc'ess'
— act
— con'duct'
— death ac'tion
— death stat'utes
— lev'y
— life ac'tion
pri'vate —

pub'lic —
— risk in·sur'ance
sol'emn —
wrong'ful·ly
— in·tend'ing

X

xen'o·do'chi·um
xe·rog'ra·phy
x'-ray'
— pho'to·graph'

Y

yacht
yard
yard'man'
yea and nay
year
— and a day
— books
— of mourn'ing
— of Our Lord
year'ling
years
es·tate' for —
year to year
ten'an·cy from —

yeas and nays
yeast
yel'low jour'nal·ism
yel'low-dog' con'tract'
yeo'man
yeo'man·ry
yeo'men of the guard
Yick Wo doc'trine
Yid'dish
yield
net —
— up·on' in·vest'ment
York, stat'ute of
young'er chil'dren
youth

Z

zeal'ot
zeal'ous
— wit'ness
zone
— of em·ploy'ment
zon'ing
ae·sthet'ic —
clus'ter —
Eu·clid'e·an —
ex·clu'sion·ar'y —
spot —
— map
zy'gote'

LEGAL CITATIONS

This section contains selected excerpts from the 13th ed. of *A Uniform System of Citation*. These excerpts are not in themselves sufficient to provide a reliable guide to correct legal citation form. Readers engaged in continuing legal research or writing should obtain a copy of *A Uniform System of Citation* from The Harvard Law Review Association, Gannett House, Cambridge, Massachusetts 02138.

I. Introduction

Most legal writing involves the use of "citation." A "citation" is an author's reference to the specific source of legal authority that substantiates a statement made in the text; essentially, it serves the same purpose as a footnote. The most common sources of legal authority are cases and statutes, and legal writers will "cite" to these sources, and others, to enable their readers to refer to the original source material.

It is useful to understand the difference between a statute and a case. A statute is a law duly passed by a legislative body (like the Congress or a state legislature) and approved by the chief executive (like the President or a governor). The Civil Rights Act of 1964 is an example of a federal statute.

A case, on the other hand, is a judicial decision in a specific case before a court. The judge's decision in a case is sometimes set forth in a written opinion, and lawyers will often refer to these opinions — or cases — in legal writing. *Griggs v. Duke Power Co.* is an example of a case.

For example, a legal writer might wish to state in a brief or legal memorandum that federal law prohibits discrimination in employment because of a person's race, color, religion, sex, or national origin. The primary federal statute that makes such discrimination illegal is known as the Civil Rights Act of 1964. Federal statutes are compiled in a set of reference books called "The United States Code" (U.S.C.). The Civil Rights Act of 1964, for example, can be found in Volume 42 of the United States Code in section 2000e-2. The legal writer's statement, with the correct citation, is as follows:

> The Civil Rights Act of 1964 prohibits employment discrimination because of race, color, religion, sex, or national origin. Civil Rights Act of 1964, § 703, 42 U.S.C. § 2000e-2 (1970).

From the above statement and citation, a reader knows that the provision of federal law that prohibits employment discrimination because of race, color, religion, sex, or national origin was enacted as section 703 of the Civil Rights Act of 1964, and can be found at "42 U.S.C. § 2000e-2 (1970)." This citation means that the federal law prohibiting such discrimination is in Volume 42 of the United States Code (42 U.S.C.) at section 2000e-2 (§ 2000e-2). The date in parentheses indicates the edition of the codification.

Citation to cases is accomplished in much the same way. For example, a legal writer might wish to say that in a certain case, the United States Supreme Court interpreted Title VII of the Civil Rights Act of 1964 to mean that even unintentional discrimination by an employer is a violation of the law. The Supreme Court did, in fact, say this in the case of *Griggs v. Duke Power Co.* in 1971. The statement, and its proper citation, might be written as follows:

> In one case, the Supreme Court has stated that even unintentional discrimination by an employer is illegal. *Griggs v. Duke Power Co.*, 401 U.S. 424, 428 (1971).

This citation shows the reader that the opinion of the Supreme Court in the case of *Griggs v. Duke Power Co.* can be found in Volume 401 of a set of books called the "United States Reports" (401 U.S.), beginning at page 424. The precise issue in question is discussed at page 428, and the year the opinion was given was 1971.

A citation can be a separate citation "sentence" (beginning with a capital letter and ending with a period) after a regular sentence or an appositive clause within a regular sentence.

A typical citation sentence may read as follows:

> Title VII of the Civil Rights Act of 1964 prohibits employment discrimination because of race, color, religion, sex, or national origin. Civil Rights Act of 1964, § 703, 42 U.S.C. § 2000e-2 (1970).

A typical citation clause may read as follows:

> The Civil Rights Act of 1964 prohibits discrimination because of race, color, religion, sex, or national origin, 42 U.S.C. § 2000e-2 (1970), and has been interpreted to mean that . . .

In addition to citations to statutes and cases, legal writers also cite to books, periodicals, congressional reports, treaties, constitutions, newspapers, and other sources. In order to make citations uniform and understandable by all legal readers, a "uniform system of citation" has been developed by various law journals. It is published as a handbook titled *A Uniform System of Citation,* commonly referred to as the "Bluebook." All citations should conform to the uniform system of citation, and examples of the most commonly used citations are given below.

II. Proper Citation Form and Content

A. Statutes

Statutes are cited in several ways, depending on where the statute is found. Statutes currently in force are usually found in a codification or code (e.g., "United States Code" is a large set of books containing current federal statutes).

Codes are generally organized according to the subject matter of the statutes. If the statute was recently enacted, however, it is probably not yet found in the code. In this event, the statute is cited to the "session law." Session laws report statutes chronologically as they are enacted. Eventually, most session laws can be found in the code, but it takes about a year for the code to be updated with the laws enacted during each session of Congress.

Statutes may also be found in "secondary sources." A secondary source is any source other than a code or session law that contains the text of a statute.

A citation to the current code must include the name of the code, the code section number, and a parenthetical that contains the year of the codification. In a citation to the current code, the name of the statute and the original section number (found in the appropriate session laws) are given only if the statute is usually cited by its name and original sections or if they would otherwise aid in identification. An official name, a popular name, or both may be used. For example, Labor Management Relations (Taft-Hartley) Act § 301(a), 29 U.S.C. § 185(a) (1970).

A citation to any other source must include the name of the act, the public law or chapter number, the original section number, the published source in which the statute is found, if any, and a parenthetical containing the year of enactment. When a statute has been amended or repealed or is otherwise no longer in force as cited, the statute's relevant history must be explained parenthetically. If a statute has no official or popular name, "Act of" with the full date of enactment should be used, for example, Act of Apr. 25, 1957, Pub. L. No. 85-24, § 3, 71 Stat. 25. The section number follows the public law or chapter number, not the name of the act, for example, Clayton Act, ch. 323, § 7, 38 Stat. 730 (1914).

Thus, the proper citation of statutes is as follows:

cited to current code	National Environmental Policy Act of 1969, § 102, 42 U.S.C. § 4332 (1970)

or

42 U.S.C. § 4332 (1970)

cited to session laws	National Environmental Policy Act of 1969, Pub. L. No. 91-190, § 102, 83 Stat. 852 (1970) (prior to 1975 amendment)
cited to secondary source	Act of Aug. 9, 1975, Pub. L. No. 94-83, § 1, 5 Envir. L. Rep. 41,014 (1975) (to be codified in 42 U.S.C. § 4332)

B. Cases

All case citations *must* give the following information so that the reader can find the source easily:

1. Name of the case
2. Location of the printed decision (volume number, name of reporter, and page number)
3. Date of decision
4. Jurisdiction and court of decision. United States courts of appeals for numbered circuits, regardless of year, are indicated: 2d Cir., *not* C.C.A. 2d, and *not* C.A.2. The Court of Appeals for the District of Columbia and all its predecessors are cited: D.C. Cir. For district court cases, give the district but not the division. Thus: S.D. Cal., *not* S.D. Cal. C.D.

    Cite the old circuit courts (abolished 1912): C.C.S.D.N.Y. And cite the Judicial Panel on Multi-District Litigation: J.P.M.D.L. Decisions of bankruptcy courts and bankruptcy appellate panels are cited: Bankr. E.D. Va. or Bankr. 4th Cir.

153

A typical case citation might look like this:

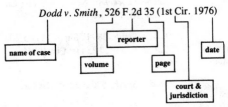

In addition, a case citation may give other important information that would be helpful to the reader. This information might include reference to specific pages within the reported decision, prior or subsequent history of the case, or specific details concerning the case.

A case citation, with helpful additional information, might look like this:

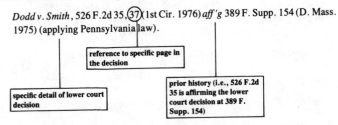

Following are typical case citation forms for the various stages of litigation, beginning when the case is first filed, all the way through to an appeal to, and decision by, the United States Supreme Court. Note that these examples are of cases in federal courts. The same format, however, can be used for state court decisions. The examples marked by an asterisk are the most commonly used.

filed but not decided	*Dodd v. Smith,* No. 74-329 (D. Mass., filed Sept. 9, 1974)
unpublished interim order	*Dodd v. Smith,* No. 74-329 (D. Mass., Oct. 10, 1974) (order granting preliminary injunction)
published interim order	*Dodd v. Smith,* 377 F. Supp. 321 (D. Mass. 1974) (order granting preliminary injunction)
unpublished decision	*Dodd v. Smith,* No. 74-329 (D. Mass., Jan. 21, 1975)
decision published in service only	*Dodd v. Smith,* [1975] Fed. Sec. L. Rep. (CCH) ¶95,098 (D. Mass., Jan. 21, 1975)
decision published in newspaper only	*Dodd v. Smith,* N.Y.L.J., Jan. 25, 1975, at 2, col. 4 (D. Mass. Jan. 21, 1975)
*published decision	*Dodd v. Smith,* 389 F. Supp. 154 (D. Mass. 1975)

appeal docketed	*Dodd v. Smith*, 389 F. Supp. 154 (D. Mass. 1975), *appeal docketed*, No. 75-699 (1st Cir. Feb. 10, 1975)
disposition in lower court showing subsequent history	*Dodd v. Smith*, 389 F. Supp. 154 (D. Mass. 1975), *aff'd*, 526 F.2d 35 (1st Cir. 1976)
*disposition on appeal	*Dodd v. Smith*, 526 F.2d 35 (1st Cir. 1976)
brief, record, or appendix	Brief for Appellee, *Dodd v. Smith*, 526 F.2d 35 (1st Cir. 1976)
petition for certiorari filed	*Dodd v. Smith*, 526 F.2d 35 (1st Cir. 1976), *petition for cert. filed*, 48 U.S.L.W. 824 (U.S. Nov. 10, 1976) (No. 76-418)
petition for certiorari granted	*Dodd v. Smith*, 526 F.2d 35 (1st Cir. 1976), *cert. granted*, 49 U.S.L.W. 101 (U.S. Jan. 25, 1977) (No. 76-418)
*Supreme Court opinion	*Dodd v. Smith*, 428 U.S. 1011 (1977)

or

Dodd v. Smith, 428 U.S. 1011, 93 S. Ct. 1480 (1977)

Aside from statutes and cases, legal writers often cite the Constitution, newspapers, periodicals, and other specialized sources. Such citations must also conform to proper citation form as the following examples show:

C. Constitutions

U.S. Const. art. I, § 9, cl. 2
U.S. Const. amend. XIV, § 2

D. Books

6 C. Wright & A. Miller, *Federal Practice and Procedure* § 1417 (1971)

E. Periodicals

Hertz, *Limits to the Naturalization Power*, 64 Geo. L.J. 1007 (1976)

F. Newspapers

Washington Post, Oct. 14, 1977, at 4, col. 2

G. Legislative Materials

1. Bills

S. 383, 83d Cong., 2d Sess. (1954)
H.R. 136, 79th Cong., 1st Sess. (1945)

  2. Reports
H.R. Rep. No. 353, 82d Cong., 1st Sess. 2 (1951)
S. Rep. No. 148, 91st Cong., 2d Sess. 181 (1973)

  3. U.S. Code Congressional & Administrative News
H.R. Rep. No. 98, 92d Cong., 1st Sess. 4 *reprinted in* [1971] U.S. Code Cong. & Ad. News 1017

  4. Congressional Record
103 Cong. Rec. 1728 (1975)
123 Cong. Rec. H12,575 (daily ed. Nov. 27, 1977)

H. Regulations

  1. Code of Federal Regulations
10 C.F.R. § 481.11 (1976)

  2. Federal Register
49 Fed. Reg. 11,234 (1977)

I. Taxation Materials

I.R.C. § 161
Treas. Reg. § 1.732 (1976)
Rev. Rul. 77-108

J. Other Sources

  1. Uniform Commercial Code
U.C.C. § 2-207

  2. Federal Rules of Evidence
Fed. R. Evid. 911

  3. Federal Rules of Civil Procedure
Fed. R. Civ. P. 61(a)

  4. Local Court Rules
1st Cir. R. 10(b)

  5. Bible
2 *Kings* 12:19

  6. Miscellaneous
9 ABA Antitrust Section 111 (1936)

ABA Canons of Professional Ethics No. 11

ABA Comm. on Professional Ethics, Opinions No. 105 (1934)

ABA-ALI Model Bus. Corp. Act. § 15 (1953)

12 Am. Jr. *Contracts* § 74 (1938)

ALI Fed. Income Tax Stat. § X105(a) (Feb. 1954 Drafts)

10 ALI Proceedings 256 (1931-1932)

5 American Law of Property § 22.30 (A.J. Casner ed. 1952)

Black's Law Dictionary 712 (4th ed. 1951)

88 C.J.S. *Trial* &192 (1955)

Model Penal Code § 305.17, Comment (Tent. Draft No. 5, 1956)

6 Moore's Federal Practice ¶ 56.07, at 2044 (2d ed. 1973)

Restatement (Second) of Agency § 20 (1957)

Restatement (Second) of Conflict of Laws § 305, Comment b, Illustration 1 (1971)

Restatement of Torts, Explanatory Notes § 3-40, Comment a at 118 (Tent. Draft No. 17, 1938)

The Federalist No. 23 (A. Hamilton)

III. General Rules for Typing Citations

A. Generally. Citation sentences begin with a capital letter and end with a period.

B. Underlining. Proper legal writing style requires that certain words in citations and text be italicized. As a general rule, to indicate italics in typewritten manuscript, *always underline the following:*

1. Case Names

Griggs v. Duke Power Co., 401 U.S. 424 (1971)

2. Book Titles

6 C. Wright & A. Miller, *Federal Practice and Procedure* § 1417 (1971)

3. Titles of Articles in Periodicals

Hertz, *Limits to the Naturalization Power,* 64 Geo. L.J. 1007 (1976)

4. Names of Newspapers

Washington Post, Dec. 3, 1977, at 2, col. 1

5. Signals and Explanatory and Procedural Phrases

Sometimes a legal writer will insert additional words in a citation sentence to explain to the reader the significance of the citation. Always underline the following words when used in a citation:

accord,
aff'd,
aff'd mem.,
aff'd [rev'd] on other grounds,
aff'd on rehearing,
aff'g [rev'g],
acq.
acq. in result
appeal denied,
appeal dismissed,
appeal filed,
argued,
but see
but cf.

cert. granted [*denied*],
cf.
compare . . . [*and*] . . . *with* . . . [*and*]
contra,
dismissing appeal from
e.g., (but only as a signal)
enforcing
id.
modified,
modifying
nonacq.
passim
petition for cert. filed,
prob. juris. noted,
reh'g granted [*denied*],
reprinted in
rev'd per curiam,
see
see also
see generally
semble
sub nom.
vacated,
withdrawn,

6. Latin Words and Phrases

Always underline the following words in typewritten manuscript when used in a citation or text:

infra
inter alia
inter se
qua
sic
supra

C. Spacing Between Certain Abbreviations.

In some instances, *there should be no space between two abbreviated words*. The rule is that whenever two adjacent abbreviated words have been abbreviated to single capital letters, there is no space between the letters. For this purpose, numerical designation such as "2d" and "3d" are considered single capital letters.

Examples:
A.L.R.2d
D.C.
D.R.I.
F.R.D.
F.2d
I.C.C.
N.Y.
S.D.N.Y.
U.S.

But:
   Cal. 3d
   F. Supp.
   So. 2d

D. More Than One Citation — "String" Citations. When there is more than one citation within a citation sentence or clause, they are separated by a semicolon.

E. Punctuation Marks in Quoted Material. Commas and periods are always placed inside the quotation marks; other punctuation marks are placed inside the quotation marks only if they are part of the quoted matter.

F. Indentation of Quotations. Quotations of 50 or more words should be indented left and right *without* quotation marks.

IV. Introductory Signals

A. Explanation

"Introductory signals" are the words or phrases used by legal writers in a citation to emphasize the importance the writer ascribes to the cited authority or for purposes of comparison or general background information. They precede or "introduce," the authorities that they explain and "signal" the reader how to interpret the material that follows and apply it to the authorities in the citation.

1. Signals That Indicate Specific Support:

When *no signal* appears, this means that the cited authority (a) directly supports the statement in the text, (b) identifies the source of a quotation, or (c) identifies an authority referred to in the text.

E.g.,: This signal means that there are other examples directly supporting the statement in the text, but citation to them would not be helpful. ("*E.g.,*" may also be used in combination with other signals, preceded by a comma: "*See, e.g.,*" "*But see, e.g.,*").

Accord,: This signal means that the cited authority directly supports the statement, but in a slightly different way than the authority(ies) first cited. "*Accord,*" is commonly used when two or more cases are on the point but the text refers to only one; the others are then introduced by "*accord,.*" Similarly, the law of one jurisdiction may be cited as in accord with that of another.

See: This signal means that the cited authority constitutes the basic source material supporting the proposition. "*See*" is used when the proposition is not stated by the cited authority but follows from it.

See also: This signal means that the cited authority constitutes additional source material that supports the proposition. "*See also*" is commonly used to cite an authority supporting a proposition when authorities that state or directly support the proposition have already been cited or discussed. Parenthetical explanations are encouraged with this signal.

Cf.: This signal means that the cited authority supports a proposition different from that in the text but is sufficiently analogous to lend support. "*Cf.*" means "compare." "*Cf.*" should always be used with an explanatory parenthetical.

2. **Signals That Suggest a Profitable Comparison:** *Compare. . . [and] . . . with . . . [and] . . .:* This signal means that comparison of authorities cited will offer support for, or illustrate, a statement in the text.

3. **Signals That Indicate Specific Contradiction:**

   Contra: This signal means that the cited authority directly supports a contrary statement.

   But see: This signal means that the cited authority suggests a contrary statement.

   But cf.: This signal means that the cited authority supports a proposition analogous to the contrary of the position stated in the text. *"But cf."* should always be used with an explanatory parenthetical.

4. **Signals That Indicate Background Material:** *See generally:* This signal means that the cited authority provides helpful background to the question examined in the text, without providing support for the specific conclusion reached. The use of a parenthetical is encouraged.

B. Order of Signals

When more than one signal is used in a citation, the signals (together with the authorities they introduce) should appear in the order listed above.

C. Order Within a Given Signal

Within a signal, authorities should be cited in the following order, subject to alteration for any good reason.

Cases are arranged within a signal according to the courts issuing the cited opinions; subsequent and prior history is irrelevant to the order of citation. Cases decided by the same court are arranged in reverse chronological order; for this purpose the several United States courts of appeals are treated as one court and all federal district courts are treated as one court. The ordering system is as follows:

Federal:

1. Supreme Court,
2. courts of appeals, Emergency Court of Appeals,
3. district courts,
4. Court of Claims,
5. Court of Customs and Patent Appeals, Court of Military Appeals, Customs Court, Tax Court (including Board of Tax Appeals), Court of International Trade,
6. bankruptcy appellate panels and judges,
7. administrative agencies (alphabetically by agency).

State (alphabetically by state):

8. courts (by rank within each state),
9. agencies (alphabetically by agency within each state).

Non-United States:

10. common-law jurisdictions (as for states),
11. civil-law jurisdictions (as for states).

Cite **statutes** according to jurisdiction in the following order:

Federal:

1. statutes in U.S.C. or U.S.C.A. or U.S.C.S. (by progressive order of U.S.C. title),
2. statutes currently in force but not in U.S.C. or U.S.C.A. or U.S.C.S. (by reverse chronological order of enactment),
3. rules of evidence and procedure,
4. repealed statutes (by reverse chronological order of enactment).

State: (alphabetically by state)

5. statutes in current codification (by order in the codification),
6. statutes currently in force but not in current codification (by reverse chronological order of enactment),
7. rules of evidence and procedure,
8. repealed statutes (by reverse chronological order of enactment).

Non-United States: (alphabetically by jurisdiction)

9. statutes currently in force,
10. repealed statutes.

International agreements, bills, and resolutions are cited in that order, in reverse chronological order within each classification.

Rules and administrative materials are cited in the following order:

Rules:

1. federal,
2. state (alphabetically by state),
3. non-United States (alphabetically by jurisdiction). These are followed by

Federal administrative regulations and rulings:

4. executive orders,
5. current treasury regulations, proposed treasury regulations,
6. all others currently in force (by progressive order of C.F.R. title),
7. all repealed regulations and rulings (by reverse chronological order of promulgation). These are followed by

Other administrative regulations and rulings:

8. state (alphabetically by state), currently in force, then repealed,
9. non-United States (alphabetically by jurisdiction), currently in force, then repealed.

Records, briefs, and petitions are cited in that order and within each classification by order of court in which filed.

Secondary sources are cited in the following order:

1. books and essays in a collection of a single author's essays (alphabetically by author — if none, by first word of title),

2. articles and essays in a collection of various authors' essays (alphabetically by author),
3. student-written law review material — special student projects, then long works such as notes, then short commentaries on recent developments (alphabetically by periodical as abbreviated in citation),
4. signed book reviews (alphabetically by reviewer),
5. student-written book reviews (alphabetically by periodical as abbreviated in citation),
6. newspapers (in reverse chronological order)
7. annotations (in reverse chronological order)
8. unpublished material and other material of limited circulation (alphabetically by author — if none, by first word of title).

V. Abbreviations

Following are proper abbreviations for the most commonly used sources for both cases and statutes.

A. Case Reporters and Statutory Compilations:

1. Federal Courts

United States Supreme Court

United States Reports	___ U.S. ___
Supreme Court Reporter	___ S. Ct. ___
United States Supreme Court Reports (Lawyers' Edition)	___ L. Ed. ___
(second series)	___ L. Ed. 2d ___
United States Law Week	___ U.S.L.W. ___

United States Courts of Appeals

a. Federal Reporter	___ F. ___
(second series)	___ F.2d ___
b. Federal Cases (1789–1800)	___ F. Cas. ___

United States District Courts

Federal Supplement	___ F. Supp. ___
Federal Rules Decisions	___ F.R.D. ___

Court of Claims and Customs Court

Court of Claims Reports	___ Ct. Cl. ___
Customs Court Reports	___ Cust. Ct. ___

Court of Customs and Patent Appeals

Court of Customs and Patent Appeals Reports	___ C.C.P.A. ___

Tax Court and Board of Tax Appeals

Tax Court of the United States Reports	___ T.C. ___
Board of Tax Appeals Reports	___ B.T.A. ___
Tax Court Memorandum Decisions	___ T.C.M. ___
	(CCH) [or (P-H)]

Board of Tax Appeals
   Memorandum Decisions   ___ B.T.A.M. (P-H)

Court of Military Appeals

a. Court of Military Appeals Reports   ___ C.M.A. ___
b. Military Justice Reports   ___ M.J. ___
c. Court-Martial Reports   ___ C.M.R.___

2. Federal Statutes

United States Code   ___ U.S.C. § ___
Internal Revenue Code of 1954   ___ I.R.C. § ___
United States Code Annotated   ___ U.S.C.A. § ___
United States Statutes at Large   ___ Stat. ___

3. Regional Reporters (state court decisions)

Regional reporters, published by the West Publishing Company, contain virtually all opinions of the highest courts of all fifty states and the District of Columbia.

Atlantic Reporter   ___ A. ___
   (second series)   ___ A.2d ___

North Eastern Reporter   ___ N.E. ___
   (second series)   ___ N.E. 2d ___

North Western Reporter   ___ N.W. ___
   (second series)   ___ N.W.2d ___

Pacific Reporter   ___ P. ___
   (second series)   ___ P.2d ___

Southern Reporter   ___ So. ___
   (second series)   ___ So. 2d ___

South Eastern Reporter   ___ S.E. ___
   (second series)   ___ S.E.2d. ___

South Western Reporter   ___ S.W. ___
   (second series)   ___ S.W.2d ___

4. Table of State Supreme Courts and Statutory Compilations

Almost every state publishes the decisions of its highest court in a separate set of books such as ''Alabama Reports'' (Ala.) or ''Arizona Reports'' (Ariz.). In those states where there is no official state reporter it is necessary to cite to the regional reporter (e.g., Alaska Supreme Court decisions are cited to P.2d).

In addition, each state compiles its statutes in a set of books such as ''Ala. Code'' (Alabama Code) and ''Ariz. Rev. Stat. Ann.'' (Arizona Revised Statutes Annotated).

Following is a table of the proper abbreviations for the source of opinions of each state's highest (or supreme) court as well as the abbreviations for each state's statutory compilation.

	Supreme Court	Statutory Compilation
Alabama	___ Ala. ___	Ala. Code tit. ___, § ___
Alaska	(Cite to P.2d)	Alaska Stat. § ___

	Supreme Court	Statutory Compilation
Arizona	___ Ariz. ___	Ariz. Rev. Stat. Ann. § ___
Arkansas	___ Ark. ___	Ark. Stat. Ann. § ___
California	___ Cal. [2d] [3d] ___	Cal.[subject] Code § ___
Colorado	___ Colo. ___	Colo. Re. Stat. § ___
Connecticut	___ Conn. ___*	Conn. Gen. Stat. § ___ Conn. Gen. Stat. Ann. § ___ (West)
Delaware	___ Del. ___ (1920-1966) (Cite to Del. and A. or A.2d)	Del. Code Ann. tit. ___, § ___
District of Columbia	(Cite to A.2d)**	D.C. Code Ann. § ___
Florida	___ Fla. ___ (1846-1948) (Cite to Fla. and So. or So.2d)	Fla. Stat. § ___
Georgia	___ Ga. ___	Ga. Code § ___
Hawaii	___ Haw. ___	Haw. Rev. Stat. § ___
Idaho	___ Idaho ___	Idaho Code § ___
Illinois	___ Ill. [2d] ___	Ill. Ann. Stat. ch. ___, § ___ (Smith-Hurd)
Indiana	___ Ind. ___	Ind. Code § ___ Ind. Code Ann. § ___ (Burns)
Iowa	___ Iowa ___ (1855-1968) (Cite to Iowa and N.W. or N.W.2d)	Iowa Code § ___ Iowa Code Ann. § ___ (West)

Kansas	___ Kan. ___	Kan. Stat. § ___
		 Kan. U.C.C. Ann. § ___ (Vernon)
		 Kan. Civ. Pro. Stat. Ann. § ___
		   (Vernon)
		 Kan. Crim. Code & Code of
		   Crim. Proc. § ___ (Vernon)

Kentucky	___ Ky. ___ (1879-1951) (Cite to Ky. and S.W. or S.W.2d)	Ky. Rev. Stat. § ___ Ky. Rev. Stat. Ann. § ___ (Baldwin)

	Supreme Court	Statutory Compilation
Louisiana	___ La. ___	La. Rev. Stat. Ann. § ___ (West)
		La. Civ. Code Ann. art. ___ (West)
		La. Code Crim. Pro. Ann. art. ___ (West)
	(1900-1972) (Cite to La. and So. or So.2d)	
Maine	___ Me. ___ (1820-1965)*** (Cite to Me. and A. or A.2d)	Me. Rev. Stat. tit. ___, § ___
Maryland	___ Md. ___**	Md. [subject] Code Ann. § ___
		Md. Ann. Code art. ___, § ___
Massachusetts	___ Mass. ___***	Mass. Gen. Laws Ann. ch. ___, § ___ (West)
		Mass. Ann. Laws Ch. ___, §___ (Michie Law. Co-op)
Michigan	___ Mich. ___	Mich. Comp. Laws § ___
		Mich. Comp. Laws Ann. § ___
		Mich. Stat. Ann. § ___
Minnesota	___ Minn. ___	Minn. Stat. § ___
		Minn. Stat. Ann. § ___ (West)
	(1851-1977) (Cite to Minn. and N.W. or N.W.2d)	
Mississippi	___ Miss. ___ (1850-1966) (Cite to Miss. and So. or So.2d)	Miss. Code Ann. § ___
Missouri	___ Mo. ___ (1821-1956) (Cite to Mo. and S.W. or S.W.2d)	Mo. Rev. Stat. § ___
		Mo. Ann. Stat. § ___ (Vernon)
Montana	___ Mont. ___	Mont. Rev. Codes Ann. § ___
Nebraska	___ Neb. ___	Neb. Rev. Stat. § ___
Nevada	___ Nev. ___	Nev. Rev. Stat. § ___
New Hampshire	___ N.H. ___	N.H. Rev. State. Ann. § ___
New Jersey	___ N.J. ___	N.J. Rev. Stat. § ___
		N.J. Stat. Ann. § ___ (West)
New Mexico	___ N.M. ___	N.M. Stat. Ann. § ___

	Supreme Court	Statutory Compilation
New York	___ N.Y. [2d] ___**	N.Y. [subject] Law (McKinney) N.Y. [subject] Law (Consol.)
North Carolina	___ N.C. ___	N.C. Gen. Stat. § ___
North Dakota	___ N.D. ___ (1890-1953) (Cite to N.D. and N.W. or N.W.2d)	N.D. Cent. Code § ___
Ohio	___ Ohio St. [2d] ___	Ohio Rev. Code Ann. § ___ (Page) Ohio Rev. Code Ann. § ___ (Baldwin) Ohio Rev. Code Ann. § ___ (Anderson)
Oklahoma	___ Okla. ___ (1890-1953) (Cite to Okla. and P. or P.2d)	Okla. Stat. tit. ___, § ___ Okla Stat. Ann. tit. ___, § ___ (West)
Oregon	___ Or. ___	Or. Rev. Stat. § ___
Pennsylvania	___ Pa. ___	___ Pa. Cons. Stat. § ___ ___ Pa. Cons. Stat. Ann. § ___ (Purdon) Pa. Stat. Ann. tit. ___, § ___ (Purdon)
Puerto Rico	___ P.R.R. ___	P.R. Laws Ann. tit. ___, § ___
Rhode Island	___ R.I. ___	R.I. Gen. Laws § ___
South Carolina	___ S.C. ___	S.C. Code §___
South Dakota	___ S.D. ___ (1890-1976) (Cite to S.D. and N.W. or N.W.2d)	S.D. Compiled Laws Ann. § ___ S.D. Uniform Prob. Code § ___
Tennessee	___ Tenn. ___ (1870-1971) (Cite to Tenn. and S.W. or S.W.2d)	Tenn. Code Ann. § ___
Texas	___ Tex. ___ (1846-1962) (Cite to Tex. and S.W. or S.W.2d)	Tex. [subject] Code Ann. tit. ___, § ___ (Vernon) Tex. Stat. Ann. § ___
Utah	___ Utah [2d] ___ (1855-1974) (Cite to Utah and P. or P.2d)	Utah Code Ann. § ___

	Supreme Court	**Statutory Compilation**
Vermont	___ Vt. ___	Vt. Stat. Ann. tit. ___, § ___
Virginia	___ Va. ___	Va. Code § ___
Washington	___ Wash. [2d] ___	Wash. Rev. Code § ___ Wash. Rev. Code Ann. § ___
West Virginia	___ W. Va. ___ (1863-1973) (Cite to W. Va. and S.E. or S.E.2d)	W. Va. Code § ___
Wisconsin	___ Wis. ___	Wis. Stat. § ___ Wis. Stat. Ann. § ___ (West)
Wyoming	___ Wyo. ___ (1870-1959) (Cite to Wyo. and P. or P.2d)	Wyo. Stat. § ___

B. Case Names:

In case names that appear in footnotes, the following words are abbreviated as indicated below. Never abbreviate "United States" or the first word of a party name. For example, a case titled *"American Brotherhood of Chemical Engineers v. General Hospital Corporation"* would be written *"American Bhd. of Chem. Eng'rs v. General Hosp. Corp."* However, always abbreviate Co., Corp., Inc., Ltd., No., and & as well as commonly used abbreviations of organizations (e.g., NAACP or UMW).

Administrator	Adm'r	Commissioner	Comm'r	Educational	Educ.
Administratrix	Adm'x	Committee	Comm.	Electric	Elec.
American	Am.	Company	Co.	Electricity	Elec.
Associate	Assoc.	Consolidated	Consol.	Electronic	Elec.
Association	Ass'n	Construction	Constr.	Engineer	Eng'r
Atlantic	Atl.	Cooperative	Coop.	Engineering	Eng'r
Authority	Auth.	Corporation	Corp.	Equipment	Equip.
Automobile	Auto.	Department	Dep't	Exchange	Exch.
Avenue	Ave.	Development	Dev.	Executor	Ex'r
Board	Bd.	Distribute	Distrib.	Executrix	Ex'x
Brotherhood	Bhd.	Distributing	Distrib.	Federal	Fed.
Brothers	Bros.	Distributor	Distrib.	Federation	Fed'n
Building	Bldg.	District	Dist.	Finance	Fin.
Casualty	Cas.	Division	Div.	General	Gen.
Central	Cent.	East	E.	Government	Gov't
Chemical	Chem.	Eastern	E.	Guaranty	Guar.
Commission	Comm'n	Education	Educ.	Hospital	Hosp.

Housing	Hous.	Market	Mkt.	Society	Soc'y
Incorporated	Inc.	Municipal	Mun.	South	S.
Indemnity	Indem.	Mutual	Mut.	Southern	S.
Industrial	Indus.	National	Nat'l	Steamship	S.S.
Industries	Indus.	North	N.	Street	St.
Industry	Indus.	Northern	N.	Surety	Sur.
Insurance	Ins.	Pacific	Pac.	System	Sys.
Institute	Inst.	Product	Prod.	Telegraph	Tel.
Institution	Inst.	Production	Prod.	Telephone	Tel.
International	Int'l	Public	Pub.	Transport	Transp.
Investment	Inv.	Railroad	R.R.	Transportation	Transp.
Liability	Liab.	Railway	Ry.	University	Univ.
Limited	Ltd.	Refining	Ref.	Utility	Util.
Machine	Mach.	Road	Rd.	West	W.
Machinery	Mach.	Savings	Sav.	Western	W.
Manufacturer	Mfr.	Securities	Sec.		
Manufacturing	Mfg.	Service	Serv.		

C. Names of Courts:

When citing to cases, it is essential to tell the reader the name of the court deciding the case. This is accomplished by placing the name of the court, properly abbreviated, in parentheses after the name of the case. For example, the case of *Fitzgerald v. Reeves,* decided by the District of Columbia Municipal Court of Appeals in 1962, might be cited as follows:

Fitzgerald v. *Reeves*, 281 A.2d 422 (D.C. Mun. Ct. App. 1962).
Following are abbreviations for court names and designations:

Admiralty Court or Division	Adm.
Appellate Department	App. Dep't
Appellate Division	App. Div.
Board of Tax Appeals	B.T.A.
Chancery Court or Division	Ch.
Children's Court	Child. Ct.
Circuit Court (old federal)	C.C.
Circuit Court (state)	Cir. Ct.
Circuit Court of Appeal (state)	Cir. Ct. App.
Circuit Court of Appeals (federal)	Cir.
City Court	[name city] City Ct.
Civil Appeals	Civ. App.
Civil Court of Record	Civ. Ct. Rec.
Common Pleas	C.P. [when appropriate, name county or similar subdivision]
Commonwealth Court	Commw. Ct.
County Court	[name county] County Ct.
County Judge's Court	County J. Ct.
Court of Appeals (federal)	Cir.
Court of Appeal[s] (state)	Ct. App.
Court of Claims	Ct. Cl.

Court of Criminal Appeals	Crim. App.
Court of Customs and Patent Appeals	C.C.P.A.
Court of Customs Appeals	Ct. Cust. App.
Court of Errors and Appeals	Ct. Err. & App.
Court of Military Appeals	C.M.A.
Court of Military Review	C.M.R.
Court of [General, Special] Sessions	Ct. [Gen., Spec.] Sess.
Criminal Appeals	Crim. App.
Customs Court	Cust. Ct.
District Court (federal)	D.
District Court (state)	Dist. Ct.
District Court of Appeal	Dist. Ct. App.
Domestic Relations Court	Dom. Rel. Ct.
Emergency Court of Appeals	Emer. Ct. App.
Equity Court or Division	Eq.
Justice of the Peace's Court	J.P. Ct.
Juvenile Court	Juv. Ct.
Law Court or Division	L. Ct. or Div.
Magistrate's Court	Magis. Ct.
Municipal Court	[name city] Mun. Ct.
Orphan's Court	Orphan's Ct.
Probate Court	P. Ct.
Police Justice's Court	Police J. Ct.
Public Utilities Commission	P.U.C.
Real Estate Commission	Real Est. Comm'n
Superior Court	Super. Ct.
Supreme Court	Sup. Ct.
Supreme Court, Appellate Division	App. Div.
Supreme Court, Appellate Term	App. T.
Supreme Judicial Court	Sup. Jud. Ct.
Surrogate's Court	Sur. Ct.
Tax Court	T.C.
Workmen's Compensation Division	Workmen's Comp. Div.
Youth Court	Youth Ct.

LEGAL FORMS

The following are suggested formats for typing some legal documents. As local rules regarding the style of forms may vary between courts, districts, and divisions, it is important to check local rules before filing any document.

All papers filed in connection with a case in court must contain a "caption." The caption is the heading on a document that shows the following: 1) name of the court, including the district or division, if any; 2) names of the parties (i.e., plaintiff and defendant); and 3) the case's number on the court docket or calendar.

IN THE UNITED STATES DISTRICT COURT
FOR
THE _____ DISTRICT OF _____
_____ DIVISION   (if applicable)

A.B., Plaintiff
      v.   Civil Action No. _____
C.D., Defendant

(Designation of paper to be filed, i.e., Complaint, Summons, Answer, Interrogatories, Motion for Summary Judgment, etc.)

Virtually all papers filed in connection with a case in court must be sent to, or "served on," all other parties connected with the case. Accordingly, it is necessary to certify to the court that the paper was served on the other parties and a certificate of service is used for this purpose. The certificate of service is usually the last paragraph of the document filed with the court.

CERTIFICATE OF SERVICE

I hereby certify that the foregoing _____
(designation of paper to be filed, i.e.,

_____ was mailed, postage prepaid, this _____day of
Answer, Interrogatories, etc.)

_____, 19__, to _____, attorney
(name and address)

for _____.
(Plaintiff, Defendant, etc.)

_____

Every complaint filed in a court must contain an allegation of jurisdiction. The allegation of jurisdiction informs the court by what statutory authority the court has to hear the case.

ALLEGATION OF JURISDICTION

(a) Jurisdiction founded on diversity of citizenship and amount.

Plaintiff is a [citizen of the State of Connecticut] [1] [corporation incorporated under the laws of the State of Connecticut having its principal place of business in the State of Connecticut] and defendant is a corporation incorporated under the laws of the State of New York having its principal place of business in a State other than the State of Connecticut. The matter in controversy exceeds, exclusive of interest and costs, the sum of ten thousand dollars.

(b) Jurisdiction founded on the existence of a Federal question and amount in controversy.

The action arises under [the Constitution of the United States, Article ____, Section ____]; [the ____ Amendment to the Constitution of the United States, Section ____]; [the Act of ____, ____ Stat. ____; U.S.C., Title ____, § ____]; [the Treaty of the United States (here describe the treaty)],[2] as hereinafter more fully appears. The matter in controversy exceeds, exclusive of interest and costs, the sum of ten thousand dollars.

(c) Jurisdiction founded on the existence of a question arising under particular statutes.

The action arises under the Act of ____, ____ Stat. ____; U.S.C., Title ____, § ____, as hereinafter more fully appears.

(d) Jurisdiction founded on the admiralty or maritime character of the claim.

This is a case of admiralty and maritime jurisdiction, as hereinafter more fully appears. [If the pleader wishes to invoke the distinctively maritime procedures referred to in Rule 9(h), add the following or its substantial equivalent: This is an admiralty or maritime claim within the meaning of Rule 9(h).]

---

[1] Form for natural person.

[2] Use the appropriate phrase or phrases. The general allegation of the existence of a Federal question is ineffective unless the matters constituting the claim for relief as set forth in the complaint raise a Federal question.

[CAPTION]

COMPLAINT ON A PROMISSORY NOTE

1. [Allegation of jurisdiction]
2. Defendant on or about ___(date)___ executed and delivered to plaintiff a promissory note [in the following words and figures: (here set out the note verbatim)]; [a copy of which is hereto annexed as Exhibit A]; [whereby defendant promised to pay to plaintiff or order on ___(date)___ the sum of _____ dollars with interest thereon at the rate of six percent per annum].
3. Defendant owes to plaintiff the amount of said note and interest.
Wherefore plaintiff demands judgment against defendant for the sum of _____ dollars, interest, and costs.

Signed: _____
Attorney for Plaintiff
Address: _____

[CAPTION]

COMPLAINT ON AN ACCOUNT

1. [Allegation of jurisdiction]
2. Defendant owes plaintiff _____ dollars according to the account hereto annexed as Exhibit A.
Wherefore plaintiff demands judgment against defendant for the sum of _____ dollars, interest, and costs.

Signed: _____
Attorney for Plaintiff
Address: _____

[CAPTION]

COMPLAINT FOR GOODS SOLD AND DELIVERED

1. [Allegation of jurisdiction]
2. Defendant owes plaintiff _____ dollars for goods sold and delivered by plaintiff to defendant between ___(date)___ and ___(date)___ .

Wherefore plaintiff demands judgment against defendant for the sum of _____ dollars, interest, and costs.

Signed: _____
Attorney for Plaintiff

Address: _____

[CAPTION]

COMPLAINT FOR MONEY LENT

1. [Allegation of jurisdiction]
2. Defendant owes plaintiff _____ dollars for money lent by plaintiff to defendant on ___(date)___ .

Wherefore plaintiff demands judgment against defendant for the sum of _____ dollars, interest, and costs.

Signed: _____
Attorney for Plaintiff

Address: _____

[CAPTION]

COMPLAINT FOR MONEY PAID BY MISTAKE

1. [Allegation of jurisdiction]
2. Defendant owes plaintiff _____ dollars for money paid by plaintiff to defendant by mistake on ___(date)___ under the following circumstances: [here state the circumstances with particularity—see Rule 9(b)] .

Wherefore plaintiff demands judgment against defendant for the sum ot _____ dollars, interest, and costs.

Signed: _____
Attorney for Plaintiff

Address: _____

[CAPTION]

COMPLAINT FOR MONEY HAD AND RECEIVED

1. [Allegation of jurisdiction]
2. Defendant owes plaintiff _____ dollars for money had and received from one G. H. on ___(date)___, to be paid by defendant to plaintiff.

Wherefore plaintiff demands judgment against defendant for the sum of _____ dollars, interest, and costs.

Signed: _____

Attorney for Plaintiff

Address: _____

[CAPTION]

ANSWER TO COMPLAINT FOR MONEY HAD AND RECEIVED WITH COUNTERCLAIM FOR INTERPLEADER

Defense

Defendant admits the allegations stated in paragraph 1 of the complaint; and denies the allegations stated in paragraph 2 to the extent set forth in the counterclaim herein.

Counterclaim for Interpleader

1. Defendant received the sum of _____ dollars as a deposit from E. F.

2. Plaintiff has demanded the payment of such deposit to him by virtue of an assignment of it which he claims to have received from E. F.

3. E. F. has notified the defendant that he claims such deposit, that the purported assignment is not valid, and that he holds the defendant responsible for the deposit.

Wherefore defendant demands:

(1) That the court order E. F. to be made a party defendant to respond to the complaint and to this counterclaim.[1]

(2) That the court order the plaintiff and E. F. to interplead their respective claims.

(3) That the court adjudge whether the plaintiff or E. F. is entitled to the sum of money.

(4) That the court discharge defendant from all liability in the premises except to the person it shall adjudge entitled to the sum of money.

(5) That the court award to the defendant its costs and attorney's fees.

---

[1] Rule 13(h) provides for the court ordering parties to a counterclaim, but who are not parties to the orginal action, to be brought in as defendants.

[CAPTION]

COMPLAINT FOR NEGLIGENCE

1. [Allegation of jurisdiction]
2. On ___(date)___, in a public highway called Boylston Street in Boston, Massachusetts, defendant negligently drove a motor vehicle against plaintiff who was then crossing said highway.
3. As a result plaintiff was thrown down and had his leg broken and was otherwise injured, was prevented from transacting his business, suffered great pain of body and mind, and incurred expenses for medical attention and hospitalization in the sum of one thousand dollars.

Wherefore plaintiff demands judgment against defendant in the sum of _____ dollars and costs.

[CAPTION]

COMPLAINT FOR CONVERSION

1. [Allegation of jurisdiction]
2. On or about ___(date)___ defendant converted to his own use ten bonds of the _____ Company (here insert brief identification as by number and issue) of the value of _____ dollars, the property of plaintiff.

Wherefore plaintiff demands judgment against defendant in the sum of _____ dollars, interest, and costs.

[CAPTION]

COMPLAINT FOR SPECIFIC PERFORMANCE OF CONTRACT TO CONVEY LAND

1. [Allegation of jurisdiction]
2. On or about ___(date)___ plaintiff and defendant entered into an agreement in writing a copy of which is hereto annexed as Exhibit A.
3. In accord with the provisions of said agreement plaintiff tendered to defendant the purchase price and requested a conveyance of the land, but defendant refused to accept the tender and refused to make the conveyance.
4. Plaintiff now offers to pay the purchase price.

Wherefore plaintiff demands (1) that defendant be required specifically to perform said agreement, (2) damages in the sum of one thousand dollars, and (3) that if specific performance is not granted plaintiff have judgment against defendant in the sum of _____ dollars.

[CAPTION]

COMPLAINT ON CLAIM FOR DEBT AND TO SET ASIDE FRAUDULENT CONVEYANCE UNDER RULE 18(b)

1. [Allegation of jurisdiction]
2. Defendant C. D. on or about _____ executed and delivered to plaintiff a promissory note [in the following words and figures: (here set out the note verbatim)]; [a copy of which is hereto annexed as Exhibit A]; [whereby defendant C. D. promised to pay to plaintiff or order on _____ the sum of five thousand dollars with interest thereon at the rate of ____ percent per annum].
3. Defendant C. D. owes to plaintiff the amount of said note and interest.
4. Defendant C. D. on or about _____ conveyed all his property, real and personal [or specify and describe] to defendant E. F. for the purpose of defrauding plaintiff and hindering and delaying the collection of the indebtedness evidenced by the note above referred to.

Wherefore plaintiff demands:

(1) That plaintiff have judgment against defendant C. D. for _____ dollars and interest; (2) that the aforesaid conveyance to defendant E. F. be declared void and the judgment herein be declared a lien on said property; (3) that plaintiff have judgment against the defendants for costs.

[CAPTION]

MOTION TO DISMISS, PRESENTING DEFENSES OR FAILURE TO STATE A CLAIM, OF LACK OF SERVICE OF PROCESS, OF IMPROPER VENUE, AND OF LACK OF JURISDICTION UNDER RULE 12(b)

The defendant moves the court as follows:

1.   To dismiss the action because the complaint fails to state a claim against defendant upon which relief can be granted.

2.   To dismiss the action or in lieu thereof to quash the return of service of summons on the grounds (a) that the defendant is a corporation organized under the laws of Delaware and was not and is not subject to service of process within the Southern District of New York, and (b) that the defendant has not been properly served with process in this action, all of which more clearly appears in the affidavits of M. N. and X. Y. hereto annexed as Exhibit A and Exhibit B respectively.

3.   To dismiss the action on the ground that it is in the wrong district because (a) the jurisdiction of this court is invoked solely on the ground that the action arises under the Constitution and laws of the United States and (b) the defendant is a corporation incorporated under the laws of the State of Delaware and is not licensed to do or doing business in the Southern District of New York, all of which more clearly appears in the affidavits of K. L. and V. W. hereto annexed as Exhibit C and D respectively.

4.   To dismiss the action on the ground that the court lacks jurisdiction because the amount actually in controversy is less than ten thousand dollars exclusive of interest and costs.

Signed: _____
Attorney for Defendant

Address: _____

Notice of Motion

To: _____
Attorney for Plaintiff

_____

Please take notice, that the undersigned will bring the above motion on for hearing before this Court at Room _____, United States Court House, Foley Square, City of New York, on the _____ day of _____, 19__, at 10 o'clock in the forenoon of that day or as soon thereafter as counsel can be heard.

Signed: _____
Attorney for Defendant

Address: _____

[CAPTION]

ANSWER PRESENTING DEFENSES UNDER RULE 12(b)

First Defense

The complaint fails to state a claim against defendant upon which relief can be granted.

Second Defense

If defendant is indebted to plaintiffs for the goods mentioned in the complaint, he is indebted to them jointly with G. H. G. H. is alive; is a citizen of the State of New York and a resident of this district, is subject to the jurisdiction of this court, as to both service of process and venue; can be made a party without depriving this court of jurisdiction of the present parties, and has not been made a party.

Third Defense

Defendant admits the allegation contained in paragraphs 1 and 4 of the complaint; alleges that he is without knowledge or information sufficient to form a belief as to the truth of the allegations contained in paragraph 2 of the complaint; and denies each and every other allegation contained in the complaint.

Fourth Defense

The right of action set forth in the complaint did not accrue within six years next before the commencement of this action.

Counterclaim

(Here set forth any claim as a counterclaim in the manner in which a claim is pleaded in a complaint. No statement of the grounds on which the court's jurisdiction depends need be made unless the counterclaim requires independent grounds of jurisdiction.)

Cross-Claim Against Defendant M. N.

(Here set forth the claim constituting a cross-claim against defendant M. N. in the manner in which a claim is pleaded in a complaint. The statement of grounds upon which the court's jurisdiction depends need not be made unless the cross-claim requires independent grounds of jurisdiction.)

[CAPTION]

NOTICE TO TAKE ORAL DEPOSITION

TO: Defendant (or Plaintiff)_____
(name and address)

and his attorney, _____
(name and address)

PLEASE TAKE NOTICE that the Plaintiff, _____,
(name)

in the above-captioned matter, will take the depositions of the following person
at _____
(address)

_____

at the time and date set forth below, said deposition to continue from day to day until completed. Such deposition will be taken upon oral examination for the purpose of discovery, or as evidence, or both, pursuant to the Federal Rules of Civil Procedure, before an officer authorized by law to administer oaths.

The said witness will please bring with him to the deposition, all correspondence, files, drawings, notes, reports, memoranda, documents, logs, contracts, agreements or other writings of any kind or character relating to _____
_____.
(the subject of the oral deposition)

You are invited to attend and participate if you desire to do so.

Person to be Deposed   Deposition Date   Time
_____   _____   _____

By: _____

[CAPTION]

SUMMONS

To the above-named Defendant:

You are hereby summoned and required to serve upon _____, plaintiff's attorney, whose address is _____, an answer to the complaint which is herewith served upon you, within 20[1] days after service of this summons upon you, exclusive of the day of service. If you fail to do so, judgment by default will be taken against you for the relief demanded in the complaint.

_____,

Clerk of Court

[Seal of the U. S. District Court]

Dated _____

[1] If the United States or an officer or agency thereof is a defendant, the time to be inserted as to it is 60 days.

[CAPTION]

SUMMONS AGAINST THIRD-PARTY DEFENDANT

A. B., Plaintiff

v.

C. D., Defendant and
Third-Party Plaintiff   *Summons*

v.

E. F., Third-Party
   Defendant

To the above-named Third-Party Defendant:

You are hereby summoned and required to serve upon _____,
plaintiff's attorney whose address is _____, and upon _____,
who is attorney for C. D., defendant and third-party plaintiff, and whose address
is _____, an answer to the third-party complaint which is herewith
served upon you within 20 days after the service of this summons upon you
exclusive of the day of service. If you fail to do so, judgment by default will be
taken against you for the relief demanded in the third-party complaint. There is
also served upon you herewith a copy of the complaint of the plaintiff which
you may but are not required to answer.

_____,

Clerk of Court

[Seal of District Court]

Dated _____

[CAPTION]

COMPLAINT AGAINST THIRD-PARTY DEFENDANT

A. B., Plaintiff
     v.
C. D., Defendant and
Third-Party Plaintiff   *Third-Party Complaint.*
     v.
E. F., Third-Party
  Defendant

    1.   Plaintiff A. B. has filed against defendant C. D. a complaint, a copy of which is hereto attached as "Exhibit A."

    2.   (Here state the grounds upon which C. D. is entitled to recover from E. F., all or part of what A. B. may recover from C. D. The statement should be framed as in an original complaint.)

    Wherefore C. D. demands judgment against third-party defendant E. F. for all sums[1] that may be adjudged against defendant C. D. in favor of plaintiff A. B.

Signed: _____
               Attorney for C. D.,
               Third-Party Plaintiff

Address: _____

[1] Make appropriate change where C. D. is entitled to only partial recovery-over against E. F.

[CAPTION]

MOTION TO BRING IN THIRD-PARTY DEFENDANT

Defendant moves for leave, as third-party plaintiff, to cause to be served upon E. F. a summons and third-party complaint, copies of which are hereto attached as Exhibit X.

Signed: _____

Attorney for Defendant C. D.

Address: _____

Notice of Motion

To: _____

Attorney for Plaintiff

_____

Please take notice, that the undersigned will bring the above motion on for hearing before this Court at Room _____, United States Court House, Foley Square, City of New York, on the _____ day of _____, 19__, at 10 o'clock in the forenoon of that day or as soon thereafter as counsel can be heard.

Signed: _____

Attorney for Defendant

Address: _____

[CAPTION]

REQUEST FOR PRODUCTION OF DOCUMENTS, ETC., UNDER RULE 34

Plaintiff A. B. requests defendant C. D. to respond within _____ days to the following requests:

(1) That defendant produce and permit plaintiff to inspect and to copy each of the following documents:

(Here list the documents either individually or by category and describe each of them.)

(Here state the time, place, and manner of making the inspection and performance of any related acts.)

(2) That defendant produce and permit plaintiff to inspect and to copy, test, or sample each of the following objects:

(Here list the objects either individually or by category and describe each of them.)

(Here state the time, place, and manner of making the inspection and performance of any related acts.)

(3) That defendant permit plaintiff to enter (here describe property to be entered) and to inspect and to photograph, test, or sample (here describe the portion of the real property and the objects to be inspected).

(Here state the time, place, and manner of making the inspection and performance of any related acts.)

Signed: _____

Attorney for Plaintiff

Address: _____

[CAPTION]

REQUEST FOR ADMISSION UNDER RULE 36

Plaintiff A. B. requests defendant C. D. within _____ days after service of this request to make the following admissions for the purpose of this action only and subject to all pertinent objections to admissibility which may be interposed at the trial:

1. That each of the following documents, exhibited with this request, is genuine.

(Here list the documents and describe each document.)

2. That each of the following statements is true.

(Here list the statements.)

Signed: _____

Attorney for Plaintiff

Address: _____

[CAPTION]

JUDGMENT ON JURY VERDICT

This action came on for trial before the Court and a jury, Honorable John Marshall, District Judge, presiding, and the issues having been duly tried and the jury having duly rendered its verdict,

It is Ordered and Adjudged

[that the plaintiff A. B. recover of the defendant C. D. the sum of _____, with interest thereon at the rate of _____ per cent as provided by law, and his costs of action.]

[that the plaintiff take nothing, that the action be dismissed on the merits, and that the defendant C. D. recover of the plaintiff A. B. his costs of action.]

Dated at New York, New York, this _____ day of _____, 19___.

_____,

Clerk of Court

[CAPTION]

JUDGMENT ON DECISION BY THE COURT

This action came on for [trial] [hearing] before the Court, Honorable John Marshall, District Judge, presiding, and the issues having been duly [tried] [heard] and a decision having been duly rendered,

It is Ordered and Adjudged

[that the plaintiff A. B. recover of the defendant C. D. the sum of _____, with interest thereon at the rate of _____ per cent as provided by law, and his costs of action.]

[that the plaintiff take nothing, that the action be dismissed on the merits, and that the defendant C. D. recover of the plaintiff A. B. his costs of action.]

Dated at New York, New York, this _____ day of _____, 19 __.

_____,
Clerk of Court

AFFIDAVITS

General forms of affidavits

State of _____,
County of _____, Sct.

E. F., after being first duly sworn, makes this his affidavit and states: [allegations].

This [date]

[Signature of affiant]

The foregoing was subscribed and sworn to before me by E. F. this [date].

(SEAL)

G. H., Notary Public
My commission expires [date].

Alternate form

State of _____,
County of _____, ss.

E. F., being first duly sworn, says that _____ [allegations].

Sworn to before me and subscribed in my presence by E. F. this _____ day of _____, 19__.

(SEAL)

G. H., Notary Public
My commission expires [date].

Specimen form of affidavit in legal proceeding

[CAPTION]

Affidavit of E. F.

State of _____,
County of _____, Sct.

E. F., being first duly sworn, makes this his affidavit and states: [allegations].

[Signature of affiant]

The foregoing was subscribed and sworn to before me by E. F. this _____ day of _____, 19__.

(SEAL)

G. H., Notary Public
My commission expires [date].

ACKNOWLEDGMENTS

The following forms of acknowledgment are taken from the Uniform Acknowledgment Act which has been adopted in the following jurisdictions:

Arizona	Massachusetts	Pennsylvania
Arkansas	Montana	South Dakota
Connecticut	New Hampshire	Utah
Hawaii	New Mexico	Virgin Islands
Idaho	North Dakota	Wisconsin
Maryland	Panama Canal Zone	Wyoming

By Individuals:

State of _____
County of _____

On this _____ day of _____, 19_____, before me, _____, the undersigned officer, personally appeared _____, known to me (or satisfactorily proven) to be the person whose name is subscribed to the within instrument and acknowledged that he executed the same for the purposes therein contained.

In witness whereof I hereunto set my hand and official seal.

                                        /s/
                        _____
                                (Title of officer)

By Corporations:

State of _____
County of _____

On this the _____ day of _____, 19_____, before me, _____, the undersigned officer, personally appeared _____, who acknowledged himself to be the _____ of _____, corporation, and that he, as such _____, being authorized to do so, executed the foregoing instrument for the purposes therein contained, by signing the name of the corporation by himself as _____.

In witness whereof I hereunto set my hand and official seal.

                                        /s/
                        _____
                                (Title of officer)

The following forms of acknowledgment are taken from the Uniform Recognition of Acknowledgments Act which has been adopted in the following states:

Arizona	Illinois	Maine
Colorado	Kansas	Michigan
Connecticut	Kentucky	Minnesota

Nebraska	Oklahoma	West Virginia
New Hampshire	Oregon	Wisconsin
North Dakota	South Carolina	
Ohio	Virginia	

By Individuals:

State of _____
County of _____

   The foregoing instrument was acknowledged before me this ___(date)___ by
___(name of person acknowledged)___ .

> (Signature of person taking acknowledgment)
> (Title or rank)
> (Serial number, if any)

By Corporations:

State of _____
County of _____

   The foregoing instrument was acknowledged before me this ___(date)___ by
(name of officer or agent, title of officer or agent)___ of ___(name of corporation acknowledging)___ a ___(state or place of incorporation)___ corporation,
on behalf of the corporation.

> (Signature of person taking acknowledgment)
> (Title or rank)
> (Serial number, if any)

By Partnerships:

State of _____
County of _____

   The foregoing instrument was acknowledged before me this ___(date)___ by
___(name of acknowledging partner or agent)___ , partner (or agent) on behalf of
___(name of partnership)___ , a partnership.

> (Signature of person taking acknowledgment)
> (Title or rank)
> (Serial number, if any)

ABBREVIATIONS

A

a., an., or **anon.** anonymous

A. [**2d**] Atlantic Reporter [second series]

A.B.A. or **ABA** American Bar Association

ABA-ALI American Bar Association-American Law Institute

Abb. N. Cas. Abbott's New Cases (New York)

Abb. Pr. [**n.s.**] Abbott's Practice Reports [new series] (New York)

abr. abridged; abridgement

A.B.R. Army Board of Review

acc'g accounting

acct. account

A.C.M.R. Army Court of Military Review

A.D. [**2d**] Appellate Division Reports [second series] (New York)

Ad. L. [**2d**] Administration Law Reporter [second]

Adm. Admiralty Court; Admiralty Division

adm'r administrator

adm'x administratrix

AEC Atomic Energy Commission

A.E.C. Atomic Energy Commission; Atomic Energy Commission Reports

A.F.B.R. Air Force Board of Review

A.F.C.M.R. Air Force Court of Military Review

aff'd affirmed

aff'g affirming

A.F. JAG L. REV. Air Force JAG Law Review

Agric. Dec. Agricultural Decisions

Aik. Aikens' Reports (Vermont Supreme Court)

Ala. Alabama; Alabama Reports (Supreme Court)

Ala. Acts Acts of Alabama

Ala. App. Alabama Appellate Court Reports

Ala. Code Code of Alabama

Alaska Sess. Laws Alaska Session Laws

Alaska Stat. Alaska Statutes

A.L.I. or **ALI** American Law Institute

All State Sales Tax Rep. All State Sales Tax Reporter

Am. America; American

amend. amendment

amends. amendments

Am. Jur. [**2d**] American Jurisprudence [second edition]

Am. Stock Ex. Guide American Stock Exchange Guide

an. anonymous

ann. annotated

ANNALS Annals of the American Academy of Political and Social Science

anon. anonymous

Antitrust & Trade Reg. Rep. Antitrust & Trade Regulation Report

app. appendix

App. D.C. Appeal Cases, District of Columbia

App. Dep't Appellate Department

App. Div. Appellate Division; Supreme Court, Appellate Division

apps. appendixes

App. T. Supreme Court, Appellate Term

App. Term Appellate Term

arb. arbitrator

Ariz. Arizona; Arizona Reports (Supreme Court)

Ariz. App. Arizona Appeals Reports

Ariz. Legis. Serv. Arizona Legislative Service

Ariz. Rev. Stat. Ann. Arizona Revised Statutes Annotated

Ariz. Sess. Laws Session Laws, Arizona

Ark. Arkansas; Arkansas Reports

Ark. Acts General Acts of Arkansas

Ark. Stat. Ann. Arkansas Statutes Annotated

art. article

arts. articles

AS, A/S, or **A/s** account sales; after sight; at sight

ASCAP American Society of Composers, Authors and Publishers

ASCAP Copyright L. Symp. Copyright Law Symposium (American Society of Composers, Authors and Publishers)

A.S. Code American Samoa Code

Ass'n Association

Assoc. Associate

Atl. Atlantic

Atom. En. L. Rep. Atomic Energy Law Reporter

Auth. Authority

Auto. Automobile

Auto. Cas. [2d] Automobile Cases [second]

Auto. Ins. Cas. Automobile Insurance Cases

Auto. L. Rep. Automobile Law Reporter

Av. Cases Aviation Cases

Ave. Avenue

Av. L. Rep. Aviation Law Reporter

B

B. Baron; British

Bankr. L. Rep. Bankruptcy Law Reporter

Barb. Barbour's Supreme Court Reports (New York)

Barb. Ch. Barbour's Chancery Reports (New York)

B.C. Bail Court; Bankruptcy Cases; before Christ; British Columbia

BCA or **B.C.A.** Board of Contract Appeals; Board of Contract Appeals Decisions

Bd. Board

Bhd. Brotherhood

Binn. Binney's Reports (Pennsylvania Supreme Court)

bk. bank; block; book

bks. banks; blocks; books

Blackf. Blackford's Reports (Indiana Supreme Court)

bldg. building

Blue Sky L. Rep. Blue Sky Law Reporter

B.R. or **BR** Board of Review

Bradf. Bradford's Reports (Iowa Supreme Court)

Brayt. Brayton's Reports (Vermont Supreme Court)

Bros. Brothers

B.T.A. United States Board of Tax Appeals

B.T.A.M. Board of Tax Appeals Memorandum Decisions

Bur. Burnett's Reports (Wisconsin Supreme Court)

C

c. or **ct.** cent

C. Chancellor

C.A.A. Civil Aeronautics Authority

CAB or **C.A.B.** Civil Aeronautics Board; Civil Aeronautics Board Reports

C.A.F. cost and freight

Cai. Cas. Caines' Cases in Error (New York)

Cai. R. Caines' Reports (New York)

Cal. [2d; 3d] California Reports [second, third series]

Cal. Adv. Legis. Serv. California Advance Legislative Service (Deering)

Cal. App. Supp. [2d; 3d] California Appellate Reports Supplement [second, third supplement]

Cal. [subject] * Code Ann. (Deering) Deering's Annotated California Code

Cal. [subject] * Code Ann. (West) West's Annotated California Code

* [Subject Abbreviations]

Bus. & Prof. Business and Professions

Civ. Civil

Civ. Proc. Civil Procedure

Com. Commercial

Corp. Corporations

Educ. Education

Elec. Elections

Evid. Evidence

Fin. Financial

Fish & Game Fish & Game

Food & Agric. Food & Agricultural

Gov't Government

Harb. & Nav. Harbors & Navigation

Health & Safety Health & Safety

Ins. Insurance

Lab. Labor

Mil. & Vet. Military & Veterans

Penal Penal

Prob. Probate

Pub. Res. Public Resources

Pub. Util. Public Utilities

Rev. & Tax. Revenue & Taxation

Sts. & Hy. Streets & Highways

U. Com. Uniform Commercial

Unemp. Ins. Unemployment Insurance

Veh. Vehicle

Water Water

Welf. & Inst. Welfare & Institutions

Cal. Gen. Laws Ann. Deering's California General Laws Annotated

Calif. L. Rev. California Law Review

Cal. Legis. Serv. California Legislative Service (West)

Cal. Rptr. West's California Reporter

Cal. Stats. Statutes of California

Cal. Unrep. California Unreported Cases

cas. casualty

ca. sa. capias ad satisfaciendum (*a writ of execution*)

c.a.v. curia advisari vult (*the court will be advised*)

c.b. common bench; chief baron

C.B. Cumulative Bulletin

C.C. Circuit Court (old Federal); United States Circuit Courts

C.C.P.A. (United States) Court of Customs and Patent Appeals

cent. central

cf. confer (*compare*)

c. & f. cost and freight

c.f.i. or **C.F.I.** cost, freight, and insurance

C.F.R. Code of Federal Regulations

ch. chaplain; chapter; check; chief; child; children; church

Ch. Chancery; Chancery Court; Chancery Division

Chand. Chandler's Reports (Wisconsin Supreme Court)

chem. chemical

Child. Ct. Children's Court

chs. chapters

c.i.f. or **C.I.F.** price covers the cost of goods, insurance, and freight

Cir. Circuit Court of Appeals (federal); Court of Appeals (federal)

Cir. Ct. Circuit Court (state)

Cir. Ct. App. Circuit Court of Appeal (state)

City Civ. Ct. Act New York City Civil Court Act (29A)

City Crim. Ct. Act New York City Criminal Court Act (29A)

Civ. App. Civil Appeals

Civ. Ct. Rec. Civil Court of Record

C.J. Chief Judge; Chief Justice

C.J.S. Corpus Juris Secundum

cl. clause

C.L. Civil Law

Cl. Ch. Clarke's Chancery Reports (New York)

cls. clauses

C.M.A. Court of Military Appeals

C.M.R. Court-Martial Reports; Court of Military Review

c/o care of

Co. Company

COD or **C.O.D.** cash on delivery; collect on delivery

Code Crim. Proc. Code of Criminal Procedure (66) (New York)

Cole. & Cai. Cas. Coleman & Caines' Cases (New York)

Cole. Cas. Coleman's Cases (New York)

Colo. Colorado; Colorado Reports (Supreme Court)

Colo. App. Colorado Court of Appeal Reports

Colo. Rev. Stat. Colorado Revised Statutes

Colo. Sess. Laws Colorado Session Laws

comm. committee

Comm. Ct. United States Commerce Court

Comm. Fut. L. Rep. Commodity Futures Law Reporter

Comm'n Commission

Comm'r Commissioner

Commw. Ct. Commonwealth Court

comp. compilation; compiled

Comp. Gen. Decision of the Comptroller General

Condit. Sale–Chat. Mort. Rep. Con-ditional Sale–Chattel Mortgage Reporter

Conn. Connecticut; Connecticut Reports (Supreme Court of Errors)

Conn. Cir. Ct. Connecticut Circuit Court Reports

Conn. Gen. Stat. General Statutes of Connecticut

Conn. Gen. Stat. Ann. Connecticut General Statutes Annotated

Conn. Legis. Serv. Connecticut Legislative Service

Conn. Pub. Acts Connecticut Public Acts

Conn. Supp. Connecticut Supplement

Cons. Cred. Guide Consumer Credit Guide

consol. consolidated

consols. consolidated annuities

constr. construction

Cont. Cas. Fed. Contract Cases Federal

Conv. [n.s.] Conveyancer & Property Lawyer [new series]

coop. cooperative

Copy. Dec. Copyright Decisions

Corp. Corporation

Corp. Guide Corporation Guide

Corp. L. Guide Corporation Law Guide

Cost Acc'g Stand. Guide Cost Accounting Standards Guide

County Ct. County Court

County J. Ct. County Judge's Court

Cow. Cowen's Reports (New York)

C.P. common pleas; Court of Common Pleas

C.P.A. Certified Public Accountant

c.r. chancery reports; curia regis (*the king's court*)

Crim. App. Court of Criminal Appeals; Criminal Appeals

crim. con. criminal conversation

Crim. L. Rep. Criminal Law Reporter

C.S.C. Civil Service Commission

ct. cent

c.t.a. cum testamento annexo (*with the will annexed*)

Ct. App. Court of Appeals (state)

Ct. Cl. United States Court of Claims

Ct. Cl. Act Court of Claims Act (29A) (New York)

Ct. Cust. App. Court of Customs Appeals

Ct. Err. & App. Court of Errors and Appeals

Ct. Gen. Sess. Court of General Sessions

Ct. Spec. Sess. Court of Special Sessions

Current Med. Current Medicine for Attorneys

Cust. B. & Dec. Customs Bulletin and Decisions

Cust. Ct. Customs Court

cwt. hundredweight

C.Z. Code Canal Zone Code

D

D. District (state); District Court (federal)

Dall. Dallas' Reports (Pennsylvania Supreme Court)

Day Day's Reports (Connecticut Supreme Court of Errors)

d.b.a. or **d/b/a** doing business as

D.C. District Court; District of Columbia

D.C. Cir. United States Court of Appeals for the District of Columbia

D.C. Code Ann. District of Columbia Code Annotated

D.C. Code Encycl. District of Columbia Code Encyclopedia

D.C. Code Legis. & Ad. Serv. D.C. Code Legislative and Administrative Service (West)

D.C. (Cranch) District of Columbia Reports (Cranch)

D. Chip. D. Chipman's Reports (Vermont Supreme Court)

D.C. (MacArth.) District of Columbia Reports (MacArthur)

D.C. (MacArth. & M.) District of Columbia Reports (MacArthur and Mackey)

D.C. (Mackey) District of Columbia Reports (Mackey)

D.C. (Tuck. & Cl.) District of Columbia Reports (Tucker and Clephane)

dec. decision

Dec. Com. Pat. Patents Decisions of the Commissioner and of U.S. Courts

Dec. Fed. Mar. Comm'n Decisions of the Federal Maritime Commission

decs. decisions

Dec. U.S. Mar. Comm'n Decision of the United States Maritime Commission

Del. Delaware; Delaware Reports (Court of Errors and Appeals)

Del. (Boyce) Delaware Reports (Boyce)

Del. Cas. Delaware Cases

Del. Ch. Delaware Chancery Reports

Del. Code Ann. Delaware Code Annotated

Del. (Harr.) Delaware Reports (Harrington)

Del. (Hous.) Delaware Reports (Houston)

Dell. Dellam's Opinions (Texas Supreme Court)

Del. Laws Laws of Delaware

Del. (Marv.) Delaware Reports (Marvel)

Del. (Penne.) Delaware Reports (Pennewill)

dem. demise

Denio Denio's Reports (New York)

Dep't or **Dept.** Department

Dep't State Bull. United States Department of State Bulletin

dev. development

dies non dies non juridicus (*not a court day*)

Dig. Digest

Dist. District

Dist. Ct. District Court (state)

Dist. Ct. App. District Court of Appeal

distrib. distribute; distributing

Div. Division

D.J. District Judge

Dom. Proc. or **D.P.** Domus Procerum (*House of Lords*)

Doug. Douglas' Reports (Michigan Supreme Court)

D.P. Also **Dom. Proc.** Domus Procerum (*House of Lords*)

dr. debtor

Dr. Doctor

Duq. Duquesne

d.w.i. died without issue; driving while under the influence

E

E. East; Eastern

econ. economic; economics; economy

Econ. Cont. Economic Controls

ed. edition; editor

educ. education; educational

Edw. Ch. Edward's Chancery Reports (New York)

EEOC or **E.E.O.C.** Equal Employment Opportunity Commission

EEOC Compl. Man. Equal Employment Opportunity Commission Compliance Manual

e.g. exempli gratia (*for example*)

elec. electric; electricity; electronic; electronics

Emer. Ct. App. United States Emergency Court of Appeals

Empl. Comp. App. Bd. Decisions of the Employees' Compensation Appeals Board

Empl. Prac. Dec. Employment Practices Decisions

Empl. Prac. Guide Employment Practices Guide

Eng. England; English

Eng'r Engineer; Engineering

Envir. Rep. Environment Reporter

envt'l environmental

e.o.e. errors and omissions excepted

Eq. Equity Court; Equity Division

equip. equipment

est. established; estimate; estimated

Est. Estate; Estates

et al. et alii (*and others*)

etc. et cetera (*and so forth*)

et seq. et sequentia (*and the following*)

et ux. et uxor (*and wife*)

Exch. Exchange

Ex'r Executor

Ex'x Executrix

F

F. Forum

F. [2d] Federal Reporter [second series]

FAA or **F.A.A.** Federal Aviation Administration

Fair Empl. Prac. Cas. Fair Employment Practices Cases

fam. family

Fam. Ct. Family Court

Fam. Ct. Act Family Court Act
(29A) (New York)

Fam. L. Rep. Family Law Reporter

f.a.s. free alongside ship

F. Cas. Federal Cases

FCC or **F.C.C.** Federal Communications Commission; Federal Communication Commission Reports

FDA or **F.D.A.** Food and Drug Administration

Fed. Federal

Fed. Banking L. Rep. Federal Banking Law Reporter

Fed. Carr. Cas. Federal Carriers Cases

Fed. Carr. Rep. Federal Carriers Reporter

Fed. Est. Gift Tax Rep. Federal Estate and Gift Tax Reporter

Fed. Ex. Tax. Rep. Federal Excise Tax Reporter

Fed'n Federation

Fed. Res. Bull. Federal Reserve Bulletin

Fed. Sec. L. Rep. Federal Securities Law Reporter

Fed. Taxes Federal Taxes

Fed. Taxes: Est. & Gift Federal Taxes: Estate and Gift Taxes

Fed. Taxes: Excise Federal Taxes: Excise Taxes

fi. fa. fieri facias (*a writ of execution*)

fin. finance

Fire & Casualty Cas. Fire & Casualty Cases

Fla. Florida; Florida Reports (Supreme Court)

Fla. Laws Laws of Florida

Fla. Sess. Law Serv. Florida Session Law Service

Fla. Stat. Florida Statutes (1975)

Fla. Stat. Ann. Florida Statutes Annotated (West)

Fla. Supp. Florida Supplement

F.O.B. or **f.o.b.** free on board

fol. folio

fols. folios

Food Drug Cos. L. Rep. Food Drug Cosmetic Law Reporter

for. forensic

fort. fortnightly

FORUM The Forum

FPC or **F.P.C.** Federal Power Commission; Federal Power Commission Reports

F.R.D. Federal Rule Decisions

F. Supp. Federal Supplement

F.T.C. Federal Trade Commission; Federal Trade Commission Decision

G

Ga. Georgia; Georgia Reports (Supreme Court)

Ga. App. Georgia Appeals Reports

Ga. Code Code of Georgia (1975)

Ga. Code Ann. Code of Georgia Annotated

Ga. Laws Georgia (session) Laws

GAO or **G.A.O.** General Accounting Office

gdn. guardian

Gen. General

Geo. Georgetown

Geo. Wash. George Washington

Gill Gill's Reports (Maryland Court of Appeals)

G. & J. Gill's and Johnson's Reports (Maryland Court of Appeals)

G. L. General Laws

Gonz. Gonzaga

Gov't Government

Gov't Cont. Rep. Government Contracts Reporter

Gov't Empl. Rel. Rep. Government Employee Relations Report

Greene Greene's Reports (Iowa Supreme Court)

GSA or **G.S.A.** General Services Administration

Guam Civ. Code Guam Civil Code

Guam Code Civ. Pro. Guam Code of Civil Procedure

Guam Gov't Code Guam Government Code

Guam Prob. Code Guam Probate Code

guar. guaranty

H

h.a. hoc anno (*this year; in this year*)

Harv. Harvard

Haw. Hawaii; Hawaii Reports (Supreme Court)

Haw. Rev. Stat. Hawaii Revised Statutes

Haw. Sess. Laws Session Laws of Hawaii

H.B. House Bill

h.c. habeas corpus (*you have the body*)

H.C. House of Commons

H. & G. Harris' & Gill's Reports (Maryland Court of Appeals)

Hill Hill's Reports (New York)

Hill & Den. Hill and Denio Supplement (Lalor) (New York)

hist. historical; history

H. & J. Harris' and Johnson's Reports (Maryland Court of Appeals)

H.L. House of Lords

H. & McH. Harris' and McHenry's Reports (Maryland Court of Appeals)

Hoff. Ch. Hoffman's Chancery Reports (New York)

Hopk. Ch. Hopkins' Chancery Reports (New York)

hosp. hospital

hous. housing

Hous. Houston

Hous. & Dev. Rep. Housing & Development Reporter

How. Howard

How. Pr. [n.s.] Howard's Practice Reports [new series] (New York)

H.R. House of Representatives

h.v. hoc verbo or hac voce (*this word* or *under this word*)

I

ib., ibid., or **id.** ibidem (*in the same place*)

I.C.C. Indian Claims Commission; Interstate Commerce Commission; Interstate Commerce Commission Reports

I.C.C. Valuation Rep. Interstate Commerce Commission Valuation Reports

Idaho Idaho Reports (Supreme Court)

Idaho Sess. Laws Idaho Session Laws

i.e. id est (*that is*)

Ill. [2d] Illinois Reports [second series], Supreme Court

Ill. Ann. Stat. Smith-Hurd Illinois Annotated Statutes

Ill. App. [2d; 3d] Illinois Appellate Court Reports [second, third series]

Ill. (Bresse) Illinois Reports (Bresse)

Ill. Ct. Cl. Illinois Court of Claims Reports

Ill. (Gilm) Illinois Reports (Gilman)

Ill. Laws Laws of Illinois (Session Laws)

Ill. Legis. Serv. Illinois Legislative Service (West)

Ill. Rev. Stat. Illinois Revised Statutes (1973; Supplement 1974)

Ill. (Scam.) Illinois Reports (Scammon)

inc. income; incorporated

Inc. Incorporated

Ind. Indiana; Indiana Reports (Supreme Court)

Ind. Acts Indiana Acts (Session Laws)

Ind. App. Indiana Court of Appeals Reports

Ind. Code Indiana Code (1971)

Ind. Code Ann. Burns' Indiana Statutes Annotated Code Edition

I. & N. Dec. Immigration and Naturalization Administrative Decisions

indem. indemnity

Ind. Rel. Industrial Relations

indus. industrial; industries; industry

Ins. Insurance

Inst. Institute; Institution

Insur. L. Rep. Insurance Law Reporter

Interior Dec. Decisions of the Department of the Interior

int'l international

intra. intramural

inv. investment

IOU I owe you

Iowa Iowa Reports (Supreme Court)

Iowa Acts Acts and Joint Resolutions of the State of Iowa

Iowa Code Code of Iowa (1971)

Iowa Code Ann. Iowa Code Annotated

Iowa Legis. Serv. Iowa Legislative Service (West)

Ir. Irish

I.R.C. Internal Revenue Code of 1954

IRS or **I.R.S.** Internal Revenue Service

J

J. Journal; Judge; Justice

J.A. Judge Advocate

JAG Judge Advocate General

JAG J. JAG Journal

J. Am. Soc'y C.L.U. Journal of American Society of Chartered Life Underwriters

J. Crim. L. C. & P.S. Journal of Criminal Law, Criminology, and Police Science

JJ. Judges; Justices

J. Mar. John Marshall

Johns. Johnson's Reports (New York)

Johns. Cas. Johnson's Cases (New York)

Johns. Ch. Johnson's Chancery Reports (New York)

J.P. Ct. Justice of the Peace's Court

jud. judicature

JUDICATURE Judicature

jur. juridical; jurist

Juris. Jurisprudence

Just. Justice

Just. Ct. Act Justice Court Act (29A) (New York)

Just. P. Justice of the Peace and Local Government Review

juv. juvenile

Juv. Ct. Juvenile Court

K

Kan. Kansas; Kansas Reports (Supreme Court)

Kan. Civ. Pro. Stat. Ann. Kansas Code of Civil Procedure

Kan. Crim. Code & Code of Crim. Proc. Kansas Criminal Code and Code of Criminal Procedure (Vernon)

Kan. Sess. Laws Session Laws of Kansas

Kan. Stat. Kansas Statutes (Supplement 1975)

Kan. U.C.C. Ann. Vernon's Kansas Statutes Annotated Uniform Commercial Code

K.B. King's Bench

K.C. King's Counsel

Ky. Kentucky; Kentucky Reports (Supreme Court, formerly Court of Appeals)

Ky. Acts Kentucky Acts (Session Laws)

Ky. (A.K. Marsh.) Kentucky Reports (A.K. Marshall)

Ky. (Bibb) Kentucky Reports (Bibb)

Ky. (B. Mon.) Kentucky Reports (Ben Monroe)

Ky. (Bush) Kentucky Reports (Bush)

Ky. (Dana) Kentucky Reports (Dana)

Ky. (Duv.) Kentucky Reports (Duvall)

Ky. (Hard.) Kentucky Reports (Hardin)

Ky. (Hughes) Kentucky Reports (Hughes)

Ky. (J.J. Marsh.) Kentucky Reports (J.J. Marshall)

Ky. (Litt.) Kentucky Reports (Littell)

Ky. (Met.) Kentucky Reports (Metcalf)

Ky. Rev. Stat. Kentucky Revised Statutes (1970)

Ky. Rev. Stat. Ann. Baldwin's Kentucky Revised Statutes Annotated

Ky. Rev. Stat. & Rules Serv. Kentucky Revised Statutes and Rules Service

Ky. (Sneed) Kentucky Reports (Sneed)

Ky. (T.B. Monroe) Kentucky Reports (T.B. Monroe)

L

L. Law; *Long Quinto* (one of the parts of the Year Books).

La. Louisiana; Louisiana Reports (Supreme Court)

L.A. Los Angeles

La. Acts State of Louisiana: Acts of the Legislature

La. Ann. Louisiana Annual Reports (Supreme Court)

La. App. Louisiana Courts of Appeal Reports

lab. labor

Lab. Arb. Awards Labor Arbitration Awards

Lab. Arb. & Disp. Settl. Labor Arbitration and Dispute Settlements

Lab. Arb. Serv. Labor Arbitration Service

Lab. Cas. Labor Cases

Lab. L. Rep. Labor Law Reporter

Lab. Rel. Rep. Labor Relations Reporter

La. Civ. Code Ann. West's Louisiana Civil Code Annotated

La. Code Civ. Pro. Ann. West's Louisiana Code of Civil Procedure Annotated

La. Code Crim. Pro. Ann. West's Louisiana Code of Criminal Procedure Annotated

Lans. Lansing's Reports (New York Supreme Court, Appellate Division)

La. Rev. Stat. Ann. West's Louisiana Revised Statutes Annotated

La. Sess. Law Serv. Louisiana Session Law Service

law. lawyer

Law. & Banker Lawyer and Banker and Central Law Journal

L.C. Leading Cases; Lord Chancellor; Lower Canada

L. Ct. Law Court

L. Div. Law Division

legis. legislation; legislative; legislature

L.F. Law French

liab. liability

lib. library

Life Cas. [2d.] Life (Health, Accident) Cases [second]

L.J. Law Journal; Law Judge; Lord Justice

ll. laws

L.L. Law Latin

LL.B. bachelor of law

LL.D. doctor of law

LL.M. master of law

Lock. Rev. Cas. Lockwood's Reversed Cases (New York)

Loy. Loyola

Loy. Chi. L. J. Loyola University of Chicago Law Journal

Loy L.A. L. Rev. Loyola University of Los Angeles Law Review

Loy L. Rev. Loyola Law Review (New Orleans)

L.R. Law Reports

L.R.R.M. Labor Relations Reference Manual

L.S. locus sigilli (*the place of the seal*)

Ltd. Limited

l.w. low water

M

mach. machine; machinery

Magis. Ct. Magistrate's Court

Man. Manhattan

mar. maritime

Marq. Marquette

marr. marriage

Mart. [n.s.] Martin's Louisiana Term Reports [new series] (Louisiana Supreme Court)

Mass. Massachusetts; Massachusetts Reports (Supreme Judicial Report)

Mass. Acts Acts and Resolves of Massachusetts

Mass. Adv. Legis. Serv. Massachusetts Advance Legislative Service (Lawyers Co-op)

Mass. Adv. Sh. Massachusetts Supreme Judicial Court Advance Sheets

Mass. (Allen) Massachusetts Reports (Allen)

Mass. Ann. Laws Annotated Laws of Massachusetts (Michie/Law. Co-op)

Mass. App. Ct. Massachusetts Appeals Court Reports

Mass. App. Ct. Adv. Sh. Massachusetts Appeals Court Advance Sheets

Mass. App. Dec. Appellate Decisions (Appellate Division of Massachusetts District Courts)

Mass. App. Div. Appellate Division Reports (Appellate Division of Massachusetts District Courts)

Mass. (Cush.) Massachusetts Reports (Cushing)

Mass. Gen. Laws Ann. Massachusetts General Laws Annotated (West)

Mass. (Gray) Massachusetts Reports (Gray)

Mass. (Met.) Massachusetts Reports (Metcalf)

Mass. (Pick.) Massachusetts Reports (Pickering)

M.C.C. Motor Carrier Cases

McCahon McCahon's Reports (Kansas Supreme Court)

McGl. McGloin's Louisiana Court of Appeals Reports

Md. Maryland; Maryland Reports (Court of Appeals)

M.D. Doctor of Medicine; Middle District

Md. Ann. Code Annotated Code of
Maryland (1957)

Md. App. Maryland Appellate
Reports

Md. [subject] * Code Ann. Anno-
tated Code of Maryland
*[Subject Abbreviations]
Agric. Agriculture (1974)
Bus. Reg. Business Regulation
Com. Law Commercial Law
(1975)
Corp. & Ass'ns Corporations and
Associations (1975)
Crim. Law Criminal Law
Cts. & Jud. Proc. Courts and
Judicial Proceedings (1974)
Educ. Education
Elec. Elections
Est. & Trusts Estates and Trusts
(1974)
Fam. Law Family Law
Gen. Prov. General Provisions
Local Gov't Local Government
Nat. Res. Natural Resources
(1974)
Occ. & Prof. Occupations and
Professions
Pub. Health Public Health
Pub. Safety Public Safety
Real Prop. Real Property (1974)
Soc. Serv. Social Services
State Gov't State Government
Tax. & Rev. Taxation and
Revenue
Transp. Transportation

Me. Maine; Maine Reports (Supreme
Judicial Court)

Me. Acts Acts, Resolves, and Constitutional Resolutions of the
State of Maine

med. mediator; medical; medicine

Melb. Melbourne

Me. Legis. Serv. Maine Legislative
Service

Mem. Memphis

Me. Rev. Stat. Maine Revised
Statutes

m.f.b.m. 1,000 feet board measure

Mfr. Manufacturer

Mich. Michigan; Michigan Reports
(Supreme Court)

Mich. App. Michigan Appeals
Reports

Mich. Comp. Laws Michigan Compiled Laws (1970)

Mich. Comp. Laws Ann. Michigan
Compiled Laws Annotated

Mich. Legis. Serv. Michigan Legislative Service (West)

Mich. Pub. Acts Public and Local
Acts of the State of Michigan

Mich. Stat. Ann. Michigan Statutes
Annotated

mil. military

min. mineral

Minn. Minnesota; Minnesota Reports
(Supreme Court)

Minn. Laws Laws of Minnesota
(Session Laws)

Minn. Sess. Law Serv. Minnesota
Session Law Service (West)

Minn. Stat. Minnesota Statutes

Minn. Stat. Ann. Minnesota Statutes
Annotated (West)

Minor Minor's Reports (Alabama
Supreme Court)

Misc. [2d] New York Miscellaneous
Reports [second series]

Miss. Mississippi; Mississippi Reports
(Supreme Court)

Miss. Code Ann. Mississippi Code
Annotated (1972)

Miss. (Howard) Howard's Reports
(Mississippi Supreme Court)

Miss. Laws General Laws of Mississippi (Session Laws)

Miss. (S. & M.) Smedes' and Marshall's Reports (Mississippi Supreme Court)

Miss. (Walker) Walker's Reports (Mississippi Supreme Court)

M.J. Military Justice Reports

mkt. market

mkts. markets

Mo. Missouri; Missouri Reports (Supreme Court)

Mo. Ann. Stat. Vernon's Annotated Missouri Statutes

Mo. App. Missouri Appeals Reports

mod. modern

Mo. Laws Laws of Missouri (Session Laws)

Mo. Legis. Serv. Missouri Legislative Service (Vernon)

Mont. Montana; Montana Reports (Supreme Court)

Mont. Laws Laws of Montana (Session Laws)

Mont. Rev. Codes Ann. Revised Codes of Montana Annotated

Mo. Rev. Stat. Missouri Revised Statutes

Morris Morris' Reports (Iowa Supreme Court)

M.R. Master of the Rolls

ms. manuscript

M.T. Michaelmas Term

Mun. Municipal

Mun. Ct. Municipal Court

Mut. Mutual

Mut. Funds Guide Mutual Funds Guide

N

n. natus (*born*); note

N. North; Northern

n.a. non allocatur (*it is not allowed*)

NASA or **N.A.S.A.** National Aeronautics and Space Administration

nat. natural

Nat'l National

n.b. nota bene (*note well*); nulla bona (*no goods*)

N.B.R. Navy Board of Review

N.C. North Carolina; North Carolina Reports (Supreme Court)

N.C. Adv. Legis. Serv. North Carolina Advance Legislative Service (Michie)

N.C. App. North Carolina Court of Appeals Reports

N.C. (Busb.) North Carolina Reports (Busbee's Law)

N.C. (Busb. Eq.) North Carolina Reports (Busbee's Equity)

N.C. (Cam. & Nor.) North Carolina Reports (Conference by Cameron & Norwood)

N.C. (Car. L. Rep.) North Carolina Reports (Carolina Law Repository)

N.C. (Dev.) North Carolina Reports (Devereux's Law)

N.C. (Dev. & Bat.) North Carolina Reports (Devereux & Battle's Law)

N.C. (Dev. & Bat. Eq.) North Carolina Reports (Devereux & Battle's Equity)

N.C. (Dev. Eq.) North Carolina Reports (Devereux's Equity)

N.C. Gen. Stat. General Statutes of North Carolina

N.C. (Hawks) North Carolina Reports (Hawks)

N.C. (Hayw.) North Carolina Reports (Haywood)

N. Chip. N. Chipman's Reports (Vermont Supreme Court)

N.C. (Ired.) North Carolina Reports (Iredell's Law)

N.C. (Ired. Eq.) North Carolina Reports (Iredell's Equity)

N.C. (Jones) North Carolina Reports (Jones' Law)

N.C. (Jones Eq.) North Carolina Reports (Jones' Equity)

N.C. (Mart.) North Carolina Reports (Martin)

N.C.M.R. Navy Court of Military Review

N.C. (Mur.) North Carolina Reports (Murphey)

N.C. (Phil. Eq.) North Carolina Reports (Phillips' Equity)

N.C. (Phil. Law) North Carolina Reports (Phillips' Law)

N.C. Sess. Laws Session Laws of North Carolina

N.C. (Tay.) North Carolina Reports (Taylor)

N.C. (Term) North Carolina Reports (Term Reports)

N.C. (Win.) North Carolina Reports (Winston)

N.D. North Dakota; North Dakota Reports (Supreme Court)

N.D. Cent. Code North Dakota Century Code

N.D. Sess. Laws Laws of North Dakota (Session Laws)

N.E. or NE Northeast; Northeastern

N.E. [2d] Northeastern Reporter [second series]

Neb. Nebraska; Nebraska Reports (Supreme Court)

Neb. Laws Nebraska Laws (Session Laws)

Neb. Rev. Stat. Revised Statutes of Nebraska

Negl. Cas. [2d] Negligence Cases [second]

Nev. Neveda; Nevada Reports (Supreme Court)

Nev. Rev. Stat. Nevada Revised Statutes

Nev. Stats. Statutes of Nevada (Session Laws)

N.H. New Hampshire; New Hampshire Reports (Supreme Court)

N.H. Laws Laws of the State of New Hampshire (Session Laws)

N.H. Rev. Stat. Ann. New Hampshire Revised Statutes Annotated

NIH or N.I.H. National Institute of Health

N. IR. L. Q. Northern Ireland Legal Quarterly

N.J. New Jersey; New Jersey Reports (Supreme Court, previously Court of Errors and Appeals)

N.J. Eq. New Jersey Equity Reports

N.J. L. New Jersey Law Reports

N.J. Laws Laws of New Jersey (Session Laws)

N.J. Misc. New Jersey Miscellaneous Reports

N.J. Rev. Stat. New Jersey Revised Statutes (1937)

N.J. Sess. Law Serv. New Jersey Session Law Service

N.J. Stat. Ann. New Jersey Statutes Annotated (West)

N.J. Super. New Jersey Superior Court Reports

NLRB or N.L.R.B. National Labor Relations Board

NLRB Dec. National Labor Relations Board Decisions

N.M. New Mexico; New Mexico Reports (Supreme Court)

N.M. (Gild., E.W.S. ed.) New Mexico Supreme Court Reports (edited by E.W.S. Gildersleeve)

N.M. Laws Laws of New Mexico (Session Laws)

N.M. Stat. Ann. New Mexico Statutes Annotated

nn. notes

no. number

NOLPE School L. J. NOLPE School Law Journal

nos. numbers

n.o.v. non obstante veredicto (*not withstanding the verdict*)

N.P. Notary Public

NRAB or N.R.A.B. National Railroad Adjustment Board; National Railroad Adjustment Board Decisions

n.s. new series

N. Trans. S. Dec. National Transportation Safety Board Decisions

N.W. Northwest; Northwestern

N.W. [2d] Northwestern Reports [second series]

N.Y. [2d] New York Reports [second series] (Court of Appeals)

N.Y. [subject] * Law (Consol.) Consolidated Laws Service (New York)

N.Y. [subject] * Law (McKinney) McKinney's Consolidated Laws (New York)

* [Subject Abbreviations]

Aband. Prop. Abandoned Property

Agric. Conserv. & Adj. Agricultural Conservation and Adjustment

Agric. & Mkts. Agriculture & Markets

Alco. Bev. Cont. Alcoholic Beverage Control

Alt. County Gov't Alternative County Government

Banking Banking

Ben. Ord. Benevolent Orders

Bus. Corp. Business Corporation

Canal Canal

Civ. Prac. Civil Practice Law & Rules

Civ. Rights Civil Rights

Civ. Serv. Civil Service

Com. Commerce

Condem. Condemnation

Coop. Corp. Cooperative Corporations

Correc. Correction

County County

Crim. Proc. Criminal Procedure

Debt. & Cred. Debtor & Creditor

Dom. Rel. Domestic Relations

Educ. Education

Elec. Election

Empl'rs Liab. Employers' Liability

Envir. Conserv. Environmental Conservation

Est., Powers & Trusts Estates, Powers & Trusts

Exec. Executive

Gen. Ass'ns General Associations

Gen. Bus. General Business

Gen. City General City

Gen. Constr. General Construction

Gen. Mun. General Municipal

Gen. Oblig. General Obligations

High. Highway

Indian Indian

Ins. Insurance

Jud. Judiciary

Lab. Labor

Legis. Legislative

Lien Lien

Local Fin. Local Finance

Mental Hyg. Mental Hygiene

Mil. Military

Mult. Dwell. Multiple Dwelling

Mult. Resid. Multiple Residence

Mun. Home Rule Municipal Home Rule

Nav. Navigation

Not-For-Profit Corp. Not-for-Profit Corporation

Opt. County Gov't Optional County Government

Parks & Rec. Parks & Recreation

Partnership Partnership

Penal Penal

Pers. Prop. Personal Property

Priv. Hous. Fin. Private Housing Finance

Pub. Auth. Public Authorities

Pub. Bldgs. Public Buildings

Pub. Health Public Health

Pub. Hous. Public Housing

Pub. Lands Public Lands

Pub. Off. Public Officers

Pub. Serv. Public Service

Rapid Trans. Rapid Transit

Real Prop. Real Property

Real Prop. Acts. Real Property Actions & Proceedings

Real Prop. Tax Real Property Tax

Relig. Corp. Religious Corporations

Retire. & Soc. Sec. Retirement & Social Security

R.R. Railroad

Rural Elec. Coop. Rural Electric Cooperative

Salt Springs Salt Springs

Second Class Cities Second Class Cities

Soc. Serv. Social Services

Soil & Water Conserv. Dist. Soil and Water Conservation Districts

State State

State Fin. State Finance

State Print. State Printing

Stat. Local Gov'ts Statute of Local Governments

Tax Tax

Town Town

Transp. Transportation

Transp. Corp. Transportation Corporations

Veh. & Traf. Vehicle & Traffic

Village Village

Vol. Fire. Ben. Volunteer Firemen's Benefit

Work. Comp. Workmen's Compensation

N.Y. Laws Laws of New York (Session Laws)

N.Y.S. [2d] West's New York Supplement [second series]

NYSE New York Stock Exchange

NYSE Guide New York Stock Exchange Guide

N.Y. Sup. Ct. Supreme Court Reports (New York)

O

OEO or O.E.O. Office of Economic Opportunity

Off. Office

Off. Gaz. Pat. Off. Official Gazette of the Patent Office

Ohio Ohio Reports (Supreme Court)

Ohio App. [2d] Ohio Appellate Reports [second series]

Ohio C.C. Ohio Circuit Court Reports (Jahn)

Ohio C.C. Dec. Ohio Circuit Court Decisions

Ohio C.C. (n.s.) Ohio Circuit Court Reports (new series)

Ohio Cir. Dec. Ohio Circuit Decisions

Ohio Dec. Ohio Decisions

Ohio Dec. Reprint Ohio Decisions (reprint)

Ohio Dep't Ohio Department Reports

Ohio Gov't Ohio Government Reports

Ohio Laws State of Ohio: Legislative Acts Passed and Joint Resolutions Adopted

Ohio Legis. Bull. Ohio Legislative Bulletin (Anderson)

Ohio Misc. Ohio Miscellaneous (case reports)

Ohio N.P. [n.s.] Ohio Nisi Prius Reports [new series]

Ohio Op. [2d] Ohio Opinions [second series]

Ohio Rev. Code Ann. (Anderson) Ohio Revised Code Annotated (Anderson)

Ohio Rev. Code Ann. (Baldwin) Ohio Revised Code Annotated (Baldwin)

Ohio Rev. Code Ann. (Page) Ohio Revised Code Annotated (Page)

Ohio St. [2d] Ohio State Reports [second series] (Supreme Court)

Okla. Oklahoma; Oklahoma Reports (Supreme Court)

Okla. Crim. Oklahoma Criminal Reports

Okla. Sess. Laws Oklahoma Session Laws

Okla. Sess. Law Serv. Oklahoma Session Law Service (West)

Okla. Stat. Oklahoma Statutes (1971 & Supplement 1975)

Okla. Stat. Ann. Oklahoma Statutes Annotated (West)

Op. Att'y Gen. Opinions of the Attorney General

Op. Solic. P.O. Dep't Official Opinion of the Solicitor for the Post Office Department

Or. Oregon; Oregon Reports (Supreme Court)

Or. App. Oregon Reports, Court of Appeal

Ord. Order

Or. Laws Oregon Laws and Resolutions (Session Laws)

Or. Laws Adv. Sh. No. Oregon Laws and Resolutions Advance Sheet Number

Or. Laws Spec. Sess. Oregon Laws and Resolutions, Special Session

Orphans' Ct. Orphans' Court

Or. Rev. Stat. Oregon Revised Statutes

Or. T.R. Oregon Tax Reporter

o.s. old style; old series

OSHA Occupational Safety and Health Administration

P

p. page

P. [2d] Pacific Reporter [second series]

Pa. Pennsylvania State Reports (Supreme Court)

Pac. Pacific

Pa. Commw. Ct. Pennsylvania Commonwealth Court Reports

Pa. Cons. Stat. Pennsylvania Consolidated Statutes

Pa. Cons. Stat. Ann. Pennsylvania Consolidated Statutes Annotated (Purdon)

Pa. D. & C. [2d] Pennsylvania District and County Reports [second series]

Pa. Fiduc. Pennsylvania Fiduciary Reporter

Paige Ch. Paige's Chancery Reports (New York)

Pa. Laws Laws of the General Assembly of the Commonwealth of Pennsylvania (Session Laws)

Pa. Legis. Serv. Pennsylvania Legislative Service (Purdon)

Pa. Stat. Ann. (Purdon) Purdon's Pennsylvania Statutes Annotated

Pa. Super. Ct. Pennsylvania Superior Court Reports

Pat. Patent

P.C. Parliamentary Cases; Patent

Cases; Penal Code; Pleas of the Crown; Political Code; Practice Cases; Privy Council

P. Ct. Probate Court

Pelt. Peltier's Orleans Reports (Louisiana)

Pens. Plan Guide Pension Plan Guide

Pen. & W. Penrose and Watts' Reports (Pennsylvania Supreme Court)

perm. permanent

PHA or **P.H.A.** Public Housing Administration

Phil. Philadelphia

Pin. Pinney's Reports (Wisconsin Supreme Court)

Pitt. Pittsburgh

Plan. Planning

p.o. post office; public officer

Pol. Politics

Police J. Ct. Police Justice's Court

pol'y policy

Port. Porter's Reports (Alabama Supreme Court)

Pov. L. Rep. Poverty Law Reporter

p.p. pages; propria persona (*in his proper person*)

p.p.i. policy proof of interest

prac. practical; practice; practitioners'

Priv. Found. Rep. Private Foundations Reporter

P.R. Laws Ann. Puerto Rico Laws Annotated

Prob. Probate; Problems

Proc. Procedures; Proceedings

prod. product; production

Prod. Liab. Rep. Products Liability Reporter

Prop. Property

P.R.R. Puerto Rico Reports (all courts)

p.s. postscript

P.S. Public Statutes

Psych. Psychiatry; Psychology

pt. part

pts. parts

Pub. Public

Pub. Lands Dec. Decisions of the Department of the Interior relating to Public Lands

Pub. U. Rep. Public Utilities Reports

PUC or **P.U.C.** Public Utilities Commission

Q

Q. Quarterly

Q.B. Queen's Bench

Q.B.D. Queen's Bench Division

Q.C. Queen's Counsel

q.c.f. or **qu. cl. fr.** quare clausum fregit (*breaking a close*)

q.d. quasi dicat (*as if he should say*)

q.e.n. quare executionem non (*execution should not be issued*)

Q.S. Quarter Sessions

q.t. qui tam (*who as well*)

Queensl. Queensland

q.v. quod vide (*which see*)

R

Rad. Reg. Radio Regulation

Rawle Rawle's Reports (Pennsylvania Supreme Court)

Rd. Road

Real Est. Comm'n Real Estate Commission

Rec. Record

Ref. Referee; Referee's; Refining; Reform

Ref. J. Journal of National Conference of Referees in Bankruptcy

Reg. Register; Regulation

Rel. Relations

Reorg. Reorganization

Rep. Reporter; Reports

repl. replacement

Res. Reserve

rev. revised; revision

Rev. Review

Rev. C. Abo. P.R. Revista del Colegio de Abogados de Puerto Rico

Rev. Jur. U. P.R. Revista Juridica de la Universidad de Puerto Rico

Rev. P.R. Revista de Derecho Puertorrinqueño

R.I. Rhode Island; Rhode Island Reports (Supreme Court)

Rich. Richmond

R.I. Gen. Laws General Laws of Rhode Island

R.I. Pub. Laws Public Laws of Rhode Island (Session Laws)

R.L. Revised Laws; Roman Laws

Rob. Robinson's Reports (Louisiana Supreme Court)

Rocky Mtn. Rocky Mountain

Root Root's Reports (Connecticut Supreme Court of Errors)

R.R. Railroad

R.S. Revised Statutes

Rut.-Cam. Rutgers-Camden

Ry. Railway

S

S. South; Southern

Sand. Ch. Sandford's Chancery Reports (New York)

San Fern. V. San Fernando Valley

Sarat. Ch. Sent. Saratoga Chancery Sentinel (New York)

Sask. Saskatchewan

Sav. Savings

S.B. Senate Bill

SBA or **S.B.A.** Small Business Administration

s.c. same case; select cases; supreme court

S.C. South Carolina Reports (Supreme Court); Supreme Court

S.C. Acts Acts and Joint Resolutions, South Carolina (Session Laws)

S.C. Code Code of Laws of South Carolina

S.C. Eq. South Carolina Equity Reports

S.C. Eq. (Bail. Eq.) South Carolina Equity Reports (Bailey's Equity)

S.C. Eq. (Chev. Eq.) South Carolina Equity Reports (Cheves' Equity)

S.C. Eq. (Des.) South Carolina Equity Reports (Desaussure's Equity)

S.C. Eq. (Dud. Eq.) South Carolina Equity Reports (Dudley's Equity)

S.C. Eq. (Harp. Eq.) South Carolina Equity Reports (Harper's Equity)

S.C. Eq. (Hill Eq.) South Carolina Equity Reports (Hill's Chancery)

S.C. Eq. (McCord Eq.) South Carolina Equity Reports (McCord's Chancery)

S.C. Eq. (McMul. Eq.) South Carolina Equity Reports (McMullan's Equity)

S.C. Eq. (Rice Eq.) South Carolina Equity Reports (Rice's Equity)

S.C. Eq. (Rich. Cas.) South Carolina Equity Reports (Richardson's Cases)

S.C. Eq. (Rich. Eq.) South Carolina Equity Reports (Richardson's Equity)

S.C. Eq. (Ril.) South Carolina Equity Reports (Riley's Chancery)

S.C. Eq. (Speers Eq.) South Carolina Equity Reports (Speers' Equity)

S.C. Eq. (Strob. Eq.) South Carolina Equity Reports (Strobhart's Equity)

Sch. School

Sci. Science; Sciences

S.C.L. South Carolina Law Reports

S.C.L. (Bail.) South Carolina Law Reports (Bailey)

S.C.L. (Bay) South Carolina Law Reports (Bay)

S.C.L. (Brev.) South Carolina Law Reports (Brevard)

S.C.L. (Chev.) South Carolina Law Reports (Cheves)

S.C.L. (Harp.) South Carolina Law Reports (Harper)

S.C.L. (Hill) South Carolina Law Reports (Hill)

S.C.L. (McCord) South Carolina Law Reports (McCord)

S.C.L. (McMul.) South Carolina Law Reports (McMullan)

S.C.L. (Mill) South Carolina Law Reports (Mill's Constitutional Court Reports)

S.C.L. (Nott & McC.) South Carolina Law Reports (Nott and McCord)

S.C.L. (Rice) South Carolina Law Reports (Rice)

S.C.L. (Rich.) South Carolina Law Reports (Richardson)

S.C.L. (Ril.) South Carolina Law Reports (Riley)

S.C.L. (Speers) South Carolina Law Reports (Speers)

S.C.L. (Strob.) South Carolina Law Reports (Strobhart)

Scot. L. Rev. Scottish Law Review and Sheriff Court Reports

S. Ct. Supreme Court Reporter

S.D. South Dakota; South Dakota Reports (Supreme Court); Southern District

S/D B/L sight draft—bill of lading attached

S.D. Compiled Laws Ann. South Dakota Compiled Laws Annotated

S.D. Sess. Laws Laws of South Dakota (Session Laws)

S.D. Uniform Prob. Code South Dakota Uniform Probate Code

S.E. [2d] Southeastern Reporter [second series]

SEC or **S.E.C.** Securities and Exchange Commission

Sec. Securities

S.E.C. Securities and Exchange Commission; Securities and Exchange Commission Decisions and Reports

Sec. Reg. Guide Securities Regulation Guide

Sec. Reg. & L. Rep. Securities Regulation and Law Report

Sel. Serv. L. Rep. Selective Service Law Reporter

ser. serial; serials; series

Ser. Series

Serg. & Rawl. Sergeant and Rawle's Reports (Pennsylvania Supreme Court)

Serv. Service

S.F. San Francisco

s.f.s. sine fraude sua (*without fraud on his part*)

S.J.C. Supreme Judicial Court

S.L. Session Laws

So. [2d] Southern Reporter [second series]

Soc. Social; Sociological; Sociology

Soc'y Society

s.p. sine prole (*without issue*)

spec. special

ss. scilicet (*to wit*)

S.S. Steamship

SSA or **S.S.A.** Social Security Administration

SSS or **S.S.S.** Selective Service System

St. State; Street

Stan. Stanford
Stand. Ex. Prof. Tax Rep. Standard
Excess Profits Tax Reporter
Stand. Fed. Tax Rep. Standard
Federal Tax Reporter
Stat. United States Statutes at large
State Tax Cas. State Tax Cases
State Tax Cas. Rep. State Tax Cases
Reporter
State & Loc. Taxes State and Local
Taxes
State Mot. Carr. Guide State Motor
Carrier Guide
Stew. Stewart's Reports (Alabama
Supreme Court)
Stew. & P. Stewart and Porter's
Reports (Alabama Supreme
Court)
Stud. Studies
Sup. Ct. Supreme Court
Super. Ct. Superior Court
Sup. Jud. Ct. Supreme Judicial
Court
Sur. Surety
Sur. Ct. Surrogate's Court
Sur. Ct. Proc. Act Surrogate's Court
Procedure Act (58A) (New York)
s.v. sub voce (*under the voice*)
S.W. Southwest; Southwestern
S.W. [2d] Southwestern Reporter
[second series]
Symp. Symposium
Sys. System

T

Tax. Taxation
Tax Ct. Mem. Dec. Tax Court Mem-
orandum Decisions
Tax Ct. Rep. Tax Court Reporter
Tax Ct. Rep. Dec. Tax Court
Reported Decisions
Tax-Exempt Orgs. Tax-Exempt
Organizations
Tax Mngm't Tax Management

T.C. United States Tax Court
Tchr. Teacher
Tchrs. Teachers
T.C.M. Tax Court Memorandum
Decisions
Tech. Technical; Technique; Tech-
nology
Teiss. Teisser's Court of Appeal,
Parish of Orleans Reports
(Louisiana)
Tel. Telegram; Telegraph; Telephone
temp. temporary
Temp. Temple
Temp. Emer. Ct. App. United States
Temporary Emergency Court of
Appeals
Tenn. Tennessee; Tennessee Reports
(Supreme Court)
Tenn. Code Ann. Tennessee Code
Annotated
Tenn. (Cold.) Tennessee Supreme
Court Reports (Coldwell)
Tenn. (Cooke) Tennessee Supreme
Court Reports (Cooke)
Tenn. (Hay.) Tennessee Supreme
Court Reports (Haywood)
Tenn. (Head) Tennessee Supreme
Court Reports (Head)
Tenn. (Heisk.) Tennessee Supreme
Court Reports (Heiskell)
Tenn. (Hum.) Tennessee Supreme
Court Reports (Humphreys)
Tenn. (Mart. & Yer.) Tennessee
Supreme Court Reports (Martin
and Yerger)
Tenn. (Meigs) Tennessee Supreme
Court Reports (Meigs)
Tenn. (Overt.) Tennessee Supreme
Court Reports (Overton)
Tenn. (Peck) Tennessee Supreme
Court Reports (Peck)
Tenn. Pub. Acts Public Acts of the
State of Tennessee (Session Laws)

Tenn. (Sneed) Tennessee Supreme Court Reports (Sneed)

Tenn. (Swan) Tennessee Supreme Court Reports (Swan)

Tenn. (Yer.) Tennessee Supreme Court Reports (Yerger)

Tex. Texas; Texas Reports (Supreme Court)

Tex. Bus. Corp. Act Ann. Texas Business Corporation Act Annotated

Tex. Civ. App. Texas Civil Appeals Reports

Tex. Civ. Cas. Texas Court of Appeals Decisions, Civil Cases (White & Willson)

Tex. [subject] * Code Ann. Texas Codes Annotated (Vernon)

[Subject Abbreviations] *

Agric. Agriculture

Alco. Bev. Alcoholic Beverage

Bus. & Com. Business and Commerce (1968)

Civ. Civil

Corp. & Ass'ns Corporations and Associations

Crim. Pro. Criminal Procedure

Educ. Education (1972)

Elec. Election

Fam. Family (1975)

Fin. Financial

Gov't Government

Health & Safety Health & Safety

High. Highway

Ins. Insurance

Lab. Labor

Occ. Occupations

Parks & Wild. Parks & Wildlife (1976)

Penal Penal (1974)

Prob. Probate

Prop. Property

Res. Resources

Tax Tax

Util. Utilities

Veh. Vehicles

Water Water (1972)

Welf. Welfare

Tex. Code Crim. Proc. Ann. Texas Code of Criminal Procedure of 1965 Annotated (Vernon)

Tex. Crim. Texas Criminal Reports (Texas Court of Appeals Reports)

Tex. Elec. Code Ann. Texas Election Code of 1951 Annotated (Vernon)

Tex. Gen. Laws General and Special Laws of the State of Texas (Session Laws)

Tex. Ins. Code Ann. Texas Insurance Code of 1951 Annotated (Vernon)

Tex. Prob. Code Ann. Texas Probate Code of 1955 Annotated (Vernon)

Tex. Rev. Civ. Stat. Ann. Texas Revised Civil Statutes Annotated (Vernon)

Tex. Sess. Law Serv. Texas Session Law Service (Vernon)

Tex. Stat. Ann. Texas Statutes Annotated

Tex. Tax-Gen. Ann. Texas Tax-General Annotated (Vernon)

tit. title

tits. titles

Tol. Toledo

T.M. Trademark

Tr. Trust

Trademark Bull. (n.s.) Bulletin of United States Trademark Association (new series)

Trade Reg. Rep. Trade Regulation Reporter

trans. translation; translator

Transnat'l Transnational

transp. transportation

Treas. Dec. Treasury Decisions under Customs and Other Laws

Treas. Dec. Int. Rev. Treasury Decisions under the Internal Revenue Laws
Tul. Tulane
Tyl. Tyler's Reports (Vermont Supreme Court)

U

U. University; Universities
U.C.C. Uniform Commercial Code
Unauth. Unauthorized
Unconsol. Laws Unconsolidated Laws (New York)
Unempl. Ins. Rep. Unemployment Insurance Reporter
Uniform City Ct. Act Uniform City Court Act (New York)
Univ. University; Universities
urb. urban
Urb. Aff. Rep. Urban Affairs Reporter
U.S. United States; United States Supreme Court Reports
U.S. App. D.C. United States Court of Appeals for District of Columbia Circuit
U.S. (Black) United States Supreme Court Reports 1861-1862 (reported by Black)
U.S.C. [A.] United States Code [Annotated]
U.S. (Cranch) United States Supreme Court Reports 1801-1815 (reported by Cranch)
U.S. (Dall.) United States Supreme Court Reports 1790-1800 (reported by Dallas)
Users Rep. Energy Users Report
U.S. (How.) United States Supreme Court Reports 1843-1860 (reported by Howard)
U.S.L.W. United States Law Week
U.S. (Pet.) United States Supreme Court Reports 1828-1842 (reported by Peters)
U.S. P. Q. United States Patent Quarterly
U.S. Tax Cas. United States Tax Cases
U.S. (Wall.) United States Supreme Court Reports 1863-1874 (reported by Wallace)
U.S. (Wheat.) United States Supreme Court Reports 1816-1827 (reported by Wheaton)
Utah [2d] Utah Reports (Supreme Court) [second series]
Utah Code Ann. Utah Code Annotated
Utah Laws Laws of Utah (Session Laws)
Util. Utility; Utilities
Util. L. Rep. Utilities Law Reporter

V

v. verb; versus; vide (*see*); voce (*voice*); volume
V. Victoria
Va. Virginia; Virginia Reports (Supreme Court, previously Supreme Court of Appeals)
Va. Acts Acts of the General Assembly of the Commonwealth of Virginia (Session Laws)
Va. (Call) Virginia Supreme Court Reports (Call)
Va. Code Code of Virginia
Va. (Gilmer) Virginia Supreme Court Reports (Gilmer)
Va. (Gratt.) Virginia Supreme Court Reports (Grattan)
Va. (Hen. & M.) Virginia Supreme Court Reports (Hening & Munford)
Val. Valparaiso
Va. (Leigh) Virginia Supreme Court (Leigh)
Va. (Munf.) Virginia Supreme Court (Munford)

Vand. Vanderbilt

Va. (Rand.) Virginia Supreme Court Reports (Randolph)

Va. (Rob.) Virginia Supreme Court (Robinson)

Va. (Va. Cas.) Virginia Supreme Court Reports (Virginia Cases, Criminal)

Va. (Wash.) Virginia Supreme Court Reports (Washington)

V.C. Vice Chancellor

V.I. Virgin Islands; Virgin Island Reports (all courts)

V.I. Code Ann. Virgin Islands Code Annotated

Vict. Victoria

Vill. Villanova

vol. volume

vols. volumes

vs. versus

Vt. Vermont; Vermont Reports (Supreme Court)

Vt. Acts Laws of Vermont (Session Laws)

Vt. Stat. Ann. Vermont Statutes Annotated

W

W. West; Western; Westminster; William

Wage and Hour Cas. Wage & Hour Cases

Wash. [2d] Washington; Washington Reports (Supreme Court) [second series]

Wash. App. Washington Appellate Reports

Wash. Laws Laws of Washington (Session Laws)

Wash. Legis. Serv. Washington Legislative Service (West)

Wash. Rev. Code Revised Code of Washington (1974)

Wash. Rev. Code Ann. Revised Code of Washington Annotated

Wash. Terr. Washington Territory Reports

W.D. Western District

Wills, Est., Tr. Wills, Estates, Trusts

Wis. Wisconsin; Wisconsin Reports (Supreme Court)

Wis. Laws Laws of Wisconsin (Session Laws)

Wis. Legis. Serv. Wisconsin Legislative Service (West)

Wis. Stat. Wisconsin Statutes

Wis. Stat. Ann. (West) Wisconsin Statutes Annotated (West)

Wm. & Mary William and Mary

Workmen's Comp. Div. Workmen's Compensation Division

Workmen's Comp. L. Rep. Workmen's Compensation Law Reporter

W. Va. West Virginia; West Virginia Reports (Supreme Court of Appeals)

W. Va. Acts Acts of the Legislature of West Virginia (Session Laws)

W. Va. Code West Virginia Code

Wyo. Wyoming; Wyoming Reports (Supreme Court)

Wyo. Sess. Laws Session Laws of Wyoming

Wyo. Stat. Wyoming Statutes

Y

Y.B. Yearbook

Youth Ct. Youth Court

UNITED STATES GOVERNMENT DIRECTORY

LEGISLATIVE BRANCH

Congress

The Senate

The Honorable _____
United States Senate
The Capitol
Washington, D.C. 20510
(202) 224-3121

The House of Representatives

The Honorable _____
United States House of
   Representatives
The Capitol
Washington, D.C. 20515
(202) 224-3121

General Accounting Office

441 G Street, N.W.
Washington, D.C. 20548
(202) 275-2812

Government Printing Office

North Capitol and H Streets, N.W.
Washington, D.C. 20401
(202) 275-2051

Library of Congress

10 First Street, S.E.
Washington, D.C. 20540
(202) 287-5000

Office of Technology Assessment

600 Pennsylvania Avenue, S.E.
Washington, D.C. 20510
(202) 224-3695 (Director)
(202) 224-8996 (Publications)

Congressional Budget Office

Second and D Streets, S.W.
Washington, D.C. 20515
(202) 225-4416

Copyright Royalty Tribunal

1111 Twentieth Street, N.W.
Washington, D.C. 20036
(202) 653-5175

JUDICIAL BRANCH

The Supreme Court of the United States

United States Supreme Court
   Building
1 First Street, N.E.
Washington, D.C. 20543
(202) 252-3000

United States Courts

See United States Court Directory

Administrative Office of United States Courts

Washington, D.C. 20544
(202) 633-6097

Federal Judicial Center

Dolley Madison House
1520 H Street, N.W.
Washington, D.C. 20005
(202) 633-6011

EXECUTIVE BRANCH

The President of the United States

The White House
Washington, D.C. 20500
(202) 456-1414

The Vice President of the United States

Executive Office Building
Washington, D.C. 20501
(202) 456-2326

The White House Office

1600 Pennsylvania Avenue, N.W.
Washington, D.C. 20500
(202) 456-1414

Office of Management and Budget

Executive Office Building
Washington, D.C. 20503
(202) 395-4747

Council of Economic Advisors

Executive Office Building
Washington, D.C. 20506
(202) 395-5084

National Security Council

Executive Office Building
Washington, D.C. 20506
(202) 395-4974

Office of Policy Development

1600 Pennsylvania Avenue, N.W.
Washington, D.C. 20500
(202) 456-1414

Office of the United States Trade Representative

1800 G Street, N.W.
Washington, D.C. 20506
(202) 395-4647

Council on Environmental Quality

722 Jackson Place, N.W.
Washington, D.C. 20006
(202) 395-5770

Office of Science and Technology Policy

Executive Office Building
Washington, D.C. 20500
(202) 456-7116

Office of the Vice President of the United States

Executive Office Building
Washington, D.C. 20501
(202) 456-2326

EXECUTIVE DEPARTMENTS

Department of Agriculture

14th Street and Independence
Avenue, S.W.
Washington, D.C. 20250
(202) 447-2791

Department of Commerce

14th Street Between Constitution
Avenue and E Street, N.W.
Washington, D.C. 20230
(202) 377-2000

Department of Defense

The Pentagon
Washington, D.C. 20301
(202) 545-6700

Department of Energy

James Forrestal Building
1000 Independence Avenue, S.W.
Washington, D.C. 20585
(202) 252-5000

Department of Health and Human Services

200 Independence Avenue, S.W.
Washington, D.C. 20201
(202) 245-6296

Department of Housing and Urban Development

451 7th Street, S.W.
Washington, D.C. 20410
(202) 655-4000

Department of the Interior

C Street Between 18th and 19th
   Streets, N.W.
Washington, D.C. 20240
(202) 343-3171

Department of Justice

Constitution Avenue and
   10th Street, N.W.
Washington, D.C. 20530
(202) 633-2007

Department of Labor

200 Constitution Avenue, N.W.
Washington, D.C. 20210
(202) 523-8165

Department of State

2201 C Street, N.W.
Washington, D.C. 20520
(202) 655-4000

Department of Transportation

400 7th Street, S.W.
Washington, D.C. 20590
(202) 426-4000

Department of the Treasury

15th Street and Pennsylvania
   Avenue, N.W.
Washington, D.C. 20220
(202) 566-2000

INDEPENDENT AGENCIES

ACTION

806 Connecticut Avenue, N.W.
Washington, D.C. 20525
(202) 393-3111

Appalachian Regional Commission

1666 Connecticut Avenue, N.W.
Washington, D.C. 20235
(202) 673-7835

Central Intelligence Agency

Washington, D.C. 20505
(703) 351-1100

Civil Aeronautics Board

1825 Connecticut Avenue, N.W.
Washington, D.C. 20428
(202) 673-5990

Commission on Civil Rights

1121 Vermont Avenue, N.W.
Washington, D.C. 20425
(202) 254-6758

Commodity Futures Trading Commission

2033 K Street, N.W.
Washington, D.C. 20581
(202) 254-8630

Community Services Administration

1200 19th Street, N.W.
Washington, D.C. 20506
(202) 254-5590

Consumer Product Safety Commission

1111 18th Street, N.W.
Washington, D.C. 20207
(202) 634-7700

Environmental Protection Agency

401 M Street, S.W.
Washington, D.C. 20460
(202) 382-2090

Equal Employment Opportunity Commission

2401 E Street, N.W.
Washington, D.C. 20506
(202) 634-6930

Export-Import Bank of the United States

811 Vermont Avenue, N.W.
Washington, D.C. 20571
(202) 566-8990

Farm Credit Administration

490 L'Enfant Plaza East, S.W.
Washington, D.C. 20578
(202) 755-2195

Federal Communications Commission

1919 M Street, N.W.
Washington, D.C. 20554
(202) 655-4000

Federal Deposit Insurance Corporation

550 17th Street, N.W.
Washington, D.C. 20429
(202) 389-4221

Federal Election Commission

1325 K Street, N.W.
Washington, D.C. 20463
(202) 523-4089

Federal Emergency Management Agency

1725 I Street, N.W.
Washington, D.C. 20472
(202) 634-6660

Federal Home Loan Bank Board

1700 G Street, N.W.
Washington, D.C. 20552
(202) 377-6000

Federal Labor Relations Authority

1900 E Street, N.W.
Washington, D.C. 20424
(202) 632-4524

Federal Maritime Commission

1100 L Street, N.W.
Washington, D.C. 20573
(202) 655-4000

Federal Mediation and Conciliation Service

2100 K Street, N.W.
Washington, D.C. 20427
(202) 653-5290

Federal Reserve System

Board of Governors of the
Federal Reserve System
20th Street and Constitution
Avenue, N.W.
Washington, D.C. 20551
(202) 452-3204

Federal Trade Commission

Pennsylvania Avenue at
6th Street, N.W.
Washington, D.C. 20580
(202) 523-3598

General Services Administration

18th and F Streets, N.W.
Washington, D.C. 20405
(202) 655-4000

International Communication Agency

1750 Pennsylvania Avenue, N.W.
Washington, D.C. 20547
(202) 655-4000

Interstate Commerce Commission

12th Street and Constitution
Avenue, N.W.
Washington, D.C. 20423
(202) 275-7252

Merit Systems Protection Board

1717 H Street, N.W.
Washington, D.C. 20419
(202) 653-7124

**National Aeronautics and
   Space Administration**

400 Maryland Avenue, S.W.
Washington, D.C. 20546
(202) 755-2320

**National Credit Union
   Administration**

1776 G Street, N.W.
Washington, D.C. 20456
(202) 357-1050

National Labor Relations Board

1717 Pennsylvania Avenue, N.W.
Washington, D.C. 20570
(202) 655-4000

National Mediation Board

1425 K Street, N.W.
Washington, D.C. 20572
(202) 523-5920

National Science Foundation

1800 G Street, N.W.
Washington, D.C. 20550
(202) 655-4000

**National Transportation
   Safety Board**

800 Independence Avenue, S.W.
Washington, D.C. 20594
(202) 382-6600

Nuclear Regulatory Commission

1717 H Street, N.W.
Washington, D.C. 20555
(301) 492-7000

**Occupational Safety and Health
   Review Commission**

1825 K Street, N.W.
Washington, D.C. 20006
(202) 634-7943

Office of Personnel Management

1900 E Street, N.W.
Washington, D.C. 20415
(202) 655-4000

**Pension Benefit Guaranty
   Corporation**

2020 K Street, N.W.
Washington, D.C. 20006
(202) 254-4817

Postal Rate Commission

2000 L Street, N.W.
Washington, D.C. 20268
(202) 655-4000

Railroad Retirement Board

844 Rush Street
Chicago, IL 60611
(312) 751-4777

Washington Liaison Office
   Room 444
425 13th Street, N.W.
Washington, D.C. 20004
(202) 724-0121

**Securities and Exchange
   Commission**

500 North Capitol Street
Washington, D.C. 20549
(202) 755-4846

Selective Service System

National Headquarters
Washington, D.C. 20435
(202) 724-0424

Small Business Administration

1441 L Street, N.W.
Washington, D.C. 20416
(202) 653-6365

Tennessee Valley Authority

400 Commerce Avenue
Knoxville, TN 37902
(615) 632-2101

Capitol Hill Office Building
412 First Street, S.E.
Washington, D.C. 20444
(202) 245-0101

United States Arms Control and Disarmament Agency

Department of State Building
Washington, D.C. 20451
(202) 655-4000

United States International Trade Commission

701 E Street, N.W.
Washington, D.C. 20436
(202) 523-0161

United States Metric Board

1600 Wilson Boulevard
Arlington, VA 22209
(703) 235-1696

United States Postal Service

475 L'Enfant Plaza West, S.W.
Washington, D.C. 20260
(202) 245-4000

Veterans Administration

810 Vermont Avenue, N.W.
Washington, D.C. 20420
(202) 393-4120

QUASI-OFFICIAL AGENCIES

Legal Services Corporation

733 15th Street, N.W.
Washington, D.C. 20005
(202) 272-4000

National Consumer Cooperative Bank

2001 S Street, N.W.
Washington, D.C. 20009
(202) 673-4300 or (800) 424-2481

National Railroad Passenger Corporation (AMTRAK)

400 North Capitol Street, N.W.
Washington, D.C. 20001
(202) 383-3000

Smithsonian Institution

1000 Jefferson Drive, S.W.
Washington, D.C. 20560
(202) 357-1300

United States Railway Association

955 L'Enfant Plaza North, S.W.
Washington, D.C. 20595
(202) 426-4250

United States Synthetic Fuels Corporation

1200 New Hampshire Avenue, N.W.
Washington, D.C. 20586
(202) 653-4363

UNITED STATES COURT DIRECTORY

Supreme Court of the United States

United States Courts of Appeals

Special Courts

United States District Courts

Federal Judicial Center

Administrative Office of the United States Courts

SUPREME COURT OF THE UNITED STATES
1 FIRST STREET, N.E.
WASHINGTON, D.C. 20543

Chief Justice
Warren E. Burger

Retired Justice
Potter Stewart

Clerk
Alexander Stevas

Associate Justices
William J. Brennan, Jr.
Byron R. White
Thurgood Marshall
Harry A. Blackmun
Lewis F. Powell, Jr.
William H. Rehnquist
John Paul Stevens
Sandra Day O'Connor

UNITED STATES COURTS OF APPEALS*

Circuit

District of Columbia Circuit

Clerk
U.S. Courthouse
3rd and Constitution Avenue, N.W.
Washington, D.C. 20001

First Circuit —
Maine, Massachusetts,
New Hampshire, Rhode Island,
Puerto Rico

Clerk
1606 John W. McCormack
  Post Office and Courthouse
  Building
Boston, MA 02109

Second Circuit —
Connecticut, New York, Vermont

Clerk
2501 U.S. Courthouse
Foley Square
New York, NY 10007

Third Circuit —
Delaware, New Jersey, Pennsylvania,
Virgin Islands

Clerk
21400 U.S. Courthouse
Independence Mall West
601 Market Street
Philadelphia, PA 19106

*The name of the court should be included in the address.
  For example: *Clerk*
             U.S. Court of Appeals
             2501 U.S. Courthouse
             Foley Square
             New York, NY 10007

Fourth Circuit —
Maryland, North Carolina,
South Carolina, Virginia,
West Virginia

Clerk
U.S. Courthouse, Room 249
Tenth and Main Streets
Richmond, VA 23219

Fifth Circuit —
Louisiana, Mississippi, Texas,
Canal Zone

Clerk
Room 100, 600 Camp Street,
New Orleans, LA 70130

Sixth Circuit —
Kentucky, Michigan, Ohio,
Tennessee

Clerk
516 U.S. Post Office and
   Courthouse Building
Cincinnati, OH 45202

Seventh Circuit —
Illinois, Indiana, Wisconsin

Clerk
U.S. Courthouse and Federal Office
   Building
219 South Dearborn Street
Chicago, IL 60604

Eighth Circuit —
Arkansas, Iowa, Minnesota,
Missouri, Nebraska, North Dakota,
South Dakota

Clerk
511 U.S. Court and Customs House
St. Louis, MO 63101

Ninth Circuit —
Arizona, California, Idaho, Montana,
Nevada, Oregon, Washington,
Alaska, Hawaii, Guam, Northern
Mariana Islands

Clerk
P.O. Box 547
San Francisco, CA 94101

Tenth Circuit —
Colorado, Kansas, New Mexico,
Oklahoma, Utah, Wyoming

Clerk
C-404 U.S. Courthouse
Denver, CO 80294

Eleventh Circuit —
Alabama, Florida, Georgia

Clerk
56 Forsyth Street, N.W.
Atlanta, GA 30303

United States Court of Appeals
Temporary Emergency Court of
   Appeals

Clerk
Room 2400, U.S. Courthouse
Washington, D.C. 20001

SPECIAL COURTS

Court

United States Court of Claims
717 Madison Place, N.W.
Washington, D.C. 20005

**United States Court of
International Trade**
One Federal Plaza
New York, NY 10007

**United States Court of Customs
and Patent Appeals**
717 Madison Place, N.W.
Washington, D.C. 20439

**Judicial Panel on
Multidistrict Litigation**
1120 Vermont Avenue, N.W.
Suite 1002
Washington, D.C. 20005

United States Court of Military Appeals
450 E Street, N.W.
Washington, D.C. 20442

UNITED STATES DISTRICT COURTS*

District

ALABAMA

Northern

Clerk
104 Federal Court House
Birmingham, AL 35203

*Divisional Office with Resident
Deputy in Charge:*
U.S. Post Office and Courthouse
101 Holmes Avenue, N.E.
Huntsville, AL 35801

Middle

Clerk
P.O. Box 711
Montgomery, AL 36101

Southern

Clerk
P.O. Box 2625
Mobile, AL 36652

*The name of the court should be included in the address.
For example: *Clerk*
      U.S. District Court
      104 Federal Court House
      Birmingham, AL 35203

ALASKA

Clerk
Federal Building
701 C Street
Anchorage, AK 99501

*Divisional Offices with Resident
Deputy in Charge:*
Federal Building and Courthouse
101 12th Avenue
Box No. 1
Fairbanks, AK 99701

Box 349
Juneau, AK 99803

Room 400
415 Main Street
Ketchikan, AK 99901

Box 130
Nome, AK 99762

ARIZONA

Clerk
Room 1400, U.S. Courthouse
Phoenix, AZ 85025

*Divisional Office with Resident
Deputy in Charge:*
55 East Broadway
Tucson, AZ 85701

ARKANSAS

Eastern

Clerk
P.O. Box 869
Little Rock, AR 72203

*Divisional Offices with Resident
Deputy in Charge:*
Room 203, Federal Building
and Courthouse
Jonesboro, AR 72401

P.O. Box 8307
Pine Bluff, AR 71611

Western

Clerk
P.O. Box 1523
Fort Smith, AR 72902

*Divisional Offices with Resident
Deputy in Charge:*
P.O. Box 1566
El Dorado, AR 71730

Room 523, Federal Building
and U.S. Courthouse
Fayetteville, AR 72701

P.O. Drawer I
Hot Springs, AR 71901

P.O. Box 2746
Texarkana, AR 75501

CALIFORNIA

Northern

Clerk
U.S. Courthouse
P.O. Box 36060
San Francisco, CA 94102

*Divisional Office with Resident
Deputy in Charge:*
U.S. Courthouse
175 West Taylor Street
San Jose, CA 95110

Eastern

Clerk
2546 U.S. Courthouse
650 Capitol Mall
Sacramento, CA 95814

*Divisional Office with Resident
Deputy in Charge:*
5408 U.S. Courthouse
1130 "O" Street
Fresno, CA 93721

Central

Clerk
U.S. Courthouse
312 North Spring Street
Los Angeles, CA 90012

Southern

Clerk
U.S. Courthouse, Room 1N20
940 Front Street
San Diego, CA 92189

CANAL ZONE, DISTRICT COURT OF THE

Clerk
Box 2006
Balboa Heights, Canal Zone
U.S.A. Postal Zone #8

Divisional Office with Resident Deputy in Charge:
Box 1175
Cristobal, Canal Zone

COLORADO

Clerk
Room C-145, U.S. Courthouse
1929 Stout Street
Denver, CO 80202

CONNECTICUT

Clerk
Federal Building
141 Church Street
New Haven, CT 06510

Divisional Offices with Resident Deputy in Charge:
915 Lafayette Boulevard
Bridgeport, CT 06604

450 Main Street
Hartford, CT 06103

DELAWARE

Clerk
Lockbox 18
Federal Building
844 N. King Street
Wilmington, DE 19801

DISTRICT OF COLUMBIA

Clerk
U.S. Courthouse
3rd and Constitution Avenue, N.W.
Washington, D.C. 20001

FLORIDA

Northern

Clerk
110 East Park Avenue
Room 122
Tallahassee, FL 32301

Divisional Office with Resident Deputy in Charge:
P.O. Box 990
Pensacola, FL 32595

Middle

Clerk
P.O. Box 53558
Jacksonville, FL 32201–3558

Divisional Offices with Resident Deputy in Charge:
Room 611, Federal Office
    and U.S. Courthouse
80 N. Hughey Avenue
Orlando, FL 32801–2278

P.O. Box 3270
Tampa, FL 33601–3270

Southern

Clerk
P.O. Box 010669
Flagler Station
Miami, FL 33101

*Divisional Offices with Resident
Deputy in Charge:*
301 North Andrews Avenue
Fort Lauderdale, FL 33301

Federal Building
701 Clematis Street
West Palm Beach, FL 33401

GEORGIA

Northern

Clerk
2211 U.S. Courthouse
75 Spring Street, S.W.
Atlanta, GA 30303

*Divisional Offices with Resident
Deputy in Charge:*
Room 201, Federal Building
Gainesville, GA 30501

Federal Building
P.O. Box 939
Newnan, GA 30264

Post Office Building
P.O. Box 1186
Rome, GA 30161

Middle

Clerk
P.O. Box 128
Macon, GA 31202

*Divisional Offices with Resident
Deputy in Charge:*
P.O. Box 1906
Albany, GA 31702

P.O. Box 124
Columbus, GA 31902

P.O. Box 68
Valdosta, GA 31601

Southern

Clerk
P.O. Box 8286
Savannah, GA 31402

*Divisional Offices with Resident
Deputy in Charge:*
P.O. Box 1130
Augusta, GA 30903

P.O. Box 1636
Brunswick, GA 31520

GUAM, DISTRICT COURT OF

Clerk
P.O. Box DC
Agana, GU 96910

HAWAII

Clerk
P.O. Box 50129
Honolulu, HI 96815

IDAHO

Clerk
U.S. Courthouse
P.O. Box 039
550 West Fort Street
Boise, ID 83724

ILLINOIS

Northern

Clerk
U.S. Courthouse
219 South Dearborn Street
Chicago, IL 60604

*Divisional Office with Resident
Deputy in Charge:*
211 South Court Street
Room 252
Rockford, IL 61101

Central

Clerk
Room 254, Federal Building
100 N.E. Monroe Street
Peoria, IL 61602

Divisional Offices with Resident
Deputy in Charge:
P.O. Box 786
Danville, IL 61832

Room 40, P.O. Building
Rock Island, IL 61201

P.O. Box 315
Springfield, IL 62705

Southern

Clerk
P.O. Box 249
East St. Louis, IL 62202

Divisional Offices with Resident
Deputy in Charge:
Federal Building
501 Belle Street
P.O. Box 654
Alton, IL 62002

U.S. Courthouse and Post Office
 Building
P.O. Box F
Benton, IL 62812

INDIANA

Northern

Clerk
Federal Building
Room 305
204 S. Main Street
South Bend, IN 46601

Divisional Offices with Resident
Deputy in Charge:
212 Federal Building
1300 South Harrison Street
Fort Wayne, IN 46802

Federal Building
507 State Street
Hammond, IN 46320

Federal Building
232 North 4th Street

P.O. Box 524
Lafayette, IN 47902

Southern

Clerk
U.S. Courthouse
Room 105
2 East Ohio Street
Indianapolis, IN 46204

Divisional Offices with Resident
Deputy in Charge:
304 Federal Building
Evansville, IN 47708

210 Federal Building
New Albany, IN 47150

210 Federal Building
Terre Haute, IN 47808

IOWA

Northern

Clerk
Federal Building
P.O. Box 4411
Cedar Rapids, IA 52407

Divisional Office with Resident
Deputy in Charge:
Federal Post Office Building
P.O. Box 1348
Sioux City, IA 51102

Southern

Clerk
Room 200, U.S. Courthouse
East 1st and Walnut Streets
Des Moines, IA 50309

Divisional Offices with Resident
Deputy in Charge:
P.O. Box 307
Council Bluffs, IA 51502

P.O. Box 256
Davenport, IA 52805

KANSAS

Clerk
P.O. Box 2201
Wichita, KS 67201

Divisional Offices with Resident
Deputy in Charge:
Room 151, Federal Building
Kansas City, KS 66101

444 S.E. Quincy
Topeka, KS 66603

KENTUCKY

Eastern

Clerk
P.O. Box 741
Lexington, KY 40586

Divisional Offices with Resident
Deputy in Charge:
P.O. Box 355
Catlettsburg, KY 41129

P.O. Box 1073
Covington, KY 41012

P.O. Box 689
London, KY 40741

P.O. Box 131
Pikeville, KY 41501

Western

Clerk
230 U.S. Courthouse Building
Louisville, KY 40202

Divisional Offices with Resident
Deputy in Charge:
213 Federal Building
Bowling Green, KY 42101

P.O. Box 538
Federal Building
Owensboro, KY 42301

224 Federal Building
Paducah, KY 42001

LOUISIANA

Eastern

Clerk
U.S. Courthouse
Chambers C-151
500 Camp Street
New Orleans, LA 70130

Middle

Clerk
Room 308
Federal Building and U.S.
  Courthouse
707 Florida Avenue
Baton Rouge, LA 70801

Western

Clerk
106 Joe D. Waggonner
  Federal Building
500 Fannin Street
Shreveport, LA 71101

Divisional Offices with Resident
Deputy in Charge:
P.O. Box 1269
Alexandria, LA 71301

237 Federal Building
705 Jefferson Street
Lafayette, LA 70501

P.O. Box 393
Lake Charles, LA 70602

Federal Building, Room 306
Union and Vine Streets
Opelousas, LA 70570

MAINE

Clerk
P.O. Box 7505 DTS
Portland, ME 04112

Divisional Office with Resident
Deputy in Charge:
212 Harlow Street
Bangor, ME 04401

MARYLAND

Clerk
U.S. Courthouse
101 West Lombard Street
Baltimore, MD 21201–2691

MASSACHUSETTS

Clerk
1525 Post Office and
   Courthouse Building
Boston, MA 02109

MICHIGAN

Eastern

Clerk
Room 133
U.S. Courthouse
Detroit, MI 48226

*Divisional Offices with Resident
Deputy in Charge:*
214 Post Office Building
Bay City, MI 48706

600 Church Street
Flint, MI 48502

Western

Clerk
458 Federal Building
110 Michigan Street, N.W.
Grand Rapids, MI 49503

*Divisional Offices with Resident
Deputy in Charge:*
U.S. Post Office and
   Federal Building
410 West Michigan
Kalamazoo, MI 49007

229 Post Office Building
Marquette, MI 49855

MINNESOTA

Clerk
708 Federal Building
316 Robert Street, North
St. Paul, MN 55101

*Divisional Offices with Resident
Deputy in Charge:*
417 U.S. Courthouse
Duluth, MN 55802

514 U.S. Courthouse
110 South 4th Street
Minneapolis, MN 55401

MISSISSIPPI

Northern

Clerk
P.O. Box 727
Oxford, MS 38655

*Divisional Offices with Resident
Deputy in Charge:*
P.O. Box 704
Aberdeen, MS 39730

P.O. Box 190
Clarksdale, MS 38614

P.O. Box 190
Greenville, MS 38701

Southern

Clerk
P.O. Box 769
Jackson, MS 39205

*Divisional Offices with Resident
Deputy in Charge:*
Box 369
Biloxi, MS 39533

Box 511
Hattiesburg, MS 39401

Box 1186
Meridian, MS 39301

MISSOURI

Eastern

Clerk
U.S. Court and Custom House
1114 Market Street
St. Louis, MO 63101

Divisional Office with Resident Deputy in Charge:
339 Broadway
Cape Girardeau, MO 63701

Western

Clerk
U.S. Courthouse
811 Grand Avenue, Room 201
Kansas City, MO 64106

Divisional Offices with Resident Deputy in Charge:
310 U.S. Courthouse
131 West High Street
Jefferson City, MO 65101

206 U.S. Courthouse
302 Joplin Street
Joplin, MO 64801

229 U.S. Courthouse
201 South Eighth Street
St. Joseph, MO 64501

305 U.S. Courthouse
870 Boonville Avenue
Springfield, MO 65801

MONTANA

Clerk
Room 5405, Federal Building
310 N. 26th Street
Billings, MT 59101

Divisional Offices with Resident Deputy in Charge:
Federal Building
Butte, MT 59701

P.O. Box 2186
Great Falls, MT 59403

P.O. Box 8537
Missoula, MT 59807

NEBRASKA

Clerk
9000 U.S. Courthouse and
    Post Office Building
P.O. Box 129
Downtown Station
Omaha, NE 68101

Divisional Office with Resident Deputy in Charge:
593 Federal Building
100 Centennial Mall North
Lincoln, NE 68508

NEVADA

Clerk
Room 3-632
300 Las Vegas Boulevard, South
Las Vegas, NV 89101

Divisional Office with Resident Deputy in Charge:
Room 5003
300 Booth Street
Reno, NV 89509

NEW HAMPSHIRE

Clerk
P.O. Box 1498
Concord, NH 03301

NEW JERSEY

Clerk
U.S. Courthouse
402 East State Street
P.O. Box 515
Trenton, NJ 08608

*Divisional Office with Resident
Deputy in Charge:*
U.S. Post Office
   and Courthouse
Newark, NJ 07102

NEW MEXICO

Clerk
P.O. Box 689
Albuquerque, NM 87103

*Divisional Offices with Resident
Deputy in Charge:*
Room C-309
200 E. Griggs
Las Cruces, NM 88001

P.O. Box 2384
Santa Fe, NM 87501

NEW YORK

Northern

Clerk
Box 950
Post Office and
   Courthouse Building
Albany, NY 12201

*Divisional Office with Resident
Deputy in Charge:*
Box 417
Post Office and
   Courthouse Building
Utica, NY 13503

Southern

Clerk
U.S. Courthouse
Foley Square
New York, NY 10007

Eastern

Clerk
U.S. Courthouse
225 Cadman Plaza East
Brooklyn, NY 11201

Western

Clerk
604 U.S. Courthouse
Buffalo, NY 14202

*Divisional Office with Resident
Deputy in Charge:*
282 U.S. Courthouse
Rochester, NY 14614

NORTH CAROLINA

Eastern

Clerk
P.O. Box 25670
Raleigh, NC 27611

*Divisional Offices with Resident
Deputy in Charge:*
P.O. Box 43
Fayetteville, NC 28302

P.O. Box 1336
New Bern, NC 28560

P.O. Box 338
Wilmington, NC 28402

Middle

Clerk
P.O. Box V-1
Greensboro, NC 27402

Western

Clerk
Post Office Building
P.O. Box 92
Asheville, NC 28802

*Divisional Offices with Resident
Deputy in Charge:*
Post Office and Courthouse
P.O. Box 31757
Charlotte, NC 28231

Post Office and Courthouse
P.O. Box 466
Statesville, NC 28677

NORTH DAKOTA

Clerk
P.O. Box 1193
Bismarck, ND 58501

*Divisional Office with Resident
Deputy in Charge:*
P.O. Box 870
Fargo, ND 58107

NORTHERN MARIANA ISLANDS

Clerk
P.O. Box 687
Saipan 96950

OHIO

Northern

Clerk
328 U.S. Courthouse
Cleveland, OH 44114

*Divisional Offices with Resident
Deputy in Charge:*
568 U.S. Courthouse
Akron, OH 44308

108 U.S. Courthouse
Toledo, OH 43624

332 U.S. Post Office Building
Youngstown, OH 44501

Southern

Clerk
328 U.S. Courthouse
85 Marconi Boulevard
Columbus, OH 43215

*Divisional Offices with Resident
Deputy in Charge:*
832 U.S. Courthouse
   and Post Office Building
5th and Walnut Streets
Cincinnati, OH 45202

P.O. Box 970
Mid-City Station
Dayton, OH 45402

OKLAHOMA

Northern

Clerk
Room 411, U.S. Courthouse
Tulsa, OK 74103

Eastern

Clerk
P.O. Box 607
U.S. Courthouse
Muskogee, OK 74401

Western

Clerk
Room 3210, U.S. Courthouse
Oklahoma City, OK 73102

OREGON

Clerk
516 U.S. Courthouse
620 S.W. Main Street
Portland, OR 97205

PENNSYLVANIA

Eastern

Clerk
2609 U.S. Courthouse
Independence Mall West
601 Market Street
Philadelphia, PA 19106

*Divisional Office with Resident
Deputy in Charge:*
Room 444
American Bank Building
35 6th Street, North
Reading, PA 19601

Middle

Clerk
P.O. Box 1148
Scranton, PA 18501

*Divisional Offices with Resident
Deputy in Charge:*
P.O. Box 983
Harrisburg, PA 17108

Box 608
Williamsport, PA 17701

Room 203, Federal Building
197 South Main Street
Wilkes-Barre, PA 18701

Western

Clerk
P.O. Box 1805
Pittsburgh, PA 15230

*Divisional Office with Resident
Deputy in Charge:*
P.O. Box 1820
Erie, PA 16507

PUERTO RICO

Clerk
P.O. Box 3671
San Juan, PR 00904

RHODE ISLAND

Clerk
119 Federal Building
U.S. Courthouse
Providence, RI 02903

SOUTH CAROLINA

Clerk
P.O. Box 867
Columbia, SC 29202

*Divisional Offices with Resident
Deputy in Charge:*
P.O. Box 835
Charleston, SC 29402

P.O. Box 10250
Greenville, SC 29603

SOUTH DAKOTA

Clerk
Room 220, Federal Building
    and U.S. Courthouse
400 South Phillips Avenue
Sioux Falls, SD 57102

*Divisional Offices with Resident
Deputy in Charge:*
Room 405, Post Office and
    U.S. Courthouse
Pierre, SD 57501

Room 302, Federal Building
    and U.S. Courthouse
515 9th Street
Rapid City, SD 57701

TENNESSEE

Eastern

Clerk
P.O. Box 2348
Knoxville, TN 37901

*Divisional Offices with Resident
Deputy in Charge:*
P.O. Box 591
Chattanooga, TN 37401

P.O. Box 149
Greeneville, TN 37743

Middle

Clerk
800 U.S. Courthouse
Nashville, TN 37203

Western

Clerk
950 Federal Building
167 Main Street, North
Memphis, TN 38103

*Divisional Office with Resident
Deputy in Charge:*
P.O. Box 756
Jackson, TN 38301

TEXAS

Northern

Clerk
U.S. Courthouse
Room 15C22
1100 Commerce Street
Dallas, TX 75242

*Divisional Offices with Resident
Deputy in Charge:*
P.O. Box 1218
Abilene, TX 79604

P.O. Box F-13240
Amarillo, TX 79109

202 U.S. Courthouse
Fort Worth, TX 76102

C-221 U.S. Courthouse
1205 Texas Avenue
Lubbock, TX 79401

Twohig and Oakes Streets
Room 202
San Angelo, TX 76903

P.O. Box 1234
Wichita Falls, TX 76307

Southern

Clerk
P.O. Box 61010
Houston, TX 77208

*Divisional Offices with Resident
Deputy in Charge:*
P.O. Box 2299
Brownsville, TX 78520

P.O. Box 2567
Corpus Christi, TX 78403

611 P.O. Building
Galveston, TX 77550

P.O. Box 597
Laredo, TX 78040

P.O. Box 1541
Victoria, TX 77901

Eastern

Clerk
Room 212, U.S. Courthouse
Beaumont, TX 77701

*Divisional Offices with Resident
Deputy in Charge:*
Federal Building
Sherman, TX 75090

P.O. Box 2667
Texarkana, TX 75501

P.O. Box 539
Tyler, TX 75710

Western

Clerk
Hemisfair Plaza
655 East Durango Boulevard
San Antonio, TX 78206

*Divisional Offices with Resident
Deputy in Charge:*
U.S. Courthouse
200 West 8th Street
Austin, TX 78701

P.O. Box 1349
Del Rio, TX 78840

Room 108, U.S. Courthouse
El Paso, TX 79901

P.O. Box 10708
Midland, TX 79702

P.O. Box 191
Pecos, TX 79772

P.O. Box 608
Waco, TX 76703

UTAH

Clerk
P.O. Box 3900
Salt Lake City, UT 84110

VERMONT

Clerk
P.O. Box 945
Federal Building
Burlington, VT 05402

*Divisional Office with Resident
Deputy in Charge:*
P.O. Box 607
Federal Building
Rutland, VT 05701

VIRGIN ISLANDS, DISTRICT
COURT OF THE

Clerk
P.O. Box 720
Charlotte Amalie
St. Thomas, VI 00801

*Divisional Office with Resident
Deputy in Charge:*
Christiansted
St. Croix, VI 00820

VIRGINIA

Eastern

Clerk
P.O. Box 1318
Norfolk, VA 23501

*Divisional Offices with Resident
Deputy in Charge:*
P.O. Box 2-AD
Richmond, VA 23205

P.O. Box 709
Alexandria, VA 22313

P.O. Box 494
Newport News, VA 23607

Western

Clerk
P.O. Box 1234
Roanoke, VA 24006

*Divisional Offices with Resident
Deputy in Charge:*
P.O. Box 398
Abingdon, VA 24210

P.O. Box 135
Charlottesville, VA 22902

P.O. Box 52
Danville, VA 24543

P.O. Box 490
Big Stone Gap, VA 24219

P.O. Box 1207
Harrisonburg, VA 22801

P.O. Box 744
Lynchburg, VA 24505

WASHINGTON

Eastern

Clerk
P.O. Box 1493
Spokane, WA 99210

Western

Clerk
308 U.S. Courthouse
Seattle, WA 98104

*Divisional Office with Resident
Deputy in Charge:*
P.O. Box 1935
Tacoma, WA 98401

WEST VIRGINIA

Northern

Clerk
P.O. Box 1518
Elkins, WV 26241

*Divisional Offices with Resident
Deputy in Charge:*
P.O. Box 471
Wheeling, WV 26003

P.O. Box 1526
Parkersburg, WV 26101

Southern

Clerk
P.O. Box 2546
Charleston, WV 25329

*Divisional Offices with Resident
Deputy in Charge:*
Federal Station Box 4128
Bluefield, WV 24701

P.O. Box 1570
Huntington, WV 25716

WISCONSIN

Eastern

Clerk
Room 362, U.S. Courthouse
517 East Wisconsin Avenue
Milwaukee, WI 53202

Western

Clerk
P.O. Box 432
Madison, WI 53701

WYOMING

Clerk
P.O. Box 727
Cheyenne, WY 82001

FEDERAL JUDICIAL CENTER

Dolley Madison House
1520 H Street, N.W.
Washington, D.C. 20005

ADMINISTRATIVE OFFICE OF THE UNITED STATES COURTS

Washington, D.C. 20544

DIRECTORY OF UNITED STATES COUNTIES AND COUNTY SEATS

County	County Seat	Zip Code

ALABAMA

County	County Seat	Zip Code
Autauga	Prattville	36067
Baldwin	Bay Minette	36507
Barbour	Clayton	36016
Bibb	Centreville	35042
Blount	Oneonta	35121
Bullock	Union Springs	36089
Butler	Greenville	36037
Calhoun	Anniston	36201
Chambers	Lafayette	36862
Cherokee	Centre	35960
Chilton	Clanton	35045
Choctaw	Butler	36904
Clarke	Grove Hill	36451
Clay	Ashland	36251
Cleburne	Heflin	36264
Coffee	Elba	36323
Colbert	Tuscumbia	35674
Conecuh	Evergreen	36401
Coosa	Rockford	35136
Covington	Andalusia	36420
Crenshaw	Luverne	36049
Cullman	Cullman	35055
Dale	Ozark	36360
Dallas	Selma	36701
De Kalb	Fort Payne	35967
Elmore	Wetumpka	36092
Escambia	Brewton	36426
Etowah	Gadsden	35901-05
Fayette	Fayette	35555
Franklin	Russellville	35653
Geneva	Geneva	36340
Greene	Eutaw	35462
Hale	Greensboro	36744
Henry	Abbeville	36310
Houston	Dothan	36301
Jackson	Scottsboro	35768
Jefferson	Birmingham	35201-43
Lamar	Vernon	35592

County	County Seat	Zip Code
Lauderdale	Florence	35630
Lawrence	Moulton	35650
Lee	Opelika	36801
Limestone	Athens	35611
Lowndes	Hayneville	36040
Macon	Tuskegee	36083
Madison	Huntsville	35801-12
Marengo	Linden	36748
Marion	Hamilton	35570
Marshall	Guntersville	35976
Mobile	Mobile	36601-19
Monroe	Monroeville	36460
Montgomery	Montgomery	36101-15
Morgan	Decatur	35601
Perry	Marion	36756
Pickens	Carrollton	35447
Pike	Troy	36081
Randolph	Wedowee	36278
Russell	Phenix City	36867
St. Clair	Ashville	35953
	and Pell City	35125
Shelby	Columbiana	35051
Sumter	Livingston	35470
Talladega	Talladega	35160
Tallapoosa	Dadeville	36853
Tuscaloosa	Tuscaloosa	35401
Walker	Jasper	35501
Washington	Chatom	36518
Wilcox	Camden	36726
Winston	Double Springs	35553

ALASKA*

Bristol Bay	Naknek	99633
Fairbanks North Star	Fairbanks	99701
Greater Anchorage Area	Anchorage	99501-41
Greater Sitka	Sitka	99835

*Alaska abolished county governments; former counties and county seats are listed here.

County	County Seat	Zip Code
Haines	Haines	99827
Juneau	Juneau	99801
Kenai		
Peninsula	Soldotna	99669
Kodiak		
Island	Kodiak	99615
Matanuska-		
Susitna	Palmer	99645

Census Divisions**

Aleutian Islands
Anchorage
Angoon
Barrow-North Slope
Bethel
Bristol Bay Borough
Bristol Bay
Cordova-McCarthy
Fairbanks
Haines
Juneau
Kenai-Cook Inlet
Ketchikan
Kobuk
Kodiak
Kuskokwim
Matanuska-Susitna
Nome
Outer Ketchikan
Prince of Wales
Seward
Sitka
Skagway-Yakuta
Southeast Fairbanks
Upper Yukon
Valdez-Chitina-Whittier
Wade Hampton
Wrangell-Petersburg
Yukon-Koyukuk

County	County Seat	Zip Code

ARIZONA

County	County Seat	Zip Code
Apache	St. Johns	85936
Cochise	Bisbee	85603
Coconino	Flagstaff	86001
Gila	Globe	85501
Graham	Safford	85546
Greenlee	Clifton	85533
Maricopa	Phoenix	85001-41
Mohave	Kingman	86401
Navajo	Holbrook	86025
Pima	Tucson	85701-24
Pinal	Florence	85232
Santa Cruz	Nogales	85621
Yavapai	Prescott	86301
Yuma	Yuma	85364

ARKANSAS

County	County Seat	Zip Code
Arkansas	De Witt	72042
	and	
	Stuttgart	72160
Ashley	Hamburg	71646
Baxter	Mountain Home	72653
Benton	Bentonville	72712
Boone	Harrison	72601
Bradley	Warren	71671
Calhoun	Hampton	71744
Carroll	Berryville	72616
	and	
	Eureka Springs	72632
Chicot	Lake Village	71653
Clark	Arkadelphia	71923
Clay	Corning	72422
	and	
	Piggott	72454
Cleburne	Heber Springs	72543
Cleveland	Rison	71665
Columbia	Magnolia	71753
Conway	Morrilton	72110

**The State of Alaska and the U.S. Bureau of the Census have established Census Divisions for use in compiling statistics for the State.

County	County Seat	Zip Code
Craighead	Jonesboro *and*	72401
	Lake City	72437
Crawford	Van Buren	72956
Crittenden	Marion	72364
Cross	Wynne	72396
Dallas	Fordyce	71742
Desha	Arkansas City	71630
Drew	Monticello	71655
Faulkner	Conway	72032
Franklin	Charleston *and*	72933
	Ozark	72949
Fulton	Salem	72576
Garland	Hot Springs	71901
Grant	Sheridan	72150
Greene	Paragould	72450
Hempstead	Hope	71801
Hot Spring	Malvern	72104
Howard	Nashville	71852
Indepen-dence	Batesville	72501
Izard	Melbourne	72556
Jackson	Newport	72112
Jefferson	Pine Bluff	71601
Johnson	Clarksville	72830
Lafayette	Lewisville	71845
Lawrence	Walnut Ridge	72476
Lee	Marianna	72360
Lincoln	Star City	71667
Little River	Ashdown	71822
Logan	Booneville *and*	72927
	Paris	72855
Lonoke	Lonoke	72086
Madison	Huntsville	72740
Marion	Yellville	72687
Miller	Texarkana	75502
Mississippi	Blytheville *and*	72315
	Osceola	72370
Monroe	Clarendon	72029

County	County Seat	Zip Code
Montgomery	Mount Ida	71957
Nevada	Prescott	71857
Newton	Jasper	72641
Ouachita	Camden	71701
Perry	Perryville	72126
Phillips	Helena	72342
Pike	Murfreesboro	71958
Poinsett	Harrisburg	72432
Polk	Mena	71953
Pope	Russellville	72801
Prairie	Des Arc *and*	72040
	De Valls Bluff	72041
Pulaski	Little Rock	72201-09
Randolph	Pocohontas	72455
St. Francis	Forrest City	72335
Saline	Benton	72015
Scott	Waldron	72958
Searcy	Marshall	72650
Sebastian	Fort Smith *and*	72901
	Greenwood	72936
Sevier	De Queen	71832
Sharp	Ash Flat	72513
Stone	Mountain View	72560
Union	El Dorado	71730
Van Buren	Clinton	72031
Washington	Fayetteville	72701
White	Searcy	72143
Woodruff	Augusta	72006
Yell	Danville *and*	72833
	Dardanelle	72834

CALIFORNIA

County	County Seat	Zip Code
Alameda	Oakland	94601-27
Alpine	Markleeville	96120
Amador	Jackson	95642
Butte	Oroville	95965
Calaveras	San Andreas	95249
Colusa	Colusa	95932

County	County Seat	Zip Code
Contra Costa	Martinez	94553
Del Norte	Crescent City	95531
El Dorado	Placerville	95667
Fresno	Fresno	93701-66
Glenn	Willows	95988
Humboldt	Eureka	95501
Imperial	El Centro	92243
Inyo	Independence	93526
Kern	Bakersfield	93301-09
Kings	Hanford	93230
Lake	Lakeport	95453
Lassen	Susanville	96130
Los Angeles	Los Angeles	90001-80
Madera	Madera	93637
Marin	San Rafael	94901-04
Mariposa	Mariposa	95338
Mendocino	Ukiah	95482
Merced	Merced	95340
Modoc	Alturas	96101
Mono	Bridgeport	93517
Monterey	Salinas	93901
Napa	Napa	94558
Nevada	Nevada City	95959
Orange	Santa Ana	92666-69
Placer	Auburn	95603
Plumas	Quincy	95971
Riverside	Riverside	92501-09
Sacramento	Sacramento	95801-60
San Benito	Hollister	95023
San Bernar-dino	San Bernar-dino	92401-10
San Diego	San Diego	92101-57
San Fran-cisco	San Fran-cisco	94101-40
San Joaquin	Stockton	95201-07
San Luis Obispo	San Luis Obispo	93401
San Mateo	Redwood City	94061-65
Santa Bar-bara	Santa Bar-bara	93101-07
Santa Clara	San Jose	95101-50

County	County Seat	Zip Code
Santa Cruz	Santa Cruz	95060
Shasta	Redding	96001
Sierra	Downieville	95936
Siskiyou	Yreka	96097
Solano	Fairfield	94533
Sonoma	Santa Rosa	95401-06
Stanislaus	Modesto	95350-54
Sutter	Yuba City	95991
Tehama	Red Bluff	96080
Trinity	Weaverville	96093
Tulare	Visalia	93277
Tuolumne	Sonora	95370
Ventura	Ventura	93001-03
Yolo	Woodland	95695
Yuba	Marysville	95901

COLORADO

County	County Seat	Zip Code
Adams	Brighton	80601
Alamosa	Alamosa	81101
Arapahoe	Littleton	80120-21
Archuleta	Pagosa Springs	81147
Baca	Springfield	81073
Bent	Las Animas	81054
Boulder	Boulder	80301-03
Chaffee	Salida	81201
Cheyenne	Cheyenne Wells	80810
Clear Creek	Georgetown	80444
Conejos	Conejos	81129
Costilla	San Luis	81152
Crowley	Ordway	81063
Custer	Westcliffe	81252
Delta	Delta	81416
Denver	Denver	80201-40
Dolores	Dove Creek	81324
Douglas	Castle Rock	80104
Eagle	Eagle	81631
Elbert	Kiowa	80117
El Paso	Colorado Springs	80901-17
Fremont	Canon City	81212
Garfield	Glenwood Springs	81601

County	County Seat	Zip Code
Gilpin	Central City	80427
Grand	Hot Sulphur Springs	80451
Gunnison	Gunnison	81230
Hinsdale	Lake City	81235
Huerfano	Walsenburg	81089
Jackson	Walden	80480
Jefferson	Golden	80401
Kiowa	Eads	81036
Kit Carson	Burlington	80807
Lake	Leadville	80461
La Plata	Durango	81301
Larimer	Fort Collins	80521
Las Animas	Trinidad	81082
Lincoln	Hugo	80821
Logan	Sterling	80751
Mesa	Grand Junction	81501
Mineral	Creede	81130
Moffat	Craig	81625
Montezuma	Cortez	81321
Montrose	Montrose	81401
Morgan	Fort Morgan	80701
Otero	La Junta	81050
Ouray	Ouray	81427
Park	Fairplay	80440
Phillips	Holyoke	80734
Pitkin	Aspen	81611
Prowers	Lamar	81052
Pueblo	Pueblo	81001-08
Rio Blanco	Meeker	81641
Rio Grande	Del Norte	81132
Routt	Steamboat Springs	80477
Saguache	Saguache	81149
San Juan	Silverton	81433
San Miguel	Telluride	81435
Sedgwick	Julesburg	80737
Summit	Breckenridge	80424
Teller	Cripple Creek	80813
Washington	Akron	80720

County	County Seat	Zip Code
Weld	Greeley	80631
Yuma	Wray	80758

CONNECTICUT*

County	County Seat	Zip Code
Fairfield	Bridgeport	06601-12
Hartford	Hartford	06101-20
Litchfield	Torrington	06790
Middlesex	Middletown	06457
New Haven	New Haven	06473
	and	
	Waterbury	06701-20
New London	New London	06320
	and	
	Norwich	06360
Tolland	Mansfield Center	06250
Windham	Willimantic	06226

DELAWARE

County	County Seat	Zip Code
Kent	Dover	19901
New Castle	Wilmington	19801-99
Sussex	Georgetown	19947

DISTRICT OF COLUMBIA**

Washington, D.C.		20001-59

FLORIDA

County	County Seat	Zip Code
Alachua	Gainesville	32601
Baker	Macclenny	32063
Bay	Panama City	32401
Bradford	Starke	32091
Brevard	Titusville	32780
Broward	Fort Lauderdale	33301-16
Calhoun	Blountstown	32424
Charlotte	Punta Gorda	33950

*Connecticut abolished county governments in 1960; former counties and county seats are listed here.

**The District of Columbia is a Federal district of the United States and is coextensive with the city of Washington.

County	County Seat	Zip Code	County	County Seat	Zip Code
Citrus	Inverness	32650	Osceola	Kissimmee	32741
Clay	Green Cove		Palm Beach	West Palm	
	Springs	32043		Beach	33401-08
Collier	Naples	33940	Pasco	Dade City	33525
Columbia	Lake City	32055	Pinellas	Clearwater	33515-18
Dade	Miami	33101-69	Polk	Bartow	33830
De Soto	Arcadia	33821	Putnam	Palatka	32077
Dixie	Cross City	32628	St. Johns	St. Augustine	32084
Duval	Jacksonville	32201-67	St. Lucie	Fort Pierce	33450
Escambia	Pensacola	32501-12	Santa Rosa	Milton	32570
Flagler	Bunnell	32010	Sarasota	Sarasota	33577-81
Franklin	Apalachicola	32320	Seminole	Sanford	32771
Gadsden	Quincy	32351	Sumter	Bushnell	33513
Gilchrist	Trenton	32693	Suwannee	Live Oak	32060
Glades	Moore Haven	33471	Taylor	Perry	32347
Gulf	Wewahitchka	32465	Union	Lake Butler	32054
Hamilton	Jasper	32052	Volusia	De Land	32720
Hardee	Wauchula	33873	Wakulla	Crawfordville	32327
Hendry	La Belle	33935	Walton	De Funiak	
Hernando	Brooksville	32512		Springs	32433
Highlands	Sebring	33870	Washington	Chipley	32428
Hillsborough	Tampa	33601-22			
Holmes	Bonifay	32425			
Indian River	Vero Beach	32960			
Jackson	Marianna	32446	Appling	Baxley	31513
Jefferson	Monticello	32344	Atkinson	Pearson	31642
Lafayette	Mayo	32066	Bacon	Alma	31510
Lake	Tavares	32778	Baker	Newton	31770
Lee	Fort Myers	33901-05	Baldwin	Milledgeville	31061
Leon	Tallahassee	32301-11	Banks	Homer	30547
Levy	Bronson	32621	Barrow	Winder	30680
Liberty	Bristol	32321	Bartow	Cartersville	30120
Madison	Madison	32340	Ben Hill	Fitzgerald	31750
Manatee	Bradenton	33500	Berrien	Nashville	31639
Marion	Ocala	32670	Bibb	Macon	31201-08
Martin	Stuart	33494	Bleckley	Cochran	31014
Monroe	Key West	33040	Brantley	Nahunta	31553
Nassau	Fernandina		Brooks	Quitman	31643
	Beach	32034	Bryan	Pembroke	31321
Okaloosa	Crestview	32536	Bulloch	Statesboro	30458
Okeechobee	Okeechobee	33472	Burke	Waynesboro	30830
Orange	Orlando	32801-99	Butts	Jackson	30233

GEORGIA

Georgia

County	County Seat	Zip Code	County	County Seat	Zip Code
Calhoun	Morgan	31766	Franklin	Carnesville	30521
Camden	Woodbine	31569	Fulton	Atlanta	30301-96
Candler	Metter	30439	Gilmer	Eliljay	30540
Carroll	Carrollton	30117	Glascock	Gibson	30810
Catoosa	Ringgold	30736	Glynn	Brunswick	31520
Charlton	Folkston	31537	Gordon	Calhoun	30701
Chatham	Savannah	31401-09	Grady	Cairo	31728
Chatta-			Greene	Greensboro	30642
hoochee	Cusseta	31805	Gwinnett	Lawrenceville	30245
Chattooga	Summerville	30747	Habersham	Clarkesville	30523
Cherokee	Canton	30114	Hall	Gainesville	30501
Clarke	Athens	30601	Hancock	Sparta	31087
Clay	Fort Gaines	31751	Haralson	Buchanan	30113
Clayton	Jonesboro	30236	Harris	Hamilton	31811
Clinch	Homerville	31634	Hart	Hartwell	30643
Cobb	Marietta	30060	Heard	Franklin	30217
Coffee	Douglas	31533	Henry	McDonough	30253
Colquitt	Moultrie	31768	Houston	Perry	31069
Columbia	Appling	30802	Irwin	Ocilla	31774
Columbus	Columbus	31901-07	Jackson	Jefferson	30549
Cook	Adel	31620	Jasper	Monticello	31064
Coweta	Newnan	30263	Jeff Davis	Hazlehurst	31539
Crawford	Knoxville	31050	Jefferson	Louisville	30434
Crisp	Cordele	31015	Jenkins	Millen	30442
Dade	Trenton	30752	Johnson	Wrightsville	31096
Dawson	Dawsonville	30534	Jones	Gray	31032
Decatur	Bainbridge	31717	Lamar	Barnesville	30204
De Kalb	Decatur	30030-34	Lanier	Lakeland	31635
Dodge	Eastman	31023	Laurens	Dublin	31021
Dooly	Vienna	31092	Lee	Leesburg	31763
Dougherty	Albany	31701-05	Liberty	Hinesville	31313
Douglas	Douglasville	30134	Lincoln	Lincolnton	30817
Early	Blakely	31723	Long	Ludowici	31316
Echols	Statenville	31648	Lowndes	Valdosta	31601
Effingham	Springfield	31329	Lumpkin	Dahlonega	30533
Elbert	Elberton	30635	McDuffie	Thomson	30824
Emanuel	Swainsboro	30401	McIntosh	Darien	31305
Evans	Claxton	30417	Macon	Oglethorpe	31068
Fannin	Blue Ridge	30513	Madison	Danielsville	30633
Fayette	Fayetteville	30214	Marion	Buena Vista	31803
Floyd	Rome	30161	Meriwether	Greenville	30222
Forsyth	Cumming	30130	Miller	Colquitt	31737

County	County Seat	Zip Code
Mitchell	Camilla	31730
Monroe	Forsyth	31029
Montgomery	Mount Vernon	30445
Morgan	Madison	30650
Murray	Chatsworth	30705
Muscogee*		
Newton	Covington	30209
Oconee	Watkinsville	30677
Oglethorpe	Lexington	30648
Paulding	Dallas	30132
Peach	Fort Valley	31030
Pickens	Jasper	30143
Pierce	Blackshear	31516
Pike	Zebulon	30295
Polk	Cedartown	30125
Pulaski	Hawkinsville	31036
Putnam	Eatonton	31024
Quitman	Georgetown	31754
Rabun	Clayton	30525
Randolph	Cuthbert	31740
Richmond	Augusta	30901-08
Rockdale	Conyers	30207
Schley	Ellaville	31806
Screven	Sylvania	30467
Seminole	Donalsonville	31745
Spalding	Griffin	30223
Stephens	Toccoa	30577
Stewart	Lumpkin	31815
Sumter	Americus	31709
Talbot	Talbotton	31827
Taliaferro	Crawfordville	30631
Tattnall	Reidsville	30453
Taylor	Butler	31006
Telfair	McRae	31055
Terrell	Dawson	31742
Thomas	Thomasville	31792
Tift	Tifton	31794
Toombs	Lyons	30436
Towns	Hiawassee	30546
Treutlen	Soperton	30457
Troup	La Grange	30240
Turner	Ashburn	31714
Twiggs	Jeffersonville	31044
Union	Blairsville	30512
Upson	Thomaston	30286
Walker	La Fayette	30728
Walton	Monroe	30655
Ware	Waycross	31501
Warren	Warrenton	30828
Washington	Sandersville	31082
Wayne	Jesup	31545
Webster	Preston	31824
Wheeler	Alamo	30411
White	Cleveland	30528
Whitfield	Dalton	30720
Wilcox	Abbeville	31001
Wilkes	Washington	30673
Wilkinson	Irwinton	31042
Worth	Sylvester	31791

HAWAII

Hawaii	Hilo	96720
Honolulu	Honolulu	96801-25
Kauai	Lihue	96766
Maui	Wailuku	96793

IDAHO

Ada	Boise	83701-07
Adams	Council	83612
Bannock	Pocatello	83201
Bear Lake	Paris	83261
Benewah	St. Maries	83861
Bingham	Blackfoot	83221
Blaine	Hailey	83333
Boise	Idaho City	83631
Bonner	Sandpoint	83864
Bonneville	Idaho Falls	83401
Boundary	Bonners Ferry	83805

*Muscogee County was replaced by a consolidated government area called Columbus.

County	County Seat	Zip Code	County	County Seat	Zip Code
Butte	Arco	83213	Calhoun	Hardin	62047
Camas	Fairfield	83327	Carroll	Mount Carroll	61053
Canyon	Caldwell	83605	Cass	Virginia	62691
Caribou	Soda Springs	83276	Champaign	Urbana	61801
Cassia	Burley	83318	Christian	Taylorville	62568
Clark	Dubois	83423	Clark	Marshall	62441
Clearwater	Orofino	83544	Clay	Louisville	62858
Custer	Challis	83226	Clinton	Carlyle	62231
Elmore	Mountain Home	83647	Coles	Charleston	61920
Franklin	Preston	83263	Cook	Chicago	60601-99
Fremont	St. Anthony	83445	Crawford	Robinson	62454
Gem	Emmett	83617	Cumberland	Toledo	62468
Gooding	Gooding	83330	De Kalb	Sycamore	60178
Idaho	Grangeville	83530	De Witt	Clinton	61727
Jefferson	Rigby	83442	Douglas	Tuscola	61953
Jerome	Jerome	83338	Du Page	Wheaton	60187
Kootenai	Coeur d'Alene	83814	Edgar	Paris	61944
Latah	Moscow	83843	Edwards	Albion	62806
Lemhi	Salmon	83467	Effingham	Effingham	62401
Lewis	Nezperce	83543	Fayette	Vandalia	62471
Lincoln	Shoshone	83352	Ford	Paxton	60957
Madison	Rexburg	83440	Franklin	Benton	62812
Minidoka	Rupert	83350	Fulton	Lewistown	61542
Nez Perce	Lewiston	83501	Gallatin	Shawneetown	62984
Oneida	Malad City	83252	Greene	Carrollton	62016
Owyhee	Murphy	83650	Grundy	Morris	60450
Payette	Payette	83661	Hamilton	McLeansboro	62859
Power	American Falls	83211	Hancock	Carthage	62321
Shoshone	Wallace	83873	Hardin	Elizabethtown	62931
Teton	Driggs	83422	Henderson	Oquawka	61469
Twin Falls	Twin Falls	83301	Henry	Cambridge	61238
Valley	Cascade	83611	Iroquois	Watseka	60970
Washington	Weiser	83672	Jackson	Murphysboro	62966
			Jasper	Newton	62448

ILLINOIS

County	County Seat	Zip Code	County	County Seat	Zip Code
			Jefferson	Mount Vernon	62864
			Jersey	Jerseyville	62052
Adams	Quincy	62301	Jo Daviess	Galena	61036
Alexander	Cairo	62914	Johnson	Vienna	62995
Bond	Greenville	62246	Kane	Geneva	60134
Boone	Belvidere	61008	Kankakee	Kankakee	60901
Brown	Mount Sterling	62353	Kendall	Yorkville	60560
Bureau	Princeton	61356	Knox	Galesburg	61401

County	County Seat	Zip Code
Lake	Waukegan	60085
La Salle	Ottawa	61350
Lawrence	Lawrenceville	62439
Lee	Dixon	61021
Livingston	Pontiac	61764
Logan	Lincoln	62656
McDonough	Macomb	61455
McHenry	Woodstock	60098
McLean	Bloomington	61701
Macon	Decatur	62521-26
Macoupin	Carlinville	62626
Madison	Edwardsville	62025
Marion	Salem	62881
Marshall	Lacon	61540
Mason	Havana	62644
Massac	Metropolis	62960
Menard	Petersburg	62675
Mercer	Aledo	61231
Monroe	Waterloo	62298
Montgomery	Hillsboro	62049
Morgan	Jacksonville	62650
Moultrie	Sullivan	61951
Ogle	Oregon	61061
Peoria	Peoria	61601-14
Perry	Pinckneyville	62274
Piatt	Monticello	61856
Pike	Pittsfield	62363
Pope	Golconda	62938
Pulaski	Mound City	62963
Putnam	Hennepin	61327
Randolph	Chester	62233
Richland	Olney	62450
Rock Island	Rock Island	61201
St. Clair	Belleville	62220-25
Saline	Harrisburg	62946
Sangamon	Springfield	62701-08
Schuyler	Rushville	62681
Scott	Winchester	62694
Shelby	Shelbyville	62565
Stark	Toulon	61483
Stephenson	Freeport	61032
Tazewell	Pekin	61554

County	County Seat	Zip Code
Union	Jonesboro	62952
Vermilion	Danville	61832
Wabash	Mount Carmel	62863
Warren	Monmouth	61462
Washington	Nashville	62263
Wayne	Fairfield	62837
White	Carmi	62821
Whiteside	Morrison	61270
Will	Joliet	60431-36
Williamson	Marion	62959
Winnebago	Rockford	61101-11
Woodford	Eureka	61530

INDIANA

County	County Seat	Zip Code
Adams	Decatur	46733
Allen	Fort Wayne	46801-19
Bartholo-mew	Columbus	47201
Benton	Fowler	47944
Blackford	Hartford City	47348
Boone	Lebanon	46052
Brown	Nashville	47448
Carroll	Delphi	46923
Cass	Logansport	46947
Clark	Jeffersonville	47130
Clay	Brazil	47834
Clinton	Frankfort	46041
Crawford	English	47118
Daviess	Washington	47501
Dearborn	Lawrenceburg	47025
Decatur	Greensburg	47240
De Kalb	Auburn	46706
Delaware	Muncie	47302-06
Dubois	Jasper	47546
Elkhart	Goshen	46526
Fayette	Connersville	47331
Floyd	New Albany	47150
Fountain	Covington	47932
Franklin	Brookville	47012
Fulton	Rochester	46975
Gibson	Princeton	47670

County	County Seat	Zip Code	County	County Seat	Zip Code
Grant	Marion	46952	Ripley	Versailles	47042
Greene	Bloomfield	47424	Rush	Rushville	46173
Hamilton	Noblesville	46060	St. Joseph	South Bend	46601-37
Hancock	Greenfield	46140	Scott	Scottsburg	47170
Harrison	Corydon	47112	Shelby	Shelbyville	46176
Hendricks	Danville	46122	Spencer	Rockport	47635
Henry	New Castle	47362	Starke	Knox	46534
Howard	Kokomo	46901	Steuben	Angola	46703
Huntington	Huntington	46750	Sullivan	Sullivan	47882
Jackson	Brownstown	47220	Switzerland	Vevay	47043
Jasper	Rensselaer	47978	Tippecanoe	Lafayette	47901-07
Jay	Portland	47371	Tipton	Tipton	46072
Jefferson	Madison	47250	Union	Liberty	47353
Jennings	Vernon	47282	Vanderburgh	Evansville	47701-27
Johnson	Franklin	46131	Vermillion	Newport	47966
Knox	Vincennes	47591	Vigo	Terre Haute	47801-09
Kosciusko	Warsaw	46580	Wabash	Wabash	46992
Lagrange	Lagrange	46761	Warren	Williamsport	47993
Lake	Crown Point	46307	Warrick	Boonville	47601
La Porte	La Porte	46350	Washington	Salem	47167
Lawrence	Bedford	47421	Wayne	Richmond	47374
Madison	Anderson	46011-17	Wells	Bluffton	46714
Marion	Indianapolis	46201-90	White	Monticello	47960
Marshall	Plymouth	46563	Whitley	Columbia City	46725
Martin	Shoals	47581			
Miami	Peru	46970			
Monroe	Bloomington	47401	**IOWA**		
Montgomery	Crawfordsville	47933	Adair	Greenfield	50849
Morgan	Martinsville	46151	Adams	Corning	50841
Newton	Kentland	47951	Allamakee	Waukon	52172
Noble	Albion	46701	Appanoose	Centerville	52544
Ohio	Rising Sun	47040	Audubon	Audubon	50025
Orange	Paoli	47454	Benton	Vinton	52349
Owen	Spencer	47460	Black Hawk	Waterloo	50701-07
Parke	Rockville	47872	Boone	Boone	50036
Perry	Cannelton	47520	Bremer	Waverly	50677
Pike	Petersburg	47567	Buchanan	Independence	50644
Porter	Valparaiso	46383	Buena Vista	Storm Lake	50588
Posey	Mount Vernon	47620	Butler	Allison	50602
Pulaski	Winamac	46996	Calhoun	Rockwell City	50579
Putnam	Greencastle	46135	Carroll	Carroll	51401
Randolph	Winchester	47394	Cass	Atlantic	50022

County	County Seat	Zip Code	County	County Seat	Zip Code
Cedar	Tipton	52772	Louisa	Wapello	52653
Cerro Gordo	Mason City	50401	Lucas	Chariton	50049
Cherokee	Cherokee	51012	Lyon	Rock Rapids	51246
Chickasaw	New Hampton	50659	Madison	Winterset	50273
Clarke	Osceola	50213	Mahaska	Oskaloosa	52577
Clay	Spencer	51301	Marion	Knoxville	50138
Clayton	Elkader	52043	Marshall	Marshalltown	50158
Clinton	Clinton	52732	Mills	Glenwood	51534
Crawford	Denison	51442	Mitchell	Osage	50461
Dallas	Adel	50003	Monona	Onawa	51040
Davis	Bloomfield	52537	Monroe	Albia	52531
Decatur	Leon	50144	Montgomery	Red Oak	51566
Delaware	Manchester	52057	Muscatine	Muscatine	52761
Des Moines	Burlington	52601	O'Brien	Primghar	51245
Dickinson	Spirit Lake	51360	Osceola	Sibley	51249
Dubuque	Dubuque	52001	Page	Clarinda	51632
Emmet	Estherville	51334	Palo Alto	Emmetsburg	50536
Fayette	West Union	52175	Plymouth	Le Mars	51031
Floyd	Charles City	50616	Pocahontas	Pocahontas	50574
Franklin	Hampton	50441	Polk	Des Moines	50301-33
Fremont	Sidney	51652	Pottawat-		
Greene	Jefferson	50129	tamie	Council Bluffs	51501
Grundy	Grundy Center	50638	Poweshiek	Montezuma	50171
Guthrie	Guthrie Center	50115	Ringgold	Mount Ayr	50854
Hamilton	Webster City	50595	Sac	Sac City	50583
Hancock	Garner	50438	Scott	Davenport	52801-08
Hardin	Eldora	50627	Shelby	Harlan	51537
Harrison	Logan	51546	Sioux	Orange City	51041
Henry	Mount Pleasant	52641	Story	Nevada	50201
Howard	Cresco	52136	Tama	Toledo	52342
Humboldt	Dakota City	50529	Taylor	Bedford	50833
Ida	Ida Grove	51445	Union	Creston	50801
Iowa	Marengo	52301	Van Buren	Keosauqua	52565
Jackson	Maquoketa	52060	Wapello	Ottumwa	52501
Jasper	Newton	50208	Warren	Indianola	50125
Jefferson	Fairfield	52556	Washington	Washington	52353
Johnson	Iowa City	52240	Wayne	Corydon	50060
Jones	Anamosa	52205	Webster	Fort Dodge	50501
Keokuk	Sigourney	52591	Winnebago	Forest City	50436
Koosuth	Algona	50511	Winneshiek	Decorah	52101
Lee	Fort Madison	52627	Woodbury	Sioux City	51101-11
Linn	Cedar Rapids	52401-07	Worth	Northwood	50459

County	County Seat	Zip Code	County	County Seat	Zip Code
Wright	Clarion	50525	Harper	Anthony	67003
			Harvey	Newton	67114
	KANSAS		Haskell	Sublette	67877
			Hodgeman	Jetmore	67854
Allen	Iola	66749	Jackson	Holton	66436
Anderson	Garnett	66032	Jefferson	Oskaloosa	66066
Atchison	Atchison	66002	Jewell	Mankato	66956
Barber	Medicine Lodge	67104	Johnson	Olathe	66061
Barton	Great Bend	67530	Kearny	Lakin	67860
Bourbon	Fort Scott	66701	Kingman	Kingman	67068
Brown	Hiawatha	66434	Kiowa	Greensburg	67054
Butler	El Dorado	67042	Labette	Oswego	67356
Chase	Cottonwood Falls	66845	Lane	Dighton	67839
Chautauqua	Sedan	67361	Leavenworth	Leavenworth	66048
Cherokee	Columbus	66725	Lincoln	Lincoln	67455
Cheyenne	St. Francis	67756	Linn	Mound City	66056
Clark	Ashland	67831	Logan	Oakley	67748
Clay	Clay Center	67432	Lyon	Emporia	66801
Cloud	Concordia	66901	McPherson	McPherson	67460
Coffey	Burlington	66839	Marion	Marion	66861
Comanche	Coldwater	67029	Marshall	Marysville	66508
Cowley	Winfield	67156	Meade	Meade	67864
Crawford	Girard	66743	Miami	Paola	66071
Decatur	Oberlin	67749	Mitchell	Beloit	67420
Dickinson	Abilene	67410	Montgomery	Independence	67301
Doniphan	Troy	66087	Morris	Council Grove	66846
Douglas	Lawrence	66044	Morton	Elkhart	67950
Edwards	Kinsley	67547	Nemaha	Seneca	66538
Elk	Howard	67349	Neosho	Erie	66733
Ellis	Hays	67601	Ness	Ness City	67560
Ellsworth	Ellsworth	67439	Norton	Norton	67654
Finney	Garden City	67846	Osage	Lyndon	66451
Ford	Dodge City	67801	Osborne	Osborne	67473
Franklin	Ottawa	66067	Ottawa	Minneapolis	67467
Geary	Junction City	66441	Pawnee	Larned	67550
Gove	Gove	67736	Phillips	Phillipsburg	67661
Graham	Hill City	67642	Pottawa-		
Grant	Ulysses	67880	tomie	Westmoreland	66549
Gray	Cimarron	67835	Pratt	Pratt	67124
Greeley	Tribune	67879	Rawlins	Atwood	67730
Greenwood	Eureka	67045	Reno	Hutchinson	67501
Hamilton	Syracuse	67878	Republic	Belleville	66935

County	County Seat	Zip Code	County	County Seat	Zip Code
Rice	Lyons	67554	Breckinridge	Hardinsburg	40143
Riley	Manhattan	66502	Bullitt	Shepherdsville	40165
Rooks	Stockton	67669	Butler	Morgantown	42261
Rush	La Crosse	67548	Caldwell	Princeton	42445
Russell	Russell	67665	Calloway	Murray	42071
Saline	Salina	67401	Campbell	Alexandria	41001
Scott	Scott City	67871	Carlisle	Bardwell	42023
Sedgwick	Wichita	67201-38	Carroll	Carrollton	41008
Seward	Liberal	67901	Carter	Grayson	41143
Shawnee	Topeka	66601-22	Casey	Liberty	42539
Sheridan	Hoxie	67740	Christian	Hopkinsville	42240
Sherman	Goodland	67735	Clark	Winchester	40391
Smith	Smith Center	66967	Clay	Manchester	40962
Stafford	St. John	67576	Clinton	Albany	42602
Stanton	Johnson	67855	Crittenden	Marion	42064
Stevens	Hugoton	67951	Cumberland	Burkesville	42717
Sumner	Wellington	67152	Daviess	Owensboro	42301
Thomas	Colby	67701	Edmonson	Brownsville	42210
Trego	Wakeeney	67672	Elliott	Sandy Hook	41171
Wabaunsee	Alma	66401	Estill	Irvine	40336
Wallace	Sharon Springs	67758	Fayette	Lexington	40501-11
Washington	Washington	66968	Fleming	Flemingsburg	41041
Wichita	Leoti	67861	Floyd	Prestonsburg	41653
Wilson	Fredonia	66736	Franklin	Frankfort	40601
Woodson	Yates Center	66783	Fulton	Hickman	42050
Wyandotte	Kansas City	66101-19	Gallatin	Warsaw	41095
			Garrard	Lancaster	40444

KENTUCKY

County	County Seat	Zip Code	County	County Seat	Zip Code
			Grant	Williamstown	41097
			Graves	Mayfield	42066
Adair	Columbia	42728	Grayson	Leitchfield	42754
Allen	Scottsville	42164	Green	Greensburg	42743
Anderson	Lawrenceburg	40342	Greenup	Greenup	41144
Ballard	Wickliffe	42087	Hancock	Hawesville	42348
Barren	Glasgow	42141	Hardin	Elizabethtown	42701
Bath	Owingsville	40360	Harlan	Harlan	40831
Bell	Pineville	40977	Harrison	Cynthiana	41031
Boone	Burlington	41005	Hart	Munfordville	42765
Bourbon	Paris	40361	Henderson	Henderson	42420
Boyd	Catlettsburg	41129	Henry	New Castle	40050
Boyle	Danville	40422	Hickman	Clinton	42031
Bracken	Brooksville	41004	Hopkins	Madisonville	42431
Breathitt	Jackson	41339	Jackson	McKee	40447

County	County Seat	Zip Code	County	County Seat	Zip Code
Jefferson	Louisville	40201-99	Pike	Pikeville	41501
Jessamine	Nicholasville	40356	Powell	Stanton	40380
Johnson	Paintsville	41240	Pulaski	Somerset	42501
Kenton	Independence	41051	Robertson	Mount Olivet	41064
Knott	Hindman	41822	Rockcastle	Mount Vernon	40456
Knox	Barbourville	40906	Rowan	Morehead	40351
Larue	Hodgenville	42748	Russell	Jamestown	42629
Laurel	London	40741	Scott	Georgetown	40324
Lawrence	Louisa	41230	Shelby	Shelbyville	40065
Lee	Beattyville	41311	Simpson	Franklin	42134
Leslie	Hyden	41749	Spencer	Taylorsville	40071
Letcher	Whitesburg	41858	Taylor	Campbellsville	42718
Lewis	Vanceburg	41179	Todd	Elkton	42220
Lincoln	Stanford	40484	Trigg	Cadiz	42211
Livingston	Smithland	42081	Trimble	Bedford	40006
Logan	Russellville	42276	Union	Morganfield	42437
Lyon	Eddyville	42038	Warren	Bowling Green	42101
McCracken	Paducah	42001	Washington	Springfield	40069
McCreary	Whitely City	42653	Wayne	Monticello	42633
McLean	Calhoun	42327	Webster	Dixon	42409
Madison	Richmond	40475	Whitley	Williamsburg	40769
Magoffin	Salyersville	41465	Wolfe	Campton	41301
Marion	Lebanon	40033	Woodford	Versailles	40383
Marshall	Benton	42025			
Martin	Inez	41224			
Mason	Maysville	41056			

LOUISIANA*

Parish	Parish Seat	Zip Code
Meade	Brandenburg	40108

County	County Seat	Zip Code	Parish	Parish Seat	Zip Code
Meade	Brandenburg	40108	Acadia	Crowley	70526
Menifee	Frenchburg	40322	Allen	Oberlin	70655
Mercer	Harrodsburg	40330	Ascension	Donaldsonville	70346
Metcalfe	Edmonton	42129	Assumption	Napoleonville	70390
Monroe	Tompkinsville	42167	Avoyelles	Marksville	71351
Montgomery	Mount Sterling	40353	Beauregard	De Ridder	70634
Morgan	West Liberty	41472	Bienville	Arcadia	71001
Muhlenberg	Greenville	42345	Bossier	Benton	71006
Nelson	Bardstown	40004	Caddo	Shreveport	71101-10
Nicholas	Carlisle	40311	Calcasieu	Lake Charles	70601
Ohio	Hartford	42347	Caldwell	Columbia	71418
Oldham	La Grange	40031	Cameron	Cameron	70631
Owen	Owenton	40359	Catahoula	Harrisonburg	71340
Owsley	Booneville	41314	Claiborne	Homer	71040
Pendleton	Falmouth	41040	Concordia	Vidalia	71373
Perry	Hazard	41701			

*Louisiana is divided into parishes rather than counties.

Parish	Parish Seat	Zip Code
De Soto	Mansfield	71052
East Baton Rouge	Baton Rouge	70801-21
East Carroll	Lake Providence	71254
East Felici- ana	Clinton	70722
Evangeline	Ville Platte	70586
Franklin	Winnsboro	71295
Grant	Colfax	71417
Iberia	New Iberia	70560
Iberville	Plaquemine	70764
Jackson	Jonesboro	71251
Jefferson	Gretna	70053
Jefferson Davis	Jennings	70546
Lafayette	Lafayette	70501
Lafourche	Thibodaux	70301
La Salle	Jena	71342
Lincoln	Ruston	71270
Livingston	Livingston	70754
Madison	Tallulah	71282
Morehouse	Bastrop	71220
Natchitoches	Natchitoches	71457
Orleans	New Orleans	70101-60
Ouachita	Monroe	71202
Plaquemines	Pointe a la Hache	70082
Pointe Coupee	New Roads	70760
Rapides	Alexandria	71301
Red River	Coushatta	71019
Richland	Rayville	71269
Sabine	Many	71449
St. Bernard	Chalmette	70043
St. Charles	Hahnville	70057
St. Helena	Greensburg	70441
St. James	Convent	70723
St. John the Baptist	Edgard	70049
St. Landry	Opelousas	70570
St. Martin	St. Martinville	70582
St. Mary	Franklin	70538
St. Tammany	Covington	70433

Parish	Parish Seat	Zip Code
Tangipahoa	Amite	70422
Tensas	St. Joseph	71366
Terrebonne	Houma	70360
Union	Farmerville	71241
Vermilion	Abbeville	70510
Vernon	Leesville	71446
Washington	Franklinton	70438
Webster	Minden	71055
West Baton Rouge	Port Allen	70767
West Carroll	Oak Grove	71263
West Felici- ana	St. Francis- ville	70775
Winn	Winnfield	71483

MAINE

County	County Seat	Zip Code
Andros- coggin	Auburn	04210
Aroostook	Houlton	04730
Cumberland	Portland	04101-12
Franklin	Farmington	04938
Hancock	Ellsworth	04605
Kennebec	Augusta	04330
Knox	Rockland	04841
Lincoln	Wiscasset	04578
Oxford	South Paris	04281
Penobscot	Bangor	04401
Piscataquis	Dover-Foxcroft	04426
Sagadahoc	Bath	04530
Somerset	Skowhegan	04976
Waldo	Belfast	04915
Washington	Machias	04654
York	Alfred	04002

MARYLAND

Allegany	Cumberland	21502
Anne Arun- del	Annapolis	21401-12
Baltimore	Towson	21204

County	County Seat	Zip Code
Baltimore (Indepen- dent City)*		21201-41
Calvert	Prince Frederick	20678
Caroline	Denton	21629
Carroll	Westminster	21157
Cecil	Elkton	21921
Charles	La Plata	20646
Dorchester	Cambridge	21613
Frederick	Frederick	21701
Garrett	Oakland	21550
Hartford	Bel Air	21014
Howard	Ellicott City	21043
Kent	Chestertown	21620
Montgomery	Rockville	20850-55
Prince Georges	Upper Marlboro	20772
Queen Annes	Centreville	21617
St. Marys	Leonardtown	20650
Somerset	Princess Anne	21853
Talbot	Easton	21601
Washington	Hagerstown	21740
Wicomico	Salisbury	21801
Worcester	Snow Hill	21863

MASSACHUSETTS

Barnstable	Barnstable	02630
Berkshire	Pittsfield	01201
Bristol	Taunton	02780
Dukes	Edgartown	02539
Essex	Salem	01970
Franklin	Greenfield	01301
Hampden	Springfield	01101-29
Hampshire	Northampton	01060
Middlesex	Cambridge	02138
Nantucket	Nantucket	02554
Norfolk	Dedham	02026
Plymouth	Plymouth	02360-64

*An Independent City has the same status as a county.

County	Shire Town	Zip Code
Suffolk	Boston	02101-215
Worcester	Worcester	01601-13

MICHIGAN

Alcona	Harrisville	48740
Alger	Munising	49862
Allegan	Allegan	49010
Alpena	Alpena	49707
Antrim	Bellaire	49615
Arenac	Standish	48658
Baraga	L'Anse	49946
Barry	Hastings	49058
Bay	Bay City	48706
Benzie	Beulah	49617
Berrien	St. Joseph	49085
Branch	Coldwater	49036
Calhoun	Marshall	49068
Cass	Cassopolis	49031
Charlevoix	Charlevoix	49720
Cheboygan	Cheboygan	49721
Chippewa	Sault Ste. Marie	49783
Clare	Harrison	48625
Clinton	St. Johns	48879
Crawford	Grayling	49738
Delta	Escanaba	49829
Dickinson	Iron Mountain	49801
Eaton	Charlotte	48813
Emmet	Petoskey	49770
Genesee	Flint	48501-59
Gladwin	Gladwin	48624
Gogebic	Bessemer	49911
Grand Traverse	Traverse City	49684
Gratiot	Ithaca	48847
Hillsdale	Hillsdale	49242
Houghton	Houghton	49931
Huron	Bad Axe	48413
Ingham	Mason	48854
Ionia	Ionia	48846
Iosco	Tawas City	48763
Iron	Crystal Falls	49920

County	County Seat	Zip Code
Isabella	Mount Pleasant	48858
Jackson	Jackson	49201-04
Kalamazoo	Kalamazoo	49001-07
Kalkaska	Kalkaska	49646
Kent	Grand Rapids	49501-11
Keweenaw	Eagle River	49924
Lake	Baldwin	49304
Lapeer	Lapeer	48446
Leelanau	Leland	49654
Lenawee	Adrian	49221
Livingston	Howell	48843
Luce	Newberry	49868
Mackinac	St. Ignace	49781
Macomb	Mount Clemens	48043
Manistee	Manistee	49660
Marquette	Marquette	49855
Mason	Ludington	49431
Mecosta	Big Rapids	49307
Menominee	Menominee	49858
Midland	Midland	48640
Missaukee	Lake City	49651
Monroe	Monroe	48161
Montcalm	Stanton	48888
Mont-morency	Atlanta	49709
Muskegon	Muskegon	49440-45
Newaygo	White Cloud	49349
Oakland	Pontiac	48053-59
Oceana	Hart	49420
Ogemaw	West Branch	48661
Ontonagon	Ontonagon	49953
Osceola	Reed City	49677
Oscoda	Mio	48647
Otsego	Gaylord	49735
Ottawa	Grand Haven	49417
Presque Isle	Rogers City	49779
Roscommon	Roscommon	48653
Saginaw	Saginaw	48601-07
St. Clair	Port Huron	48060
St. Joseph	Centreville	49032
Sanilac	Sandusky	48471
Schoolcraft	Manistique	49854

County	County Seat	Zip Code
Shiawassee	Corunna	48817
Tuscola	Caro	48723
Van Buren	Paw Paw	49079
Washtenaw	Ann Arbor	48103-08
Wayne	Detroit	48201-42
Wexford	Cadillac	49601

MINNESOTA

County	County Seat	Zip Code
Aitkin	Aitkin	56431
Anoka	Anoka	55303
Becker	Detroit Lakes	56501
Beltrami	Bemidji	56601
Benton	Foley	56329
Big Stone	Ortonville	56278
Blue Earth	Mankato	56001
Brown	New Ulm	56073
Carlton	Carlton	55718
Carver	Chaska	55318
Cass	Walker	56484
Chippewa	Montevideo	56265
Chisago	Center City	55012
Clay	Moorhead	56560
Clearwater	Bagley	56621
Cook	Grand Marais	55604
Cottonwood	Windom	56101
Crow Wing	Brainerd	56401
Dakota	Hastings	55033
Dodge	Mantorville	55955
Douglas	Alexandria	56308
Faribault	Blue Earth	56013
Fillmore	Preston	55965
Freeborn	Albert Lea	56007
Goodhue	Red Wing	55066
Grant	Elbow Lake	56531
Hennepin	Minneapolis	55401-80
Houston	Caledonia	55921
Hubbard	Park Rapids	56470
Isanti	Cambridge	55008
Itasca	Grand Rapids	55744
Jackson	Jackson	56143
Kanabec	Mora	55051

County	County Seat	Zip Code
Kandiyohi	Willmar	56201
Kittson	Hallock	56728
Koochiching	International Falls	56649
Lac qui Parle	Madison	56256
Lake	Two Harbors	55616
Lake of the Woods	Baudette	56623
Le Sueur	Le Center	56057
Lincoln	Ivanhoe	56142
Lyon	Marshall	56258
McLeod	Glencoe	55336
Mahnomen	Mahnomen	56557
Marshall	Warren	56762
Martin	Fairmont	56031
Meeker	Litchfield	55355
Mille Lacs	Milaca	56353
Morrison	Little Falls	56345
Mower	Austin	55912
Murray	Slayton	56172
Nicollet	St. Peter	56082
Nobles	Worthington	56187
Norman	Ada	56510
Olmsted	Rochester	55901
Otter Tail	Fergus Falls	56537
Pennington	Thief River Falls	56701
Pine	Pine City	55063
Pipestone	Pipestone	56164
Polk	Crookston	56716
Pope	Glenwood	56334
Ramsey	St. Paul	55101-77
Red Lake	Red Lake Falls	56750
Redwood	Redwood Falls	56283
Renville	Olivia	56277
Rice	Faribault	55021
Rock	Luverne	56156
Roseau	Roseau	56751
St. Louis	Duluth	55801-14
Scott	Shakopee	55379
Sherburne	Elk River	55330
Sibley	Gaylord	55334
Stearns	St. Cloud	56301

County	County Seat	Zip Code
Steele	Owatonna	55060
Stevens	Morris	56267
Swift	Benson	56215
Todd	Long Prairie	56347
Traverse	Wheaton	56296
Wabasha	Wabasha	55981
Wadena	Wadena	56482
Waseca	Waseca	56093
Washington	Stillwater	55082
Watonwan	St. James	56081
Wilkin	Breckenridge	56520
Winona	Winona	55987
Wright	Buffalo	55313
Yellow Medicine	Granite Falls	56241

MISSISSIPPI

County	County Seat	Zip Code
Adams	Natchez	39120
Alcorn	Corinth	38834
Amite	Liberty	39645
Attala	Kosciusko	39090
Benton	Ashland	38603
Bolivar	Cleveland	38732
Calhoun	Pittsboro	38951
Carroll	Vaiden and Carrollton	39176 38917
Chickasaw	Houston and Okolona	38851 38860
Choctaw	Ackerman	39735
Claiborne	Port Gibson	39150
Clarke	Quitman	39355
Clay	West Point	39733
Coahoma	Clarksdale	38614
Copiah	Hazlehurst	39083
Covington	Collins	39428
De Soto	Hernando	38632
Forrest	Hattiesburg	39401
Franklin	Meadville	39653
George	Lucedale	39452

County	County Seat	Zip Code	County	County Seat	Zip Code
Greene	Leakesville	39451	Panola	Sardis	38666
Grenada	Grenada	38901		and	
Hancock	Bay St. Louis	39520		Batesville	38606
Harrison	Gulfport	39501	Pearl River	Poplarville	39470
	and		Perry	New Augusta	39462
	Biloxi	39530-34	Pike	Magnolia	39652
Hinds	Jackson	39201-18	Pontotoc	Pontotoc	38863
	and		Prentiss	Booneville	38829
	Raymond	39154	Quitman	Marks	38646
Holmes	Lexington	39095	Rankin	Brandon	39042
Humphreys	Belzoni	39038	Scott	Forest	39074
Issaquena	Mayersville	39113	Sharkey	Rolling Fork	39159
Itawamba	Fulton	38843	Simpson	Mendenhall	39114
Jackson	Pascagoula	39567	Smith	Raleigh	39153
Jasper	Bay Springs	39422	Stone	Wiggins	39577
	and		Sunflower	Indianola	38751
	Paulding	39348	Tallahatchie	Charleston	38921
Jefferson	Fayette	39069		and	
Jefferson				Sumner	38957
Davis	Prentiss	39474	Tate	Senatobia	38668
Jones	Ellisville	39437	Tippah	Ripley	38663
	and		Tishomingo	Iuka	38852
	Laurel	39440	Tunica	Tunica	38676
Kemper	De Kalb	39328	Union	New Albany	38652
Lafayette	Oxford	38655	Walthall	Tylertown	39667
Lamar	Purvis	39475	Warren	Vicksburg	39180
Lauderdale	Meridian	39301	Washington	Greenville	38701
Lawrence	Monticello	39654	Wayne	Waynesboro	39367
Leake	Carthage	39051	Webster	Walthall	39771
Lee	Tupelo	38801	Wilkinson	Woodville	39669
Leflore	Greenwood	39830	Winston	Louisville	39339
Lincoln	Brookhaven	39601	Yalobusha	Coffeeville	38922
Lowndes	Columbus	39701		and	
Madison	Canton	39046		Water Valley	38965
Marion	Columbia	39429	Yazoo	Yazoo City	39194
Marshall	Holly Springs	38635			
Monroe	Aberdeen	39730			

MISSOURI

County	County Seat	Zip Code
Montgomery	Winona	38967			
Neshoba	Philadelphia	39350	Adair	Kirksville	63501
Newton	Decatur	39327	Andrew	Savannah	64485
Noxubee	Macon	39341	Atchison	Rockport	64482
Oktibbeha	Starkville	39759	Audrain	Mexico	65265

County	County Seat	Zip Code	County	County Seat	Zip Code
Barry	Cassville	65625	Howell	West Plains	65775
Barton	Lamar	64759	Iron	Ironton	63650
Bates	Butler	64730	Jackson	Independence	64050-54
Benton	Warsaw	65355	Jasper	Carthage	64836
Bollinger	Marble Hill	63764	Jefferson	Hillsboro	63050
Boone	Columbia	65201	Johnson	Warrensburg	64093
Buchanan	St. Joseph	64501-08	Knox	Edina	63537
Butler	Poplar Bluff	63901	Laclede	Lebanon	65536
Caldwell	Kingston	64650	Lafayette	Lexington	64067
Callaway	Fulton	65251	Lawrence	Mount Vernon	65712
Camden	Camdenton	65020	Lewis	Monticello	63457
Cape			Lincoln	Troy	63379
Girardeau	Jackson	63755	Linn	Linneus	64653
Carroll	Carrollton	64633	Livingston	Chillicothe	64601
Carter	Van Buren	63965	McDonald	Pineville	64856
Cass	Harrisonville	64701	Macon	Macon	63552
Cedar	Stockton	65785	Madison	Fredericktown	63645
Chariton	Keytesville	65261	Maries	Vienna	65582
Christian	Ozark	65721	Marion	Palmyra	63461
Clark	Kahoka	63445	Mercer	Princeton	64673
Clay	Liberty	64068	Miller	Tuscumbia	65082
Clinton	Plattsburg	64477	Mississippi	Charleston	63834
Cole	Jefferson City	65101	Moniteau	California	65018
Cooper	Boonville	65233	Monroe	Paris	65275
Crawford	Steelville	65565	Montgomery	Montgomery	
Dade	Greenfield	65661		City	63361
Dallas	Buffalo	65622	Morgan	Versailles	65084
Daviess	Gallatin	64640	New Madrid	New Madrid	63869
De Kalb	Maysville	64469	Newton	Neosho	64850
Dent	Salem	65560	Nodaway	Maryville	64468
Douglas	Ava	65608	Oregon	Alton	65606
Dunklin	Kennett	63857	Osage	Linn	65051
Franklin	Union	63084	Ozark	Gainesville	65655
Gasconade	Hermann	65041	Pemiscot	Caruthersville	63830
Gentry	Albany	64402	Perry	Perryville	63775
Greene	Springfield	65801-06	Pettis	Sedalia	65301
Grundy	Trenton	64683	Phelps	Rolla	65401
Harrison	Bethany	64424	Pike	Bowling Green	63334
Henry	Clinton	64735	Platte	Platte City	64079
Hickory	Hermitage	65668	Polk	Bolivar	65613
Holt	Oregon	64473	Pulaski	Waynesville	65583
Howard	Fayette	65248	Putnam	Unionville	63565

County	County Seat	Zip Code
Ralls	New London	63459
Randolph	Huntsville	65259
Ray	Richmond	64085
Reynolds	Centerville	63633
Ripley	Doniphan	63935
St. Charles	St. Charles	63301
St. Clair	Osceola	64776
St. Francois	Farmington	63640
St. Louis	Clayton	63105
St. Louis (Independent City)*		63101-99
Ste. Genevieve	Ste. Genevieve	63670
Saline	Marshall	65340
Schuyler	Lancaster	63548
Scotland	Memphis	63555
Scott	Benton	63736
Shannon	Eminence	65466
Shelby	Shelbyville	63469
Stoddard	Bloomfield	63825
Stone	Galena	65656
Sullivan	Milan	63556
Taney	Forsyth	65653
Texas	Houston	65483
Vernon	Nevada	64772
Warren	Warrenton	63383
Washington	Potosi	63664
Wayne	Greenville	63944
Webster	Marshfield	65706
Worth	Grant City	64456
Wright	Hartville	65667

MONTANA

County	County Seat	Zip Code
Beaverhead	Dillon	59725
Big Horn	Hardin	59034
Blaine	Chinook	59523
Broadwater	Townsend	59644
Carbon	Red Lodge	59068

*An Independent City has the same status as a county.

County	County Seat	Zip Code
Carter	Ekalaka	59324
Cascade	Great Falls	59401-05
Chouteau	Fort Benton	59442
Custer	Miles City	59301
Daniels	Scobey	59263
Dawson	Glendive	59330
Deer Lodge	Anaconda	59711
Fallon	Baker	59313
Fergus	Lewistown	59457
Flathead	Kalispell	59901
Gallatin	Bozeman	59715
Garfield	Jordan	59337
Glacier	Cut Bank	59427
Golden Valley	Ryegate	59074
Granite	Philipsburg	59858
Hill	Havre	59501
Jefferson	Boulder	59632
Judith Basin	Stanford	59479
Lake	Polson	59860
Lewis and Clark	Helena	59601
Liberty	Chester	59522
Lincoln	Libby	59923
McCone	Circle	59215
Madison	Virginia City	59755
Meagher	White Sulphur Springs	59645
Mineral	Superior	59872
Missoula	Missoula	59801
Musselshell	Roundup	59072
Park	Livingston	59047
Petroleum	Winnett	59087
Phillips	Malta	59538
Pondera	Conrad	59425
Powder River	Broadus	59317
Powell	Deer Lodge	59722
Prairie	Terry	59349
Ravalli	Hamilton	59840
Richland	Sidney	59270
Roosevelt	Wolf Point	59201

County	County Seat	Zip Code
Rosebud	Forsyth	59327
Sanders	Thompson Falls	59873
Sheridan	Plentywood	59254
Silver Bow	Butte	59701
Stillwater	Columbus	59019
Sweet Grass	Big Timber	59011
Teton	Choteau	59422
Toole	Shelby	59474
Treasure	Hysham	59038
Valley	Glasgow	59230
Wheatland	Harlowton	59036
Wibaux	Wibaux	59353
Yellowstone	Billings	59101-03

NEBRASKA

County	County Seat	Zip Code
Adams	Hastings	68901
Antelope	Neligh	68756
Arthur	Arthur	69121
Banner	Harrisburg	69345
Blaine	Brewster	68821
Boone	Albion	68620
Box Butte	Alliance	69301
Boyd	Butte	68722
Brown	Ainsworth	69210
Buffalo	Kearney	68847
Burt	Tekamah	68061
Butler	David City	68632
Cass	Plattsmouth	68048
Cedar	Hartington	68739
Chase	Imperial	69033
Cherry	Valentine	69201
Cheyenne	Sidney	69162
Clay	Clay Center	68933
Colfax	Schuyler	68661
Cuming	West Point	68788
Custer	Broken Bow	68822
Dakota	Dakota City	68731
Dawes	Chadron	69337
Dawson	Lexington	68850
Deuel	Chappell	69129
Dixon	Ponca	68770

County	County Seat	Zip Code
Dodge	Fremont	68025
Douglas	Omaha	68101-64
Dundy	Benkelman	69021
Fillmore	Geneva	68361
Franklin	Franklin	68939
Frontier	Stockville	69042
Furnas	Beaver City	68926
Gage	Beatrice	68310
Garden	Oshkosh	69154
Garfield	Burwell	68823
Gosper	Elwood	68937
Grant	Hyannis	69350
Greeley	Greeley Center	68842
Hall	Grand Island	68801
Hamilton	Aurora	68818
Harlan	Alma	68920
Hayes	Hayes Center	69032
Hitchcock	Trenton	69044
Holt	O'Neill	68763
Hooker	Mullen	69152
Howard	St. Paul	68873
Jefferson	Fairbury	68352
Johnson	Tecumseh	68450
Kearney	Minden	68959
Keith	Ogallala	69153
Keya Paha	Springview	68778
Kimball	Kimball	69145
Knox	Center	68724
Lancaster	Lincoln	68501-32
Lincoln	North Platte	69101
Logan	Stapleton	69163
Loup	Taylor	68879
McPherson	Tryon	69167
Madison	Madison	68748
Merrick	Central City	68826
Morrill	Bridgeport	69336
Nance	Fullerton	68638
Nemaha	Auburn	68305
Nuckolls	Nelson	68961
Otoe	Nebraska City	68410
Pawnee	Pawnee City	68420
Perkins	Grant	69140

County	County Seat	Zip Code
Phelps	Holdrege	68949
Pierce	Pierce	68767
Platte	Columbus	68601
Polk	Osceola	68651
Red Willow	McCook	69001
Richardson	Falls City	68355
Rock	Bassett	68714
Saline	Wilber	68465
Sarpy	Papillion	68046
Saunders	Wahoo	68066
Scotts Bluff	Gering	69341
Seward	Seward	68434
Sheridan	Rushville	69360
Sherman	Loup City	68853
Sioux	Harrison	69346
Stanton	Stanton	68779
Thayer	Hebron	68370
Thomas	Thedford	69166
Thurston	Pender	68047
Valley	Ord	68862
Washington	Blair	68008
Wayne	Wayne	68787
Webster	Red Cloud	68970
Wheeler	Bartlett	68622
York	York	68467

NEVADA

County	County Seat	Zip Code
Carson City (Independent City)*		89701
Churchill	Fallon	89406
Clark	Las Vegas	89101-14
Douglas	Minden	89423
Elko	Elko	89801
Esmeralda	Goldfield	89013
Eureka	Eureka	89316
Humboldt	Winnemucca	89445
Lander	Austin	89310
Lincoln	Pioche	89043

*An Independent City has the same status as a county.

County	County Seat	Zip Code
Lyon	Yerington	89447
Mineral	Hawthorne	89415
Nye	Tonopah	89049
Pershing	Lovelock	89419
Storey	Virginia City	89440
Washoe	Reno	89501-10
White Pine	Ely	89301

NEW HAMPSHIRE

Belknap	Laconia	03246
Carroll	Ossipee	03864
Cheshire	Keene	03431
Coos	Lancaster	03584
Grafton	Woodsville	03785
Hillsborough	Nashua	03060
Merrimack	Concord	03301
Rockingham	Exeter	03833
Strafford	Dover	03820
Sullivan	Newport	03773

NEW JERSEY

Atlantic	Mays Landing	08330
Bergen	Hackensack	07601-08
Burlington	Mount Holly	08060
Camden	Camden	08101-10
Cape May	Cape May Court House	08210
Cumberland	Bridgeton	08302
Essex	Newark	07101-14
Gloucester	Woodbury	08096
Hudson	Jersey City	07301-08
Hunterdon	Flemington	08822
Mercer	Trenton	08601-91
Middlesex	New Brunswick	08901-04
Monmouth	Freehold	07728
Morris	Morristown	07960
Ocean	Toms River	08753
Passaic	Paterson	07501-24

County	County Seat	Zip Code
Salem	Salem	08079
Somerset	Somerville	08876
Sussex	Newton	07860
Union	Elizabeth	07201-08
Warren	Belvidere	07823

NEW MEXICO

County	County Seat	Zip Code
Bernalillo	Albuquerque	87101-23
Catron	Reserve	87830
Chaves	Roswell	88201
Colfax	Raton	87740
Curry	Clovis	88101
De Baca	Fort Sumner	88119
Dona Ana	Las Cruces	88001
Eddy	Carlsbad	88220
Grant	Silver City	88061
Guadalupe	Santa Rosa	88435
Harding	Mosquero	87733
Hidalgo	Lordsburg	88045
Lea	Lovington	88260
Lincoln	Carrizozo	88301
Los Alamos	Los Alamos	87544
Luna	Deming	88030
McKinley	Gallup	87301
Mora	Mora	87732
Otero	Alamogordo	88310
Quay	Tucumcari	88401
Rio Arriba	Tierra Amarilla	87575
Roosevelt	Portales	88130
Sandoval	Bernalillo	87004
San Juan	Aztec	87410
San Miguel	Las Vegas	87701
Santa Fe	Santa Fe	87501
Sierra	Truth or Consequences	87901
Socorro	Socorro	87801
Taos	Taos	87571
Torrance	Estancia	87016
Union	Clayton	88415
Valencia	Los Lunas	87031

County	County Seat	Zip Code

NEW YORK

County	County Seat	Zip Code
Albany	Albany	12201-26
Allegany	Belmont	14813
Bronx	Bronx	10451
Broome	Binghamton	13901-05
Cattaraugus	Little Valley	14755
Cayuga	Auburn	13021
Chautauqua	Mayville	14757
Chemung	Elmira	14901-05
Chenango	Norwich	13815
Clinton	Plattsburg	12901
Columbia	Hudson	12534
Cortland	Cortland	13045
Delaware	Delhi	13753
Dutchess	Poughkeepsie	12601-03
Erie	Buffalo	14201-40
Essex	Elizabethtown	12932
Franklin	Malone	12953
Fulton	Johnstown	12095
Genesee	Batavia	14020
Greene	Catskill	12414
Hamilton	Lake Pleasant	12108
Herkimer	Herkimer	13350
Jefferson	Watertown	13601
Kings	Brooklyn	11201
Lewis	Lowville	13367
Livingston	Geneseo	14454
Madison	Wampsville	13163
Monroe	Rochester	14601-55
Montgomery	Fonda	12068
Nassau	Mineola	11501
New York	New York	10001-99
Niagara	Lockport	14094
Oneida	Utica	13501-03
Onondaga	Syracuse	13201-25
Ontario	Canandaigua	14424
Orange	Goshen	10924
Orleans	Albion	14411
Oswego	Oswego	13126
Otsego	Cooperstown	13326
Putnam	Carmel	10512

County	County Seat	Zip Code
Queens	Jamaica	11431
Rensselaer	Troy	12180-83
Richmond	Staten Island	10301
Rockland	New City	10956
St. Lawrence	Canton	13617
Saratoga	Ballston Spa	12020
Schenectady	Schenectady	12301-09
Schoharie	Schoharie	12157
Schuyler	Watkins Glen	14891
Seneca	Waterloo	13165
Steuben	Bath	14810
Suffolk	Riverhead	11901
Sullivan	Monticello	12701
Tioga	Owego	13827
Tompkins	Ithaca	14850
Ulster	Kingston	12401
Warren	Lake George	12845
Washington	Hudson Falls	12839
Wayne	Lyons	14489
Westchester	White Plains	10601-07
Wyoming	Warsaw	14569
Yates	Penn Yan	14527

NORTH CAROLINA

County	County Seat	Zip Code
Alamance	Graham	27253
Alexander	Taylorsville	28681
Alleghany	Sparta	28675
Anson	Wadesboro	28170
Ashe	Jefferson	28640
Avery	Newland	28657
Beaufort	Washington	27889
Bertie	Windsor	27983
Bladen	Elizabethtown	28337
Brunswick	Southport	28461
Buncombe	Asheville	28801-07
Burke	Morganton	28655
Cabarrus	Concord	28025
Caldwell	Lenoir	28645
Camden	Camden	27921
Carteret	Beaufort	28516
Caswell	Yanceyville	27379

County	County Seat	Zip Code
Catawba	Newton	28658
Chatham	Pittsboro	27312
Cherokee	Murphy	28906
Chowan	Edenton	27932
Clay	Hayesville	28904
Cleveland	Shelby	28150
Columbus	Whiteville	28472
Craven	New Bern	28560
Cumberland	Fayetteville	28301-08
Currituck	Currituck	27929
Dare	Manteo	27954
Davidson	Lexington	27292
Davie	Mocksville	27028
Duplin	Kenansville	28349
Durham	Durham	27701-09
Edgecombe	Tarboro	27886
Forsyth	Winston-Salem	27101-09
Franklin	Louisburg	27549
Gaston	Gastonia	28052
Gates	Gatesville	27938
Graham	Robbinville	28771
Granville	Oxford	27565
Greene	Snow Hill	28580
Guilford	Greensboro	27401-20
Halifax	Halifax	27839
Harnett	Lillington	27546
Haywood	Waynesville	28786
Henderson	Hendersonville	28739
Hertford	Winton	27986
Hoke	Raeford	28376
Hyde	Swanquarter	27885
Iredell	Statesville	28677
Jackson	Sylva	28779
Johnston	Smithfield	27577
Jones	Trenton	28585
Lee	Sanford	27330
Lenoir	Kinston	28501
Lincoln	Lincolnton	28092
McDowell	Marion	28752
Macon	Franklin	28734
Madison	Marshall	28753

County	County Seat	Zip Code
Martin	Williamston	27892
Mecklenburg	Charlotte	28201-17
Mitchell	Bakersville	28705
Montgomery	Troy	27371
Moore	Carthage	28327
Nash	Nashville	27856
New Hanover	Wilmington	28401
Northampton	Jackson	27845
Onslow	Jacksonville	28540
Orange	Hillsboro	27278
Pamlico	Bayboro	28515
Pasquotank	Elizabeth City	27909
Pender	Burgaw	28425
Perquimans	Hertford	27944
Person	Roxboro	27573
Pitt	Greenville	27834
Polk	Columbus	28722
Randolph	Asheboro	27203
Richmond	Rockingham	28379
Robeson	Lumberton	28358
Rockingham	Wentworth	27375
Rowan	Salisbury	28144
Rutherford	Rutherfordton	28139
Sampson	Clinton	28328
Scotland	Laurinburg	28352
Stanly	Albemarle	28001
Stokes	Danbury	27016
Surry	Dobson	27017
Swain	Bryson City	28713
Transylvania	Brevard	28712
Tyrrell	Columbia	27925
Union	Monroe	28110
Vance	Henderson	27536
Wake	Raleigh	27601-11
Warren	Warrenton	27589
Washington	Plymouth	27962
Watauga	Boone	28607
Wayne	Goldsboro	27530
Wilkes	Wilkesboro	28697
Wilson	Wilson	27893
Yadkin	Yadkinville	27055

County	County Seat	Zip Code
Yancey	Burnsville	28714

NORTH DAKOTA

County	County Seat	Zip Code
Adams	Hettinger	58639
Barnes	Valley City	58072
Benson	Minnewaukan	58351
Billings	Medora	58645
Bottineau	Bottineau	58318
Bowman	Bowman	58623
Burke	Bowbells	58721
Burleigh	Bismarck	58501
Cass	Fargo	58102
Cavalier	Langdon	58249
Dickey	Ellendale	58436
Divide	Crosby	58730
Dunn	Manning	58642
Eddy	New Rockford	58356
Emmons	Linton	58552
Foster	Carrington	58421
Golden Valley	Beach	58621
Grand Forks	Grand Forks	58201
Grant	Carson	58529
Griggs	Cooperstown	58425
Hettinger	Mott	58646
Kidder	Steele	58482
La Moure	La Moure	58458
Logan	Napoleon	58561
McHenry	Towner	58788
McIntosh	Ashley	58413
McKenzie	Watford City	58854
McLean	Washburn	58577
Mercer	Stanton	58571
Morton	Mandan	58554
Mountrail	Stanley	58784
Nelson	Lakota	58344
Oliver	Center	58530
Pembina	Cavalier	58220
Pierce	Rugby	58368
Ramsey	Devils Lake	58301
Ransom	Lisbon	58054

County	County Seat	Zip Code
Renville	Mohall	58761
Richland	Wahpeton	58075
Rolette	Rolla	58367
Sargent	Forman	58032
Sheridan	McClusky	58463
Sioux	Fort Yates	58538
Slope	Amidon	58620
Stark	Dickinson	58601
Steele	Finley	58230
Stutsman	Jamestown	58401
Towner	Cando	58324
Traill	Hillsboro	58045
Walsh	Grafton	58237
Ward	Minot	58701
Wells	Fessenden	58438
Williams	Williston	58801

OHIO

County	County Seat	Zip Code
Adams	West Union	45693
Allen	Lima	45801-09
Ashland	Ashland	44805
Ashtabula	Jefferson	44047
Athens	Athens	45701
Auglaize	Wapakoneta	45895
Belmont	St. Clairsville	43950
Brown	Georgetown	45121
Butler	Hamilton	45011-15
Carroll	Carrollton	44615
Champaign	Urbana	43078
Clark ·	Springfield	45501-06
Clermont	Batavia	45103
Clinton	Wilmington	45177 ·
Columbiana	Lisbon	44432
Coshocton	Coshocton	43812
Crawford	Bucyrus	44820
Cuyahoga	Cleveland	44101-99
Darke	Greenville	45331
Defiance	Defiance	43512
Delaware	Delaware	43015
Erie	Sandusky	44870
Fairfield	Lancaster	43130

County	County Seat	Zip Code
Fayette	Washington Court House	43160
Franklin	Columbus	43201-30
Fulton	Wauseon	43567
Gallia	Gallipolis	45631
Geauga	Chardon	44024
Greene	Xenia	45385
Guernsey	Cambridge	43725
Hamilton	Cincinnati	45201-99
Hancock	Findlay	45840
Hardin	Kenton	43326
Harrison	Cadiz	43907
Henry	Napoleon	43545
Highland	Hillsboro	45133
Hocking	Logan	43138
Holmes	Millersburg	44654
Huron	Norwalk	44857
Jackson	Jackson	45640
Jefferson	Steubenville	43952
Knox	Mount Vernon	43050
Lake	Painesville	44077
Lawrence	Ironton	45638
Licking	Newark	43055
Logan	Bellefontaine	43311
Lorain	Elyria	44035-39
Lucas	Toledo	43601-24
Madison	London	43140
Mahoning	Youngstown	44501-15
Marion	Marion	43302
Medina	Medina	44256
Meigs	Pomeroy	45769
Mercer	Celina	45822
Miami	Troy	45373
Monroe	Woodsfield	43793
Montgomery	Dayton	45400
Morgan	McConnelsville	43756
Morrow	Mount Gilead	43338
Muskingum	Zanesville	43701
Noble	Caldwell	43724
Ottawa	Port Clinton	43452
Paulding	Paulding	45879
Perry	New Lexington	43764

County	County Seat	Zip Code	County	County Seat	Zip Code
Pickaway	Circleville	43113	Comanche	Lawton	73501
Pike	Waverly	45690	Cotton	Walters	73572
Portage	Ravenna	44266	Craig	Vinita	74301
Preble	Eaton	45320	Creek	Sapulpa	74066
Putnam	Ottawa	45875	Custer	Arapaho	73620
Richland	Mansfield	44901-07	Delaware	Jay	74346
Ross	Chillicothe	45601	Dewey	Taloga	73667
Sandusky	Fremont	43420	Ellis	Arnett	73832
Scioto	Portsmouth	45662	Garfield	Enid	73701
Seneca	Tiffin	44883	Garvin	Pauls Valley	73075
Shelby	Sidney	45365	Grady	Chickasha	73018
Stark	Canton	44701-30	Grant	Medford	73759
Summit	Akron	44301-21	Greer	Mangum	73554
Trumbull	Warren	44481-85	Harmon	Hollis	73550
Tuscarawas	New Philadelphia	44663	Harper	Buffalo	73834
Union	Marysville	43040	Haskell	Stigler	74462
Van Wert	Van Wert	45891	Hughes	Holdenville	74848
Vinton	McArthur	45651	Jackson	Altus	73521
Warren	Lebanon	45036	Jefferson	Waurika	73573
Washington	Marietta	45750	Johnston	Tishomingo	73460
Wayne	Wooster	44691	Kay	Newkirk	74647
Williams	Bryan	43506	Kingfisher	Kingfisher	73750
Wood	Bowling Green	43402	Kiowa	Hobart	73651
Wyandot	Upper Sandusky	43351	Latimer	Wilburton	74578
			Le Flore	Poteau	74953

OKLAHOMA

County	County Seat	Zip Code	County	County Seat	Zip Code
			Lincoln	Chandler	74834
			Logan	Guthrie	73044
Adair	Stilwell	74960	Love	Marietta	73448
Alfalfa	Cherokee	73728	McClain	Purcell	73080
Atoka	Atoka	74525	McCurtain	Idabel	74745
Beaver	Beaver	73932	McIntosh	Eufaula	74432
Beckham	Sayre	73662	Major	Fairview	73737
Blaine	Watonga	73772	Marshall	Madill	73446
Bryan	Durant	74701	Mayes	Pryor Creek	74361
Caddo	Anadarko	73005	Murray	Sulphur	73086
Canadian	El Reno	73036	Muskogee	Muskogee	74401
Carter	Ardmore	73401	Noble	Perry	73077
Cherokee	Tahlequah	74464	Nowata	Nowata	74048
Choctaw	Hugo	74743	Okfuskee	Okemah	74859
Cimarron	Boise City	73933	Oklahoma	Oklahoma	
Cleveland	Norman	73069		City	73101-81
Coal	Coalgate	74538	Okmulgee	Okmulgee	74447

County	County Seat	Zip Code
Osage	Pawhuska	74056
Ottawa	Miami	74354
Pawnee	Pawnee	74058
Payne	Stillwater	74074
Pittsburg	McAlester	74501
Pontotoc	Ada	74820
Pottawat-omie	Shawnee	74801
Pushmataha	Antlers	74523
Roger Mills	Cheyenne	73628
Rogers	Claremore	74017
Seminole	Wewoka	74884
Sequoyah	Sallisaw	74955
Stephens	Duncan	73533
Texas	Guymon	73942
Tillman	Frederick	73542
Tulsa	Tulsa	74101-56
Wagoner	Wagoner	74467
Washington	Bartlesville	74003
Washita	Cordell	73632
Woods	Alva	73717
Woodward	Woodward	73801

OREGON

County	County Seat	Zip Code
Baker	Baker	97814
Benton	Corvallis	97330
Clackamas	Oregon City	97045
Clatsop	Astoria	97103
Columbia	St. Helens	97051
Coos	Coquille	97423
Crook	Prineville	97754
Curry	Gold Beach	97444
Deschutes	Bend	97701
Douglas	Roseburg	97470
Gilliam	Condon	97823
Grant	Canyon City	97820
Harney	Burns	97720
Hood River	Hood River	97031
Jackson	Medford	97501
Jefferson	Madras	97741
Josephine	Grants Pass	97526

County	County Seat	Zip Code
Klamath	Klamath Falls	97601
Lake	Lakeview	97630
Lane	Eugene	97401-05
Lincoln	Newport	97365
Linn	Albany	97321
Malheur	Vale	97918
Marion	Salem	97301-10
Morrow	Heppner	97836
Multnomah	Portland	97201-68
Polk	Dallas	97338
Sherman	Moro	97039
Tillamook	Tillamook	97141
Umatilla	Pendleton	97801
Union	La Grande	97850
Wallowa	Enterprise	97828
Wasco	The Dalles	97058
Washington	Hillsboro	97123
Wheeler	Fossil	97830
Yamhill	McMinnville	97128

PENNSYLVANIA

County	County Seat	Zip Code
Adams	Gettysburg	17325
Allegheny	Pittsburgh	15201-44
Armstrong	Kittanning	16201
Beaver	Beaver	15009
Bedford	Bedford	15522
Berks	Reading	19601-10
Blair	Hollidaysburg	16648
Bradford	Towanda	18848
Bucks	Doylestown	18901
Butler	Butler	16001
Cambria	Ebensburg	15931
Cameron	Emporium	15834
Carbon	Jim Thorpe	18229
Centre	Bellefonte	16823
Chester	West Chester	19380
Clarion	Clarion	16214
Clearfield	Clearfield	16830
Clinton	Lock Haven	17745
Columbia	Bloomsburg	17815
Crawford	Meadville	16335

County	County Seat	Zip Code
Cumberland	Carlisle	17013
Dauphin	Harrisburg	17101-28
Delaware	Media	19063-65
Elk	Ridgway	15853
Erie	Erie	16501-12
Fayette	Uniontown	15401
Forest	Tionesta	16353
Franklin	Chambersburg	17201
Fulton	McConnellsburg	17233
Greene	Waynesburg	15370
Huntingdon	Huntingdon	16652
Indiana	Indiana	15701
Jefferson	Brookville	15825
Juniata	Mifflintown	17059
Lackawanna	Scranton	18501-19
Lancaster	Lancaster	17601-04
Lawrence	New Castle	16101-05
Lebanon	Lebanon	17042
Lehigh	Allentown	18101-06
Luzerne	Wilkes-Barre	18701-10
Lycoming	Williamsport	17701
McKean	Smethport	16749
Mercer	Mercer	16137
Mifflin	Lewistown	17044
Monroe	Stroudsburg	18360
Montgomery	Norristown	19401-09
Montour	Danville	17821
Northampton	Easton	18042
Northumberland	Sunbury	17801
Perry	New Bloomfield	17068
Philadelphia	Philadelphia	19101-55
Pike	Milford	18337
Potter	Coudersport	16915
Schuylkill	Pottsville	17901
Snyder	Middleburg	17842
Somerset	Somerset	15501
Sullivan	Laporte	18626
Susquehanna	Montrose	18801
Tioga	Wellsboro	16901
Union	Lewisburg	17837
Venango	Franklin	16323

County	County Seat	Zip Code
Warren	Warren	16365
Washington	Washington	15301
Wayne	Honesdale	18431
Westmoreland	Greensburg	15601
Wyoming	Tunkhannock	18657
York	York	17401-07

RHODE ISLAND

Bristol	Bristol	02809
Kent	East Greenwich	02818
Newport	Newport	02840
Providence	Providence	02901-20
Washington	West Kingston	02892

SOUTH CAROLINA

Abbeville	Abbeville	29620
Aiken	Aiken	29801
Allendale	Allendale	29810
Anderson	Anderson	29621
Bamberg	Bamberg	29003
Barnwell	Barnwell	29812
Beaufort	Beaufort	29902
Berkeley	Moncks Corner	29461
Calhoun	St. Matthews	29135
Charleston	Charleston	29401-12
Cherokee	Gaffney	29340
Chester	Chester	29706
Chesterfield	Chesterfield	29709
Clarendon	Manning	29102
Colleton	Walterboro	29488
Darlington	Darlington	29532
Dillon	Dillon	29536
Dorchester	St. George	29477
Edgefield	Edgefield	29824
Fairfield	Winnsboro	29180
Florence	Florence	29501
Georgetown	Georgetown	29440
Greenville	Greenville	29601-14
Greenwood	Greenwood	29646

County	County Seat	Zip Code
Hampton	Hampton	29924
Horry	Conway	29526
Jasper	Ridgeland	29936
Kershaw	Camden	29020
Lancaster	Lancaster	29720
Laurens	Laurens	29360
Lee	Bishopville	29010
Lexington	Lexington	29072
McCormick	McCormick	29835
Marion	Marion	29571
Marlboro	Bennettsville	29512
Newberry	Newberry	29108
Oconee	Walhalla	29691
Orangeburg	Orangeburg	29115
Pickens	Pickens	29671
Richland	Columbia	29201-11
Saluda	Saluda	29138
Spartanburg	Spartanburg	29301-03
Sumter	Sumter	29150
Union	Union	29379
Williams-burg	Kingstree	29556
York	York	29745

SOUTH DAKOTA

County	County Seat	Zip Code
Aurora	Plankinton	57368
Beadle	Huron	57350
Bennett	Martin	57551
Bon Homme	Tyndall	57066
Brookings	Brookings	57006
Brown	Aberdeen	57401
Brule	Chamberlain	57325
Buffalo	Gannvalley	57341
Butte	Belle Fourche	57717
Campbell	Mound City	57646
Charles Mix	Lake Andes	57356
Clark	Clark	57225
Clay	Vermillion	57609
Codington	Watertown	57201
Corson	McIntosh	57641
Custer	Custer	57730

County	County Seat	Zip Code
Davison	Mitchell	57301
Day	Webster	57274
Deuel	Clear Lake	57226
Dewey	Timber Lake	57656
Douglas	Armour	57313
Edmunds	Ipswich	57451
Fall River	Hot Springs	57747
Faulk	Faulkton	57438
Grant	Milbank	57252
Gregory	Burke	57523
Haakon	Philip	57567
Hamlin	Hayti	57241
Hand	Miller	57362
Hanson	Alexandria	57311
Harding	Buffalo	57720
Hughes	Pierre	57501
Hutchinson	Olivet	57052
Hyde	Highmore	57345
Jackson	Kadoka	57543
Jerauld	Wessington Springs	57382
Jones	Murdo	57559
Kingsbury	De Smet	57231
Lake	Madison	57042
Lawrence	Deadwood	57732
Lincoln	Canton	57013
Lyman	Kennebec	57544
McCook	Salem	57058
McPherson	Leola	57456
Marshall	Britton	57430
Meade	Sturgis	57785
Mellette	White River	57579
Miner	Howard	57349
Minnehaha	Sioux Falls	57101-07
Moody	Flandreau	57028
Pennington	Rapid City	57701
Perkins	Bison	57620
Potter	Gettysburg	57442
Roberts	Sisseton	57262
Sanborn	Woonsocket	57385
Shannon	Hot Springs	57747
Spink	Redfield	57469

County	County Seat	Zip Code
Stanley	Fort Pierre	57532
Sully	Onida	57564
Todd	Winner	57580
Tripp	Winner	57580
Turner	Parker	57053
Union	Elk Point	57025
Walworth	Selby	57472
Washabaugh	Kadoka	57543
Yankton	Yankton	57078
Ziebach	Dupree	57623

TENNESSEE

County	County Seat	Zip Code
Anderson	Clinton	37716
Bedford	Shelbyville	37160
Benton	Camden	38320
Bledsoe	Pikeville	37367
Blount	Maryville	37801
Bradley	Cleveland	37311
Campbell	Jacksboro	37757
Cannon	Woodbury	37190
Carroll	Huntingdon	38344
Carter	Elizabethton	37643
Cheatham	Ashland City	37015
Chester	Henderson	38340
Claiborne	Tazewell	37879
Clay	Celina	38551
Cocke	Newport	37821
Coffee	Manchester	37355
Crockett	Alamo	38001
Cumberland	Crossville	38555
Davidson	Nashville	37201-21
Decatur	Decaturville	38329
De Kalb	Smithville	37166
Dickson	Charlotte	37036
Dyer	Dyersburg	38024
Fayette	Somerville	38068
Fentress	Jamestown	38556
Franklin	Winchester	37398
Gibson	Trenton	38382
Giles	Pulaski	38478
Grainger	Rutledge	37861

County	County Seat	Zip Code
Greene	Greeneville	37743
Grundy	Altamont	37301
Hamblen	Morristown	37814
Hamilton	Chattanooga	37401-21
Hancock	Sneedville	37869
Hardeman	Bolivar	38008
Hardin	Savannah	38372
Hawkins	Rogersville	37857
Haywood	Brownsville	38012
Henderson	Lexington	38351
Henry	Paris	38242
Hickman	Centerville	37033
Houston	Erin	37061
Humphreys	Waverly	37185
Jackson	Gainesboro	38562
Jefferson	Dandridge	37725
Johnson	Mountain City	37683
Knox	Knoxville	37901-21
Lake	Tiptonville	38079
Lauderdale	Ripley	38063
Lawrence	Lawrenceburg	38464
Lewis	Hohenwald	38462
Lincoln	Fayetteville	37334
Loudon	Loudon	37774
McMinn	Athens	37303
McNairy	Selmer	38375
Macon	Lafayette	37083
Madison	Jackson	38301
Marion	Jasper	37347
Marshall	Lewisburg	37091
Maury	Columbia	38401
Meigs	Decatur	37322
Monroe	Madisonville	37354
Montgomery	Clarksville	37040
Moore	Lynchburg	37352
Morgan	Wartburg	37887
Obion	Union City	38261
Overton	Livingston	38570
Perry	Linden	37096
Pickett	Byrdstown	38549
Polk	Benton	37307
Putnam	Cookeville	38501

County	County Seat	Zip Code
Rhea	Dayton	37321
Roane	Kingston	37763
Robertson	Springfield	37172
Rutherford	Murfreesboro	37130
Scott	Huntsville	37756
Sequatchie	Dunlap	37327
Sevier	Sevierville	37862
Shelby	Memphis	38101-34
Smith	Carthage	37030
Stewart	Dover	37058
Sullivan	Blountville	37617
Sumner	Gallatin	37066
Tipton	Covington	38019
Trousdale	Hartsville	37074
Unicoi	Erwin	37650
Union	Maynardville	37807
Van Buren	Spencer	38585
Warren	McMinnville	37110
Washington	Jonesboro	37659
Wayne	Waynesboro	38485
Weakley	Dresden	38225
White	Sparta	38583
Williamson	Franklin	37064
Wilson	Lebanon	37087

TEXAS

County	County Seat	Zip Code
Anderson	Palestine	75801
Andrews	Andrews	79714
Angelina	Lufkin	75901
Aransas	Rockport	78382
Archer	Archer City	76351
Armstrong	Claude	79019
Atascosa	Jourdanton	78026
Austin	Bellville	77418
Bailey	Muleshoe	79347
Bandera	Bandera	78003
Bastrop	Bastrop	78602
Baylor	Seymour	76380
Bee	Beeville	78102
Bell	Belton	76513
Bexar	San Antonio	78201-46

County	County Seat	Zip Code
Blanco	Johnson City	78636
Borden	Gail	79738
Bosque	Meridian	76665
Bowie	Boston	75557
Brazoria	Angleton	77515
Brazos	Bryan	77801
Brewster	Alpine	79830
Briscoe	Silverton	79257
Brooks	Falfurrias	78355
Brown	Brownwood	76801
Burleson	Caldwell	77836
Burnet	Burnet	78611
Caldwell	Lockhart	78644
Calhoun	Port Lavaca	77979
Callahan	Baird	79504
Cameron	Brownsville	78520
Camp	Pittsburg	75686
Carson	Panhandle	79068
Cass	Linden	75563
Castro	Dimmitt	79027
Chambers	Anahuac	77514
Cherokee	Rusk	75785
Childress	Childress	79201
Clay	Henrietta	76365
Cochran	Morton	79346
Coke	Robert Lee	76945
Coleman	Coleman	76834
Collin	McKinney	75069
Collings- worth	Wellington	79095
Colorado	Columbus	78934
Comal	New Braunfels	78130
Comanche	Comanche	76442
Concho	Paint Rock	76866
Cooke	Gainesville	76240
Coryell	Gatesville	76528
Cottle	Paducah	79248
Crane	Crane	79731
Crockett	Ozona	76943
Crosby	Crosbyton	79322
Culberson	Van Horn	79855
Dallam	Dalhart	79022

County	County Seat	Zip Code	County	County Seat	Zip Code
Dallas	Dallas	75201-99	Hardeman	Quanah	79252
Dawson	Lamesa	79331	Hardin	Kountze	77625
Deaf Smith	Hereford	79045	Harris	Houston	77001-92
Delta	Cooper	75432	Harrison	Marshall	75670
Denton	Denton	76201	Hartley	Channing	79018
De Witt	Cuero	77954	Haskell	Haskell	79521
Dickens	Dickens	79229	Hays	San Marcos	78666
Dimmit	Carrizo Springs	78834	Hamphill	Canadian	79014
Donley	Clarendon	79226	Henderson	Athens	75751
Duval	San Diego	78384	Hidalgo	Edinburg	78539
Eastland	Eastland	76448	Hill	Hillsboro	76645
Ector	Odessa	79760	Hockley	Levelland	79336
Edwards	Rocksprings	78880	Hood	Granbury	76048
Ellis	Waxahachie	75165	Hopkins	Sulphur Springs	75482
El Paso	El Paso	79901-99	Houston	Crockett	75835
Erath	Stephenville	76401	Howard	Big Spring	79720
Falls	Marlin	76661	Hudspeth	Sierra Blanca	79851
Fannin	Bonham	75418	Hunt	Greenville	75401
Fayette	La Grange	78945	Hutchinson	Stinnett	79083
Fisher	Roby	79543	Irion	Mertzon	76941
Floyd	Floydada	79235	Jack	Jacksboro	76056
Foard	Crowell	79227	Jackson	Edna	77957
Fort Bend	Richmond	77469	Jasper	Jasper	75951
Franklin	Mount Vernon	75457	Jeff Davis	Fort Davis	79734
Freestone	Fairfield	75840	Jefferson	Beaumont	77701-09
Frio	Pearsall	78061	Jim Hogg	Hebbronville	78361
Gaines	Seminole	79360	Jim Wells	Alice	78332
Galveston	Galveston	77550	Johnson	Cleburne	76031
Garza	Post	79356	Jones	Anson	79501
Gillespie	Fredericksburg	78624	Karnes	Karnes City	78118
Glasscock	Garden City	79739	Kaufman	Kaufman	75142
Goliad	Goliad	77963	Kendall	Boerne	78006
Gonzales	Gonzales	78629	Kenedy	Sarita	78385
Gray	Pampa	79065	Kent	Jayton	79528
Grayson	Sherman	75090	Kerr	Kerrville	78028
Gregg	Longview	75601	Kimble	Junction	76849
Grimes	Anderson	77830	King	Guthrie	79236
Guadalupe	Seguin	78155	Kinney	Brackettville	78832
Hale	Plainview	79072	Kleberg	Kingsville	78363
Hall	Memphis	79245	Knox	Benjamin	79505
Hamilton	Hamilton	76531	Lamar	Paris	75460
Hansford	Spearman	79081	Lamb	Littlefield	79339

County	County Seat	Zip Code	County	County Seat	Zip Code
Lampasas	Lampasas	76550	Palo Pinto	Palo Pinto	76072
La Salle	Cotulla	78014	Panola	Carthage	75633
Lavaca	Hallettsville	77964	Parker	Weatherford	76086
Lee	Giddings	78942	Parmer	Farwell	79325
Leon	Centerville	75833	Pecos	Fort Stockton	79735
Liberty	Liberty	77575	Polk	Livingston	77351
Limestone	Groesbeck	76642	Potter	Amarillo	79101-10
Lipscomb	Lipscomb	79056	Presidio	Marfa	79843
Live Oak	George West	78022	Rains	Emory	75440
Llano	Llano	78643	Randall	Canyon	79015
Loving	Mentone	79754	Reagan	Big Lake	76932
Lubbock	Lubbock	79401-17	Real	Leakey	78873
Lynn	Tahoka	79373	Red River	Clarksville	75426
McCulloch	Brady	76825	Reeves	Pecos	79772
McLennan	Waco	76701-11	Refugio	Refugio	78377
McMullen	Tilden	78072	Roberts	Miami	79059
Madison	Madisonville	77864	Robertson	Franklin	77856
Marion	Jefferson	75657	Rockwall	Rockwall	75087
Martin	Stanton	79782	Runnels	Ballinger	76821
Mason	Mason	76856	Rusk	Henderson	75652
Matagorda	Bay City	77414	Sabine	Hemphill	75948
Maverick	Eagle Pass	78852	San Augus-tine	San Augus-tine	75972
Medina	Hondo	78861	San Jacinto	Coldspring	77331
Menard	Menard	76859	San Patricio	Sinton	78387
Midland	Midland	79701	San Saba	San Saba	76877
Milam	Cameron	76520	Schleicher	Eldorado	76936
Mills	Goldthwaite	76844	Scurry	Snyder	79549
Mitchell	Colorado City	79512	Shackelford	Albany	76430
Montague	Montague	76251	Shelby	Center	75935
Montgomery	Conroe	77301	Sherman	Stratford	79084
Moore	Dumas	79029	Smith	Tyler	75701
Morris	Daingerfield	75638	Somervell	Glen Rose	76043
Motley	Matador	79244	Starr	Rio Grande City	78582
Nacogdoches	Nacogdoches	75961	Stephens	Breckenridge	76024
Navarro	Corsicana	75110	Sterling	Sterling City	76951
Newton	Newton	75966	Stonewall	Aspermont	79502
Nolan	Sweetwater	79556	Sutton	Sonora	76950
Nueces	Corpus Christi	78401-19	Swisher	Tulia	79088
Ochiltree	Perryton	79070	Tarrant	Fort Worth	76101-79
Oldham	Vega	79092	Taylor	Abilene	79601-07
Orange	Orange	77630	Terrell	Sanderson	79848

County	County Seat	Zip Code
Terry	Brownfield	79316
Throck-morton	Throckmorton	76083
Titus	Mount Pleasant	75455
Tom Green	San Angelo	76901
Travis	Austin	78701-67
Trinity	Groveton	75845
Tyler	Woodville	75979
Upshur	Gilmer	75644
Upton	Rankin	79778
Uvalde	Uvalde	78801
Val Verde	Del Rio	78840
Van Zandt	Canton	75103
Victoria	Victoria	77901
Walker	Huntsville	77340
Waller	Hempstead	77445
Ward	Monahans	79756
Washington	Brenham	77833
Webb	Laredo	78040
Wharton	Wharton	77488
Wheeler	Wheeler	79096
Wichita	Wichita Falls	76301-11
Wilbarger	Vernon	76384
Willacy	Raymondville	78580
Williamson	Georgetown	78626
Wilson	Floresville	78114
Winkler	Kermit	79745
Wise	Decatur	76234
Wood	Quitman	75783
Yoakum	Plains	79355
Young	Graham	76046
Zapata	Zapata	78076
Zavala	Crystal City	78839

UTAH

County	County Seat	Zip Code
Beaver	Beaver	84713
Box Elder	Brigham City	84302
Cache	Logan	84321
Carbon	Price	84501
Daggett	Manila	84046
Davis	Farmington	84025

County	County Seat	Zip Code
Duchesne	Duchesne	84021
Emery	Castle Dale	84513
Garfield	Panguitch	84759
Grand	Moab	84532
Iron	Parowan	84761
Juab	Nephi	84648
Kane	Kanab	84741
Millard	Fillmore	84631
Morgan	Morgan	84050
Piute	Junction	84740
Rich	Randolph	84064
Salt Lake	Salt Lake City	84101-21
San Juan	Monticello	84535
Sanpete	Manti	84642
Sevier	Richfield	84701
Summit	Coalville	84017
Tooele	Tooele	84074
Uintah	Vernal	84078
Utah	Provo	84601
Wasatch	Heber City	84032
Washington	St. George	84770
Wayne	Loa	84747
Weber	Ogden	84401-06

VERMONT

County	County Seat	Zip Code
Addison	Middlebury	05753
Bennington	Bennington	05201
	and	
	Manchester	05254
Caledonia	St. Johnsbury	05819
Chittenden	Burlington	05401
Essex	Guildhall	05905
Franklin	St. Albans	05478
Grand Isle	North Hero	05474
Lamoille	Hyde Park	05655
Orange	Chelsea	05038
Orleans	Newport	05855
Rutland	Rutland	05701
Washington	Montpelier	05602
Windham	Newfane	05345
Windsor	Woodstock	05091

County	County Seat	Zip Code	County	County Seat	Zip Code
			Gloucester	Gloucester	23061
	VIRGINIA		Goochland	Goochland	23063
			Grayson	Independence	24348
Accomac	Accomac	23301	Greene	Standardsville	22973
Albemarle	Charlottes-		Greensville	Emporia*	23847
	ville	22901-05	Halifax	Halifax	24558
Alleghany	Covington*	24426	Hanover	Hanover	23069
Amelia	Amelia		Henrico	Richmond*	23273
	Courthouse	23002	Henry	Martinsville*	24112
Amherst	Amherst	24521	Highland	Monterey	24465
Appomattox	Appomattox	24522	Isle of		
Arlington	Arlington	22201-16	Wight	Isle of Wight	23397
Augusta	Staunton*	24401	James City	Williamsburg*	23185
Bath	Warm Springs	24484	King and	King and	
Bedford	Bedford*	24523	Queen	Queen Court-	
Bland	Bland	24315		house	23085
Botetourt	Fincastle	24090	King George	King George	22485
Brunswick	Lawrenceville	23868	King		
Buchanan	Grundy	24614	William	King William	23086
Buckingham	Buckingham	23921	Lancaster	Lancaster	22503
Campbell	Rustburg	24588	Lee	Jonesville	24263
Caroline	Bowling Green	22427	Loudoun	Leesburg	22075
Carroll	Hillsville	24343	Louisa	Louisa	23093
Charles City	Charles City	23030	Lunenburg	Lunenburg	23952
Charlotte	Charlotte		Madison	Madison	22727
	Courthouse	23923	Mathews	Mathews	23109
Chesterfield	Chesterfield	23832	Mecklenburg	Boydton	23917
Clarke	Berryville	22611	Middlesex	Saluda	23149
Craig	New Castle	24127	Montgomery	Christianburg	24073
Culpeper	Culpeper	22701	Nelson	Lovingston	22949
Cumberland	Cumberland	23040	New Kent	New Kent	23124
Dickenson	Clintwood	24228	Northampton	Eastville	23347
Dinwiddie	Dinwiddie	23841	Northum-		
Essex	Tappahannock	22560	berland	Heathsville	22473
Fairfax	Fairfax*	22030	Nottoway	Nottoway	23955
Fauquier	Warrenton	22186	Orange	Orange	22960
Floyd	Floyd	24091	Page	Luray	22835
Fluvanna	Palmyra	22963	Patrick	Stuart	24171
Franklin	Rocky Mount	24151	Pittsylvania	Chatham	24531
Frederick	Winchester*	22601	Powhatan	Powhatan	23139
Giles	Pearisburg	24134			

*Independent Cities that serve as county seats but are administratively independent of the county.

County	County Seat	Zip Code
Prince Edward	Farmville	23901
Prince George	Prince George	23875
Prince William	Manassas	22110
Pulaski	Pulaski	24301
Rappa-hannock	Washington	22747
Richmond	Warsaw	22572
Roanoke	Salem*	24153
Rockbridge	Lexington*	24450
Rockingham	Harrisonburg*	22801
Russell	Lebanon	24266
Scott	Gate City	24251
Shenandoah	Woodstock	22664
Smyth	Marion	24354
Southampton	Courtland	23837
Spotsylvania	Spotsylvania	22553
Stafford	Stafford	22554
Surry	Surry	23883
Sussex	Sussex	23884
Tazewell	Tazewell	24651
Warren	Front Royal	22630
Washington	Abingdon	24210
Westmore-land	Montross	22520
Wise	Wise	24293
Wythe	Wytheville	24382
York	Yorktown	23490

Independent Cities*	Zip Code
Alexandria	22301-14
Bedford	24523
Bristol	24201
Buena Vista	24416
Charlottesville	22901-05
Chesapeake	23320-25
Clifton Forge	24422

*These 38 Independent Cities have the status of counties.

Independent Cities	Zip Code
Colonial Heights	23834
Covington	24426
Danville	24541
Emporia	23847
Fairfax	22030
Falls Church	22040-46
Franklin	23851
Fredericksburg	22401
Galax	24333
Hampton	23360-69
Harrisonburg	22801
Hopewell	23860
Lexington	24450
Lynchburg	24501-05
Martinsville	24112
Newport News	23601-07
Norfolk	23501-23
Norton	24273
Petersburg	23803
Portsmouth	23701-10
Radford	24141
Richmond	23201-40
Roanoke	24001-20
Salem	24153
South Boston	24592
Staunton	24401
Suffolk	23434
Virginia Beach	23450-62
Waynesboro	22980
Williamsburg	23185
Winchester	22601

WASHINGTON

County	County Seat	Zip Code
Adams	Ritzville	99169
Asotin	Asotin	99402
Benton	Prosser	99350
Chelan	Wenatchee	98801
Clallam	Port Angeles	98362
Clark	Vancouver	98660-65

County	County Seat	Zip Code	County	County Seat	Zip Code
Columbia	Dayton	99328	Cabell	Huntington	25701-25
Cowlitz	Kelso	98626	Calhoun	Grantsville	26147
Douglas	Waterville	98858	Clay	Clay	25043
Ferry	Republic	99166	Doddridge	West Union	26456
Franklin	Pasco	99301	Fayette	Fayetteville	25840
Garfield	Pomeroy	99347	Gilmer	Glenville	26351
Grant	Ephrata	98823	Grant	Petersburg	26847
Grays			Greenbrier	Lewisburg	24901
Harbor	Montesano	98563	Hampshire	Romney	26757
Island	Coupeville	98239	Hancock	New Cumberland	26047
Jefferson	Port Townsend	98368	Hardy	Moorefield	26836
King	Seattle	98101-99	Harrison	Clarksburg	26301
Kitsap	Port Orchard	98366	Jackson	Ripley	25271
Kittitas	Ellensburg	98926	Jefferson	Charles Town	25414
Klickitat	Goldendale	98620	Kanawha	Charleston	25301-32
Lewis	Chehalis	98532	Lewis	Weston	26452
Lincoln	Davenport	99122	Lincoln	Hamlin	25523
Mason	Shelton	98584	Logan	Logan	25601
Okanogan	Okanogan	98840	McDowell	Welch	24801
Pacific	South Bend	98586	Marion	Fairmont	26554
Pend Oreille	Newport	99156	Marshall	Moundsville	26041
Pierce	Tacoma	98401-99	Mason	Point Pleasant	25550
San Juan	Friday Harbor	98250	Mercer	Princeton	24740
Skagit	Mount Vernon	98273	Mineral	Keyser	26726
Skamania	Stevenson	98648	Mingo	Williamson	25661
Snohomish	Everett	98201-03	Monongalia	Morgantown	26505
Spokane	Spokane	99201-20	Monroe	Union	24983
Stevens	Colville	99114	Morgan	Berkeley Springs	25411
Thurston	Olympia	98501-03	Nicholas	Summersville	26651
Wahkiakum	Cathlamet	98612	Ohio	Wheeling	26003
Walla Walla	Walla Walla	99362	Pendleton	Franklin	26807
Whatcom	Bellingham	98225	Pleasants	St. Marys	26170
Whitman	Colfax	99111	Pocahontas	Marlinton	24954
Yakima	Yakima	98901-06	Preston	Kingwood	26537
			Putnam	Winfield	25213

WEST VIRGINIA

County	County Seat	Zip Code
Raleigh	Beckley	25801
Randolph	Elkins	26241
Barbour	Philippi	26416
Ritchie	Harrisville	26362
Berkeley	Martinsburg	25401
Roane	Spencer	25276
Boone	Madison	25130
Summers	Hinton	25951
Braxton	Sutton	26601
Taylor	Grafton	26354
Brooke	Wellsburg	26070

County	County Seat	Zip Code
Tucker	Parsons	26287
Tyler	Middlebourne	26149
Upshur	Buckhannon	26201
Wayne	Wayne	25570
Webster	Webster Springs	26288
Wetzel	New Martinsville	26155
Wirt	Elizabeth	26143
Wood	Parkersburg	26101
Wyoming	Pineville	24874

WISCONSIN

County	County Seat	Zip Code
Adams	Friendship	53934
Ashland	Ashland	54806
Barron	Barron	54812
Bayfield	Washburn	54891
Brown	Green Bay	54301-06
Buffalo	Alma	54610
Burnett	Grantsburg	54840
Calumet	Chilton	53014
Chippewa	Chippewa Falls	54729
Clark	Neillsville	54456
Columbia	Portage	53901
Crawford	Prairie du Chien	53821
Dane	Madison	53701-19
Dodge	Juneau	53039
Door	Sturgeon Bay	54235
Douglas	Superior	54880
Dunn	Menomonie	54751
Eau Claire	Eau Claire	54701
Florence	Florence	54121
Fond du Lac	Fond du Lac	54935
Forest	Crandon	54520
Grant	Lancaster	53813
Green	Monroe	53566
Green Lake	Green Lake	54941
Iowa	Dodgeville	53533
Iron	Hurley	54534
Jackson	Black River Falls	54615
Jefferson	Jefferson	53549
Juneau	Mauston	53948
Kenosha	Kenosha	53140
Kewaunee	Kewaunee	54216
La Crosse	La Crosse	54601
Lafayette	Darlington	53530
Langlade	Antigo	54409
Lincoln	Merrill	54452
Manitowoc	Manitowoc	54220
Marathon	Wausau	54401
Marinette	Marinette	54143
Marquette	Montello	53949
Menominee	Keshena	54135
Milwaukee	Milwaukee	53201-46
Monroe	Sparta	54656
Oconto	Oconto	54153
Oneida	Rhinelander	54501
Outagamie	Appleton	54911
Ozaukee	Port Washington	53074
Pepin	Durand	54736
Pierce	Ellsworth	54011
Polk	Balsam Lake	54810
Portage	Stevens Point	54481
Price	Phillips	54555
Racine	Racine	53401-06
Richland	Richland Center	53581
Rock	Janesville	53545
Rusk	Ladysmith	54848
St. Croix	Hudson	54016
Sauk	Baraboo	53913
Sawyer	Hayward	54843
Shawano	Shawano	54166
Sheboygan	Sheboygan	53081
Taylor	Medford	54451
Trempealeau	Whitehall	54773
Vernon	Viroqua	54665
Vilas	Eagle River	54521
Walworth	Elkhorn	53121
Washburn	Shell Lake	54871
Washington	West Bend	53095
Waukesha	Waukesha	53186
Waupaca	Waupaca	54981
Waushara	Wautoma	54982
Winnebago	Oshkosh	54901
Wood	Wisconsin Rapids	54494

WYOMING

County	County Seat	Zip Code
Albany	Laramie	82070
Big Horn	Basin	82410
Campbell	Gillette	82716
Carbon	Rawlins	82301
Converse	Douglas	82633
Crook	Sundance	82729
Fremont	Lander	82520
Goshen	Torrington	82240
Hot Springs	Thermopolis	82443
Johnson	Buffalo	82834
Laramie	Cheyenne	82001
Lincoln	Kemmerer	83101
Natrona	Casper	82601
Niobrara	Lusk	82225
Park	Cody	82414
Platte	Wheatland	82201
Sheridan	Sheridan	82801
Sublette	Pinedale	82941
Sweetwater	Green River	82935
Teton	Jackson	83001
Uinta	Evanston	82930
Washakie	Worland	82401
Weston	Newcastle	82701

DIRECTORY OF UNITED STATES EMBASSIES AND CONSULATES

Afghanistan

U.S. Embassy
Wazir Akbar Khan Mina
Kabul, Afghanistan

Algeria

U.S. Embassy
4 Chemin Cheich Bachir Brahimi
Algiers, Algeria

Antigua and Barbudo

U.S. Embassy
F.P.O. Miami 34054

Argentina

U.S. Embassy
4300 Colombia, 1425
Buenos Aires, Argentina

Australia

U.S. Embassy
Moonah Place
Yarralumla
Australian Capital Territory
Canberra, Australia

U.S. Consulate General
36th Floor
T & G Tower
Hyde Park Square
Sydney, Australia

U.S. Consulate General
24 Albert Road
Melbourne, Australia

U.S. Consulate
264 St. George's Terrace
Perth, Australia

Austria

U.S. Embassy
IX Boltzmanngasse 16
A-1091
Vienna, Austria

Bahamas

U.S. Embassy
Mosmar Building
Queen Street
Nassau, Bahamas

Bahrain

U.S. Embassy
P.O. Box 26431
Manama, Bahrain

Bangladesh

U.S. Embassy
Fifth Floor
Adamjee Court Building
Montijheel Area
Dacca, Bangladesh

Barbados

U.S. Embassy
P.O. Box 302
Bridgetown, Barbados

Belgium

U.S. Embassy
27 Boulevard du Régent
Brussels, Belgium

U.S. Consulate General
Rubenscenter, Nationalestraat 5
Antwerp, Belgium

U.S. Mission to the European
    Communities
40 Boulevard du Régent
Brussels, Belgium

U.S. Mission to the North Atlantic
Treaty Organization
Autoroute de Zaventem
Brussels, Belgium

Belize

U.S. Embassy
Gabourel Lane and Hutson Street
Belize City, Belize

Benin

U.S. Embassy
Rue Caporal Anani Bernard
Boîte Postale 2012
Cotonou, Benin

Bermuda

U.S. Consulate General
Vallis Building
Front Street
Hamilton, Bermuda

Bolivia

U.S. Embassy
Banco Popular del Peru Building
Corner of Callas Mercado y Colón
La Paz, Bolivia

Botswana

U.S. Embassy
P.O. Box 90
Gaborone, Botswana

Brazil

U.S. Embassy
Lote No. 3 Avenida das Nocoes
Brasilia, Brazil

U.S. Consulate General
Avenida Presidente Wilson 147
Rio de Janeiro, Brazil

U.S. Consulate General
Rua Padre Jõao Manuel
São Paulo, Brazil

U.S. Consulate
Rua Coronel Genuino
Porto Alegre, Brazil

U.S. Consulate
Rua Gonçalves Maia 163
Recife, Brazil

U.S. Consulate
Avenida Presidente Vargas
Salvador, Brazil

Bulgaria

U.S. Embassy
One Alexander Stamboliski Boulevard
Sofia, Bulgaria

Burma

U.S. Embassy
581 Merchant Street
Rangoon, Burma

Burundi

U.S. Embassy
Chaussée Prince Louise Rwagasore
Boîte Postale 1720
Bujumbura, Burundi

Cameroon

U.S. Embassy
Rue Nachtigal
Boîte Postale 817
Yaoundé, Cameroon

U.S. Consulate
21 Avenue du Général
De Gaulle
Boîte Postale 4006
Douala, Cameroon

Canada

U.S. Embassy
100 Wellington Street
Ottawa, Ontario
Canada

U.S. Consulate General
Room 1050
615 Macleod Trail, S.E.
Calgary, Alberta
Canada

U.S. Consulate General
360 University Avenue
Toronto, Ontario
Canada

U.S. Consulate General
6 Donald Street
Winnipeg, Manitoba
Canada

U.S. Consulate General
P.O. Box 65
Place Desjardins
Montreal, Quebec
Canada

U.S. Consulate General
Cogswell Tower (Suite 910)
Scotia Square
Halifax, Nova Scotia
Canada

U.S. Consulate General
1199 West Hastings
Vancouver, British Columbia
Canada

U.S. Consulate
One Avenue Ste. Geneviève
Quebec, Quebec
Canada

Cape Verde

U.S. Embassy
Rua Hoji Ya Yenna
Praia, Cape Verde

Central African Republic

U.S. Embassy
Avenue President Dacko
Bangui, Central African Republic

Chad

U.S. Embassy
Rue du Lt. Colonel Colonna
    D'oranano
Boîte Postale 413
N'Djamena, Chad

Chile

U.S. Embassy
Codina Building
1343 Augustinas
Santiago, Chile

China, People's Republic of

U.S. Embassy
Guang Hua Lu
Beijing, China

U.S. Consulate General
Dong Fang Hotel
Guangzhou, China

U.S. Consulate General
1469 Huai Huai Middle Road
Shanghai, China

Colombia

U.S. Embassy
Calle 37 8–40
Bogotá, Colombia

U.S. Consulate
Hotel El Prado
Carrera 54 No. 70–10
Barranquilla, Colombia

U.S. Consulate
Edificio Pielroja
Carrera, No. 3 11–55
Cali, Colombia

Congo

U.S. Embassy
Avenue Amilcar Cabral
Brazzaville, Republic of the Congo

Costa Rica

U.S. Embassy
Avenida 3 and Calle 1
San José, Costa Rica

Cyprus

U.S. Embassy
Therissos Street and Dositheos Street
Nicosia, Cyprus

Czechoslovakia

U.S. Embassy
Trziste 15–12548
Prague, Czechoslovakia

Denmark

U.S. Embassy
Dag Hammarskjölds Alle 24
Copenhagen, Denmark

Djibouti

U.S. Embassy
Villa Plateau du Serpent Blvd.
Maréchal Joffre
Djibouti

Dominican Republic

U.S. Embassy
Corner of Calle César Nicholas
   Pensen and Calle Leopoldo
   Navarro
Santo Domingo, Dominican
   Republic

Ecuador

U.S. Embassy
120 Avenida Patria
Quito, Ecuador

U.S. Consulate General
9 de Octubre y Garcia Moreno
Guayaquil, Ecuador

Egypt

U.S. Embassy
5 Sharia Latin America
Box 10
Cairo, Arab Republic of Egypt

U.S. Consulate General
110 Avenue Horreya
Alexandria, Arab Republic of Egypt

El Salvador

U.S. Embassy
1230 25 Avenida Norte
San Salvador, El Salvador

England (United Kingdom)

U.S. Embassy
24/31 Grosvenor Square, W. 1
London, England

Equatorial Guinea

U.S. Embassy
Armengol Coll and Asturias Streets
Malabo, Equatorial Guinea

Ethiopia

U.S. Embassy
Entoto Street
P.O. Box 1014
Addis Ababa, Ethiopia

Fiji

U.S. Embassy
31 Loftus Street
P.O. Box 218
Suva, Fiji

Finland

U.S. Embassy
Itainen Puistotie 14a
Helsinki, Finland

France

U.S. Embassy
2 Avenue Gabriel 75382
Paris, France

U.S. Consulate General
9 Rue Armeny
Marseilles, France

U.S. Consulate General
15 Avenue d'Alsace
Strasbourg, France

U.S. Consulate General
22 Cours du Maréchal Foch
Bordeaux, France

U.S. Consulate General
7 Quai Général Sarrail
Lyons, France

U.S. Consulate
3 Rue Dr. Barety
Nice, France

French West Indies

U.S. Consulate
14 Rue Blenac
Boîte Postale 561
Fort-de-France 97206
Martinique, French West Indies

Gabon

U.S. Embassy
Boulevard de la Mer
Boîte Postale 4000
Libreville, Gabon

Gambia

U.S. Embassy
16 Buckle Street
Banjul, The Gambia

German Democratic Republic (East Germany)

U.S. Embassy
108 Berlin
Neustaedtische Kirchstrasse 4–5
East Berlin, German Democratic
    Republic

Germany, Federal Republic of (West Germany)

U.S. Embassy
Deichmannsaue 5300 Bonn 2
Bonn, Federal Republic of Germany

U.S. Consulate General
Koeniginstrasse 5
8000 Muenchen 22
Munich, Federal Republic of
    Germany

U.S. Consulate General
Urbanstrasse 7
7000 Stuttgart
Stuttgart, Federal Republic of
    Germany

U.S. Consulate General
Alsterufer 27/28
2000 Hamburg 36
Box 2
Hamburg, Federal Republic of
    Germany

U.S. Consulate General
Cecilienallee 5
4000 Düsseldorf
30 Germany
Box 515
Düsseldorf, Federal Republic of
 Germany

U.S. Consulate General
Siesmayerstrasse 21
Frankfurt am Main, Federal Republic
 of Germany

U.S. Mission
Clayallee 170
D-1000 Berlin 33
West Berlin, Federal Republic of
 Germany

Ghana

U.S. Embassy
Liberia and Kinbu Roads
P.O. Box 194
Accra, Ghana

Greece

U.S. Embassy
91 Vasilissis Sophias Boulevard
Athens, Greece

U.S. Consulate General
59 Vasileos Constantinou Street
Thessaloniki, Greece

Guatemala

U.S. Embassy
7–01 Avenida de la Reforma
Zone 10
Guatemala

Guinea

U.S. Embassy
Second Boulevard and Ninth Avenue
Boîte Postale 603
Conakry, Guinea

Guinea-Bissau

U.S. Embassy
Avenida Domingos Ramos
CP 297
Bissau, Guinea-Bissau

Guyana

U.S. Embassy
31 Main Street
Georgetown, Guyana

Haiti

U.S. Embassy
Harry Truman Boulevard
Port-au-Prince, Haiti

Honduras

U.S. Embassy
Avenida La Paz
Tegucigalpa, Honduras

Hong Kong

U.S. Consulate General
26 Garden Road
Hong Kong

Hungary

U.S. Embassy
V. Szabadsag Ter 12
Budapest, Hungary

Iceland

U.S. Embassy
Laufasvegur 21
Reykjavik, Iceland

India

U.S. Embassy
Shanti Path
Chanakyapuri 21
New Delhi, India

U.S. Consulate General
5/1 Ho Chi Minh Sarani
Calcutta, India

U.S. Consulate General
Lincoln House
78 Bhulabhai Desai Road
Bombay, India

U.S. Consulate General
Mount Road 6
Madras, India

Indonesia

U.S. Embassy
Medan Merdeka
Selaton 5
Jakarta, Indonesia

U.S. Consulate
Jalan Imam Bonjoi 13
Medan, Indonesia

U.S. Consulate
Jalan Raya Drive
Sutomo 33
Surabaya, Indonesia

Republic of Ireland

U.S. Embassy
42 Elgin Road
Ballsbridge
Dublin, Ireland

Northern Ireland

U.S. Consulate General
Queen's House
14 Queen Street
Belfast, Northern Ireland

Israel

U.S. Embassy
71 Hayarkon Street
Tel Aviv, Israel

Italy

U.S. Embassy
Via Veneto 119A
Rome, Italy

U.S. Consulate General
Banco d'America e d'Italia Building
Piazza Portello 6
Box G
Genoa, Italy

U.S. Consulate General
Piazza della Repubblica
80122 Naples
Box 18
Naples, Italy

U.S. Consulate General
Piazza Della Repubblica 32
Milan, Italy

U.S. Consulate General
Via Baccarini 1
Palermo, Italy

U.S. Consulate
38 Lungarmo Amerigo Vespucci
Florence, Italy

U.S. Consulate
Via Roma 9 (4th floor)
Trieste, Italy

Ivory Coast

U.S. Embassy
5 Rue Jesse Owens
Boîte Postale 1712
Abidjan, Ivory Coast

Jamaica

U.S. Embassy
2 Oxford Road
Kingston, Jamaica

Japan

U.S. Embassy
10–5 Akasaka 1-chome
Minatoku (107)
Tokyo, Japan

U.S. Consulate General
Sankei Building 4–9 (9th floor)
Umeda 2-chome, Kitaku,
    Osaka (530)
Osaka, Japan

U.S. Consulate General
3–1 Kano-sho 6-chome
Chuoku Kobe (650)
Kobe, Japan

U.S. Consulate
Kita 1–Jyo Nishi 28-chome Chuoku,
    Sapporo (064)
Sapporo, Japan

U.S. Consulate
5–26 Ohari 2-chome
Chuaku Fukuokashi (810)
Box 10
Fukuoka, Japan

Jordan

U.S. Embassy
Jebel Amman
Amman, Jordan

Kenya

U.S. Embassy
Moi/Haile Selassie Avenue
Haile Selassie Avenue
P.O. Box 30137
Nairobi, Kenya

Korea

U.S. Embassy
82 Sejong-Ro
Seoul, Korea

Kuwait

U.S. Embassy
c/o 77 P.O. Box SAFAT
Kuwait

Laos

U.S. Embassy
Rue Bartholonie
Boîte Postale 114
Vientiane, Laos

Lebanon

U.S. Embassy
Corniche at Rue Ain Mreisseh
Beirut, Lebanon

Lesotho

U.S. Embassy
P.O. Box 333
Maseru, Lesotho

Liberia

U.S. Embassy
111 United Nations Drive
Monrovia, Liberia

Libya

U.S. Embassy
Shari Mohammad Thabit
Tripoli, Libya

Luxembourg

U.S. Embassy
22 Boulevard Emmanuel Servais
Luxembourg, Luxembourg

Madagascar

U.S. Embassy
14 and 16 Rue Rainitovo
Antsahavola
Boîte Postale 620
Tananarive, Madagascar

Malawi
U.S. Embassy
P.O. Box 30016
Lilongwe, Malawi

Malaysia
U.S. Embassy
A I A Building
Jalan Ampang
P.O. Box 35
Kuala Lumpur, Malaysia

Mali
U.S. Embassy
Rue Testard and Rue Mohamed V
Bamako, Mali

Malta
U.S. Embassy
Development House (2nd floor)
Saint Anne Street
Floriana Malta
Valletta, Malta

Mauritania
U.S. Embassy
B.P. 222
Nouakchott, Mauritania

Mauritius
U.S. Embassy
Rogers Building (4th floor)
John Kennedy Street
Port Louis, Mauritius

Mexico
U.S. Embassy
Paseo de la Reforma 305
Colonia Cuauhtémoc
Mexico City, Mexico

U.S. Consulate General
Istenson Building (3rd floor)
Miguel Hidalgo y Costilla 15
Hermosillo, Mexico

U.S. Consulate General
924 Avenue Lopez Mateos
Ciudad Juárez, Mexico

U.S. Consulate General
Avenida Constitución
411 Poniente
Monterrey, Mexico

U.S. Consulate General
Progreso 175
Guadalajara, Mexico

U.S. Consulate General
Tapachula 96
Tijuana, Mexico

U.S. Consulate
Avenida Allende 3330
Colonia Jardín
Nuevo Laredo, Mexico

U.S. Consulate
Paseo Montejo 453
Apartado Postal 130
Mérida, Mexico

U.S. Consulate
6 Circunvalación No. 6 at Venusti-
    ana Carranza
Mazatlán, Mexico

U.S. Consulate
Avenida Primera No. 232
Matamoros, Mexico

Morocco
U.S. Embassy
2 Avenue de Marrakech
Rabat, Morocco

U.S. Consulate General
8 Boulevard Moulay Youssef
Casablanca, Morocco

U.S. Consulate General
Chemin des Amoureux
Tangier, Morocco

Mozambique

U.S. Embassy
35 Rua Da Mesquita (3rd floor)
Maputo, Mozambique

Nepal

U.S. Embassy
Pani-pokhari
Katmandu, Nepal

Netherlands

U.S. Embassy
102 Lange Voorhout
The Hague, Netherlands

U.S. Consulate General
Vlasmarkt 1
Rotterdam, Netherlands

U.S. Consulate General
Museumplein 19
Amsterdam, Netherlands

Netherlands Antilles

U.S. Consulate General
St. Anna Boulevard 19
P.O. Box 158
Curaçao, Netherlands Antilles

New Zealand

U.S. Embassy
29 Fitzherbert Terrace
Thornden
Wellington, New Zealand

U.S. Consulate General
Yorkshire General Building

Shortland and O'Connell Streets
Auckland, New Zealand

Nicaragua

U.S. Embassy
Km 4–1/2 Carretera Sur.
2 South Highway
Managua, Nicaragua

Niger

U.S. Embassy
Boîte Postale 11201
Niamey, Niger

Nigeria

U.S. Embassy
2 Eleke Crescent
Lagos, Nigeria

U.S. Consulate
5 Ahmadu Bellow Way
Kaduna, Nigeria

Norway

U.S. Embassy
Drammensveien 18
Oslo, Norway

Oman

U.S. Embassy
P.O. Box 966
Muscat, Oman

Okinawa

U.S. Consulate General
2129 Gusukuma, Urasoe City
Naha, Okinawa

Pakistan

U.S. Embassy
AID/UN Building
P.O. Box 1048
Islamabad, Pakistan

U.S. Consulate General
8 Abdullah Haroon Road
Karachi, Pakistan

U.S. Consulate
50 Zafar Ali Road
Lahore, Pakistan

U.S. Consulate
11 Hospital Road
Peshawar, Pakistan

Panama

U.S. Embassy
Avenida Balboa at 38th Street
Panama City, Panama

Papua New Guinea

U.S. Embassy
Armit Street
P.O. Box 3492
Port Moresby, Papua New Guinea

Paraguay

U.S. Embassy
1776 Mariscal López Avenue
Asunción, Paraguay

Peru

U.S. Embassy
Corner Avenidas Inca Garcilaso de la
    Vega and España
P.O. Box 1995
Lima, Peru

Philippines

U.S. Embassy
1201 Roxas Boulevard
Manila, Philippines

U.S. Consulate General
Philippine America Life Insurance
    Building (3rd floor)
Jones Avenue
Cebu, Philippines

Poland

U.S. Embassy
Aleje Ujazdowskie 29/31
Warsaw, Poland

U.S. Consulate
Ulica Stolarka 9
31043 Kraków
Kraków, Poland

U.S. Consulate
Ulica Chopino 4
Poznań, Poland

Portugal

U.S. Embassy
Avenida Duque de Loulé, 39
Lisbon, Portugal

U.S. Consulate
Apartado 88
Rua Julio Dinis 826–30
Oporto, Portugal

U.S. Consulate
Avenida D. Henrique
Ponta Delgada, São Miguel
Azores, Portugal

Qatar

U.S. Embassy
Farig Bin Omran
P.O. Box 2399
Doha, Qatar

Romania

U.S. Embassy
Strada Tudor Argezhi 7–9
Bucharest, Rumania

Rwanda

U.S. Embassy
Boulevard de la Revolution
Kigali, Rwanda

Saudi Arabia

U.S. Embassy
Palestine Road, Ruwais
Jidda, Saudi Arabia

U.S. Consulate General
Between Aramco Headquarters and
    Dhahran International Airport
Dhahran, Saudi Arabia

Scotland

U.S. Consulate General
3 Regent Terrace
Edinburgh, Scotland

Senegal

U.S. Embassy
Boîte Postale 49
Avenue Jean XXIII
Dakar, Senegal

Seychelles

U.S. Embassy
Box 148
Victoria, Seychelles

Sierra Leone

U.S. Embassy
Corner Walpole and Siaka Stevens
    Streets
Freetown, Sierra Leone

Singapore

U.S. Embassy
30 Hill Street
Singapore

Somalia

U.S. Embassy
Corso Primo Luglio
Mogadishu, Somalia

South Africa, Republic of

U.S. Embassy
Thibault House
225 Pretorius Street
Pretoria, Republic of South Africa

U.S. Consulate General
Durban Bay House (29th floor)
333 Smith Street
Durban, Republic of South Africa

U.S. Consulate General
Broadway Industries Center
Heerengracht, Foreshore
Cape Town, Republic of South
    Africa

U.S. Consulate General
Kine Center (11th floor)
Commissioner and Kruis Streets
P.O. Box 2155
Johannesburg, Republic of South
    Africa

Spain

U.S. Embassy
Serrano 75
Madrid, Spain

U.S. Consulate General
Via Layetana 33
Barcelona, Spain

U.S. Consulate General
Paseo de las Delicias 7
Seville, Spain

U.S. Consulate
Avenida del Ejército, 11–3rd
    floor, Duesto-Bilbao
Bilbao, Spain

Sri Lanka

U.S. Embassy
44 Galle Road, Colombo 3
Colombo, Sri Lanka

Sudan

U.S. Embassy
Gamhouria Avenue
P.O. Box 699
Khartoum, Sudan

Surinam

U.S. Embassy
Dr. Sophie Redmondstraat 129
Paramaribo, Surinam

Swaziland

U.S. Embassy
Central Bank Building
P.O. Box 199
Mbabane, Swaziland

Sweden

U.S. Embassy
Strandvagen 101
Stockholm, Sweden

Switzerland

U.S. Embassy
93/95 Jubilaumsstrasse
Bern, Switzerland

U.S. Embassy (Branch Office)
11 Route de Pregny
Geneva, Switzerland

U.S. Consulate General
Zollikerstrasse 141
Zurich, Switzerland

Syria

U.S. Embassy
Abu Rumaneh, Al Mansur Street 2
P.O. Box 29
Damascus, Syria

Tanzania

U.S. Embassy
36 Laibon Road

P.O. Box 9123
Dar es Salaam, Tanzania

Thailand

U.S. Embassy
95 Wireless Road
Bangkok, Thailand

U.S. Consulate
35/6 Supakitjanya Road
WBO 96237
Udorn, Thailand

U.S. Consulate
9 Sadao Road
Songkhla, Thailand

U.S. Consulate
Vidhayanond Road
Chiang Mai, Thailand

Togo

U.S. Embassy
Rue Pelletier Caventou and
    Rue Vouban
BP 852
Lomé, Togo

Trinidad and Tobago

U.S. Embassy
15 Queen's Park West
Port-of-Spain, Trinidad

Tunisia

U.S. Embassy
144 Avenue de la Liberté
Tunis, Tunisia

Turkey

U.S. Embassy
110 Ataturk Boulevard
Ankara, Turkey

U.S. Consulate
386 Ataturk Caddesi
Izmir, Turkey

U.S. Consulate
104–108 Mesrutiyet Caddesi,
Tepebasi
Istanbul, Turkey

U.S. Consulate
Ataturk Caddesi
Adana, Turkey

Uganda

U.S. Embassy
Kampala, Uganda

Union of Soviet Socialist Republics

U.S. Embassy
Ulitsa Chaykoyskogo 19/21/23
Moscow, Union of Soviet Socialist
Republics

U.S. Consulate General
UL, Petra Lavrova Street 15
Box L
Leningrad, Union of Soviet Socialist
Republics

United Arab Emirates

U.S. Embassy
Shaikh Khalid Building
Pnornidnherd
Abu Dhabi, United Arab Emirates

Upper Volta

U.S. Embassy
Boîte Postale 35
Ouagadougou, Upper Volta

Uruguay

U.S. Embassy
Calle Lauro Muller 1776
Montevideo, Uruguay

Venezuela

U.S. Embassy
Avenida Francisco de Miranda and
Avenida Principal de la Floresta
Caracas, Venezuela

U.S. Consulate
Edificio Matema, 1 Piso
Avenida 15 Calle 78
Maracaibo, Venezuela

Yemen Arab Republic

U.S. Embassy
P.O. Box 1088
Sana, Yemen Arab Republic

Yugoslavia

U.S. Embassy
Kneza Milosa 50
Belgrade, Yugoslavia

U.S. Consulate General
Brace Kavurica 2
Zagreb, Yugoslavia

Zaire

U.S. Embassy
310 Avenue des Aviateurs
Kinshasa, Zaire

U.S. Consulate General
1029 Boulevard Kamanyole
Boîte Postale 1196
Lubumbashi, Zaire

U.S. Consulate
Boîte Postale 3037
Avenue Mobutu
Bukavu, Zaire

Zambia

U.S. Embassy
P.O. Box 31617
Lusaka, Zambia

Zimbabwe

U.S. Embassy
78 Enterprise Road, Highlands
Salisbury
Harare, Zimbabwe

FORMS OF ADDRESS

Forms of address do not always follow set guidelines; the type of salutation is often determined by the relationship between correspondents or by the purpose and content of the letter. However, a general style applies to most occasions. In formal salutations, when the addressee is a woman, "Madam" should be sub-

stituted for "Sir." When the salutation is informal, "Mrs." or "Miss" or "Ms." should be substituted for "Mr." If a woman addressee has previously stated a preference for a particular form of address this form should be used.

	Form of Address	Salutation
Academics		
assistant professor, college or university	Dr. (*or* Mr.) Joseph Stone Assistant Professor Department of ___	Dear Professor Stone:
associate professor, college or university	Dr. (*or* Mr.) Joseph Stone Associate Professor Department of ___	Dear Professor Stone:
chancellor, university	Chancellor Joseph Stone	Dear Chancellor Stone:
dean, college or university	Dean Joseph Stone *or* Dr. (*or* Mr.) Joseph Stone Dean, School of ___	Dear Dean Stone: Dear Dr. (*or* Mr.) Stone:
president, college or university	President Joseph Stone *or* Dr. (*or* Mr.) Joseph Stone President, ___	Dear President Stone: Dear Dr. (*or* Mr.) Stone:

	Envelope and Inside Address	Salutation
professor, college or university	Professor Joseph Stone / *or* / Dr. (*or* Mr.) Joseph Stone / Department of ___	Dear Professor Stone: / Dear Dr. (*or* Mr.) Stone:
Clerical and Religious Orders		
abbot, Roman Catholic	The Right Reverend Joseph Stone, O.S.B. / Abbot of ___	Right Reverend Abbot:
archbishop, Armenian Church	His Eminence the Archbishop of ___	Your Eminence: / *or* / Your Excellency:
archbishop, Greek Orthodox	His Eminence Archbishop Joseph Stone	Your Eminence:
archbishop, Roman Catholic	The Most Reverend Joseph Stone / Archbishop of ___	Your Excellency:
archbishop, Russian Orthodox	His Eminence the Archbishop of ___ / *or* / The Most Reverend Archbishop of ___	Your Grace: / Right Reverend Joseph:
archdeacon, Episcopal	The Venerable Joseph Stone, / Archdeacon of ___	Venerable Sir: / Dear Archdeacon Stone: / Dear Father Stone:
archimandrite, Russian Orthodox	Very Reverend Father Joseph Stone	Very Reverend Father: / Very Reverend Father Stone:
archpriest, Russian Orthodox	Very Reverend Father Joseph Stone	Very Reverend Father: / Very Reverend Father Stone:

	Form of Address	Salutation
Clerical and Religious Orders		
bishop, Episcopal	The Right Reverend Joseph Stone Bishop of ___	Right Reverend Sir: Dear Bishop Stone:
bishop, Greek Orthodox	The Right Reverend Joseph Stone	Your Grace:
bishop, Methodist	Bishop Joseph Stone	Dear Bishop Stone:
bishop, Roman Catholic	The Most Reverend Joseph Stone Bishop of ___	Your Excellency:
brotherhood, Roman Catholic, member of	Brother Joseph Stone, C.F.C.	Dear Brother: Dear Brother Joseph:
canon, Episcopal	The Reverend Canon Joseph Stone	Dear Canon Stone:
cantor	Cantor Joseph Stone	Dear Cantor Stone:
cardinal	His Eminence Joseph Cardinal Stone	Your Eminence:
clergyman, Protestant	The Reverend Joseph Stone *or* The Reverend Joseph Stone, D.D.	Dear Mr. (*or* Dr.) Stone:
elder, Presbyterian	Elder Joseph Stone	Dear Elder Stone:
dean of a cathedral, Episcopal	The Very Reverend Joseph Stone Dean of ___	Very Reverend Sir: Dear Dean Stone:

metropolitan, Russian Orthodox	His Eminence the Metropolitan of ___ *or* The Most Reverend Metropolitan of ___	Your Grace: Right Reverend Joseph:
monsignor, Roman Catholic	Reverend Monsignor Joseph Stone	Reverend Monsignor: Dear Monsignor: Dear Monsignor Stone:
patriarch, Armenian Church	His Beatitude the Patriarch of ___	Your Beatitude:
patriarch, Greek Orthodox	His All Holiness Patriarch Demetrios	Your All Holiness:
patriarch, Russian Orthodox	His Beatitude the Patriarch of ___	Your Beatitude:
pope	His Holiness Pope John XXIII *or* His Holiness the Pope	Your Holiness:
president, Mormon Church	President Joseph Stone Church of Jesus Christ of Latter-day Saints	Dear President Stone:
priest, Greek Orthodox	Reverend Father Joseph Stone	Dear Reverend Stone: Dear Reverend Father:
priest, Roman Catholic	The Reverend Joseph Stone, S.J.	Dear Reverend Father: Dear Father: Dear Father Stone:
priest, Russian Orthodox	The Reverend Joseph Stone	Reverend Father: Reverend Father Stone:
protopresbyter, Russian Orthodox	Very Reverend Father Joseph Stone	Very Reverend Father: Very Reverend Father Stone:

	Form of Address	Salutation
Clerical and Religious Orders		
rabbi	Rabbi Joseph Stone *or* Joseph Stone, D.D.	Dear Rabbi (*or* Dr.) Stone:
sisterhood, Roman Catholic, member of	Sister Mary Stone, C.S.J.	Dear Sister: Dear Sister Mary:
supreme patriarch, Armenian Church	His Holiness the Supreme Patriarch and Catholicos of all Armenians	Your Holiness:
Diplomats		
ambassador, U.S.	The Honorable Joseph Stone The Ambassador of the United States	Sir: Dear Mr. Ambassador:
ambassador to the U.S.	His Excellency Joseph Stone The Ambassador of ____	Excellency: Dear Mr. Ambassador:
chargé d'affaires, U.S.	Joseph Stone, Esq. American Chargé d'Affaires	Dear Sir:
chargé d'affaires to the U.S.	Joseph Stone, Esq. Chargé d'Affaires of ____	Dear Sir:
consul, U.S.	Mr. Joseph Stone American Consul	Sir: Dear Mr. Consul:
minister, U.S.	The Honorable Joseph Stone The Minister of the United States	Sir: Dear Mr. Minister:

minister to the U.S.	The Honorable Joseph Stone The Minister of ____	Sir: Dear Mr. Minister:
secretary general, United Nations	His Excellency Joseph Stone Secretary General of the United Nations	Excellency: Dear Mr. Secretary General:
U.S. representative to the United Nations	The Honorable Joseph Stone United States Representative to the United Nations	Sir: Dear Mr. Stone:
Federal, state, and local officials (government)		
alderman	The Honorable Joseph Stone	Dear Mr. Stone:
assistant to the President	The Honorable Joseph Stone Assistant to the President The White House	Dear Mr. Stone:
Attorney General, U.S.	The Honorable Joseph Stone Attorney General of the United States	Dear Mr. Attorney General:
attorney general, state	The Honorable Joseph Stone Attorney General State of ____	Dear Mr. Attorney General:
assemblyman, state	The Honorable Joseph Stone ____ Assembly State Capitol	Dear Mr. Stone:
cabinet member	The Honorable Joseph Stone Secretary of ____	Dear Mr. Secretary:

Form of Address

Federal, state, and local officials (government)	Form of Address	Salutation
assistant secretary of a department	The Honorable Joseph Stone Assistant Secretary of _____	Dear Mr. Stone:
undersecretary of a department	The Honorable Joseph Stone Undersecretary of _____	Dear Mr. Stone:
deputy secretary of a department	The Honorable Joseph Stone Deputy Secretary of _____	Dear Mr. Stone:
chairman, House Committee	The Honorable Joseph Stone Chairman, Committee on _____ United States House of Representatives	Dear Mr. Chairman:
chairman, joint committee of Congress	The Honorable Joseph Stone Chairman, Joint Committee on _____ Congress of the United States	Dear Mr. Chairman:
chairman, Senate Committee	The Honorable Joseph Stone Chairman, Committee on _____ United States Senate	Dear Mr. Chairman:
chief justice, U.S. Supreme Court	The Chief Justice of the United States The Supreme Court of the United States	Dear Mr. Chief Justice:
associate justice, U.S. Supreme Court	Mr. Justice Stone The Supreme Court of the United States	Dear Mr. Justice:
commissioner (federal, state, or local)	The Honorable Joseph Stone	Dear Mr. Stone:

delegate, state	The Honorable Joseph Stone _____ House of Delegates State Capitol	Dear Mr. Stone:
governor	The Honorable Joseph Stone Governor of _____	Dear Governor Stone:
judge, federal	The Honorable Joseph Stone Judge of the United States Tax Court	Dear Judge Stone:
judge, state or local	The Honorable Joseph Stone Judge of the Superior Court of _____	Dear Judge Stone:
lieutenant governor	The Honorable Joseph Stone Lieutenant Governor of _____	Dear Mr. Stone:
mayor	The Honorable Joseph Stone Mayor of _____	Dear Mayor Stone:
Postmaster General	The Honorable Joseph Stone Postmaster General of the United States	Dear Mr. Postmaster General:
President, U.S.	The President The White House	Dear Mr. President:
former President, U.S.	The Honorable Joseph Stone	Dear Mr. Stone:
representative, state	The Honorable Joseph Stone House of Representatives State Capitol	Dear Mr. Stone:
representative, U.S.	The Honorable Joseph Stone United States House of Representatives	Dear Mr. Stone:
secretary of state, state	The Honorable Joseph Stone Secretary of State State Capitol	Dear Mr. Secretary:

	Form of Address	Salutation
Federal, state, and local officials (government)		
senator, state	The Honorable Joseph Stone The State Senate State Capitol	Dear Senator Stone:
senator, U.S.	The Honorable Joseph Stone United States Senate	Dear Senator Stone:
Speaker, U.S. House of Representatives	The Honorable Joseph Stone Speaker of the House of Representatives	Dear Mr. Speaker:
Vice President, U.S.	The Vice President United States Senate	Dear Mr. Vice President:
Professions		
attorney	Mr. Joseph Stone Attorney at Law *or* Joseph Stone, Esq.	Dear Mr. Stone:
chiropractor	Joseph Stone, D.C. (office) *or* Dr. Joseph Stone (residence)	Dear Dr. Stone:
dentist	Joseph Stone, D.D.S. (office) *or* Dr. Joseph Stone (residence)	Dear Dr. Stone:

physician	Joseph Stone, M.D. (office) *or* Dr. Joseph Stone (residence)	Dear Dr. Stone:
veterinarian	Joseph Stone, D.V.M. (office) *or* Dr. Joseph Stone (residence)	Dear Dr. Stone:
Military		
admiral vice admiral rear admiral	Full rank, full name, abbreviation of service branch	Dear Admiral Stone:
airman first class airman airman basic	Full rank. full name, abbreviation of service branch	Dear Airman Stone:
cadet (air force, army)	Cadet Joseph Stone United States Air Force Academy United States Military Academy	Dear Cadet Stone: *or* Dear Mr. Stone:
captain, (air force, army, coast guard, marine corps, navy)	Full rank, full name, abbreviation of service branch	Dear Captain Stone:
chief petty officer (coast guard, navy)	Full rank, full name, abbreviation of service branch	Dear Mr. Stone: *or* Dear Chief Stone:

Military	Form of Address	Salutation
chief warrant officer, warrant officer (air force, army, marine corps, navy)	Full rank, full name, abbreviation of service branch	Dear Mr. Stone:
colonel, lieutenant colonel (air force, army, marine corps)	Full rank, full name, abbreviation of service branch	Dear Colonel Stone:
commander (coast guard, navy)	Full rank, full name, abbreviation of service branch	Dear Commander Stone:
commodore (navy)	Full rank, full name, abbreviation of service branch	Dear Commodore Stone:
corporal (army), lance corporal (marine corps)	Full rank, full name, abbreviation of service branch	Dear Corporal Stone:
ensign (coast guard, navy)	Full rank, full name, abbreviation of service branch	Dear Mr. Stone: *or* Dear Ensign Stone:
first lieutenant, second lieutenant (air force, army, marine corps)	Full rank, full name, abbreviation of service branch	Dear Lieutenant Stone:
general, lieutenant general, major general, brigadier general (air force, army, marine corps)	Full rank, full name, abbreviation of service branch	Dear General Stone:

lieutenant commander, lieutenant, lieutenant (jg) (coast guard, navy)	Full rank, full name, abbreviation of service branch	Dear Mr. Stone: *or* Dear Lieutenant Stone:
major (air force, army, marine corps)	Full rank, full name, abbreviation of service branch	Dear Major Stone:
midshipman	Midshipman Joseph Stone United States Coast Guard Academy United States Naval Academy	Dear Midshipman Stone:
petty officer (coast guard, navy)	Full rank, full name, abbreviation of service branch	Dear Mr. Stone:
private first class, private (air force, army, marine corps)	Full rank, full name, abbreviation of service branch	Dear Private Stone:
seaman, seaman apprentice, seaman recruit (coast guard, navy)	Full rank, full name, abbreviation of service branch	Dear Seaman Stone:
master sergeant (air force, army, marine corps)	Full rank, full name, abbreviation of service branch	Dear Sergeant Stone:

Note: Other compound titles in enlisted ranks are not shown here. They all follow forms indicated for this example.

specialist (army)	Full rank, full name, abbreviation of service branch	Dear Specialist Stone:

PROOFREADERS' MARKS

Instruction	Mark in Margin	Mark in Type	Corrected Type
Delete	ℐ	the ~~good~~ word	the word
Insert indicated material	good	the word	the good word
Let it stand	stet	the ~~good~~ word	the good word
Make capital	cap	the word	the Word
Make lower case	lc	The Word	the Word
Set in small capitals	sc	See word	See WORD.
Set in italic type	ital	The word is word.	The word is *word*.
Set in roman type	rom	the word	the word
Set in boldface type	bf	the entry word	the entry **word**
Set in lightface type	lf	the entry word	the entry word
Transpose	tr	the word good	the good word
Close up space	⌒	the wo rd	the word
Delete and close up space	ℐ	the w ord	the word
Spell out	sp	2 words	two words
Insert: space	#	the word	the word
period	⊙	This is the word	This is the word.
comma	⌃	words words, words	words, words, words
hyphen	=⁄=	word for word test	word-for-word test
colon	⊙	The following words	The following words:
semicolon	⌃;	Scan the words skim the words.	Scan the words; skim the words.
apostrophe	∨	Johns words	John's words
quotation marks	∨/∨/	the word word	the word ''word''
parentheses	(/)/	The word word is in parentheses.	The word (word) is in parentheses.
brackets	[/]	He read from the Word the Bible.	He read from the Word [the Bible].
en dash	⅟N	1964 1972	1964–1972
em dash	⅟M /	The dictionary how often it is needed belongs in every home.	The dictionary—how often it is needed— belongs in every home.
superior type	∨	2 = 4	$2^2 = 4$
inferior type	∧	HO	H_2O
asterisk	∨	word	word*
dagger	†	a word	a word†
double dagger	‡	words and words	words and words‡
section symbol	§	Book Reviews	§Book Reviews
virgule	/	either or	either/or
Start paragraph	¶	''Where is it?'' ''It's on the shelf.''	''Where is it?'' ''It's on the shelf.''

Instruction	Mark in Margin	Mark in Type	Corrected Type
Run in	*run in*	The entry word is printed in boldface. ⌐The pronunciation follows.	The entry word is printed in boldface. The pronunciation follows.
Turn right side up	ꝺ	the word	the word
Move left	⌐	⌐the word	the word
Move right	⌐	the word	the word
Move up	⌐	the word	the word
Move down	⌐	the word	the word
Align	‖	the word the word the word	the word the word the word
Straighten line	=	the word	the word
Wrong font	*wf*	the word	the word
Broken type	×	the word	the word

ROMAN NUMERALS

Roman numerals are often used to list topics in outlines and legal memoranda, pagination of the front matter in books, in copyright dates, documents, and dates on monuments. The Roman numeral system is made up of seven symbols: I(1), V(5), X(10), L(50), C(100), D(500), and M(1000). Zero is not used in the system. The following table lists Roman numerals that are used frequently.

I	1	XCVIII	98
II	2	IC	99
III	3	C	100
IV	4	CI	101
V	5	CL	150
VI	6	CC	200
VII	7	CCL	250
VIII	8	CCC	300
IX	9	CCCL	350
X	10	CD	400
XI	11	CDL	450
XII	12	D	500
XIII	13	DL	550
XIV	14	DC	600
XV	15	DCL	650
XVI	16	DCC	700
XVII	17	DCCL	750
XVIII	18	DCCC	800
XIX	19	DCCCL	850
XX	20	CM	900
XXI	21	CML	950
XXIX	29	M	1000
XXX	30	MDCLXVI	1666
XL	40	MCMLXX	1970
XLVIII	48	MCMLXXVI	1976
IL	49	MCMLXXVII	1977
L	50	MCMLXXVIII	1978
LX	60	MCMLXXIX	1979
LXX	70	MCMLXXX	1980
LXXX	80	MCMXC	1990
XC	90	MM	2000

PERPETUAL CALENDAR

Our present calendar — the Gregorian calendar — was calculated by Pope Gregory XIII in 1582. Great Britain and her colonies did not adopt the Gregorian calendar until 1752. Eleven of the months in this calendar have 30 or 31 days. The month of February has 28 days except every fourth year, or leap year, when its days "leap" to 29. However, century years that cannot be divided by 400, such as 1700, 1800, and 1900, are not leap years and February will have 28 days. The century year 2000 will be a leap year. This is necessary so that calendar and solar years will remain the same.

Directions: Pick desired year from chart below. The number shown with each year indicates what calendar to use for that year.

1776... 9	1806... 4	1836...13	1866... 2	1896...11	1926... 6	1956... 8	1986... 4	2016...13	2046... 2
1777... 4	1807... 5	1837... 1	1867... 3	1897... 6	1927... 7	1957... 3	1987... 5	2017... 1	2047... 3
1778... 5	1808...13	1838... 2	1868...11	1898... 7	1928... 8	1958... 4	1988...13	2018... 2	2048...11
1779... 6	1809... 1	1839... 3	1869... 6	1899... 1	1929... 3	1959... 5	1989... 1	2019... 3	2049... 6
1780...14	1810... 2	1840...11	1870... 7	1900... 2	1930... 4	1960...13	1990... 2	2020...11	2050... 7
1781... 2	1811... 3	1841... 6	1871... 1	1901... 3	1931... 5	1961... 1	1991... 3	2021... 6	2051... 1
1782... 3	1812...11	1842... 7	1872... 9	1902... 4	1932...13	1962... 2	1992...11	2022... 7	2052... 9
1783... 4	1813... 6	1843... 1	1873... 4	1903... 5	1933... 1	1963... 3	1993... 6	2023... 1	2053... 4
1784...12	1814... 7	1844... 9	1874... 5	1904...13	1934... 2	1964...11	1994... 7	2024... 9	2054... 5
1785... 7	1815... 1	1845... 4	1875... 6	1905... 1	1935... 3	1965... 6	1995... 1	2025... 4	2055... 6
1786... 1	1816... 9	1846... 5	1876...14	1906... 2	1936...11	1966... 7	1996... 9	2026... 5	2056...14
1787... 2	1817... 4	1847... 6	1877... 2	1907... 3	1937... 6	1967... 1	1997... 4	2027... 6	2057... 2
1788...10	1818... 5	1848...14	1878... 3	1908...11	1938... 7	1968... 9	1998... 5	2028...14	2058... 3
1789... 5	1819... 6	1849... 2	1879... 4	1909... 6	1939... 1	1969... 4	1999... 6	2029... 2	2059... 4
1790... 6	1820...14	1850... 3	1880...12	1910... 7	1940... 9	1970... 5	2000...14	2030... 3	2060...12
1791... 7	1821... 2	1851... 4	1881... 7	1911... 1	1941... 4	1971... 6	2001... 2	2031... 4	2061... 7
1792... 8	1822... 3	1852...12	1882... 1	1912... 9	1942... 5	1972... 7	2002... 3	2032...12	2062... 1
1793... 3	1823... 4	1853... 7	1883... 2	1913... 4	1943... 6	1973... 2	2003... 4	2033... 7	2063... 2
1794... 4	1824...12	1854... 1	1884...10	1914... 5	1944...14	1974... 3	2004...12	2034... 1	2064...10
1795... 5	1825... 7	1855... 2	1885... 5	1915... 6	1945... 2	1975... 4	2005... 7	2035... 2	2065... 5
1796...13	1826... 1	1856...10	1886... 6	1916...14	1946... 3	1976...12	2006... 1	2036...10	2066... 6
1797... 1	1827... 2	1857... 5	1887... 7	1917... 2	1947... 4	1977... 7	2007... 2	2037... 5	2067... 7
1798... 2	1828...10	1858... 6	1888... 8	1918... 3	1948...12	1978... 1	2008...10	2038... 6	2068... 8
1799... 3	1829... 5	1859... 7	1889... 3	1919... 4	1949... 7	1979... 2	2009... 5	2039... 7	2069... 3
1800... 4	1830... 6	1860... 8	1890... 4	1920...12	1950... 1	1980...10	2010... 6	2040... 8	2070... 4
1801... 5	1831... 7	1861... 3	1891... 5	1921... 7	1951... 2	1981... 5	2011... 7	2041... 3	2071... 5
1802... 6	1832... 8	1862... 4	1892...13	1922... 1	1952...10	1982... 6	2012... 8	2042... 4	2072...13
1803... 7	1833... 3	1863... 5	1893... 1	1923... 2	1953... 5	1983... 7	2013... 3	2043... 5	2073... 1
1804... 8	1834... 4	1864...13	1894... 2	1924...10	1954... 6	1984... 8	2014... 4	2044...13	2074... 2
1805... 3	1835... 5	1865... 1	1895... 3	1925... 5	1955... 7	1985... 3	2015... 5	2045... 1	2075... 3

1   1978

JANUARY
S M T W T F S
1 2 3 4 5 6 7
8 9 10 11 12 13 14
15 16 17 18 19 20 21
22 23 24 25 26 27 28
29 30 31

FEBRUARY
S M T W T F S
1 2 3 4
5 6 7 8 9 10 11
12 13 14 15 16 17 18
19 20 21 22 23 24 25
26 27 28

MARCH
S M T W T F S
1 2 3 4
5 6 7 8 9 10 11
12 13 14 15 16 17 18
19 20 21 22 23 24 25
26 27 28 29 30 31

APRIL
S M T W T F S
1
2 3 4 5 6 7 8
9 10 11 12 13 14 15
16 17 18 19 20 21 22
23 24 25 26 27 28 29
30

MAY
S M T W T F S
1 2 3 4 5 6
7 8 9 10 11 12 13
14 15 16 17 18 19 20
21 22 23 24 25 26 27
28 29 30 31

JUNE
S M T W T F S
1 2 3
4 5 6 7 8 9 10
11 12 13 14 15 16 17
18 19 20 21 22 23 24
25 26 27 28 29 30

JULY
S M T W T F S
1
2 3 4 5 6 7 8
9 10 11 12 13 14 15
16 17 18 19 20 21 22
23 24 25 26 27 28 29
30 31

AUGUST
S M T W T F S
1 2 3 4 5
6 7 8 9 10 11 12
13 14 15 16 17 18 19
20 21 22 23 24 25 26
27 28 29 30 31

SEPTEMBER
S M T W T F S
1 2
3 4 5 6 7 8 9
10 11 12 13 14 15 16
17 18 19 20 21 22 23
24 25 26 27 28 29 30

OCTOBER
S M T W T F S
1 2 3 4 5 6 7
8 9 10 11 12 13 14
15 16 17 18 19 20 21
22 23 24 25 26 27 28
29 30 31

NOVEMBER
S M T W T F S
1 2 3 4
5 6 7 8 9 10 11
12 13 14 15 16 17 18
19 20 21 22 23 24 25
26 27 28 29 30

DECEMBER
S M T W T F S
1 2
3 4 5 6 7 8 9
10 11 12 13 14 15 16
17 18 19 20 21 22 23
24 25 26 27 28 29 30
31

2   1979

JANUARY
S M T W T F S
1 2 3 4 5 6
7 8 9 10 11 12 13
14 15 16 17 18 19 20
21 22 23 24 25 26 27
28 29 30 31

FEBRUARY
S M T W T F S
1 2 3
4 5 6 7 8 9 10
11 12 13 14 15 16 17
18 19 20 21 22 23 24
25 26 27 28

MARCH
S M T W T F S
1 2 3
4 5 6 7 8 9 10
11 12 13 14 15 16 17
18 19 20 21 22 23 24
25 26 27 28 29 30 31

APRIL
S M T W T F S
1 2 3 4 5 6 7
8 9 10 11 12 13 14
15 16 17 18 19 20 21
22 23 24 25 26 27 28
29 30

MAY
S M T W T F S
1 2 3 4 5
6 7 8 9 10 11 12
13 14 15 16 17 18 19
20 21 22 23 24 25 26
27 28 29 30 31

JUNE
S M T W T F S
1 2
3 4 5 6 7 8 9
10 11 12 13 14 15 16
17 18 19 20 21 22 23
24 25 26 27 28 29 30

JULY
S M T W T F S
1 2 3 4 5 6 7
8 9 10 11 12 13 14
15 16 17 18 19 20 21
22 23 24 25 26 27 28
29 30 31

AUGUST
S M T W T F S
1 2 3 4
5 6 7 8 9 10 11
12 13 14 15 16 17 18
19 20 21 22 23 24 25
26 27 28 29 30 31

SEPTEMBER
S M T W T F S
1
2 3 4 5 6 7 8
9 10 11 12 13 14 15
16 17 18 19 20 21 22
23 24 25 26 27 28 29
30

OCTOBER
S M T W T F S
1 2 3 4 5 6
7 8 9 10 11 12 13
14 15 16 17 18 19 20
21 22 23 24 25 26 27
28 29 30 31

NOVEMBER
S M T W T F S
1 2 3
4 5 6 7 8 9 10
11 12 13 14 15 16 17
18 19 20 21 22 23 24
25 26 27 28 29 30

DECEMBER
S M T W T F S
1
2 3 4 5 6 7 8
9 10 11 12 13 14 15
16 17 18 19 20 21 22
23 24 25 26 27 28 29
30 31

3

```
     JANUARY              FEBRUARY               MARCH
S  M  T  W  T  F  S   S  M  T  W  T  F  S   S  M  T  W  T  F  S
         1  2  3  4  5               1  2                  1  2
 6  7  8  9 10 11 12   3  4  5  6  7  8  9   3  4  5  6  7  8  9
13 14 15 16 17 18 19  10 11 12 13 14 15 16  10 11 12 13 14 15 16
20 21 22 23 24 25 26  17 18 19 20 21 22 23  17 18 19 20 21 22 23
27 28 29 30 31        24 25 26 27 28        24 25 26 27 28 29 30
                                            31

      APRIL                  MAY                   JUNE
S  M  T  W  T  F  S   S  M  T  W  T  F  S   S  M  T  W  T  F  S
    1  2  3  4  5  6            1  2  3  4                     1
 7  8  9 10 11 12 13   5  6  7  8  9 10 11   2  3  4  5  6  7  8
14 15 16 17 18 19 20  12 13 14 15 16 17 18   9 10 11 12 13 14 15
21 22 23 24 25 26 27  19 20 21 22 23 24 25  16 17 18 19 20 21 22
28 29 30              26 27 28 29 30 31     23 24 25 26 27 28 29
                                            30

      JULY                 AUGUST              SEPTEMBER
S  M  T  W  T  F  S   S  M  T  W  T  F  S   S  M  T  W  T  F  S
    1  2  3  4  5  6            1  2  3   1  2  3  4  5  6  7
 7  8  9 10 11 12 13   4  5  6  7  8  9 10   8  9 10 11 12 13 14
14 15 16 17 18 19 20  11 12 13 14 15 16 17  15 16 17 18 19 20 21
21 22 23 24 25 26 27  18 19 20 21 22 23 24  22 23 24 25 26 27 28
28 29 30 31           25 26 27 28 29 30 31  29 30

     OCTOBER              NOVEMBER              DECEMBER
S  M  T  W  T  F  S   S  M  T  W  T  F  S   S  M  T  W  T  F  S
       1  2  3  4  5               1  2   1  2  3  4  5  6  7
 6  7  8  9 10 11 12   3  4  5  6  7  8  9   8  9 10 11 12 13 14
13 14 15 16 17 18 19  10 11 12 13 14 15 16  15 16 17 18 19 20 21
20 21 22 23 24 25 26  17 18 19 20 21 22 23  22 23 24 25 26 27 28
27 28 29 30 31        24 25 26 27 28 29 30  29 30 31
```

4

```
     JANUARY              FEBRUARY               MARCH
S  M  T  W  T  F  S   S  M  T  W  T  F  S   S  M  T  W  T  F  S
            1  2  3  4                     1                     1
 5  6  7  8  9 10 11   2  3  4  5  6  7  8   2  3  4  5  6  7  8
12 13 14 15 16 17 18   9 10 11 12 13 14 15   9 10 11 12 13 14 15
19 20 21 22 23 24 25  16 17 18 19 20 21 22  16 17 18 19 20 21 22
26 27 28 29 30 31     23 24 25 26 27 28     23 24 25 26 27 28 29
                                            30 31

      APRIL                  MAY                   JUNE
S  M  T  W  T  F  S   S  M  T  W  T  F  S   S  M  T  W  T  F  S
       1  2  3  4  5            1  2  3   1  2  3  4  5  6  7
 6  7  8  9 10 11 12   4  5  6  7  8  9 10   8  9 10 11 12 13 14
13 14 15 16 17 18 19  11 12 13 14 15 16 17  15 16 17 18 19 20 21
20 21 22 23 24 25 26  18 19 20 21 22 23 24  22 23 24 25 26 27 28
27 28 29 30           25 26 27 28 29 30 31  29 30

      JULY                 AUGUST              SEPTEMBER
S  M  T  W  T  F  S   S  M  T  W  T  F  S   S  M  T  W  T  F  S
       1  2  3  4  5               1  2   1  2  3  4  5  6
 6  7  8  9 10 11 12   3  4  5  6  7  8  9   7  8  9 10 11 12 13
13 14 15 16 17 18 19  10 11 12 13 14 15 16  14 15 16 17 18 19 20
20 21 22 23 24 25 26  17 18 19 20 21 22 23  21 22 23 24 25 26 27
27 28 29 30 31        24 25 26 27 28 29 30  28 29 30
                      31

     OCTOBER              NOVEMBER              DECEMBER
S  M  T  W  T  F  S   S  M  T  W  T  F  S   S  M  T  W  T  F  S
         1  2  3  4                     1   1  2  3  4  5  6
 5  6  7  8  9 10 11   2  3  4  5  6  7  8   7  8  9 10 11 12 13
12 13 14 15 16 17 18   9 10 11 12 13 14 15  14 15 16 17 18 19 20
19 20 21 22 23 24 25  16 17 18 19 20 21 22  21 22 23 24 25 26 27
26 27 28 29 30 31     23 24 25 26 27 28 29  28 29 30 31
                      30
```

5

```
     JANUARY              FEBRUARY               MARCH
S  M  T  W  T  F  S   S  M  T  W  T  F  S   S  M  T  W  T  F  S
            1  2  3   1  2  3  4  5  6  7   1  2  3  4  5  6  7
 4  5  6  7  8  9 10   8  9 10 11 12 13 14   8  9 10 11 12 13 14
11 12 13 14 15 16 17  15 16 17 18 19 20 21  15 16 17 18 19 20 21
18 19 20 21 22 23 24  22 23 24 25 26 27 28  22 23 24 25 26 27 28
25 26 27 28 29 30 31                        29 30 31

      APRIL                  MAY                   JUNE
S  M  T  W  T  F  S   S  M  T  W  T  F  S   S  M  T  W  T  F  S
         1  2  3  4               1  2   1  2  3  4  5  6
 5  6  7  8  9 10 11   3  4  5  6  7  8  9   7  8  9 10 11 12 13
12 13 14 15 16 17 18  10 11 12 13 14 15 16  14 15 16 17 18 19 20
19 20 21 22 23 24 25  17 18 19 20 21 22 23  21 22 23 24 25 26 27
26 27 28 29 30        24 25 26 27 28 29 30  28 29 30
                      31

      JULY                 AUGUST              SEPTEMBER
S  M  T  W  T  F  S   S  M  T  W  T  F  S   S  M  T  W  T  F  S
         1  2  3  4                     1   1  2  3  4  5
 5  6  7  8  9 10 11   2  3  4  5  6  7  8   6  7  8  9 10 11 12
12 13 14 15 16 17 18   9 10 11 12 13 14 15  13 14 15 16 17 18 19
19 20 21 22 23 24 25  16 17 18 19 20 21 22  20 21 22 23 24 25 26
26 27 28 29 30 31     23 24 25 26 27 28 29  27 28 29 30
                      30 31

     OCTOBER              NOVEMBER              DECEMBER
S  M  T  W  T  F  S   S  M  T  W  T  F  S   S  M  T  W  T  F  S
            1  2  3   1  2  3  4  5  6  7   1  2  3  4  5
 4  5  6  7  8  9 10   8  9 10 11 12 13 14   6  7  8  9 10 11 12
11 12 13 14 15 16 17  15 16 17 18 19 20 21  13 14 15 16 17 18 19
18 19 20 21 22 23 24  22 23 24 25 26 27 28  20 21 22 23 24 25 26
25 26 27 28 29 30 31  29 30                 27 28 29 30 31
```

6

```
     JANUARY              FEBRUARY               MARCH
S  M  T  W  T  F  S   S  M  T  W  T  F  S   S  M  T  W  T  F  S
               1  2            1  2  3  4  5  6            1  2  3  4  5  6
 3  4  5  6  7  8  9   7  8  9 10 11 12 13   7  8  9 10 11 12 13
10 11 12 13 14 15 16  14 15 16 17 18 19 20  14 15 16 17 18 19 20
17 18 19 20 21 22 23  21 22 23 24 25 26 27  21 22 23 24 25 26 27
24 25 26 27 28 29 30  28                    28 29 30 31
31

      APRIL                  MAY                   JUNE
S  M  T  W  T  F  S   S  M  T  W  T  F  S   S  M  T  W  T  F  S
            1  2  3                     1   1  2  3  4  5
 4  5  6  7  8  9 10   2  3  4  5  6  7  8   6  7  8  9 10 11 12
11 12 13 14 15 16 17   9 10 11 12 13 14 15  13 14 15 16 17 18 19
18 19 20 21 22 23 24  16 17 18 19 20 21 22  20 21 22 23 24 25 26
25 26 27 28 29 30     23 24 25 26 27 28 29  27 28 29 30
                      30 31

      JULY                 AUGUST              SEPTEMBER
S  M  T  W  T  F  S   S  M  T  W  T  F  S   S  M  T  W  T  F  S
            1  2  3   1  2  3  4  5  6  7            1  2  3  4
 4  5  6  7  8  9 10   8  9 10 11 12 13 14   5  6  7  8  9 10 11
11 12 13 14 15 16 17  15 16 17 18 19 20 21  12 13 14 15 16 17 18
18 19 20 21 22 23 24  22 23 24 25 26 27 28  19 20 21 22 23 24 25
25 26 27 28 29 30 31  29 30 31              26 27 28 29 30

     OCTOBER              NOVEMBER              DECEMBER
S  M  T  W  T  F  S   S  M  T  W  T  F  S   S  M  T  W  T  F  S
               1  2            1  2  3  4  5  6            1  2  3  4
 3  4  5  6  7  8  9   7  8  9 10 11 12 13   5  6  7  8  9 10 11
10 11 12 13 14 15 16  14 15 16 17 18 19 20  12 13 14 15 16 17 18
17 18 19 20 21 22 23  21 22 23 24 25 26 27  19 20 21 22 23 24 25
24 25 26 27 28 29 30  28 29 30              26 27 28 29 30 31
31
```

7 — 1977

```
        JANUARY                  FEBRUARY                   MARCH
  S  M  T  W  T  F  S      S  M  T  W  T  F  S      S  M  T  W  T  F  S
                    1            1  2  3  4  5            1  2  3  4  5
  2  3  4  5  6  7  8      6  7  8  9 10 11 12      6  7  8  9 10 11 12
  9 10 11 12 13 14 15     13 14 15 16 17 18 19     13 14 15 16 17 18 19
 16 17 18 19 20 21 22     20 21 22 23 24 25 26     20 21 22 23 24 25 26
 23 24 25 26 27 28 29     27 28                    27 28 29 30 31
 30 31

         APRIL                      MAY                      JUNE
  S  M  T  W  T  F  S      S  M  T  W  T  F  S      S  M  T  W  T  F  S
                 1  2      1  2  3  4  5  6  7               1  2  3  4
  3  4  5  6  7  8  9      8  9 10 11 12 13 14      5  6  7  8  9 10 11
 10 11 12 13 14 15 16     15 16 17 18 19 20 21     12 13 14 15 16 17 18
 17 18 19 20 21 22 23     22 23 24 25 26 27 28     19 20 21 22 23 24 25
 24 25 26 27 28 29 30     29 30 31                 26 27 28 29 30

         JULY                     AUGUST                  SEPTEMBER
  S  M  T  W  T  F  S      S  M  T  W  T  F  S      S  M  T  W  T  F  S
                 1  2         1  2  3  4  5  6                  1  2  3
  3  4  5  6  7  8  9      7  8  9 10 11 12 13      4  5  6  7  8  9 10
 10 11 12 13 14 15 16     14 15 16 17 18 19 20     11 12 13 14 15 16 17
 17 18 19 20 21 22 23     21 22 23 24 25 26 27     18 19 20 21 22 23 24
 24 25 26 27 28 29 30     28 29 30 31              25 26 27 28 29 30
 31

        OCTOBER                  NOVEMBER                  DECEMBER
  S  M  T  W  T  F  S      S  M  T  W  T  F  S      S  M  T  W  T  F  S
                    1            1  2  3  4  5                  1  2  3
  2  3  4  5  6  7  8      6  7  8  9 10 11 12      4  5  6  7  8  9 10
  9 10 11 12 13 14 15     13 14 15 16 17 18 19     11 12 13 14 15 16 17
 16 17 18 19 20 21 22     20 21 22 23 24 25 26     18 19 20 21 22 23 24
 23 24 25 26 27 28 29     27 28 29 30              25 26 27 28 29 30 31
 30 31
```

8

```
        JANUARY                  FEBRUARY                   MARCH
  S  M  T  W  T  F  S      S  M  T  W  T  F  S      S  M  T  W  T  F  S
  1  2  3  4  5  6  7            1  2  3  4                  1  2  3
  8  9 10 11 12 13 14      5  6  7  8  9 10 11      4  5  6  7  8  9 10
 15 16 17 18 19 20 21     12 13 14 15 16 17 18     11 12 13 14 15 16 17
 22 23 24 25 26 27 28     19 20 21 22 23 24 25     18 19 20 21 22 23 24
 29 30 31                 26 27 28 29              25 26 27 28 29 30 31

         APRIL                      MAY                      JUNE
  S  M  T  W  T  F  S      S  M  T  W  T  F  S      S  M  T  W  T  F  S
  1  2  3  4  5  6  7            1  2  3  4  5                  1  2
  8  9 10 11 12 13 14      6  7  8  9 10 11 12      3  4  5  6  7  8  9
 15 16 17 18 19 20 21     13 14 15 16 17 18 19     10 11 12 13 14 15 16
 22 23 24 25 26 27 28     20 21 22 23 24 25 26     17 18 19 20 21 22 23
 29 30                    27 28 29 30 31           24 25 26 27 28 29 30

         JULY                     AUGUST                  SEPTEMBER
  S  M  T  W  T  F  S      S  M  T  W  T  F  S      S  M  T  W  T  F  S
  1  2  3  4  5  6  7            1  2  3  4                        1
  8  9 10 11 12 13 14      5  6  7  8  9 10 11      2  3  4  5  6  7  8
 15 16 17 18 19 20 21     12 13 14 15 16 17 18      9 10 11 12 13 14 15
 22 23 24 25 26 27 28     19 20 21 22 23 24 25     16 17 18 19 20 21 22
 29 30 31                 26 27 28 29 30 31        23 24 25 26 27 28 29
                                                   30

        OCTOBER                  NOVEMBER                  DECEMBER
  S  M  T  W  T  F  S      S  M  T  W  T  F  S      S  M  T  W  T  F  S
     1  2  3  4  5  6               1  2  3                        1
  7  8  9 10 11 12 13      4  5  6  7  8  9 10      2  3  4  5  6  7  8
 14 15 16 17 18 19 20     11 12 13 14 15 16 17      9 10 11 12 13 14 15
 21 22 23 24 25 26 27     18 19 20 21 22 23 24     16 17 18 19 20 21 22
 28 29 30 31              25 26 27 28 29 30        23 24 25 26 27 28 29
                                                   30 31
```

9

```
        JANUARY                  FEBRUARY                   MARCH
  S  M  T  W  T  F  S      S  M  T  W  T  F  S      S  M  T  W  T  F  S
     1  2  3  4  5  6               1  2  3                     1  2
  7  8  9 10 11 12 13      4  5  6  7  8  9 10      3  4  5  6  7  8  9
 14 15 16 17 18 19 20     11 12 13 14 15 16 17     10 11 12 13 14 15 16
 21 22 23 24 25 26 27     18 19 20 21 22 23 24     17 18 19 20 21 22 23
 28 29 30 31              25 26 27 28              24 25 26 27 28 29 30
                                                   31

         APRIL                      MAY                      JUNE
  S  M  T  W  T  F  S      S  M  T  W  T  F  S      S  M  T  W  T  F  S
     1  2  3  4  5  6            1  2  3  4                        1
  7  8  9 10 11 12 13      5  6  7  8  9 10 11      2  3  4  5  6  7  8
 14 15 16 17 18 19 20     12 13 14 15 16 17 18      9 10 11 12 13 14 15
 21 22 23 24 25 26 27     19 20 21 22 23 24 25     16 17 18 19 20 21 22
 28 29 30                 26 27 28 29 30 31        23 24 25 26 27 28 29
                                                   30

         JULY                     AUGUST                  SEPTEMBER
  S  M  T  W  T  F  S      S  M  T  W  T  F  S      S  M  T  W  T  F  S
     1  2  3  4  5  6               1  2  3      1  2  3  4  5  6  7
  7  8  9 10 11 12 13      4  5  6  7  8  9 10      8  9 10 11 12 13 14
 14 15 16 17 18 19 20     11 12 13 14 15 16 17     15 16 17 18 19 20 21
 21 22 23 24 25 26 27     18 19 20 21 22 23 24     22 23 24 25 26 27 28
 28 29 30 31              25 26 27 28 29 30 31     29 30

        OCTOBER                  NOVEMBER                  DECEMBER
  S  M  T  W  T  F  S      S  M  T  W  T  F  S      S  M  T  W  T  F  S
        1  2  3  4  5                     1  2      1  2  3  4  5  6  7
  6  7  8  9 10 11 12      3  4  5  6  7  8  9      8  9 10 11 12 13 14
 13 14 15 16 17 18 19     10 11 12 13 14 15 16     15 16 17 18 19 20 21
 20 21 22 23 24 25 26     17 18 19 20 21 22 23     22 23 24 25 26 27 28
 27 28 29 30 31           24 25 26 27 28 29 30     29 30 31
```

10

```
        JANUARY                  FEBRUARY                   MARCH
  S  M  T  W  T  F  S      S  M  T  W  T  F  S      S  M  T  W  T  F  S
        1  2  3  4  5                  1  2                        1
  6  7  8  9 10 11 12      3  4  5  6  7  8  9      2  3  4  5  6  7  8
 13 14 15 16 17 18 19     10 11 12 13 14 15 16      9 10 11 12 13 14 15
 20 21 22 23 24 25 26     17 18 19 20 21 22 23     16 17 18 19 20 21 22
 27 28 29 30 31           24 25 26 27 28 29        23 24 25 26 27 28 29
                                                   30 31

         APRIL                      MAY                      JUNE
  S  M  T  W  T  F  S      S  M  T  W  T  F  S      S  M  T  W  T  F  S
        1  2  3  4  5                  1  2  3      1  2  3  4  5  6  7
  6  7  8  9 10 11 12      4  5  6  7  8  9 10      8  9 10 11 12 13 14
 13 14 15 16 17 18 19     11 12 13 14 15 16 17     15 16 17 18 19 20 21
 20 21 22 23 24 25 26     18 19 20 21 22 23 24     22 23 24 25 26 27 28
 27 28 29 30              25 26 27 28 29 30 31     29 30

         JULY                     AUGUST                  SEPTEMBER
  S  M  T  W  T  F  S      S  M  T  W  T  F  S      S  M  T  W  T  F  S
        1  2  3  4  5                     1  2         1  2  3  4  5  6
  6  7  8  9 10 11 12      3  4  5  6  7  8  9      7  8  9 10 11 12 13
 13 14 15 16 17 18 19     10 11 12 13 14 15 16     14 15 16 17 18 19 20
 20 21 22 23 24 25 26     17 18 19 20 21 22 23     21 22 23 24 25 26 27
 27 28 29 30 31           24 25 26 27 28 29 30     28 29 30
                          31

        OCTOBER                  NOVEMBER                  DECEMBER
  S  M  T  W  T  F  S      S  M  T  W  T  F  S      S  M  T  W  T  F  S
           1  2  3  4                        1         1  2  3  4  5  6
  5  6  7  8  9 10 11      2  3  4  5  6  7  8      7  8  9 10 11 12 13
 12 13 14 15 16 17 18      9 10 11 12 13 14 15     14 15 16 17 18 19 20
 19 20 21 22 23 24 25     16 17 18 19 20 21 22     21 22 23 24 25 26 27
 26 27 28 29 30 31        23 24 25 26 27 28 29     28 29 30 31
                          30
```

11

JANUARY

S	M	T	W	T	F	S
			1	2	3	4
5	6	7	8	9	10	11
12	13	14	15	16	17	18
19	20	21	22	23	24	25
26	27	28	29	30	31	

FEBRUARY

S	M	T	W	T	F	S
						1
2	3	4	5	6	7	8
9	10	11	12	13	14	15
16	17	18	19	20	21	22
23	24	25	26	27	28	29

MARCH

S	M	T	W	T	F	S
1	2	3	4	5	6	7
8	9	10	11	12	13	14
15	16	17	18	19	20	21
22	23	24	25	26	27	28
29	30	31				

APRIL

S	M	T	W	T	F	S
			1	2	3	4
5	6	7	8	9	10	11
12	13	14	15	16	17	18
19	20	21	22	23	24	25
26	27	28	29	30		

MAY

S	M	T	W	T	F	S
					1	2
3	4	5	6	7	8	9
10	11	12	13	14	15	16
17	18	19	20	21	22	23
24	25	26	27	28	29	30
31						

JUNE

S	M	T	W	T	F	S
	1	2	3	4	5	6
7	8	9	10	11	12	13
14	15	16	17	18	19	20
21	22	23	24	25	26	27
28	29	30				

JULY

S	M	T	W	T	F	S
			1	2	3	4
5	6	7	8	9	10	11
12	13	14	15	16	17	18
19	20	21	22	23	24	25
26	27	28	29	30	31	

AUGUST

S	M	T	W	T	F	S
						1
2	3	4	5	6	7	8
9	10	11	12	13	14	15
16	17	18	19	20	21	22
23	24	25	26	27	28	29
30	31					

SEPTEMBER

S	M	T	W	T	F	S
		1	2	3	4	5
6	7	8	9	10	11	12
13	14	15	16	17	18	19
20	21	22	23	24	25	26
27	28	29	30			

OCTOBER

S	M	T	W	T	F	S
				1	2	3
4	5	6	7	8	9	10
11	12	13	14	15	16	17
18	19	20	21	22	23	24
25	26	27	28	29	30	31

NOVEMBER

S	M	T	W	T	F	S
1	2	3	4	5	6	7
8	9	10	11	12	13	14
15	16	17	18	19	20	21
22	23	24	25	26	27	28
29	30					

DECEMBER

S	M	T	W	T	F	S
		1	2	3	4	5
6	7	8	9	10	11	12
13	14	15	16	17	18	19
20	21	22	23	24	25	26
27	28	29	30	31		

12

JANUARY

S	M	T	W	T	F	S
				1	2	3
4	5	6	7	8	9	10
11	12	13	14	15	16	17
18	19	20	21	22	23	24
25	26	27	28	29	30	31

FEBRUARY

S	M	T	W	T	F	S
1	2	3	4	5	6	7
8	9	10	11	12	13	14
15	16	17	18	19	20	21
22	23	24	25	26	27	28
29						

MARCH

S	M	T	W	T	F	S
	1	2	3	4	5	6
7	8	9	10	11	12	13
14	15	16	17	18	19	20
21	22	23	24	25	26	27
28	29	30	31			

APRIL

S	M	T	W	T	F	S
				1	2	3
4	5	6	7	8	9	10
11	12	13	14	15	16	17
18	19	20	21	22	23	24
25	26	27	28	29	30	

MAY

S	M	T	W	T	F	S
						1
2	3	4	5	6	7	8
9	10	11	12	13	14	15
16	17	18	19	20	21	22
23	24	25	26	27	28	29
30	31					

JUNE

S	M	T	W	T	F	S
		1	2	3	4	5
6	7	8	9	10	11	12
13	14	15	16	17	18	19
20	21	22	23	24	25	26
27	28	29	30			

JULY

S	M	T	W	T	F	S
				1	2	3
4	5	6	7	8	9	10
11	12	13	14	15	16	17
18	19	20	21	22	23	24
25	26	27	28	29	30	31

AUGUST

S	M	T	W	T	F	S
1	2	3	4	5	6	7
8	9	10	11	12	13	14
15	16	17	18	19	20	21
22	23	24	25	26	27	28
29	30	31				

SEPTEMBER

S	M	T	W	T	F	S
			1	2	3	4
5	6	7	8	9	10	11
12	13	14	15	16	17	18
19	20	21	22	23	24	25
26	27	28	29	30		

OCTOBER

S	M	T	W	T	F	S
					1	2
3	4	5	6	7	8	9
10	11	12	13	14	15	16
17	18	19	20	21	22	23
24	25	26	27	28	29	30
31						

NOVEMBER

S	M	T	W	T	F	S
	1	2	3	4	5	6
7	8	9	10	11	12	13
14	15	16	17	18	19	20
21	22	23	24	25	26	27
28	29	30				

DECEMBER

S	M	T	W	T	F	S
			1	2	3	4
5	6	7	8	9	10	11
12	13	14	15	16	17	18
19	20	21	22	23	24	25
26	27	28	29	30	31	

13

JANUARY

S	M	T	W	T	F	S
					1	2
3	4	5	6	7	8	9
10	11	12	13	14	15	16
17	18	19	20	21	22	23
24	25	26	27	28	29	30
31						

FEBRUARY

S	M	T	W	T	F	S
	1	2	3	4	5	6
7	8	9	10	11	12	13
14	15	16	17	18	19	20
21	22	23	24	25	26	27
28	29					

MARCH

S	M	T	W	T	F	S
		1	2	3	4	5
6	7	8	9	10	11	12
13	14	15	16	17	18	19
20	21	22	23	24	25	26
27	28	29	30	31		

APRIL

S	M	T	W	T	F	S
					1	2
3	4	5	6	7	8	9
10	11	12	13	14	15	16
17	18	19	20	21	22	23
24	25	26	27	28	29	30

MAY

S	M	T	W	T	F	S
1	2	3	4	5	6	7
8	9	10	11	12	13	14
15	16	17	18	19	20	21
22	23	24	25	26	27	28
29	30	31				

JUNE

S	M	T	W	T	F	S
			1	2	3	4
5	6	7	8	9	10	11
12	13	14	15	16	17	18
19	20	21	22	23	24	25
26	27	28	29	30		

JULY

S	M	T	W	T	F	S
					1	2
3	4	5	6	7	8	9
10	11	12	13	14	15	16
17	18	19	20	21	22	23
24	25	26	27	28	29	30
31						

AUGUST

S	M	T	W	T	F	S
	1	2	3	4	5	6
7	8	9	10	11	12	13
14	15	16	17	18	19	20
21	22	23	24	25	26	27
28	29	30	31			

SEPTEMBER

S	M	T	W	T	F	S
				1	2	3
4	5	6	7	8	9	10
11	12	13	14	15	16	17
18	19	20	21	22	23	24
25	26	27	28	29	30	

OCTOBER

S	M	T	W	T	F	S
						1
2	3	4	5	6	7	8
9	10	11	12	13	14	15
16	17	18	19	20	21	22
23	24	25	26	27	28	29
30	31					

NOVEMBER

S	M	T	W	T	F	S
		1	2	3	4	5
6	7	8	9	10	11	12
13	14	15	16	17	18	19
20	21	22	23	24	25	26
27	28	29	30			

DECEMBER

S	M	T	W	T	F	S
				1	2	3
4	5	6	7	8	9	10
11	12	13	14	15	16	17
18	19	20	21	22	23	24
25	26	27	28	29	30	31

14

JANUARY

S	M	T	W	T	F	S
						1
2	3	4	5	6	7	8
9	10	11	12	13	14	15
16	17	18	19	20	21	22
23	24	25	26	27	28	29
30	31					

FEBRUARY

S	M	T	W	T	F	S
		1	2	3	4	5
6	7	8	9	10	11	12
13	14	15	16	17	18	19
20	21	22	23	24	25	26
27	28	29				

MARCH

S	M	T	W	T	F	S
			1	2	3	4
5	6	7	8	9	10	11
12	13	14	15	16	17	18
19	20	21	22	23	24	25
26	27	28	29	30	31	

APRIL

S	M	T	W	T	F	S
						1
2	3	4	5	6	7	8
9	10	11	12	13	14	15
16	17	18	19	20	21	22
23	24	25	26	27	28	29
30						

MAY

S	M	T	W	T	F	S
	1	2	3	4	5	6
7	8	9	10	11	12	13
14	15	16	17	18	19	20
21	22	23	24	25	26	27
28	29	30	31			

JUNE

S	M	T	W	T	F	S
				1	2	3
4	5	6	7	8	9	10
11	12	13	14	15	16	17
18	19	20	21	22	23	24
25	26	27	28	29	30	

JULY

S	M	T	W	T	F	S
						1
2	3	4	5	6	7	8
9	10	11	12	13	14	15
16	17	18	19	20	21	22
23	24	25	26	27	28	29
30	31					

AUGUST

S	M	T	W	T	F	S
		1	2	3	4	5
6	7	8	9	10	11	12
13	14	15	16	17	18	19
20	21	22	23	24	25	26
27	28	29	30	31		

SEPTEMBER

S	M	T	W	T	F	S
					1	2
3	4	5	6	7	8	9
10	11	12	13	14	15	16
17	18	19	20	21	22	23
24	25	26	27	28	29	30

OCTOBER

S	M	T	W	T	F	S
1	2	3	4	5	6	7
8	9	10	11	12	13	14
15	16	17	18	19	20	21
22	23	24	25	26	27	28
29	30	31				

NOVEMBER

S	M	T	W	T	F	S
			1	2	3	4
5	6	7	8	9	10	11
12	13	14	15	16	17	18
19	20	21	22	23	24	25
26	27	28	29	30		

DECEMBER

S	M	T	W	T	F	S
					1	2
3	4	5	6	7	8	9
10	11	12	13	14	15	16
17	18	19	20	21	22	23
24	25	26	27	28	29	30
31						

POSTAL ABBREVIATIONS

Alabama	AL	Maine	ME	Pennsylvania	PA
Alaska	AK	Maryland	MD	Rhode Island	RI
Arizona	AZ	Massachusetts	MA	South Carolina	SC
Arkansas	AR	Michigan	MI	South Dakota	SD
California	CA	Minnesota	MN	Tennessee	TN
Colorado	CO	Mississippi	MS	Texas	TX
Connecticut	CT	Missouri	MO	Utah	UT
Delaware	DE	Montana	MT	Vermont	VT
District of Columbia	DC	Nebraska	NE	Virginia	VA
Florida	FL	Nevada	NV	Washington	WA
Georgia	GA	New Hampshire	NH	West Virginia	WV
Hawaii	HI	New Jersey	NJ	Wisconsin	WI
Idaho	ID	New Mexico	NM	Wyoming	WY
Illinois	IL	New York	NY		
Indiana	IN	North Carolina	NC		
Iowa	IA	North Dakota	ND		
Kansas	KS	Ohio	OH	Guam	GU
Kentucky	KY	Oklahoma	OK	Puerto Rico	PR
Louisiana	LA	Oregon	OR	Virgin Islands	VI

TELEPHONE AREA CODES

Place	Area Code	Place	Area Code	Place	Area Code
ALABAMA		**CALIFORNIA** (Cont'd)		**CALIFORNIA** (Cont'd)	
All points	205				
		El Monte	213	Newport Beach	714
ALASKA		Escondido	714	North Highlands	916
All points	907	Eureka	707	Norwalk	213
		Fairfield	707	Novato	415
ARIZONA		Fountain Valley	714	Oakland	415
All points	602	Fremont	415	Oceanside	714
		Fresno	209	Ontario	714
		Fullerton	714	Orange	714
ARKANSAS		Gardena	213	Oxnard	805
All points	501	Garden Grove	714	Pacifica	415
		Glendale	213	Palo Alto	415
CALIFORNIA		Glendora	213	Palos Verdes	213
Alameda	415	Hacienda Heights	213	Paramount	213
Alhambra	213	Hawthorne	213	Pasadena	213
Altadena	213	Hollywood	213	Petaluma	707
Anaheim	714	Huntington Beach	714	Pico Rivera	213
Arcadia	213	Huntington Park	213	Pleasant Hill	415
Azusa	213	Inglewood	213	Rancho Cordova	916
Bakersfield	805	La Habra	213	Redlands	714
Baldwin Park	213	Lakewood	213	Redondo Beach	213
Bell Gardens	213	La Mesa	714	Redwood City	415
Bellflower	213	La Mirada	714	Rialto	714
Belmont	415	Lancaster	805	Richmond	415
Berkeley	415	La Puente	213	Riverside	714
Beverly Hills	213	Lawndale	213	Rosemead	213
Burbank	213	Livermore	415	Sacramento	916
Burlingame	415	Lodi	209	Salinas	408
Buena Pk.	714	Lompoc	805	San Bernardino	714
Campbell	408	Long Beach	213	San Bruno	415
Carmichael	916	Los Altos	415	San Carlos	415
Carson	213	Los Angeles	213	San Diego	714
Castro Valley	415	Los Gatos	408	San Francisco	415
Chula Vista	714	Lynwood	213	San Gabriel	213
Claremont	714	Manhattan Beach	213	San Jose	408
Compton	213	Menlo Park	415	San Leandro	415
Concord	415	Merced	209	San Lorenzo	415
Corona	714	Milpitas	408	San Luis Obispo	805
Costa Mesa	714	Modesto	209	San Rafael	415
Covina	213	Monrovia	213	Santa Ana	714
Culver City	213	Montclair	714	Santa Barbara	805
Cypress	714	Montebello	213	Santa Clara	408
Daly City	415	Monterey	408	Santa Cruz	408
Davis	916	Monterey Park	213	Santa Maria	805
Downey	213	Mountain View	415	Santa Monica	213
East Los Angeles	213	Napa	707	Santa Rosa	707
El Cerrito	415	National City	714	Seal Beach	213
		Newark	415	Seaside	408

Place	Area Code	Place	Area Code	Place	Area Code

CALIFORNIA (Cont'd)

Place	Area Code
Simi Valley	805
South Gate	213
South Pasadena	213
South San Francisco	415
South Whittier	213
Spring Valley	714
Stockton	209
Sunnyvale	408
Temple City	213
Thousand Oaks	805
Torrance	213
Upland	714
Vallejo	707
Ventura	805
Visalia	209
Vista	714
Walnut Creek	415
West Covina	213
West Hollywood	213
Westminster	714
Whittier	213

COLORADO

Place	Area Code
All points	303

CONNECTICUT

Place	Area Code
All points	203

DELAWARE

Place	Area Code
All points	302

DISTRICT OF COLUMBIA

Place	Area Code
Washington	202

FLORIDA

Place	Area Code
Boca Raton	305
Carol City	305
Clearwater	813
Coral Gables	305
Daytona Beach	904
Fort Lauderdale	305
Fort Myers	813
Fort Pierce	305
Gainesville	904

FLORIDA (Cont'd)

Place	Area Code
Hallandale	305
Hialeah	305
Jacksonville	904
Kendall	305
Key West	305
Lakeland	813
Lake Worth	305
Melbourne	305
Merritt Island	305
Miami	305
Miami Beach	305
Miramar	305
North Miami	305
North Miami Beach	305
Ocala	904
Orlando	305
Panama City	904
Pensacola	904
Plantation	305
Pompano Beach	305
St. Petersburg	813
Sarasota	813
Tallahassee	904
Tampa	813
Titusville	305
West Palm Beach	305

GEORGIA

Place	Area Code
Albany	912
Athens	404
Atlanta	404
Augusta	404
Columbus	404
East Point	404
Fort Benning	404
Gainesville	404
Griffin	404
La Grange	404
Macon	912
Marietta	404
Rome	404
Savannah	912
Valdosta	912
Warner Robins	912

HAWAII

Place	Area Code
All points	808

IDAHO

Place	Area Code
All points	208

ILLINOIS

Place	Area Code
Addison	312
Alton	618
Arlington Heights	312
Aurora	312
Belleville	618
Berwyn	312
Bloomington	309
Blue Island	312
Calumet City	312
Carbondale	618
Carpentersville	312
Champaign	217
Chicago	312
Chicago Heights	312
Cicero	312
Danville	217
Decatur	217
De Kalb	815
Des Plaines	312
Dolton	312
Downers Grove	312
East St. Louis	618
Elgin	312
Elk Grove Village	312
Elmhurst	312
Elmwood Park	309
Evanston	312
Evergreen Park	312
Freeport	815
Galesburg	309
Granite City	618
Harvey	312
Highland Park	312
Hinsdale	312
Hoffman Estates	312
Joliet	815
Kankakee	815
La Grange	312
Lansing	312
Lombard	312
Maywood	312
Melrose Park	312
Moline	309
Morton Grove	312
Mount Prospect	312
Naperville	312

Place	Area Code	Place	Area Code	Place	Area Code
ILLINOIS (Cont'd)		**IOWA**		**LOUISIANA** (Cont'd)	
		Ames	515		
Niles	312	Burlington	319	Kenner	504
Normal	309	Cedar Falls	319	Lafayette	318
Northbrook	312	Cedar Rapids	319	Lake Charles	318
North Chicago	312	Clinton	319	Marrero	504
Oak Lawn	312	Council Bluffs	712	Metairie	504
Oak Park	312	Davenport	319	Monroe	318
Palatine	312	Des Moines	515	New Iberia	318
Park Forest	312	Dubuque	319	New Orleans	504
Park Ridge	312	Fort Dodge	515	Scotlandville	504
Pekin	309	Iowa City	319	Shreveport	318
Peoria	309	Marshalltown	515		
Rantoul	217	Ottumwa	515	**MAINE**	
Rockford	815	Sioux City	712	All points	207
Rock Island	309	Waterloo	319		
Schaumburg	312			**MARYLAND**	
Skokie	312	**KANSAS**		All points	301
South Holland	312	Emporia	316		
Springfield	217	Hutchinson	316	**MASSACHUSETTS**	
Urbana	217	Kansas City	913	Amherst	413
Villa Park	312	Lawrence	913	Andover	617
Waukegan	312	Leavenworth	913	Arlington	617
Wheaton	312	Manhattan	913	Attleboro	617
Wilmette	312	Overland Park	913	Barnstable	617
		Salina	913	Belmont	617
		Topeka	913	Beverly	617
INDIANA		Wichita	316	Billerica	617
Anderson	317			Boston	617
Bloomington	812	**KENTUCKY**		Braintree	617
Columbus	812	Ashland	606	Brockton	617
East Chicago	219	Bowling Green	502	Brookline	617
Elkhart	219	Covington	606	Cambridge	617
Evansville	812	Fort Knox	502	Chelmsford	617
Fort Wayne	219	Frankfort	502	Chelsea	617
Gary	219	Henderson	502	Chicopee	413
Hammond	219	Lexington	606	Danvers	617
Highland	219	Louisville	502	Dedham	617
Indianapolis	317	Newport	606	Everett	617
Kokomo	317	Owensboro	502	Fall River	617
Lafayette	317	Paducah	502	Fitchburg	617
Marion	317	Pleasure Ridge Park	502	Framingham	617
Merrillville	219	Valley Station	502	Gardner	617
Michigan City	219			Gloucester	617
Mishawaka	219	**LOUISIANA**		Greenfield	413
Muncie	317	Alexandria	318	Haverhill	617
New Albany	812	Baton Rouge	504	Holyoke	413
Richmond	317	Bossier City	318	Lawrence	617
South Bend	219	Gretna	504	Leominster	617
Terre Haute	812	Houma	504	Lexington	617

Place	Area Code	Place	Area Code	Place	Area Code
MASSACHUSETTS (Cont'd)		**MICHIGAN** (Cont'd)		**MINNESOTA** (Cont'd)	
Longmeadow	413	Dearborn	313	Columbia Heights	612
Lowell	617	Detroit	313	Coon Rapids	612
Lynn	617	East Detroit	313	Crystal	612
Malden	617	East Lansing	517	Duluth	218
Marblehead	617	Ferndale	313	Edina	612
Marlboro	617	Flint	313	Fridley	612
Medford	617	Garden City	313	Mankato	507
Melrose	617	Grand Rapids	616	Minneapolis	612
Methuen	617	Hamtramck	313	Minnetonka	612
Milton	617	Hazel Park	313	Moorhead	218
Natick	617	Highland Park	313	New Hope	612
Needham	617	Holland	616	Rochester	507
New Bedford	617	Inkster	313	Roseville	612
Newton	617	Jackson	517	St. Cloud	612
North Adams	413	Kalamazoo	616	St. Louis Park	612
Northampton	413	Lansing	517	St. Paul	612
Norwood	617	Livonia	313	White Bear Lake	612
Peabody	617	Madison Heights	313	Winona	507
Pittsfield	413	Marquette	906		
Quincy	617	Midland	517	**MISSISSIPPI**	
Randolph	617	Monroe	313	All points	601
Reading	617	Muskegon	616		
Revere	617	Niles	616	**MISSOURI**	
Roxbury	617	Oak Park	313	Affton	314
Saugus	617	Pontiac	313	Cape Girardeau	314
Salem	617	Portage	616	Columbia	314
Somerville	617	Port Huron	313	Ferguson	314
Springfield	413	Roseville	313	Florissant	314
Stoughton	617	Royal Oak	313	Fort Leonard Wood	314
Taunton	617	Saginaw	517	Gladstone	816
Tewksbury	617	St. Clair Shores	313	Independence	816
Wakefield	617	St. Joseph	616	Jefferson City	314
Waltham	617	Southfield	313	Joplin	417
Watertown	617	Southgate	313	Kansas City	816
Wellesley	617	Sterling Heights	313	Kirkwood	314
Westfield	413	Taylor	313	Lemay	314
West Springfield	413	Trenton	313	Overland	314
Weymouth	617	Troy	313	Raytown	816
Woburn	617	Warren	313	Sedalia	816
Worcester	617	Westland	313	Springfield	417
		Wyandotte	313	St. Charles	314
MICHIGAN		Wyoming	616	St. Joseph	816
Allen Park	313	Ypsilanti	313	St. Louis	314
Ann Arbor	313			University City	314
Battle Creek	616	**MINNESOTA**		Webster Groves	314
Bay City	517	Austin	507		
Benton Harbor	616	Bloomington	612	**MONTANA**	
Birmingham	313	Brooklyn Center	612	All points	406

Place	Area Code	Place	Area Code	Place	Area Code
NEBRASKA		**NEW JERSEY**		**NEW JERSEY**	
Fremont	402	(Cont'd)		(Cont'd)	
Grand Island	308	Hawthorne	201	South River	201
Hastings	402	Hoboken	201	Summit	201
Lincoln	402	Irvington	201	Teaneck	201
North Platte	308	Jersey City	201	Trenton	609
Omaha	402	Kearny	201	Union City	201
		Lakewood	201	Verona	201
NEVADA		Linden	201	Vineland	609
All points	702	Long Branch	201	Weehawken	201
		Madison	201	Westfield	201
NEW HAMPSHIRE		Maplewood	201	West New York	201
All points	603	Mendham	201	West Orange	201
		Metuchen	201	Wildwood	609
NEW JERSEY		Middlesex	201	Woodbridge	201
Asbury Park	201	Millburn	201	Woodbury	609
Atlantic City	609	Millville	609	Wyckoff	201
Barnegat	609	Montclair	201		
Bayonne	201	Morristown	201	**NEW MEXICO**	
Belleville	201	Mount Holly	609	All points	505
Bellmawr	609	Newark	201		
Bergenfield	201	New Brunswick	201	**NEW YORK**	
Bloomfield	201	New Milford	201	Albany & Suburbs	518
Bound Brook	201	North Arlington	201	Amagansett	516
Bridgeton	609	North Plainfield	201	Amityville	516
Burlington	609	Nutley	201	Amsterdam	518
Camden	609	Old Bridge	201	Armonk Village	914
Carteret	201	Orange	201	Auburn	315
Cliffside Park	201	Paramus	201	Babylon	516
Clifton	201	Passaic	201	Baldwin	516
Collingswood	609	Paterson	201	Batavia	716
Dover	201	Perth Amboy	201	Bay Shore	516
Dumont	201	Phillipsburg	201	Bedford Village	914
East Orange	201	Plainfield	201	Bellmore	516
East Paterson	201	Pleasantville	609	Bethpage	516
Eatontown	201	Point Pleasant	201	Binghamton	607
Elizabeth	201	Pompton Lakes	201	Brentwood	516
Englewood	201	Princeton	609	Brewster	914
Ewing	609	Rahway	201	Bridgehampton	516
Fair Lawn	201	Red Bank	201	Bronx	212
Flemington	201	Ridgefield	201	Bronxville	914
Fort Dix	609	Ridgewood	201	Brooklyn	212
Fort Lee	201	Roselle	201	Brookville	516
Garfield	201	Rutherford	201	Buffalo & Suburbs	716
Glassboro	609	Sayreville	201	Callicoon	914
Glen Ridge	201	Somerville	201	Carmel	914
Gloucester	609	South Amboy	201	Center Moriches	516
Hackensack	201	South Orange	201	Central Islip	516
Haddonfield	609	South Plainfield	201	Chappaqua	914
Hasbrouck Heights	201				

Place	Area Code	Place	Area Code	Place	Area Code
NEW YORK (Cont'd)		**NEW YORK** (Cont'd)		**NEW YORK** (Cont'd)	
Cohoes	518	Hicksville	516	New Rochelle	914
Cold Spring	914	Hudson	518	New York City	212
Commack	516	Huntington	516	Niagara	716
Congers	914	Huntington Station	516	North Babylon	516
Copiague	516	Hurleyville	914	North Bellmore	516
Corning	607	Irvington	914	North Massapequa	516
Cortland	607	Islip	516	North Tonawanda	716
Croton-on-Hudson	914	Ithaca	607	Norwich	607
Deer Park	516	Jamestown	716	Nyack	914
Depew	716	Jeffersonville	914	Oceanside	516
Dobbs Ferry	914	Johnson City	607	Olean	716
Dunkirk	716	Kenmore	716	Oneida	315
Eastchester	914	Kerhonkson	914	Oneonta	607
East Hampton	516	Kiamesha	914	Ossining	914
East Massapequa	516	Kingston	914	Oswego	315
East Meadow	516	Lackawanna	716	Oyster Bay	516
Eastport	516	Lake Huntington	914	Patchogue	516
Ellenville	914	Lakeland	914	Pearl River	914
Elmira	607	Lake Success	516	Peekskill	914
Elmsford	914	Larchmont	914	Pelham	914
Elwood	516	Levittown	516	Piermont	914
Endicott	607	Liberty	914	Plainview	516
Endwell	607	Lindenhurst	516	Plattsburgh	518
Fairmount	315	Livingston Manor	914	Pleasantville	914
Fallsburg	914	Lockport	716	Port Chester	914
Farmingdale	516	Long Beach	516	Port Jefferson	516
Fire Island	516	Long Island	516	Port Washington	516
Fishers Island	516	Lynbrook	516	Potsdam	315
Floral Park	516	Mahopac	914	Poughkeepsie	914
Franklin Square	516	Mamaroneck	914	Queens County	212
Freeport	516	Manhasset	516	Riverhead	516
Fulton	315	Manhattan	212	Rochester	716
Garden City	516	Massapequa	516	Rockville Centre	516
Garrison	914	Massapequa Park	516	Roosevelt	516
Geneva	315	Massena	315	Rome	315
Glen Cove	516	Merrick	516	Ronkonkoma	516
Glens Falls	518	Middletown	914	Roscoe	607
Gloversville	518	Mineola	516	Roslyn	516
Grahamsville	914	Montauk Point	516	Rye	914
Great Neck	516	Monticello	914	Sag Harbor	516
Grossinger	914	Mount Kisco	914	Saratoga Springs	518
Hamilton	315	Mount Vernon	914	Sayville	516
Hampton Bays	516	Nanuet	914	Scarsdale	914
Harrison	914	Narrowsburg	914	Schenectady	518
Hastings-on-Hudson	914	Newark	315	Seaford	516
Haverstraw	914	Newburgh	914	Shelter Island	516
Hempstead	516	New City	914	Sloatsburg	914

Place	Area Code	Place	Area Code	Place	Area Code

NEW YORK (Cont'd)

Smithtown	516
Southampton	516
Spring Valley	914
Staten Island	212
Stony Point	914
Suffern	914
Syracuse & Suburbs	315
Tarrytown	914
Ticonderoga	518
Tonawanda	716
Troy	518
Tuckahoe	914
Uniondale	516
Utica & Suburbs	315
Valley Stream	516
Wantagh	516
Watertown	315
Westbury	516
Westchester Co.	914
Westhampton	516
West Hempstead	516
West Islip	516
Wheatley Hills	516
White Lake	914
White Plains	914
Woodbourne	914
Woodmere	516
Woodridge	914
Woodstock	914
Wyandanch	516
Yonkers	914
Yorktown Heights	914

NORTH CAROLINA

Asheville	704
Burlington	919
Camp Le Jeune	919
Chapel Hill	919
Charlotte	704
Durham	919
Fayetteville	919
Fort Bragg	919
Gastonia	704
Goldsboro	919
Greensboro	919
Greenville	919
High Point	919

NORTH CAROLINA (Cont'd)

Kannapolis	704
Kinston	919
Lexington	704
Raleigh	919
Rocky Mount	919
Salisbury	704
Wilmington	919
Wilson	919
Winston-Salem	919

NORTH DAKOTA

All points	701

OHIO

Akron	216
Alliance	216
Ashtabula	216
Athens	614
Austintown	216
Barberton	216
Boardman	216
Brook Park	216
Canton	216
Chillicothe	614
Cincinnati	513
Cleveland	216
Columbus	614
Cuyahoga Falls	216
Dayton	513
East Cleveland	216
East Liverpool	216
Elyria	216
Euclid	216
Fairborn	513
Findlay	419
Garfield Heights	216
Hamilton	513
Kent	216
Kettering	513
Lakewood	216
Lancaster	614
Lima	419
Lorain	216
Mansfield	419
Maple Heights	216
Marion	614
Massillon	216
Mentor	216

OHIO (Cont'd)

Middletown	513
Newark	614
North Olmsted	216
Norwood	513
Parma	216
Parma Heights	216
Portsmouth	614
Rocky River	216
Sandusky	419
Shaker Heights	216
South Euclid	216
Springfield	513
Steubenville	614
Toledo	419
Upper Arlington	614
Warren	216
Whitehall	614
Xenia	513
Youngstown	216
Zanesville	614

OKLAHOMA

Altus	405
Bartlesville	918
Bethany	405
Dill City	405
Enid	405
Lawton	405
Midwest City	405
Muskogee	918
Oklahoma City	405
Ponca City	405
Shawnee	405
Stillwater	405
Tulsa	918

OREGON

All points	503

PENNSYLVANIA

Allentown	215
Altoona	814
Beaver Falls	412
Bellefonte	814
Bethel Park	412
Bethlehem	215
Bloomsburg	717
Bradford	814

Place	Area Code	Place	Area Code	Place	Area Code

PENNSYLVANIA
(Cont'd)

Chambersburg	717
Chester	215
Columbia	717
DuBois	814
Easton	215
Erie	814
Greensburg	412
Harrisburg	717
Hazelton	717
Indiana	412
Johnstown	814
Lancaster	717
Lebanon	717
Levittown	215
Lock Haven	717
McKeesport	412
Monroeville	412
New Castle	412
Norristown	215
Philadelphia	215
Pittsburgh	412
Pottstown	215
Reading	212
Scranton	717
Sharon	412
State College	814
Stroudsburg	717
Sunbury	717
Uniontown	814
Warren	814
Washington	412
Wayne	215
West Chester	215
West Mifflin	412
Wilkes Barre	717
Wilkinsburg	412
Williamsport	717
York	717

RHODE ISLAND
| All points | 401 |

SOUTH CAROLINA
| All points | 803 |

SOUTH DAKOTA
| All points | 605 |

TENNESSEE

Chattanooga	615
Clarksville	615
Jackson	901
Johnson City	615
Kingsport	615
Knoxville	615
Memphis	901
Murfreesboro	615
Nashville	615
Oak Ridge	615

TEXAS

Abilene	915
Amarillo	806
Arlington	817
Austin	512
Baytown	713
Beaumont	713
Big Spring	915
Brownsville	512
Bryan	713
Corpus Christi	512
Dallas	214
Denison	214
Denton	817
El Paso	915
Farmers Branch	214
Fort Hood	817
Fort Worth	817
Galveston	713
Garland	214
Grand Prairie	214
Harlingen	512
Houston	713
Hurst	817
Irving	214
Killeen	817
Kingsville	512
Laredo	512
Longview	214
Lubbock	806
Lufkin	713
Marshall	214
McAllen	512
Mesquite	214
Midland	915
Nacogdoches	713
Odessa	915
Orange	713

TEXAS
(Cont'd)

Paris	214
Pasadena	713
Port Arthur	713
Richardson	214
San Angelo	915
San Antonio	512
Sherman	214
Temple	817
Texarkana	214
Texas City	713
Tyler	214
Victoria	512
Waco	817
Wharton	713
Wichita Falls	817

UTAH
| All points | 801 |

VERMONT
| All points | 802 |

VIRGINIA
Alexandria	703
Annandale	703
Arlington	703
Charlottesville	804
Chesapeake	804
Covington	703
Danville	804
Hampton	804
Hopewell	804
Jefferson	804
Lynchburg	804
Newport News	804
Norfolk	804
Petersburg	804
Portsmouth	804
Richmond	804
Roanoke	703
Staunton	703
Virginia Beach	804
Woodbridge	703

WASHINGTON
Bellevue	206
Bellingham	206
Bremerton	206

Place	Area Code	Place	Area Code	Place	Area Code

WASHINGTON
(Cont'd)

Edmonds	206
Everett	206
Fort Lewis	206
Longview	206
Olympia	206
Renton	206
Richland	509
Seattle	206
Spokane	509
Tacoma	206
Vancouver	206
Walla Walla	509
Yakima	509

WEST VIRGINIA

All points	304

WISCONSIN

Appleton	414
Beloit	608
Brookfield	414
Eau Claire	715
Fond Du Lac	414
Green Bay	414
Greenfield	414
Janesville	608
Kenosha	414
La Crosse	608
Madison	608
Manitowoc	414
Menomonee Falls	414
Milwaukee	414
Neenah	414
New Berlin	414
Oshkosh	414

WISCONSIN
(Cont'd)

Racine	414
Sheboygan	414
South Milwaukee	414
Stevens Point	715
Superior	715
Waukesha	414
Wausau	715
Wauwatosa	414
West Allis	414

WYOMING

All points	307

WIDE AREA TELEPHONE SERVICE

All points	800

CANADIAN PROVINCES

ALBERTA

All points	403

BRITISH COLUMBIA

All points	604

MANITOBA

All points	204

NEW BRUNSWICK

All points	506

NEWFOUNDLAND

All points	709

NOVA SCOTIA

All points	902

ONTARIO

Fort William	807
London	519
North Bay	705
Ottawa	613
Toronto	416

PRINCE EDWARD ISLAND

All points	902

QUEBEC

Montreal	514
Quebec	418
Sherbrooke	819

SASKATCHEWAN

All points	306

MEXICO

Las Palomas	903
Mexicali	903
Mexico City	905
Tijuana	903

BERMUDA

All points	809

PUERTO RICO

All points	809

VIRGIN ISLANDS

All points	809